GO GIRL!

The Black Woman's Book of Travel and Adventure

Elaine Lee, Editor

The Eighth Mountain Press

Portland ✦ Oregon ✦ 1997

Cover illustration and design © 1997 by Linda Dalal Sawaya
Cover production and typography by Marcia Barrentine
Photo on cover of Elaine Lee by Stanley Hébert, III
Book design by Ruth Gundle and Marcia Barrentine

Manufactured in the United States of America
This book is printed on acid-free paper.
First printing 1997
10 9 8 7 6 5 4 3 2 1

Library of Congress Cataloging-in-Publication Data

 Go girl! : the black woman's book of travel and
  adventure / Elaine Lee, editor.
   p. cm.
  ISBN 0-933377-43-6 (cloth : alk. paper)
  ISBN 0-933377-42-8 (trade paper : alk. paper)
  1. Voyages and travels. 2. Afro-American women travelers.
  I. Lee, Elaine, 1952–
  G465.G6 1997
  910.4'08996073--dc21   97–25233

THE EIGHTH MOUNTAIN PRESS
624 Southeast Twenty-ninth Avenue
Portland, Oregon 97214
phone: 503 / 233-3936
fax: 503 / 233-0774

It is customary in many African cultures, to pay tribute to the ancestors prior to engaging in any significant endeavor. In the spirit of that tradition, I give thanks and praise to early African American women travelers for showing us by example that neither chains nor indoctrination can successfully harness the human spirit. I salute their vision, their adventuresome spirits, their ability to overcome fear of the unknown, and their success against the odds.

I call the name of **Phillis Wheatley**, poet and writer, who sailed to England in 1773. Her poem, "Farewell to America" commemorates her journey.

I call the name of **Nancy Prince**, businesswoman and missionary, who sailed to Russia and throughout the Caribbean during the 1820s.

I call the name of **Sojourner Truth**, abolitionist and suffragist, who traveled extensively throughout the United States between the 1840s and 1880s, speaking for equal rights for African Americans and women.

I call the name of **Harriet Tubman**, "conductor" of the Underground Railroad, who made nineteen dangerous trips between the South and the North and between the United States and Canada during the 1850s and 1860s to usher slaves to freedom.

I call the name of **Ida B. Wells**, author, journalist, and activist, who traveled to England and Scotland in the 1890s to place the issue of lynching and the widespread disenfranchisement of African Americans in the international arena.

I call the name of **Bessie Coleman**, the first licensed African American pilot, who after being repeatedly turned down from U.S. flying schools, went to school to become a manicurist in order to raise money to send herself to flying school in France. She received her license from the Federation Aeronautique Internationale in 1921.

These pathfinders, these mavericks, show us that travel is a time-honored tradition among African American women. I offer up their names and their voyages to honor African American women travelers and our journey from the slaveship to the spaceship.

—*Elaine Lee*

✳ 2 SISTREN TRAVELING THE DIASPORA

✳ 3 Trippin' All Over The World

INTRODUCTION

MY LOVE OF TRAVEL WAS INSTILLED IN ME BY MY MOTHER WHO, AS A CHILD, OFTEN envisioned herself as an adult living and working in Africa. She shared those dreams with me and even though she never made it across the great waters, her travels spanned this continent and many of them were with me in tow.

I began traveling on my own at the age of twenty-three when I went to the Bahamas for three weeks during summer break from graduate school. Serendipity caught and cradled me through many exciting, enriching and heartwarming adventures, and I've been traveling regularly ever since. Initially, I was reluctant to travel on my own but I never seemed to be able to find someone with the time and money to travel with me, so I accepted my destiny as a solo traveler. I can truly say I have never experienced loneliness or boredom in my twenty years of international solo travel. Actually, I'm never alone for very long. Within twenty-four hours of my arrival in a new place I meet fellow travelers or locals who are happy to share in my journey. And when I consider the alternatives—not traveling at all, or expensive short-term group travel—traveling on my own wins out every time.

It wasn't until I was thirty-eight that I realized I could do more than take vacations. I could be a *traveler*. While visiting Paris that year, I met a brother at a dinner party for whom international travel was a way of life. He was a fashion and travel photographer as well as a photojournalist for UNESCO. Looking at his passport was orgasmic! The pages were so full of stamps that he not only had to add several accordion pages but after having filled those, he had to renew his passport two years early because of the wear and tear. I thumbed through it and turned green with envy (eight shades at least). I counted forty-three stamps to Africa alone. During the dinner party he was asked, "How is it that you manage to take so many vacations?" He looked at the questioner with a somewhat perplexed glare and announced "I don't take vacations. My travels and time off are lifestyle choices. On average, I work two months and take off two months." I was awestruck by his response; witnessing that encounter ultimately transformed me. At that moment, I knew I would become a traveler.

Shortly after returning home I started a travel fund. I knew I would have to be creative, disciplined, and persistent (since I wasn't particularly lucky or rich). I converted my underutilized two-car garage into a one-bedroom apartment and faithfully deposited the rent I received into a special account. And I consulted a financial planner who helped me rethink my attitudes about saving, spending, and investing. Eventually I was able to semiretire for two years during which I took a trip around the world followed by many other (shorter) journeys. The story of how I figured out how to make that round-the-world trip happen is the concluding story in *Go Girl*.

When I travel to places of exquisite natural beauty or witness the rich tapestry of beliefs, customs, and aesthetics in a foreign country, I am humbled. I feel an extraordinary sense of gratitude: to be alive to witness the awesomeness of nature or the diversity of humanity, grateful for my sight, for the activity of my limbs, for my ability to get myself there. And I am infused with a *joie de vivre* that awakens my senses and heals my soul. It's when I'm traveling that I most deeply celebrate life.

So often in my day-to-day life my focus is narrowly set on tasks, places to go, things to do, and there isn't much room for serendipity. But when I travel I have the freedom to take risks, follow my hunches, and trust my intuition. I am open to whatever comes my way, and much does. One night in Paris, I set out to go to a reggae concert. When I got there the show was sold out and I thought, Now what? It was getting late, and I'd already trekked across town. Then I remembered hearing about an African American hangout called Randy and Jay's, and I decided to try to find it.

I got lost repeatedly, yet stumbled in at just the right moment. After introducing myself to Randy and telling him I was a friend of one of his former regulars, he seated me at a table where a dinner party was in full swing. The folks welcomed me warmly, and we laughed and danced and became fast friends. We all went from there to a nightclub and then to a house party and I didn't land in bed until dawn. Had I gotten into the concert, had I gone back to my hotel, had I not gotten lost, I would have missed one of the best nights of my life.

On another trip I was in Luxor, Egypt, and was scheduled to leave for Thailand in three days, but I still had no contact for that country despite four months of trying. I shared my concern with a group of travelers, and one of them said, "I know someone in Thailand, come up to my room and I'll give you her address and a letter of introduction." Hallelujah! It turned out the name she gave me was of a multimillionaire industrialist who took me under her wing. She was brilliant and gracious, and it was an honor to share a month with her and her family, friends, and staff. While in Bangkok, I stayed in one of her homes and had my own car and driver. When I traveled around the country I stayed in a network of her homes; everything was provided for me. It was an opportunity not only to understand another culture but another class as well. Why did I get such royal treatment? Many Thais view visitors as gifts from God. She also felt that she had a duty to my mother to protect and care for me. She was operating out of a deep sense of sisterhood as well, and loved the opportunity to improve her English.

Some believe that wanderers have a fear of intimacy and like the loose attachments that traveling affords, but I disagree. I find that travel relationships can foster a kind of intimacy unparalleled in ordinary daily interactions. The people I've met have often bared their souls to me and trusted me with their truths. As a traveler, I'm viewed as a free spirit who is less judgmental than the people in their daily lives. It turns out to be a way to balance the energy: their hospitality and our open hearts. I've been blessed with many opportunities to help others as we share our lives across cultural barriers, meeting at that sacred juncture on the quest for wholeness.

Travel is both mind expanding and a brain awakener. Being forced to deal with so many new and different things within a short period of time exercises my brain in ways nothing else does. After returning from a trip, my thinking is sharper and my problem-solving abilities enhanced.

Perhaps the biggest surprise about traveling internationally was to discover that in many parts of the world it is an asset to be a black woman, unlike in North America, where it is often a liability. When I am abroad, I am usually afforded a level of respect and appreciation that I do not get in my own country. It's when I travel that I am told I'm attractive, courageous, and smart. In some parts of the world, I am even considered beautiful, yet in the U.S., I'm just a short, brown, skinny, ordinary woman who's been cursed with a good education, ambition, and an American Express gold card.

For a couple of days, weeks, or months a year, I kinda like the idea of being consistently treated like a human being. I like going into stores and not being followed or going into a restaurant and not being immediately shuttled to the back table by the kitchen. I enjoy being graciously extended service on a first-come-first-served basis without having to insist on it. It does wonders for my self-esteem and peace of mind, which, in turn, contributes to my overall well-being. Most of us are not fully aware of the stress involved in being an African American until it's absent. Then it feels like a weight has been lifted off your shoulders and your soul.

In view of our well-known (and documented) shorter life span than whites, as well as our higher incidence of heart attacks, hypertension, obesity, and certain types of cancer, I think it behooves us to look at ways to nurture our bodies, minds and spirits. For me, international travel is a surefire way to do just that.

Many black women, when they heard I had taken a trip around the world by myself told me, "I could *never* do that!" or "I could never get enough money together" or "I could never take that much time off work" or "I'd be too scared." I understood where those feelings came from, and at the same time I knew that travel was more accessible and less threatening than they perceived it to be. I so wanted them to experience travel as I did, as a form of empowerment, survival, and renewal, and as an avenue to the economic opportunities available outside our national borders.

So, for many years, I had been looking for ways to encourage other black women to pack their bags and set off to explore the planet when the idea of editing the very first travel book by and for African American women was suggested to me by my sista' friend Evelyn C. White. The result is *Go Girl*, fifty-two wonderful travel stories (and dozens of snippets of stories and advice) that cover the globe and every kind of travel experience. They are by women who are old, young, and in-between; women traveling on a budget and those with no limits; first-time travelers and old hands; women traveling alone or with friends or a group; women traveling for adventure, for education, for enlightenment, for business, or just for fun. All the stories explore and illuminate the joys, frustrations, and lasting impact of travel for black women.

The first section of *Go Girl*, "Back to Africa," gathers stories of travel to Kenya, Nigeria, Ghana, South Africa, Egypt, Sierra Leone, and South Africa. I've put them together as a group (and put them first) because visiting Africa is a travel experience like no other for us, children of the diaspora. I urge every black woman to visit Africa at least once in her life, if at all possible. (I think we should have a tenet like the *hajj*, which requires Muslims to visit Mecca once in their lives.) I had no idea how deep my African roots were until I returned "home" and witnessed so many commonalities of food, culture, sensibility, and temperament. It was my experience, and I've heard it said over and over by others, "It is when you go to Africa that you get part of your soul back." Seeing all the familiar faces on the heads of strangers made me realize with a shock that I was no longer in the minority but part of the majority; even the guy on the dollar bill looked a whole lot like my Uncle Jr. When I got back to the U.S. I noticed my back was straighter and my head was higher and I felt a rootedness and inner strength I had never felt before. That fortification has remained with me to this day.

The second section, "Sistren Travel the Diaspora," gathers stories of travel to the places our ancestors were taken as slaves. Jamaica, Haiti, the United States, the Bahamas, Guyana, and other places in the Caribbean are wonderful travel destinations for black women not only for escape and relaxation but also for the immersion in African-infused cultures. Here, also, are fascinating stories of trips to Bahia, a predominantly black area in Brazil, El Carmen, an all-black town in the mountains of Peru, rural Mississippi, and the Sea Islands, all places rich in black history and culture.

The third section, "Trippin' All over the World" collects stories of black women traveling the world over, from Iceland to Japan, from Austria to Australia, from China to Colombia. These traveling sisters testify to the myriad destinations, styles of travel, and opportunities for adventure available to us as black women.

The resource guide at the end of *Go Girl* lists books, travel clubs, festivals, and other important resources.

By lighting the way, by sharing our stories, we can inspire and encourage one another. It is my fervent hope that after reading *Go Girl*, you will be as buoyed up as I have been by these sisters' courage, ingenuity, and adventuresome spirits, and realize that you, too, can take the trip you've been dreaming of.

Blessed be your journey,
Elaine Lee

PART ONE

BACK TO AFRICA

Andrea Benton Rushing

Goin' There and Knowin' There

When Zora Neale Hurston's Janie Starks gets back from her travels and trials to Florida's Everglades, she tells her best friend, "Pheoby, you got tuh go there tuh know there."

I am witness. I had taught and written about Africa for ten years by the time I finally got to Nigeria in 1983. Although I went to teach in the Department of Literature in English at the University of Ife, I knew I'd come back having learned much more than I could possibly teach.

I arrived in Lagos already owning some African cloth and jewelry and having worn my hair in cornrows for years. By the time I came home the following August, I'd worn a dozen different braid styles (from star and crown to crossroads) and amassed a wardrobe of Yoruba designs in various styles and fabrics. And though I never mastered the body language of women's hip-rocking walks, I had learned that what Yoruba women wore was a language I could "speak" with my own hairstyles, jewelry, and cloth, and I had mastered translating that language for non-Yoruba. I left for the U.S. knowing I'd have to return to strident, unpredictable, fascinating, generous Nigeria as surely as if my umbilical cord were buried there.

One of the first things that struck me as soon as I left the Babel of the Lagos airport, was that Nigerian women were remarkably untouched by Western fashion, and I also didn't see any of the bracelets, necklaces, and shoulder-length earrings—the cultural nationalism of "Black Is Beautiful" defined as African. As they strode under head loads with babies on their backs, squatted beside the road selling snacks and cigarettes, perched on the backs of motorcycles, and clung to the sides of rickety *molue* passenger buses, they looked like gorgeous kinetic artworks.

I was eager to get to know these women, but I found myself in a family-centered society where one isn't an adult unless one is (these words are almost synonymous) married and a parent. Although I arrived with two children, I was divorced, which made me a threat in a polygynous culture, and did not have Yoruba in-laws. Furthermore, a calabash of things separated me from Yoruba women: my Ph.D., faculty rank, and salary. I was unschooled in—and it took what felt like forever to learn— even the basics of the Yoruba's elaborate and necessary greetings. And women were, as I learned on return trips, uneasy about speaking English to a native-speaker. Unaware that I'd learned to "swallow" traditional food and eat it with the "natural fork" of my hand, and despite the Yoruba's deserved reputation for both hospitality and arrogance, they worried that my U.S. origin would make me sneer at their table manners.

Unable to speak with Yoruba women, I focused on them as though I were a camera, and I asked my best friend Lanre (my guide in Yorubaland the way I'd been hers when we met in Amherst, Massachusetts) about puzzling aspects of their attire. Dowdily layered against New England cold when I knew her in Amherst, in Nigeria, Lanre almost always wore traditional attire and looked stunning. I carefully observed what she wore, listened to comments people made about women's ensembles, and paid close attention when I accompanied Lanre and her daughters on trips to shop for cloth in open-air markets where designs included umbrellas, skulls, and alphabet letters, and patterns had names like "Capable Woman" and "If My Husband Goes Out, I Go Out." Our expeditions to seamstresses to have cloth sewn into clothes were crash courses in both Yoruba aesthetics and the African feminism that Sierra Leonean anthropologist Filomina Steady describes.

Eventually I wore traditional dress myself, which enabled me to "converse" with the Yoruba without a single spoken word. Though I rarely wore my hair braided as elaborately as the crafters at Express Salon thought suited my position as mother and senior lecturer, when I went out, my cloth and jewelry signed my age and status and pleased the Yoruba (who are dismayed at the way most *oyinbo* foreigners just hang African cloth on their walls) by showing that I was learning to see their culture through Yoruba eyes.

What Yoruba women wear is articulate in several ways. It can reveal social facts like ethnicity, religion, marital status, city of origin, and relation to others. For example: Their standard *buba* blouse, *iro* skirt, *iborun* shawl, and *gèlè* head-tie not only distinguish them from Senegalese women in their grand *boubou* but also set them apart from such Nigerian ethnic groups as the Ibibo and the Kalabari; white cloth draped atop a *gèlè* head-tie means the woman is a Muslim (though not all Muslims follow this practice); *iborun* shawl over the right shoulder indicates marriage and motherhood; the more cloth one displays, the older, wealthier, more sophisticated, and higher in social class one is thought to be (that, rather than modesty or sexist strictures, accounts for adult women's full-length *iro* skirts).

Yoruba fashion, with its emphasis on full-figured women and its focus on the head and the skilled arrangement of cloth, does not revolve around scrawny adolescents. It fuels my feminism to know about an African culture which conceives of different manifestations of beauty, poise, and elegance in all the phases of girls' and women's lives from menarche past menopause.

—Andrea Benton Rushing

Emphasis on attire is neither confined to the elite nor a sign of women's peripheral economic and social roles: 95 percent of Nigerian women work, and they work (for money) no matter how wealthy their father or husband is. Their attire is an idiom in which they express a daily creativity that still astounds, fascinates, challenges, and instructs me.

I am particularly fascinated by groups in outfits of identical fabric. Women wearing it are in *"aso-ebi"* (association cloth) and may be friends, sisters, co-wives, sisters-in-law, or members of a market association and are demonstrating and celebrating the social webs the Yoruba find more natural and satisfying than individualism. I have, for example, *aso-ebi* association cloth with my best friend and her youngest daughter in one ensemble and with the Yoruba husband of an African American who considers me her sister in another. People seeing us in it know we're related, although they don't know exactly how.

In the ancient city of Ile-Ife, I learned a lot about hair when I enrolled my eleven-year-old daughter in the prestigious Moremi secondary school. She had her hair in a loose braid style and it was long, even by U.S. standards. Yoruba girls in their age group are expected to have closely cropped naturals. The school only allowed her to sign up with the firm understanding that she would keep her hair very neatly braided. (When a girl reaches her teens, braids are appropriate, and she can choose from a dizzying array of traditional and contemporary cornrow, threaded, and loose braids patterns with evocative names like the bucket, pineapple, pig, centipede, spider's web, snake, and tortoise.)

The Yoruba consider the head the site of one's *ori* (spirit/soul/destiny). Neatly arranged hair is much more than a matter of personal choice; tousled hair is a sign of chaos rather than a free-spirit sexiness. It is the special province of the powerful, elegant, female *orisa* deity Osun—one of whose *oriki* praise-names is "owner of the beaded comb."

For the Yoruba, hairdos are human manifestations of the harmony and order they discern in the natural world and strive for in social relationships. They also provide social and cultural commentary. When Nigeria changed from left-side driving to right-side, women wore braided hairdos that showed the new traffic pattern. Coiffures are named for heads of state, major architectural feats like the Eko bridge, and, currently, satellite dishes. A hairstyle is named for the Afro-British pop singer Sade and, seven thousands miles from the U.S., one can see Sulphur-8, named for the African American hair product.

> *T*he roots of the modernist movement are right here in Africa. Complex communication reduced to the essence of symbol and form. When the modernists imported the primitive into their work, they left behind the one thing that could not be exported. The soul. Soul arrived in the West in the minds and bones of African people and was reintroduced to the modern world through African American music. It is fascinating to imagine that African people travel thousands of miles to America to meet up with their own cultural "stuff" in the form of modern art!
>
> —Sylvia Harris Woodard,
> "Postcards from the Global Village"

According to Yoruba cosmology, women and men have separate and complementary spheres and roles, and so they don't produce androgynous or unisex fashions, although the *agbada* robes men wear would be considered dresses in the U.S. No women's wide hips squished into parking meter officer, police, or transit authority trousers. No fashions that present men's wear as sexy on women. No ambitious professional women imagining that wearing navy pinstripes will pry open portals of power: The more successful a woman becomes, the more elaborately feminine her ensembles, especially her head-tie. A TV anchor is renowned for having to go through doorways sideways so her ostentatious *gèlè* will fit. When my best friend had two sons graduating from the University of Ife at the same time she proclaimed, "My *gèlè* is going to touch the sky!"

In the same way that Yoruba women are baffled by the idea of marrying for romantic love or having joint checking accounts with their husbands, they would not understand having their hair styled by men. Women create both the myriad braid styles one sees on cardboard signs at beauty salons and the dazzling three dimensional, sometimes architectonic *gèlè* head-tie designs. Men don't invent women's clothing styles either. There are no Yoruba equivalents to Ralph Lauren, Calvin Klein, Bill Blass, Yves Saint Laurent, Giorgio Armani, or even African Americans like Willi Smith, Patrick Kelly, Stephen Burrows, and Byron Lars.

Rather than buying a fully accessorized "look," mimicking male fashions, or seeing concern with one's attire as frivolous, Yoruba women claim the power to invent themselves every time they get dressed. Although upscale urban neighborhoods have boutiques that sell expensive ready-made clothing, most women buy cloth in open-air markets and, becoming co-creators of what they wear, take it to tailors or seamstresses who sew and decorate it with the color and pattern of embroidery or appliqué chosen. Of the four pieces in the customary ensemble, only the *buba* blouse is sewn. The *iro* wraparound skirt, *iborun* shawl, and *gèlè* head-tie are all formed from rectangular pieces of cloth and tucked into place without any pins, buttons, zippers, or other fasteners.

The culture provides unwritten rules that decree where the *iro* skirt should be tied and how the *iborun* shawl should be draped. Individual artistry shines forth in the selection of fabric, decisions about style and color of embroidery and appliqué and other decorations, and, most impressively, the arrangement of the *gèlè* head-tie. Over and over men surprised me by praising women's *gèlès* (which have names and shapes as varied as "ivory cone," "peacock," "spiral," "paddle your own canoe," and "loop the slanderer in the head-tie"). When I realized that men's headwear comes already sewn into shapes, I understood why men see deftly tied, often asymmetrical *gèlès*—like women's power to give birth and prepare life-sustaining food—as an outward and visible sign of their formidable creative and transformative gifts.

For me, too, the *gèlè* conveyed a woman's power that cannot be directly observed or controlled. It is a cool power, detected, yet hidden, in the beauty of a composed face. It is fascinating in its complexity and has an awesome and consuming power. The perfect complement to an artful *gèlè* is the smile I've discovered in my photographs of Yoruba women, an expression that radiates calm, composure, and restraint.

Long before I went to Nigeria I had heard the joke about how if a man's mother and wife are in a sinking boat he will save his mother, because he can always get another wife. And I knew the Yoruba dictum, "mother is gold." I had done a comparative study of the idea of mother in African American and African poetry. I knew and admired Filomina Steady's bold and groundbreaking exposition of an African feminism that differs from and antedates European and Euro-American feminism, insisting on the centrality of motherhood in African cultures and contrasting the sanctity of women's bodies—as bearers of life—in Africa with the cynical use of women's bodies in U.S. advertising and pornography.

Impressed as I am with this part of her argument, what strikes me as equally feminist in Yoruba culture is its accepting attitude toward women's bodies of every size and shape. Some young urban elites diet and exercise, but most women focus their attention on putting their bodies in fabrics, colors, and patterns they find elegant, rather than in altering their bodies with shoulder pads, push-up bras, diets, or liposuction. Thin is not "in" in Nigeria. Rather than envying my five-foot-three-inch, 105 lb., size 5 figure, the Yoruba found it childlike. In a society where most women are producers (rather than consumers), tall, large-boned, full-figured women are the ideal. Instead of the flat stomachs many in the U.S. groan and grunt to achieve and maintain, the Yoruba consider rounded stomachs (which testify to women's child-bearing potential or experience) the ideal. The *iro* skirts of girls and women, including those of prepubescent girls and matronly priestesses, are wrapped to accentuate the stomach by draping horizontal folds across it.

And instead of the contemporary Euro-American sexual focus on women's legs and breasts, Yoruba culture (where breast-feeding is widespread and traditionally lasts about three years) is like its Caribbean and African American offshoots in seeing women's hips and buttocks as the locus of sexual interest and procreative power. I would have had a hard time *giving* a Yoruba woman a girdle. Women dress to call attention to these areas with, for example, tops with fitted waists and short, flared peplums that graze the buttocks and ensembles that combine and contrast *buba* blouses with vertical stripes (which minimize the breasts), with *iro* skirts of the same fabric (where the horizontal stripes emphasize hips and buttocks). The way girls and women walk, their bottoms undulating effortlessly, intensifies the effect.

Although one-half of the population of Nigeria is under fifteen and contemporary U.S. styles like concealing gray hair have made inroads into ancient Yoruba values, age is still the most important hierarchy: an aged, toothless woman who has never seen the inside of a schoolroom commands respect from all, including men who are intellectuals, business tycoons, military officers, and heads of state who may prostrate forehead-on-the-floor before her.

Where do they all come from?
Tall men?
From the woman's crotch!
Short men?
From the woman's crotch!
Hunters and warriors?
From the woman's crotch!
Chiefs and court clerks?
From the woman's crotch!
Even the White man?
*From the woman's crotch!**

All too often, African American women ethnocentrically assume that we have nothing to learn from (and everything to teach) African women.

Without minimizing the differences between us, romanticizing Yoruba women's lives, or ignoring the scourges of economic poverty, limited access to formal education and political power, AIDS, and "female circumcision" that beset them, I still turn to their brand of feminism in order to stoke my own. And, a decade after I first touched down in Nigeria, I continue to wear Yoruba attire (over cotton or silk thermals when winter insists) every chance I get.

Our decisions about self-presentation can be among our most feminist acts. When I put on *aso-oke* attire or *ankara* cloth, when I tuck my *iro* on my right hip and fold my *iborun* on my right shoulder, when I get a *gèlè* wrapped and tilted at exactly the right asymmetrical angle, a parasol of memories unfurls: where I bought the cloth or who gave it to me; which seamstress cut and sewed it, what my Nigerian friends thought of it; which woman artist wove, dyed, and sold me the cloth; which Yoruba has this *aso-ebi* association cloth with me.

The 1970s taught us that the personal is political. RuPaul says, "We're born naked and the rest is drag." The more I speak the language of Yoruba women's attire and the better my pronunciation in this expressively tonal idiom becomes, the more concisely and resonantly I sign myself an African feminist.

*From the Nigerian novel *I Saw the Sky Catch Fire* by T. Obinkaram Echewa.

Adrienne Johnson

Going to Ghana

MY MOTHER WAS FIRST. WE HAD JUST LEFT A DARK ROOM TO SIT IN A ROW OF STOOLS in the center of the Ghanaian town of Akutukope. We had received wisdom from elders, been wrapped in fine handwoven cloth, and adorned in strands of beads culled from the earth. And now, amid the noise of celebration, the head of the village—a woman—guided my mother in front of a man with a short black sword. My mother looked back at me and widened her eyes in an expression that was partly fear but mostly anticipation.

The man with the sword raised it above her head and the crowd quieted. Then he began speaking in his language, Ewe, in a tone I could recognize as one of pronouncement. The crowd cheered. My mother was being embraced by these people. And she was being renamed. Bea Johnson was now Queen Mother Amertoryor.

We hadn't set out for Ghana looking to be reclaimed. My mother, my sister, and I were simply looking for a place to go together. We had visited the African continent many times, returning home gift-laden, informed, and filled with the desire to see more. That year we wanted to explore Ghana, knowing only that it is the home of *kente* cloth, colonized Africa's first independent president, Kwame Nkrumah, and a family friend. Since my sister, always good at games of chance, had won two round-trip tickets to Italy in a raffle, she bowed out. So it was Mom and me, on the lookout for a group tour that promised education, adventure, and shopping.

What we found was a tour filled with other mothers and daughters, traveling to West Africa to fulfill a sacred ritual, the rites of passage of a girl into womanhood. The sponsoring group was African Womanhood Is Mine, a Brooklyn-based organization founded in 1991 by Barbara Gathers, a middle-school teacher whose goal is to teach girls responsibility to themselves, their families, and their communities, as well as entrepreneurial skills. After a year of classes and counseling, they go through rites in a Ghanaian village. That year, there would be a rite for adult women too, so we signed up enthusiastically.

Drums sounded a welcome as we took our seats at the hotel's poolside restaurant on our first night in Accra. In Africa, the drum has a voice telling tales of death, life, anger, and war. These drums accompanied the Novisi Cultural Group. Despite the hard concrete, the young people danced unreservedly, leaping, extending, and shimmying, all the while smiling at our enjoyment and their own. The drums—the From Tom From, Kpalogo, Djembe, and Kagau—spoke to us. After a while, the young people came to our tables, taking our hands and encouraging us to join them. So, between bites of curried meats and ground-nut stews, we danced. They were delighted at how well and willingly we matched their steps.

The next day we toured Accra. As our bus wove through the commercial area of Adabraka, in search of a place to exchange dollars for *cedis*, our guide entertained us with an Anansi story. These are folk tales that feature a lazy, conniving spider who sometimes gets his comeuppance and sometimes just reveals the whys of the world. This day's tale told why wisdom was spread among all people instead of hoarded by one.

With nearly one million people, Accra's streets are continually crowded, active with the hum and roar of cars, and people sauntering and scurrying, definitely going somewhere to do something. From the window of our bus we saw students in two-toned uniforms, housewives going to market, vendors selling to passing cars, beggars pleading for survival, and taxis galore. In fact, in Accra there were more taxis than I have ever seen anywhere.

The most magnetic images were the women, balancing seemingly impossible loads on their heads, often with babies bound to their backs. We learned later that carrying things this way is considered a sign of beauty, and I could see why. When they do it, the women have a languid ease and a lazy grace—I was spellbound by each example of sangfroid elegance.

And the wave of color in Ghanaian fabrics only heightened the vibrancy of the streets. Between the *ntama*, the smooth cotton of which most everyday clothes are made, and the *adinkra*, a stamped, hand-stitched material, the city streets were an animated patchwork quilt. I longed to be off our bus, walking amid that color, moving at its pace. Later, when we finally did walk along Accra's streets, we could keep up just fine (we're New Yorkers). With no tall buildings as landmarks, however, one wrong turn left us lost. A policeman smiled at our dilemma, hailed a taxi, and negotiated a fare for us. That turned out to be typical of Ghanaian hospitality.

At the National Museum we learned about *kente* (which means "handwoven"), the now popular fabric indigenous to Ghana. Pieces of it hang in the museum with the names, meanings, and regional origins of particular patterns. One black-and-white pattern (originally all *kente* was black and white) was named Nyawoho, meaning "you have become rich," because only a man worth a certain price in gold who had the king's approval could wear that pattern. Another, Adweneasa, or "skill is exhausted," was so named because the weaver was convinced he had put all he knew into his creation.

Afterward, we paid our respects at Kwame Nkrumah's burial site. Ghana was the first African country to gain independence. Nkrumah led it from Great Britain's grasp in 1957 and became its first president. His tomb sits on the former polo grounds of British expatriates. The memorial park is immaculately manicured and absolutely spotless; when we walked onto the square, we felt an immediate sense of reverence. Four Ghanaian flags—red, gold, and green with a black star in the center—fly in pairs; between them is the sloping gray granite building that harbors Nkrumah's grave. Before it is a cast bronze statue of the late leader striding and pointing forever forward as he wanted his nation to do.

A T-shaped walkway is partly formed by two squares of water with seven statues squatting on white tile pedestals rising out of the water. The statues are men crouched on one knee, blowing horns that spout water. The horns blow in perpetual announcement of Nkrumah's death, while the continuous flow of water symbolizes that his ideals live on. Behind the tomb is a small but thorough museum devoted to Nkrumah's life and work, including his many books. Also on the grounds are trees planted by various dignitaries; the most recently planted was a mango tree, perhaps four feet tall, in a slated wooden box to protect its slow growth. The black sign with white lettering says it was planted by Nelson Mandela in 1991.

After a typical Ghanaian lunch of *kenkey* (doughnut-shaped patties of ground fermented maize), *kelewele* (fried and spiced plantains), *red red* (a red bean sauce over fried plantains), salad, roasted chicken, fish, and mutton, we headed to the village of Osudoku, an hour-long drive east of Accra. Osudoku is populated by people of the Ga-Adagme ethnic group and was to be the scene of the girls' two-day rites. Along the way, our bus passed artisans selling their wares—wicker hampers, baskets, and chairs, and intricately carved blond-wood doors and similarly sturdy bed frames. We drove by lush fields in shades of green ranging from lime to emerald. Elementary schoolchildren in uniforms of brown and cream stared as we passed, some smiling and waving, others just noting our presence. Storefronts displayed the spirituality of their owners by boasting signs in English with names such as: As It Is in Heaven Fashion.

The people of Osudoku were awaiting our arrival at the village gathering place, a two-story stone building with a porch and a verandah on the top floor. The elder women of the village sat on benches in front of the building. It was the home of the area's head chief, Nene Klagbordzor Animle V, and we were to be presented to him. We removed our shoes at the door and were led upstairs, with warnings not to present our left hands because in Muslim culture that is considered offensive.

The chief was a smooth-skinned man in his sixties swathed in navy batik and wearing thick glasses. Around his living room were six of the kind of chairs you sink into, upholstered in wool despite the temperate climate, and on the tables, the lace doilies found in a grandparents'

> *I* was struck by a sense of dignity in the people of West Africa that I have seldom seen in blacks in America. Is it because these Africans, unlike many of us, have never been taught to believe that their lives are worthless? I doubt that. I think that in the days of Dutch, French, and English rule they, too, were told that they were nothing. No, I don't think it is a matter of what anyone outside of their African communities taught them. I think the difference is what those inside of their communities have taught and continue to teach them.
>
> The Africans I met were from close-knit communities. In fact, when we were leaving Ghana, we saw large groups of people at the airport and were told that when one person from a particular community comes home, the entire village goes to the airport to meet them.
>
> I met an older man who took a particular interest in a younger man, so much so that he took him into his home to live and is teaching the younger man his business.
>
> In the marketplace, if one vendor didn't have what we were looking for, we weren't sent away empty-handed. Instead, the vendor sent a message to a seller who had what we wanted and then helped them make the sale.
>
> I came back deeply impressed by these and other examples of unity and community and started to question folks back home who sit around complaining about what the white man won't do for us. I understood on a profound level, in Africa, that we are the descendants of a proud, wonderful people. If we just tapped the surface of the vast resources that are innately ours, there would be no limit to the success we could attain.
>
> —Gail A. Clanton, "My Trip Back Home"

home. He explained that he was named chief in 1944, "abducted" on the street, he said, at nineteen while he was attending school in Accra. Dead set on studying abroad, he abdicated and spent the next thirty-five years in the United Kingdom where he married a Jamaican woman and had three children. When his successor died, he came back to his post as chief reluctantly. He'd hoped for a quiet retirement.

The purpose of the rites had changed somewhat, he explained. It still aimed to prepare young women for life as wives and mothers, but now it was also intended to help prevent teen pregnancy. Of course, the rites would not include clitoridectomies. Even the Ghanaian girls in the villages we went to were not circumcised. Although an estimated eighty million Africans girls, from Senegal to Somalia, have undergone female circumcision, the villages we visited did not follow the practice.

Some call the rites of passage "initiation rites," but the former term seems more accurate. The girls who undergo the rites don't so much join a special sorority as go through a transition. The ceremonies are filled with symbols of this transition, this journey from what they were to what they must become. And they must go through it without their mothers. So, all of us adult women sat outside while the girls were undressed in preparation for the rites.

The village was noisy and active. Children stared openly at us. Young men sat watching us on the wall enclosing the area and nearly everyone else milled about on benches or on the verandah. It was a weird standoff: We looked at them, discussed them, talked among ourselves and they seemed to do the same. We had no idea what to do. Finally, two women in our group asked if they could approach and greet the elders. They did, and the women returned the gesture. Bowing slightly, they shook our hands while smiling shyly. It was the only way we could communicate, but it was effective in breaking the ice.

Barbara Gathers was privy to all the goings on. She reported back periodically, assuring the mothers that the girls were fine, although at first uncomfortable with undressing in front of strangers. "I told them, 'These are all women, no one wants your breasts!'" she said. Still, unlike the other girls from the village also going through rites, they would not appear topless publicly. Instead, the girls were wrapped in colorful prints from the chest down. Underneath, they wore waist beads with white calico cloth looped through in front and back. On their heads were toquelike straw hats.

When the girls came out, things got even noisier and more frenetic. They were led to a concrete area just beyond the chief's house, where the elders had just poured libations—palm wine or water poured onto the ground to acknowledge ancestors and show faith. Some of the elders sang a melodic chant, shook gourds, and danced around the girls as others tied a strand of straw around the girls' necks. A man who spoke some

English translated the verse: "Our lost friends are back home, rejoice that they have returned home." Other initiates from the village were brought out of the isolation they are put in during the much longer traditional rites and matched with one of our girls as a special friend with whom they would share new names.

Once they were matched, the girls and their friends were taken to a quarter of the village filled with mud-brick homes with tin and thatched roofs. There, they had to visit the Dipo stone, a place where all initiates go to swear their virginity. We had wondered why one of the villages' initiates had blue and white waist beads while the others had red; we discovered she had not been to the Dipo stone yet and would join our girls.

Another libation was given at the stone with a prayer for the girls' marriage, fertility, and sense of responsibility. Then, one at a time, they

*O*n my first trip to Ghana in 1969, I met three African American women who became like sisters to me. Cheryl and Eileen shared a room, and Pattie and I took a room right next to theirs in the hostel that Nkrumah had built for Africans from other countries. Living together and sharing meals every day at the hostel we came to respect, understand, and love one another.

All four of us took classes at the University of Ghana in Legon. On warm tropical mornings before class, we'd drop tiny sugar cubes into warm coffee in clear glass cups, enjoying the scents of the flowering bushes that adorned the beautiful whitewashed buildings. We read Chinua Achebe's *Things Fall Apart* and *Man of the People* and James Ngugi's *Weep Not Child* for our modern African literature class. We brought each other goodies from parties when one of us stayed home and we hitched rides together from Legon to the hostel, often having the luck to have a big old Mercedes stop for us. We traveled to Sumanya to visit Pattie's friend Joe and eat chicken with the feet still on. We drank warm beer and ate hot bread in a *tro tro* on our way into the bush where we hiked to a pristine waterfall with bats circling and beeping at the black stones at the top of the falls.

Cheryl made African-print dresses and Pattie cooked okra with onions and tomatoes. Eileen and Cheryl spent a long weekend in Lagos with our modern African literature teacher and Wole Soyinka; I did not go because it cost $30 and that was all the money I had at the time. Pattie and I taught classes at an American school. Our driver picked us up in the school station wagon in the morning, and we often went out to a Chinese or Lebanese restaurant for a long, quiet lunch after school. That was the life! We were never in a hurry, never stressed.

The hostel had no screens on the windows and we slept under mosquito nets rigged up on narrow wooden slats over the bed; every night the mosquitoes flew in formation taunting us. We relied on the tiny pink geckos to reduce their numbers. We took quinine once a week and prayed that we would not get malaria. The watchman sat every night beside the open sewer in front of our door, his machete over his lap. He often spent his nights embroidering the tops of grand *bubas* with bright red, yellow, and blue threads. Most nights he just slept, but we felt safe.

were led to the stone. The elders held them, lowering them once, twice, and on the third time allowing them to sit. Their hats were removed behind a piece of material designed to keep the method a secret. Then they were lifted up slowly and told not to look back until they were away from this sacred area.

There was more singing and dancing and people poured talcum powder on the girls' shoulders and faces, a sign of purity. It took three hours, and the heat and the celebrating had left us exhausted. Nearly all of us slept on the way back to Accra.

The next day in Osudoku was an even noisier one. The children were out in full force. Soon, two of the women in our group had them form a circle and taught them the Hokey Pokie and Ring around the Rosey. I'd brought two packs of Polaroid film and began taking pictures and giving

---

People estranged from home, family, and support systems talk openly, frankly, seeking their truth and at least a temporary stability. In the hostel, there was an honesty that came of fleeing war and fighting for life—or, in our case, of being young and searching. We met Ibos from Biafra who had fled Nigeria. Wellington Nyangone, from what was then Rhodesia, told us stories of the political underground there. Men from the Gambia and a family from Cameroon lived with us too. We even had our own personal money changer from Somalia. He knew the Lebanese business men who would give us the most *cedis* for our dollars. And the four of us talked, discussed, and argued about everything and anything every day, savoring the rich brew of experiences.

At the end of that year, when I left Ghana on a hot August afternoon, my friend Larry Kojo Lee, who had grown up in Ghana, took me to the airport. I hugged him and said, "You'll see my smile in the sunset." We both laughed, believing we would someday share a tall bottle of Star beer at the Continental Hotel in Legon once again. We would talk about his chicken farm we had set up together in Leecrom, where his father had built a house with a rainwater shower and where he grew cashews, guava, and papaya. We would reminisce about the motorcycle ride to Leecrom and the rabbit stew that his mother had made specially for us. We would remind each other of the day we first met and stood side by side in our bathing suits singing the Negro National Anthem on the coast of Ghana in an old slave castle that was to become a hostel for African Americans

I would return to Ghana, but I would never see Larry again.

One Sunday afternoon Eileen called to tell me that Larry had gotten into some political difficulties. This was soon after the coup that made his close friend, flight lieutenant Jerry Rawlings, Ghana's president. The details were sketchy, but someone had ordered his execution.

When I returned to Ghana in 1995 for the twenty-fifth anniversary celebration of the Asantehene, I remembered how optimistic Larry had been about Ghana's future and his own. But Larry was gone, and the Ghana I remembered was gone.

—Margaret Musgrove, "Ghana, Sweet and Bittersweet"

them out as small gifts. They loved having their pictures taken and cheered whenever a flash went off. Soon I was overwhelmed by requests. Twenty pictures were gone in less than ten minutes!

The drums began to speak and the village's initiates came out. They were still topless, but this time they had multiple strands of beads adorning their chests and backs and perhaps twenty strands of thick waist beads. Their white calico was replaced by prints and their skin was decoratively striped with dried clay. In their right hands they held thin sticks taller than they were. They entered the concrete area united in a dance, stepping twice quickly on each foot—almost a step up, so the big toe curled in slightly—arms out, palms down. At first they faced the crowd, but after a while they did the step while slowly turning. It seemed a step they were born knowing.

Our girls came out, one at a time, with their partners from the day before. They, too, were adorned with beads and clay and though their partners had their heads covered, our girls had plastic combs secured by bands on their heads as decoration. The women of the village watched as our girls entered to see if they did the step correctly. The first girl did, down to the toe curl. The women smiled with approval. We beamed. I pointed out to one mother that her daughter was next. "Where?" she asked. She didn't recognize her daughter in all the finery! I looked at her and saw the mixture of astonishment and pride.

Soon they were all in line with the village girls, turning as they did the step over and over, some moving easily, some moving unsteadily, amid a clamorous swirl of pounding drum beats, clanging cowbells, melodic intonations and shouts in a language we could not understand. And it was hot. For one girl in our group, it was all too much. She suddenly burst into tears; she wanted to drop out. But her adult cousin was there to comfort her and urge her on. The girl got back in line.

The sticks were taken away and each initiate was given a second stick with a white flag, another sign of purity. Pots were placed on their heads and then quickly collected. The often-seen practice of carrying a pot on one's head is considered a sign of beauty because of the grace and balance it takes to pull it off successfully. It also symbolized the daily chores for which the women are traditionally responsible. Just as it had grown to its intensity, the ceremony petered to a close.

Next came a dance the girls performed with their mothers, symbolizing the trek to womanhood. They wore pink *bubus* (an ankle-length dress with draped sleeves); their mothers wore purple. The dance started with birth, then the mothers raising, helping, and ultimately freeing their daughters to stand alone. At the end, the mothers rejoined the dance, but now they danced with women and these new women opened up their circle and allowed the mothers to enter. During the dance, our girls smiled, relieved that they were finally doing something familiar.

The girl who nearly dropped out looked especially relaxed and happy. At the end, the crowd hooted in appreciation as mothers and daughters bowed, arm in arm.

The women's rites were held in Akutukope, a town in southeastern Ghana, the home of the Ewe people. There is a memory passed along among the people of Akutukope that survives from the seventeenth century, when white men first came to their village. The villagers had never seen such people before, but they grew to trust and befriend them. Then one day, during a celebration, the men invited them onto their ship. It was a trick. They went dancing and singing to their enslavement.

That's why, when we arrived in Akutukope for the *tagaye* or women's rites, we were treated not as special visitors but as people returning. Our guide told us we were seen as those long-lost people who they always hoped would come back.

Our reception was of a magnitude that would humble anyone. If Osodoku was overwhelming with noise and crowds, Akutukope surpassed it by matching both, then exceeding it with color and pageantry. There was royalty, relaxing under huge umbrellas of red, blue, yellow, pink, and green triangles, the men holding staffs topped with ivory figures, the women awash in multiple necklaces. The queen mother of the village, who was also a teacher, greeted us and led us to our places of honor. We were treated to traditional dances and songs by the village's children, just like a grade school performance. Everything was translated by a passionate young man.

The celebration went on after the women participating in the rites were led into a private room. There we met with the women elders. Traditionally, the rites are for those getting married or who have had children. It focuses on fertility and productivity, emphasizing the need to learn many skills to help support a family.

In Akutukope the rites are typically three weeks long. Since our time was limited, we asked the elders questions as they showed us weaving techniques, special to their village. At first, the questions were benign: someone asked advice on keeping a marriage happy. Things loosened up with the question, "What do you do when your husband gets on your nerves?" From there, we asked about domestic abuse, childlessness, herbal hygiene formulas and how men are prepared for marriage.

Then one of the elders said she had a question for us. How, she wondered, could they raise their children these days when they were moving into the cities, watching videos, and losing their sense of tradition? We laughed ruefully at the familiar dilemma.

As we talked, other women and elders began adorning us with beads knotted with strands of splayed raffia. *Kente* that had been woven for us for the occasion, then tied around us, first under our arms to the right, then over left, and tucked. The top of the cloth was rolled and secured by another strip knotted in back.

We were led outside and seated on stools. In front of us was a table covered in white with large bowls of scented powders, perfumes, and soaps. My mother, as the oldest, was called forward. A member of the royal family stood her before him and held a black metal sword with shapes cut out of it above her head. He intoned: "Upon this sword I swear before the gods and ancestors that today you have been identified as a true daughter of this town. I give you this name." And then he re-named my mother Queen Mother Ametoryor, a name of a prominent woman in the village, meaning "what is hers is hers." When my turn came, I was named Borborloe, meaning "gentleness and tolerance is essential in achieving great things in life." The ceremony ended as all do, with dancing. Those who were especially good got a thousand *cedi* bill slapped on their forehead in appreciation.

Our trip ended on the coast of Ghana with a visit to the Elmina and Cape Coast forts, once used for slave trading. Elmina is a town peppered with palm and coconut trees with roads of red dirt. It has the feel of all old coastal areas: a patient pace borne from an appreciation of, and reliance on, nature. As we headed through gates up a hill toward the fort, we passed the central fishing village. It was packed with skiffs, canoes, dories, and catamarans docked neatly and flying flags of various nations. Hundreds of people were shopping in the area, which was surrounded by quaint faded stone houses.

From the outside, the fort looks almost new. It's a soft white color with strong stone barricades and a cannon peaking over a high wall. But standing within its vast courtyard, you can see its age. That cannon is crumbling and the walls are mildewed from more than five hundred years of ocean air. The feeling of sorrow and agony still lingers. A guide showed us the iron balls shackled to a captive's legs as part of a punishment that included hours standing in the sun. We saw two cells with skull and crossbones symbols over the entrance. One was for soldiers who broke regulations. The other was for those condemned to death. Some of those were pirates, but most were captives who tried to start rebellions. They were put in the room and starved to death, then tied to rocks and dropped to the bottom of the ocean.

The guide led us through dungeons where the men and women were held, where more than a hundred people might be packed into a room large enough for twenty. It was after I came out of the dungeons, my eyes stinging from the sudden shock of sunlight, that I realized just how dark and cramped it must have been. Near the women's dungeons, we were shown a small staircase leading to a trap door just beyond the governor's room. It was common, our guide said, for the reigning governor to point out a female captive from his balcony. A soldier would bring her up the staircase to the governor's room where she would be raped.

Then our guide led us to the Door of No Return. This was the entryway where ships pulled up to load the captives. The opening was deliberately small to make escape difficult. Many of us walked to the door and stood in it, looking out at the ocean and the fishing boats. We were all quiet, the only sound was the Atlantic's pounding surf. I thought of the captured Africans hearing the waves, a sound so familiar, a sound of home. And yet they would hear that same sound as it carried them away—to South America, the Caribbean, and the United States.

We were all emotionally drained and went to the Cape Coast fort wearily. We got a brief tour of the dungeons and the trading room that still smelled of the kerosene used to clean the floors hundreds of years ago. The guide then led us to the courtyard where a stage had been set up. Students from the University of Ghana School of Performing Arts put on the play *Ghana Is Home: The Return* for us. The play chronicles the advent of colonialism in Ghana and the changes it wrought on the people. It ended with the actors taking us into one of the dungeons. As we entered the darkness, we were given lighted white candles. Once inside, we were told to blow them out so that we could experience the darkness as the captives did. Many in our group cried, but the actors wanted to end on a note of hope. As we left, they sang: "Come with me on this happy trip back to the Promised Land. Welcome Home."

Of the many trips my mother and I have taken, we agreed this was the most fulfilling. This time, instead of returning home with the notion of seeing more of Africa, we returned with the notion of seeing more of Ghana. It is a welcoming place with honest and friendly people. As for the rites, the girls returned as girls, several still cuddling dolls, but they are girls a little differently than when they left, girls who know more about their world, more about themselves, more about their strengths. And that's certainly a solid step toward womanhood. Whether I am more productive or fertile or will be a good wife remains to be seen. Those qualities are a part of me. But another part of me knows that choosing the right time is also an aspect of womanhood.

Maya Angelou

from All God's Children Need Traveling Shoes

"GOOD DAY." I SPOKE IN FANTI, AND SHE RESPONDED. I CONTINUED, "I BEG YOU, I am a stranger looking for a place to stay."

She repeated, "Stranger?" and laughed. "You are a stranger? No. No."

To many Africans only whites could be strangers. All Africans belonged somewhere, to some clan. All Akan-speaking people belong to one of eight blood lines (Abosua) and one of eight spirit lines (Ntoro).

I said, "I am not from here."

For a second fear darted in her eyes. There was the possibility that I was a witch or some unhappy ghost from the country of the dead. I quickly said, "I am from Accra." She gave me a good smile. "Oh, one Accra. Without a home." She laughed. The Fanti word *Nkran,* for which the capital was named, means the large ant that builds ten-foot-high domes of red clay and lives with millions of other ants.

"Come with me." She turned quickly, steadying the bucket on her head and led me between two corrugated tin shacks. The baby bounced and slept on her back, secured by the large piece of cloth wrapped around her body. We passed a compound where women were pounding the dinner *foo foo* in wooden bowls.

The woman shouted, "Look what I have found. One Nkran has no place to sleep tonight." The women laughed and asked, "One Nkran? I don't believe it."

"Are you taking it to the old man?"

"Of course."

"Sleep well, alone, Nkran, if you can." My guide stopped before a

*T*raveling in Africa has helped me better understand and appreciate the uniqueness of black folks' language on the continent and in America. In the Ghanaian village of Amafie, where I lived during the summer of 1981, something as simple as a greeting was harmonic and almost poetic. When a woman comes into the village, those who greet her say "ma nU ooh." She acknowledges by saying, "ah yah." Her greeters follow by saying, "akwabaa" which means welcome. Then the woman will melodically say, "yoooo." The greeting gets more involved depending on the number of people involved and the gender. When there is more than one woman returning to the village, those who greet them say "ma, ma nU ooh." When a man is returning, the greeting is "enja nuo" or "enja, enja nuo," if there is more than one man.

If a mixed group is returning the greeters say, "enja, enja, ma, ma, nUo." The incoming group responds, "ah yah." The greeters then say "akwabaa," and finally the others say "yooo." It's almost like a short song. "Yo." Sound familiar? It's African American lexicon for Hello.

Don't tell me that our language is not rich.

—Linda Jones

small house. She put the water on the ground and told me to wait while she entered the house. She returned immediately followed by a man who rubbed his eyes as if he had just been awakened.

He walked close and peered hard at my face. "This is the Nkran?" The woman was adjusting the bucket on her head.

"Yes, Uncle. I have brought her." She looked at me, "Goodbye, Nkran. Sleep in peace. Uncle, I am going." The man said, "Go and come, child," and resumed studying my face. "You are not Ga." He was reading my features.

A few small children had collected around his knees. They could barely hold back their giggles as he interrogated me.

"Aflao?"

I said, "No."

"Brong-ahafo?"

I said, "No. I am—." I meant to tell him the truth, but he said, "Don't tell me. I will soon know." He continued staring at me. "Speak more. I will know from your Fanti."

"Well, I have come from Accra and I need to rent a room for the night. I told that woman that I was a stranger...."

He laughed. "And you are. Now, I know. You are Bambara from Liberia. It is clear you are Bambara." He laughed again. "I always can tell. I am not easily fooled." He shook my hand. "Yes, we will find you a place for the night. Come." He touched a boy at his right. "Find Patience Aduah, and bring her to me."

The children laughed and all ran away as the man led me into the house. He pointed me to a seat in the neat little parlor and shouted, "Foriwa, we have a guest. Bring beer." A small black woman with an imperial air entered the room. Her knowing face told me that she had witnessed the scene in her front yard.

She spoke to her husband. "And, Kobina, did you find who the stranger was?" She walked to me. I stood and shook her hand. "Welcome, stranger." We both laughed. "Now don't tell me, Kobina, I have ears, also. Sit down, Sister, beer is coming. Let me hear you speak."

We sat facing each other while her husband stood over us smiling. "You, Foriwa, you will never get it."

I told her my story, adding a few more words I had recently learned. She laughed grandly. "She is Bambara. I could have told you when Abaa first brought her. See how tall she is? See her head? See her color? Men, huh. They only look at a woman's shape."

Two children brought beer and glasses to the man who poured and handed the glasses around. "Sister, I am Kobina Artey; this is my wife Foriwa and some of my children."

I introduced myself, but because they had taken such relish in detecting my tribal origin I couldn't tell them that they were wrong. Or, less admirably, at that moment I didn't want to remember that I was an American. For the first time since my arrival, I was very nearly home. Not a Ghanaian, but at least accepted as an African. The sensation was worth a lie.

Voices came to the house from the yard.

"Brother Kobina," "Uncle," "Auntie."

Foriwa opened the door to a group of people who entered speaking fast and looking at me. "So this is the Bambara woman? The stranger?" They looked me over and talked with my hosts. I understood some of their conversation. They said that I was nice looking and old enough to have a little wisdom. They announced that my car was parked a few blocks away. Kobina told them that I would spend the night with the newlyweds, Patience and Kwame Duodu. Yes, they could see clearly that I was a Bambara.

"Give us the keys to your car, Sister; someone will bring your bag." I gave up the keys and all resistance. I was either at home with friends, or I would die wishing that to be so.

Later, Patience, her husband, Kwame, and I sat out in the yard around a cooking fire near to their thatched house which was much smaller than the Artey bungalow. They explained that Kobina Artey was not a chief, but a member of the village council, and all small matters in that area of Dunkwa were taken to him. As Patience stirred the stew in the pot, which was balanced over the fire, children and women appeared sporadically out of the darkness carrying covered plates. Each time Patience thanked the bearers and directed them to the house, I felt the distance narrow between my past and present.

In the United States, during segregation, black American travelers, unable to stay in hotels restricted to white patrons, stopped at churches and told the black ministers or deacons of their predicaments. Church officials would select a home and then inform the unexpecting hosts of the decision. There was never a protest, but the new hosts relied on the generosity of their neighbors to help feed and even entertain their guests. After the travelers were settled, surreptitious knocks would sound on the back door.

In Stamps, Arkansas, I heard so often, "Sister Henderson, I know you've got guests. Here's a pan of biscuits."

"Sister Henderson, Mama sent a half a cake for your visitors."

"Sister Henderson, I made a lot of macaroni and cheese. Maybe this will help with your visitors."

My grandmother would whisper her thanks and finally when the family and guests sat down at the table, the offerings were so different and plentiful it appeared that days had been spent preparing the meal.

Patience invited me inside, and when I saw the table I was confirmed in my earlier impression. Ground nut stew, garden egg stew, hot pepper soup, *kenke, kotomre,* fried plantain, *dukuno,* shrimp, fish cakes, and more, all crowded together on variously patterned plates.

---

*G*oree is a beautiful beach front island just off the coast of Senegal, West Africa with a bright warm sun and a friendly breeze that invites you to enjoy the water, the sand and the sun. To get there we took a thirty minute ferry ride from Dakar. As the island came into view, the sky is lined with strange buildings that look like forts, with iron bars and iron guns and fortified walls. The buildings annoyed my senses for they didn't belong in this otherwise beautiful place.

As we approached and drew nearer to the island there was a hush in the air and for the African Americans on board there was a heaviness in the air. Everyone was very still and quiet. Everyone knew why we have come to this island and where we are going once we disembark. We are going to see and touch and feel and smell and hear the pain and anguish of our ancestors. We are going to reclaim that part of ourselves that has been lying dormant since our ancestors were last here.

The quietness still hangs heavily around us as we approach the House of the Slaves. This is the last place our ancestors knew African soil. We wait patiently as the big heavy wooden doors are opened and there before us lies the courtyard that millions of Africans passed through on their way to a land of toll, pain, and suffering. We see the small cell rooms where fifteen to twenty of our foremothers and forefathers were shackled together with chains around their necks and around their ankles waiting for the white slavers to arrive in their slave vessels.

We hear the stories of how families were separated by sending the father to Louisiana in the United States, the mother to Cuba or Puerto Rico and the child to the Virgin Islands. We are all visibly shaken but it is not over yet.

There at the end of the courtyard stands the "Door of No Return." It was through this door that the African passed never to return home again. We have returned to this spot to reclaim what was taken from us, to put to rest the souls of our ancestors.

—Ruth E. Gough, "The Door of No Return"

In Arkansas, the guests would never suggest, although they knew better, that the host had not prepared every scrap of food, especially for them.

I said to Patience, "Oh, Sister, you went to such trouble."

She laughed, "It is nothing, Sister. We don't want our Bambara relative to think herself a stranger anymore. Come, let us wash and eat."

After dinner I followed Patience to the outdoor toilet, then they gave me a cot in a very small room.

In the morning I wrapped my cloth under my arms, sarong fashion, and walked with Patience to the bathhouse. We joined about twenty women in a walled enclosure that had no ceiling. The greetings were loud and cheerful as we soaped ourselves and poured buckets of water over our shoulders.

Patience introduced me. "This is our Bambara sister."

"She's a tall one all right. Welcome, Sister."

"I like her color."

"How many children, Sister?" The woman was looking at my breasts.

I apologized, "I only have one."

"One?"

"One?"

"One!" Shouts reverberated over the splashing water. I said, "One, but I'm trying."

They laughed. "Try hard, sister. Keep trying."

We ate leftovers from the last night feast and I said a sad goodbye to my hosts. The children walked me back to my car with the oldest boy carrying my bag. I couldn't offer money to my hosts, Arkansas had taught me that, but I gave change to the children. They bobbed and jumped and grinned.

"Goodbye, Bambara Auntie."

"Go and come, Auntie."

"Go and come."

I drove into Cape Coast before I thought of the gruesome castle and out of its environs before the ghosts of slavery caught me. Perhaps their attempts had been halfhearted. After all, in Dunkwa, although I let a lie speak for me, I had proved that one of their descendants, at least one, could just briefly return to Africa, and that despite cruel betrayals, bitter ocean voyages and hurtful centuries, we were still recognizable.

Evelyn C. White

Egypt: Body and Soul

SISTERS (AND BROTHERS) OF ALL RACES WHO WANT TO EXPERIENCE THE FULL FORCE of the achievements of people of color should make a visit to Egypt a top priority. It's impossible to believe the negative stereotypes American society perpetuates about the aspirations and abilities of blacks after seeing the great civilization the Egyptians developed centuries ago. People of color have a grand and glorious heritage that has been systematically kept from us for far too long. In Egypt, black accomplishments are reflected in architecture, books, art, song, science, and agriculture. At every turn, there is something to remind one that African Americans are descendants of some of the most brilliant and sophisticated people that ever walked the earth. As the late black writer James Baldwin said, "Our crown has already been bought and paid for. All we have to do is wear it." I'm here to tell you that they're wearing it big time on the shores of the Nile.

My two-week visit to Egypt was the fulfillment of a lifelong dream. As a child growing up in Gary, Indiana, I was always fascinated by the storybook images I saw of the Pyramids. Stylized drawings of Egyptians with their hands pointed in opposite directions never failed to catch my eye. A word and phonics addict, I was enchanted by the secret codes and language waiting to be revealed in hieroglyphics. While living in Seattle during the late 1970s, I got up one morning before dawn to stand in line with thousands of people hoping to gain entry to the local museum's exhibition of treasures from the tomb of King Tutankhamen. "This little brother was bad," I thought to myself as I slowly walked past one dazzling gold display after another. "He was something else." My decision to visit Egypt was sealed by my friend Candace, who has lived in Spain for nearly two decades and traveled widely. When I asked her to name the most memorable country of all she has visited, she said "Egypt" without hesitation. I was on my way.

Even for seasoned travelers, Egypt can be difficult to manage because of unfamiliar customs, delays with transportation, the heat, and language (Arabic) barriers. I took an organized tour and strongly recommend this approach for first-time visitors. I felt it best to leave the details to travel industry experts who understood Egyptian culture better than I. Most tours are designed to ensure that a traveler cruises the Nile and visits the Pyramids, the Sphinx, the Cairo Museum, the Valley of the Kings (where King Tut's treasures were found), and several other magnificent temples.

The first thing I noticed upon arrival in Cairo was the thick smog that envelopes the city. Stringent environmental regulations and pollution controls are simply not a priority in a country that is still primarily agriculturally based. The air quality in Cairo is disheartening, but apparently (unlike Mexico City) has not yet been deemed an immediate health hazard. The air in Cairo is cleansed somewhat by the majestic Nile River that dissects the city, as it does all of Egypt. Bringing forth

On an all-day trip down the Nile to Luxor I had lunch on the upper deck, under colorful canopies. There were three kinds of soup, four kinds of fresh fish, and three kinds of beans served in several delicious ways: baked beans with tomatoes, pinto beans served with tahini, and green beans, pole beans and string beans cooked with ham and bacon. Fresh mixed green salads, mixed fruit of the country, and a Jell-O like salad served on palm leaves. Pie, cake, and ice cream were served on deck and came as a big surprise considering the hot weather. All this was topped off with cinnamon tea spiced with clove, coffee, beer, and wine.

The river was alive with boats and feluccas, gliding up, down and across from one bank to the other. Horns tooted, bells rang, their passengers smiled and waved, sometimes greeting us as we passed. We returned the greetings as we walked up and down on the upper deck. On the shore, mothers with babies on their hips and smaller children clinging to their skirts came closer the edge to smile and wave when we passed.

In the late afternoon women with shrouded heads carrying water in gleaming brass water jugs perched on their shoulders passed between the palm trees. The cane fields formed a back drop, and in the distance, now and then could be seen straw cones of villages scattered here and there. Naked boys waded up to their knees in the water netting fish, their bodies glistening with the sweat of labor and tanned by the sun. These scenes brought back memories of long forgotten summers from my childhood and I oddly felt very at home.

—Mary J. Miller, "My Cruise on the Nile"

fertile land, food, and power, the Nile is considered the Mother of Egypt.

Seven and a half miles outside of Cairo, in the suburb of Giza, are the towering Pyramids. I first saw them out of the corner of my left eye as the tour bus rambled down the road. They span the horizon, appearing larger and more impressive than any photo could ever depict. As we drove closer, I realized that I was actually in the storybook picture that had bedazzled me as a child—the image that had maintained its black allure and power, even as it was juxtaposed against those of German shepherds snarling at black children, the mule-drawn cart bearing the body of Martin Luther King, Jr., and other horrific images from my youth.

When I stepped out of the bus in front of a caravan of camels sprawled lazily on the desert sand, my jaw dropped and tears formed in my eyes. I could hear the voice of Aretha wailing, as she does on her album *Amazing Grace* about the rocky road on her way home.

The Pyramids (the tombs of the pharaohs Cheops, Chephren, and Mycerinus) were erected as royal burial grounds and are the star attractions of Egyptian tourism. Nearby, guarding the Pyramids, sits the enigmatic Sphinx, sculpted in the shape of a lion with a human head wearing a headdress. Unlike the massive structures it watches over, the Sphinx is actually much smaller than its picture postcard images. Despite the throngs of camera-clicking tourists who flock to the site, the Pyramids and the Sphinx retain a regal dignity that has left people breathless for centuries. For me, seeing and touching the time-honored structures, reinforced my belief that any obstacle can be overcome, no matter how formidable. The Pyramids and the Sphinx are living proof that people of color have accomplished great feats. Surely we can conquer drug addiction, teen pregnancy, unemployment, spiritual despair, ruthless politicians, and the other contemporary ills we face.

After several days in Cairo (during which I stumbled upon a festive Egyptian wedding), my group flew to Luxor to board a ship that cruised the Nile. In the heart of Upper Egypt, Luxor is the site of Thebes, the "hundred-gated city" immortalized by Homer. Among its many treasures is the divine city of Karnak, a temple of stones, statues, and obelisks that covers more than forty acres. Down the road a bit is the temple of Luxor, which, experts say, the Egyptians used only to commemorate New Year's with a raucous celebration. The temple of Luxor is also the site where soprano Leontyne Price once performed her signature opera *Aida*. It was sheer bliss to imagine her singing in the midst of these sensuous ruins on the bank of the Nile.

Luxor is also the starting point for visits to the nearly one hundred tombs in the Valley of the Kings and the Valley of the Queens. Dug into hillsides are the cavernous tombs where the mummies of pharaohs once lay and the temples in which they stored the treasures they would need to survive in the afterlife. From floor to ceiling, the tombs are graced with shimmering blue and emerald green hieroglyphics that tell the story of each pharaoh's victories and defeats. The tombs helped me—a product of America's death-fearing and -denying culture—gain a new perspective on life. According to the ancient Egyptians, life never ended, but rather continued into eternity. They greeted death not with sorrow, but rather with a joyous acceptance and anticipation of experiencing an even better afterlife. In fact, the legendary Queen-Pharaoh Hatshepshut was so exhilarated by the prospect of death that she ordered a mortuary temple to be built especially for her embalming. The huge split-level necropolis is built into the side of a mountain top in the Valley of the Queens and is heralded as one of the most spectacular architectural achievements in the world.

From Luxor, the deluxe cruise ship would sail to temple sites at Esna, Edfu, and Kom Ombo before arriving in Aswan. After visiting the Valley of the Queens, our group was dropped off in the commercial waterfront of Luxor, not far from where the ship was docked. We were directed to make our way back to the boat for lunch, after which, we were scheduled to depart for Esna.

Until one's body clock adjusts, the combination of early morning outings and (in my view) the mystical impact of Egypt can leave a first-time visitor disoriented and dazed. I believe that African Americans are especially susceptible to this phenomenon because of the ways in which the splendor and power of Egypt contradicts the denigrating messages we've internalized about our roots. That's exactly what happened to me in Luxor.

*O*utdoor sightseeing excursions in Egypt are routinely scheduled between 5 a.m. and 11 a.m. to avoid the heat, which can easily reach a surreal 110–120 degrees by noon. Be sure to check with a travel expert about seasonal temperatures before booking a trip to Egypt. I visited the country during the relatively "comfortable" month of September and still, several people in my group were affected by the heat.

—Evelyn C. White

Overwhelmed by my experiences at the tombs, I spaced out. I meandered along the waterfront, walking in and out of shops for who knows how long before coming out of my stupor and heading back to the boat. As I approached the dock, I could see a huge cruise ship moving down the Nile. My stomach sank. I knew instinctively that it was the Ramses—the boat I was supposed to be on.

There were several men on the dock, coiling ropes, oiling wenches, and tending to other nautical chores. I ran toward them, hoping they'd tell me it was the Prince Ra-hetep or the Khufu sailing away, not the Ramses. No such luck. Stunned, I stood on the dock, gazing out at the water as the ship moved steadily toward the horizon. "I can't believe it," I said to myself. "I've really and truly missed the boat."

Luckily, I'd made a point of memorizing the ship's itinerary and knew for sure that the next stop would be Esna. Lesson learned: When traveling with an organized tour, be sure to know your group's daily destinations. Don't count on the guides to fill you in on all the details. Travelers can easily get separated from their guides. Don't I know it.

When I visit a new place and encounter a new culture, I look first to identify some similarities to my own. When I've done that I find that I can start to notice how people are different—how they are in their communities, how they treat each other, and how they treat visitors. For example, one thing that often amazes me when I visit another country or even another state is how many people say "hello, good morning, etc." They welcome friendly faces. If a stranger greets me in New York City, I wonder to myself, "what does this person want?" Traveling offers me the chance to see the limits of what I take for granted.

—Coreen L. Jones, "Travel: My Passion"

I had my passport, driver's license, and plenty of cash in my backpack. I had noticed, during the trip, that folks in the group often divvied up their personal belongings with partners or friends. One person would place, say, the water bottles, wallets, cabin room keys, etc. of both travelers in one pack. Then they would trade-off carrying the bag. This was done, I'm sure, so that each person would be periodically unencumbered during often strenuous days. Although I was traveling with a dear friend, we'd decided to maintain control over our own money and personal documents. Lesson learned: Never leave money, passport, plane tickets, or other valuables in the care of a traveling companion. Graciously decline to be responsible for another traveler's belongings.

Working also to my advantage was the decade I'd spent working at a major metropolitan newspaper. As a reporter, I'd covered riots, explosions, murders, earthquakes, conventions, etc., in cities both large and small. I was accustomed to finding myself in unfamiliar situations that demanded my full concentration. Thus, when it sunk in that the Ramses was not going to make a U-turn and retrieve me, I shifted immediately into reporter mode. My assignment was to meet the ship in Esna without getting raped, robbed, or killed.

My concern about safety was not particular to being black or the fact that I was traveling in Egypt. Common sense dictates that safety should be of paramount importance to any female, anywhere, anytime. In this case, I knew that I'd thrown myself into a crisis situation and was therefore more vulnerable to making hasty decisions. So, as I turned from the dock and walked toward a row of about a dozen taxis, I offered a silent prayer to the Gods asking them to help me choose a driver who would deliver me to Esna in one piece. His name was Aesop.

What I remember most about Aesop is that he was wearing a tan, crisply ironed, full-length *jelaba*, or shirtdress, that contrasted beautifully with his cocoa-brown skin. Indeed, I'm sure I was drawn to Aesop because he exuded a cool, calm, serenity in what was by then, brain-broiling midday heat. There was not a bead of sweat on his body. Discreetly flashing a $20 bill, I asked Aesop if he'd take me to Esna. He looked around nervously, as if trying, mentally, to fend off other taxi drivers who might have swooped upon me for the fare. Having vibed away the competition, he gently hustled me into the cab. Lesson learned: When in a tight spot abroad, let your greenbacks do the talking.

Off we went. If you're thinking speedy, sprawling interstate highways, think again. We're talking back roads, dusty roads, gutted roads, twisted roads, to who knew where? Surely not I, for whom Esna could have just as well been Edinborough for all I knew of its whereabouts. For two hours, Aesop and I rambled through rustic villages and lush Egyptian farmland that I would never have seen had I not missed the boat. Along the way, he explained many of his country's customs to me with the whimsical pride that I came to know as characteristic of Egyptian people. Delivering me to the site where the Ramses would dock several hours before its scheduled arrival (land travel is much faster than water), Aesop suggested that I visit a nearby temple and purchased an entry ticket for me. As he drove away, I thought about the often fractious relationship between black men and black women, and how in America, we've become so far removed from our best selves. My time with Aesop gave a meaning to the word *brother* that I'll carry with me for the rest of my life.

After visiting the temple, I found myself strolling through Esna's open-air market. I was soon greeted by Nubie, a poor, barefoot Egyptian boy of about ten, who ran to my side and asked, in halting English, if I knew Mike Tyson, Bill Cosby, or Michael Jackson. Quick to shrug off his disappointment when I answered no, Nubie lit a cigarette (quite common among Egyptian boys), and then offered to take me on a carriage ride through town. With the grace and charm of a refined gentleman, Nubie took my arm and led me around the corner where a speckled gray horse, hitched to a black carriage, stood in the sun swatting flies with its tail. Just as we were about to start clip-clopping down the street, a thin boy with a thatch of dark curls, wearing a soiled and tattered *jelaba*, came running toward us, shouting excitedly. The boy, apparently a friend of Nubie's, was begging to join us on the ride. With an officious nod, Nubie granted permission, and the boy, all elbows and knees, scampered into the carriage.

With the horse's hooves tapping out a steady, syncopated beat on the pavement, we rode along Esna's waterfront. After a while, Nubie pulled the reins and we turned left into a dusty, mazelike neighborhood of whitewashed houses with tightly shuttered windows. Stopped at an intersection, Nubie leaned back and asked if he could take me home to meet his mother. I said sure, and his face lit up like Times Square.

Nubie's house was a plain, primitive structure crafted out of baked earth. The peeling paint, rickety door, and other signs of poverty were diminished by its coziness and the fact that the temperature inside was a full 20 to 30 degrees cooler than outside. Nubie's mother, a short, dark-skinned woman dressed in black, responded to Nubie's Arabic commands by extending her weathered hand to me and then scurrying to the kitchen to make tea. His sister, a girl of about twelve, grabbed a broom made of palm fronds and began sweeping a patch of dirt in front of a battered gold couch she motioned me to sit on. When the sweet, fragrant, cinnamon tea was ready, Nubie's mother poured three glasses—for me, Nubie, and his friend. I waved my hand toward Nubie's mother and sister, encouraging them to join us; they both giggled nervously, shaking their heads from side to side. In a flash, my mother wit kicked in and I understood what was happening. Though only about four feet tall, Nubie was clearly the man of the house. And I, the smiling, polite, then thirty-four-year-old black woman from America, was being showcased to Nubie's mother as a "love interest." It was so poignant, I nearly started to cry.

Word must have gotten out about Nubie's "girlfriend" because the next thing I knew a stream of neighbors was outside the house. Smoking a cigarette and speaking proudly in Arabic, Nubie opened the shuttered windows and allowed the people to peep in. There was soon a huge crowd gazing lovingly at me, including several women in brightly colored wraps, who were holding babies. These women were especially animated and seemed quite eager to enter the house. After a rapid-fire exchange in front of the window, Nubie went to the door and ushered the women with babies into the living room. One after the other, they came forward with their kicking, cooing infants and held them before me to touch. For this, I needed no translation. The Egyptian mothers clearly considered me a sign of good luck.

I snuggled, nuzzled, bounced, cradled, and rocked a good two dozen babies before realizing that if we didn't leave soon, I might again miss the boat. I gestured to Nubie (who was now standing about six feet tall), that it was time to go, and after making my farewell to the glowing crowd, we climbed into the carriage and left. As the horse made its way back to the waterfront, with both Nubie and his friend beaming, I reflected on my amazing afternoon. Missed boat, fantastic taxi ride, adorable babies, and ten-year-old Egyptian "boyfriend." What a life!

About fifteen minutes after we arrived at the dock, the Ramses pulled in. I waved—as cavalierly as I'd walked through the shops in Luxor—to friends on the ship who had come out on the deck and were leaning over the railing, looking for me. I wondered how I could possibly thank the gods for such a memorable day. While I knew it was meaningless in terms of the cosmos and my profound sense of gratitude, I handed Nubie a wad of bills before I walked down the gangplank to the Ramses. He took them, kissed me on the cheek, and burst into a smile that is forever etched in my heart. A blazing, magnificent smile that is the body and soul of Egypt.

Opal Palmer Adisa

Accra Drums Me Home

I EMERGED FROM KATOKA AIRPORT IN ACCRA, GHANA, AND FACED A WALL OF people, nutmeg to charcoal colored, some with shiny, sweaty faces, others dry and smooth as silk. They were dressed in brightly patterned clothes—deep greens, browns, oranges, yellows, reds, in various floral and geometric designs—each pulling my eyes to its beauty. Then suddenly I felt people pressed in on me, their bodies forming an impenetrable wall, and my head swam. Their voices were loud, almost defiant, as people called out to relatives and friends emerging, like me, from the bowels of the airport; their speech was as rapid as if they were in a race to see who could speak the fastest. I felt shut out from their conversations, but something about their presence, the smell and intimacy of being squashed among them, was very familiar. I closed my eyes and for a few moments I was back in Jamaica at downtown parade during a Saturday evening shopping frenzy.

Bata, bum-bum. Bata, bata, bum-bum. The sound of the conga drums pulled me back into the moment. I opened my eyes, looked up at the sky and realized it was that time of day just before the sun waves goodbye and darkness descends. The sky was swollen pink with a mauve haze shadowing it. The moment felt magical, unreal. *Bu-dum. Bu-dum.* The chatter of the people gained my attention once again. I looked into their faces, seeing expressions of cousins, aunts, uncles and friends—Jamaica in Ghana, I thought—historical connections made real. A calm euphoria descended on me. I certainly would have floated but for all the people swarming around me.

I searched the crowd hoping to recognize Afiwa, my childhood pen pal with whom I had been communicating and exchanging photographs for over fifteen years. There were so many people, most of whom were taller than I. I'll never find her, I thought. Then a large man with a moon-shaped face and chiseled features tapped me on my shoulder and said, "Welcome, my sister. You must be Opal." I smiled, recognizing Kofi, Afiwa's husband. Kofi pointed way beyond the crowd and I spied Afiwa waving at me. Kofi grabbed my luggage and cleared a path for me by shoving his way through.

As we got to the periphery of the crowd, Afiwa came up and hugged and held on to me as if she would never let go. When we pulled apart, she smiled into my face and said, "My sister, I never thought this day would come. I'm so happy to meet you at last. Welcome home." I had to fight away tears as we made our way from the airport grounds, Kofi on one side of me, asking about my trip, and Afiwa on the other, saying again how happy she was to see me.

Once on the street, I breathed deeply. People were no longer pressing in on me, their sweat and ardor no longer stung my nostrils and I suddenly felt exposed. Just then the sun tipped its hat and for a minute the day folded in on itself, but it was not yet ready to relinquish its place to night. Afiwa reached for my hand and squeezed it. Her gesture was like a warm shawl draped over my body. I smiled at her and followed along.

I glanced around, certain that a car was going to pull up to take us to Afiwa and Kofi's home, but instead, Kofi hoisted the larger of my two suitcases on his head, Afiwa did likewise with the smaller one, and they walked down the road. I looked around but saw no car approaching. After walking five blocks, we stopped, and Kofi said his friend, a cab driver, would pick us up shortly. My throat felt parched and the heat clung to my body. Twenty minutes later the cab arrived and before we were settled safely, the driver sped off, swerving in and out of traffic. The landscape zoomed by like a high-speed movie reel: red soil, large, leafy trees, and people, vibrant in colorful clothes, both native and western. I had to close my eyes to seal the images into memory, so when the cab stopped, I was jolted.

Kofi announced we would walk the rest of the way to their home. Night was creeping in, but as I looked around at the open gutters, peeling paint, zinc fences, and dilapidated housing, I realized that this was not the middle-class setting I had pictured, knowing that Afiwa was a secretary at the television station and Kofi an accountant.

Kofi and Afiwa once again hoisted my luggage and I followed behind. There were no roads, merely dirt tracks. Shacks in need of repair told the story of poverty. Women throwing dirty basins of water and rubbish in the open gutters, as well as children balancing enamel and plastic containers of water indicated that there was no indoor plumbing. My eyes darted from one scene to the next as we wound our way through James Town, one of the largest ghettos in Accra.

My nostrils flared from the stench. I marveled at the children who were everywhere, running in and out, frolicking around, seemingly happy, with white-toothed grins. I was weary and sweat glued my clothes to my body as I tried to keep up with Afiwa's and Kofi's fast pace. The evening was a concert of voices and sounds, and were it not for the conga drums tom-tomming, *ba-ta-ta, ba-ta-ta,* I would have sat right down in the middle of the path.

After what seemed like an eternity, we arrived at their compound. Kofi pushed the gate open and I was greeted with loud tongue-clicking and hand-clapping. Many people rushed up to touch my shoulder in welcome. Afiwa introduced each one, including Kofi's brother and his wife and their children, whose cottage was adjacent to theirs. I smiled and shook hands with each one. Then Afiwa presented her three sons and the nine-year-old niece she was raising. They bowed shyly, addressing me as "auntie" before scampering off.

Several people offered me food and drink. Exhausted from the long trip, I ate what was presented to me and smiled, not understanding much of what was being said. Afiwa tried to translate. Someone said she and I resembled each other in a small way. I nodded in agreement. I started to feel uncomfortable being waited on and wanted to be doing something, so I asked for my suitcase and distributed the gifts I had brought for the children. They were delighted with the toys and books and took them to show their cousins who stood off, watching us.

At this point, I wanted the welcome to be over with as I needed to urinate. I asked to be shown the bathroom and was taken to the outhouse. At the sight of the wooden, boxlike closet, I was on the verge of saying, Take me to a hotel, but my need was urgent. Nonetheless, I began to sweat under my arms. I felt as if I was thrust back into my childhood. Each summer after I turned eight, my mother sent my sister and me to her relatives for a week in one of the most remote rural regions of Jamaica. Although I usually enjoyed myself, the trip played havoc with my bowel movements because they had an outhouse and I was always afraid I would fall in the pit or be bitten by the lizards and insects that inhabited it.

I breathed deeply, and Abena, Afiwa's niece, held the lantern high and opened the door. It was clean and I didn't spy any insects. I stepped in and Abena closed the wooden door, leaving me in complete darkness. I felt a scream coming up my throat and without thinking kicked the door open. With the light streaming in from the compound, I hastily relieved myself and stumbled out. Abena awaited me five yards away with a cup of water to wash my hands.

I was ready for bed. I desperately wanted to be in a quiet room by myself. Afiwa read my mind. She brought me a basin and towel to wash my face, then made me sit on a chair while Abena washed my feet. Afterward, Afiwa led me through a crammed living room/kitchen area into a back room with a full-size bed neatly spread. "This is your room now," she said. " Rest well." I pulled off my clothes, stumbled into bed, and as my head hit the pillow, the drums in the distance uttered, *bat-ta, ba-um, ba-um, bu-dum, bu-dum...* and I felt my eyes closing.

The next morning I awoke to a quiet house. I pulled on the same dress I had worn the day before and walked outside where the glaring sun greeted me. No one appeared to be around. I stood on the little patio and took in my surroundings starting with the dirt ground swept clean. On one side of the compound were four cottages, including the one in which I stood, each with a little patio enclosed by a brick wall. On the other side of the compound were the outhouse and the washing/shower area, a rectangular box without a roof. In the center was a large tree, from which ran clotheslines fully draped with washed clothes. There were three or so dilapidated chicken coops and chickens running around the yard. A few wobbly looking tables on which were eating and cooking utensils were also placed around the compound, and two large covered barrels stood beside each cottage. Other paraphernalia were scattered about the yard. It looked like a well lived-in and efficiently used space shared by how many, I was unsure. My survey was interrupted by a lilting voice: "Good morning Sister Opal. I hope you had a good sleep."

"Yes, I did," I replied, and wished Afiwa's sister-in-law, whose name I did not remember, good morning. With her baby strapped to her back, she gave me a basin to wash my face and brush my teeth, then fed me breakfast. While I ate she suckled her baby and after apologizing about her poor English (which I had no difficulty understanding) she asked if I had any children, whether Jamaica was close to America, if all black Americans were rich and looked like the people in Ebony magazine, what did I do in America, and if it was true that I wanted to come and live in Ghana. I answered her questions as best I could, and she seemed surprised by many of the answers, especially that many black Americans are poor. I don't think she believed me. When the baby fell asleep she went to put her down, then handed me a pail of water to take my bath.

When I emerged from the shower, Kofi was waiting for me on the patio. He was a broad-chested man with cool, velvety charcoal skin, and short cropped hair. His voice was lazy, but his eyes were inviting. The first thing he asked me after exchanging pleasantries was if there were lots of jobs in America. He spoke about his frustration at not being able to find employment since the company he worked for folded two years ago. He had gotten a visa to Nigeria, where he had secured work and from where he had been able to send money home. But after six months his visa expired and they refused to extend it. He was dispirited and said he felt useless.

I didn't know what to say. I certainly had no job to offer. We sat quietly, Kofi tapping on the table on the patio. When I stood up and stretched, Kofi sprang to life. He laughed, light and full, and offered to be my tour guide. "What would you like to do?" he asked in a formal tone.

"I want to stand under the Black Star," I declared and Kofi smiled approvingly. He went inside to change his shirt, then pulled the door behind him and we entered one of the many paths of James Town. We passed open markets teeming with people, mostly women, selling fruits, cooked food, gorgeous fabric, and all manner of things. There was a riot of color everywhere. Women strolled about assured, elegant, in ankle-length wrapped skirts, *gèlès* adorning their heads, babies strapped to their backs, many with baskets on their heads and a load in one or both hands, yet stepping as if they owned the world.

I kept falling behind Kofi be-

I'm sure other folks have had long plane trips, but surely a five-day journey is right up there in the record books. In 1962 I was working for the U.S. Agency for International Development and had accepted a job as the missions's first records supervisor in Mali, a former French colony in West Africa. The newly established government was cautious of all foreigners and travel restrictions were stringent and complicated. (Photography was strictly forbidden. Just possessing a camera without a permit from the Minister of Information engendered serious consequences.)

After a grueling flight from Washington, D.C., via Paris to Dakar, I was relieved to be on the last leg of my journey. I *just* missed my flight to Bamako (I watched it taxi down the runway) but was confident that there would be space on the next plane when I was told: "You have just seen the very last plane leave Dakar for Bamako. The borders between Senegal and Mali were closed at six-thirty this morning. There will be no communication between our two countries, riding or walking."

Exhausted, and with a weak grasp of French, I set about to find a way to Bamako, which turned out to be a flight back to Paris (!), where I stayed overnight before heading south once again, this time directly to Bamako. I finally arrived five days after leaving home!

—Mary J. Miller, "Assignment Mali"

cause my eyes could not stop feasting on all the sights. My people, I kept saying inside my head. I was proud just observing them but also sad that they had been kept from me so long that I was unable to communicate with them. There was so much I wanted to ask, to know. I felt my heart beating against my chest, and I heard the drums drumming in my ears.

We arrived at Independence Square and I stood under the Black Star and paid homage to Kwame Nkrumah, the great African visionary. Ghana had been the promise not only of Africa but for many in the diaspora who came from North and South America and the Caribbean to realize the vision. "What happened to prevent its realization?" I spoke my thoughts aloud. Kofi shook his head as if trying to shake off a blow. His shoulders drooped. We sat close to each other as Kofi, his voice choked, talked about Nkrumah's assassination. For him, it signaled the end of the dream of Africa's independence. Everything he had hoped for was buried with the great leader. His anger came to the surface and his eyes were red when he spat, "I don't want to leave Ghana, but I can't feed my family here anymore." I wanted to put my arms around his shoulders, but he turned from me and stood up.

We returned to the compound just as Afiwa arrived home from work. It was my first opportunity to be alone with her and really see this woman who had so generously welcomed me as her sister. She was cinnamon colored, tight as a rope, and strong. Her eyes were probing and bright and she wore her hair in an Afro. When she pulled me to her side, I noticed that she was no more than two inches taller than I. I could tell from the instructions she gave her niece and sons before we left for the market to purchase food for dinner that she was precise and accustomed to being in charge.

We clasped arms like schoolgirls as we strolled among children heading home and women, like Afiwa, shopping for dinner. She pointed out food items; some I recognized, others were unfamiliar. She carefully explained everything I inquired about and set about teaching me Twi. We talked with the ease I feel with the people I've known all my life. We laughed and swapped secret desires until darkness draped us, then we made our way back to the compound. It was after seven o'clock, but Afiwa and Abena squatted with ease, pounding spices and crushing tomatoes to prepare a delicious tomato fish stew with *fufu* that they cooked in the open on a coal-burning stove and a portable two-flame gas burner.

After dinner, although it was after nine o'clock, Aiwa said she had to take me to meet her mother who lived about a mile away. The heat of the day had cooled, and as we walked I noticed the sky, an assured blue sprinkled with stars. As we approached Aiwa's mother's compound, I heard the drums, *bata-bata, batter,* and asked Aiwa if they never ceased. She said they were announcing the death of someone, but she didn't know the person. I reached for Aiwa and pulled her to stop; I listened with my whole body but could not decipher the rhythm. I felt like a child in her presence. "Come," she insisted, pulling me along.

Anna, an elegant woman of eighty-seven, squatted gracefully near the door to her cottage, a lantern on a stool close by. She smoked a pipe and scrutinized my face before declaring to Aiwa that I was one of them, and therefore her daughter. While Anna waited for her daughter to translate, she held me firmly by the wrist as if she didn't want me to escape. Aiwa said she reprimanded her for bringing me so late and told her to bring me earlier the next day. Her penetrating gaze and the utterance of the drums followed me all the way back to Aiwa's home.

Early the next morning Anna came to see me at Aiwa's compound; she couldn't wait until the evening to ask her questions. She wanted me to describe Jamaica and tell her about my family, especially the matrilineal line. She asked me if we had queen mothers too and whether all Jamaicans were Ghana people like me. It was a long and reflecting conversation, one of many that I would have with her during my three-week stay.

Sometimes, when I visited Anna, she would pull me to squat beside her or sit on a low stool, and we would stay like that for thirty minutes or more without talking. Every so often she would reach out and pat my arm, look into my eyes, smile, nod her head in satisfaction, utter a clicking sound with her tongue, then resume smoking her pipe. Whenever I was beside her, I felt cloaked in a warm towel and I yearned to rest my head on her bosom and be cradled by her.

The day Kofi took me to Cape Coast Castle, however, not even Anna could have comforted me. Visiting one of the slave forts was one of my reasons for wanting to go to the motherland. I didn't know what to expect, but I certainly was not prepared for the aching feeling that gripped me. The view from the castle was ironically beautiful, the waves swelled and swirled, and the ocean breeze was soothing. I took off my shoes and walked along the beach and imagined I saw myself bound and naked, being led away. I was scared and could not look out to sea, believing that if I did, I would be carried away, never to return. I was reluctant to go inside the fort, to wander through the damp, dark passages. Eventually I did, urged by Kofi who stayed outside talking to the guard.

My eyes were slow adjusting to the dimness; my feet literally led the way. I didn't wander throughout. I couldn't. I was overwhelmed and after a while just crouched, close to a square window that was about nine inches by nine inches. My mind left my body then and I became a woman, younger than I, eighteen at the most, squatting there, with tear-stained cheeks but hard eyes in which were imprinted the bloody body of her lover. She was squatting there just minutes before she was prodded on board a boat, still hopeful that her brother, father, or someone would come and rescue her. But the ship sailed with her hope. I was that young woman and fear, pain, and anger clasped my body. I fell like a block of ice. I could not move, not until the guard came and told me it was time to leave.

I shivered as I rejoined Kofi on the landing. When I rubbed my eyes, I was surprised to find them dry; salt had eaten my tears. We did not talk on the long drive back to Accra and I did not hear any drums. By the time we arrived at the compound, night had fallen and the sky was indigo. My head throbbing, I refused Aiwa's offer of food and retreated to my room, but sleep eluded me for a long, long time.

❖ ❖ ❖

The day before I was scheduled to depart, Aiwa and Kofi planned a Christian marriage ceremony and accepted my offer to withstand the cost of the feast. In keeping with their tradition, Aiwa and Kofi had already exchanged fabric before becoming man and wife, but Aiwa was nevertheless enticed by the Western ritual. I was one of only three people who accompanied them to church to exchange their vows, Aiwa looking smart in a simple beige suit, Kofi looking slightly uncomfortable in his western clothes. The Caucasian priest did not appear enthused, and although the ceremony was short, I found the whole affair quite boring. Moreover, I was upset at the colonial practice that required Aiwa and Kofi to take European names before they could be married.

Once the church affair was over, we returned to the compound. Anna and Aiwa's sisters and their children were there as were Kofi's brother and uncle. The compound, now overflowing with family and friends, had been transformed into a festive place with chairs and tables arranged in groups. No clothes hung from the lines and even the chickens had been put away. Colorful cloth had been draped over the back fence and over the railings, giving the appearance of a sea of color. Three drummers under the large tree pounded their hearts into their drums. The tables were piled with food and laughter abounded. Afiwa and Kofi had changed into traditional dress and Afiwa took me around and introduced me to the family members and friends I had not yet met. The women clicked their tongues loudly, singing *lululu* rapidly and clapped their hands. The men stamped their feet. The children darted in and out. After a great deal of food was consumed, the women, elegant in their long wrapped skirts and flounce-sleeved tops, got up to dance.

Dancing was their providence, and they danced with one another, not with the men. I was pulled to my feet to dance with one woman after another. They thrust their breasts forward, contracted and released their pelvises, shuffled their feet on the ground, extending their arms in a half-moon away and toward their bodies. Then all the women formed a circle, holding one another around the waist and swishing their hips from side to side. Sweat snaked down my clothes. I danced until I was out of breath, then rested, then got Abena and danced with her, then danced with Anna, who moved only from the waist up, in a gently, seductive sway. Her smile was a firefly in a dark sky.

The drums blared, *batata, batata, budum, budum*. The women encircled me and I danced, forgetting myself, only hearing the drums telling me to prance and leap, to come home, that I *was* home. Tears smarted my eyes. The women embraced me; Afiwa said I was her long-lost sister returned. I clapped and laughed until I felt stitches in my side. I was dizzy. Ghana and Jamaica merged. I evoked my ancestors and their spirits swelled out to meet me. The drums rang, *batata, ba!*

Barbara Ellis-Van de Water

Harvest out of Africa

THERE IS A PLACE IN THE HEART OF AFRICA'S GREAT RIFT VALLEY WHERE WINE grapes grow. The Masai named this place E-Nai-Posha, "that which is heaving, that which flows to and fro." Perhaps it is the ancestral way of describing Lake Naivasha, a remarkably beautiful place and the home of Elli, my sister-in-law, and her husband, John. In 1982 they started Kenya's first commercial winery with vines from some of California's most prestigious wineries, purchased or generously donated by friends in the winemaking trade.

Many might think it foolhardy to start a winery fifty miles south of the equator; and yet, it is easy to explain why a vineyard can thrive there. With the exception of two rainy seasons, most of the days in the valley are hot and dry. The evenings are cool because of the high altitude and moist breezes off Lake Naivasha, whose waters are used to irrigate the vines.

Elli is from Los Angeles. She met John, a third-generation Kenyan farmer of Irish-English descent on a blind date while visiting Kenya. Elli's letters were full of stories about her life and the progress and perils of the young vineyard. She wrote about the giraffe that wandered through the grapevines, dining on the tops of thorn trees, and the hippopotamus that chased her from the lake to the steps of her verandah. Her letters contained as much real-life drama as any that Karen Blixen sent out of Africa.

Her letters and a love of family, wine, and travel made a visit inevitable.

❦ ❦ ❦

As we approached Lake Naivasha Vineyards, riding over the crest of the escarpment, we had a breathtaking view of the Great Rift Valley and Mt. Longonot rising 9,000 feet above sea level amid the vast, endless plains. This enormous seismic fault in the earth's crust, we learned, provided the sandy volcanic soil that nurtures the vines.

The harvest was well underway when my husband and I arrived. The crop of sauvignon blanc grapes had already been harvested and was fermenting in thousand-gallon fiberglass vats inside the winery. But there were rows and rows of vines—thirteen acres in all—burdened with clusters of green-gold colombard grapes waiting to be picked. We had come to Kenya to go on safari, but for a few weeks we would harvest wine grapes with Elli and John and the crew.

"*Habarai asubuhi.*" The melodious Swahili greeting rang out from the workers gathered outside the winery ready to begin the day's tasks.

"*Jambo sana,*" I answered, enjoying the opportunity to use the Swahili I was learning.

"*Kazi mengi,*" the workers said, and I knew that had to mean "lots of work."

We picked the grapes in the cool morning hours between six and ten when they are freshest. As the sun rose over the vineyard, there was singing and laughter. The men sang comical songs about women and love, often raising their voices in falsetto to mimic the women they were singing about.

I looked forward to my mornings with the harvest because it was a chance for me to become acquainted with people who live and work in the surrounding villages. (These were mostly men, the majority of whom were from the Luo, Kikuyu, and Kamba tribes. Few women participated.) They were curious about the cost of things in the United States, everything from T-shirts and blue jeans to a plane ticket to Kenya. I told them the *kikapus* (colorfully woven straw bags) we were filling with grapes sold for as much as $25 in many stores. For these men who earn a few dollars a month as grape pickers and farm laborers, America seemed like a place where only millionaires could live. But they didn't believe anyone with so much money could be happy.

I was also curious about them. "What is the cost of a child's education?" I asked a man whose child was attending the village school. "A bag of flour," he told me. "Women walk with children and firewood strapped on their backs," I said. "It is such a heavy load. How far do you walk in a day?" The answer came with arms and palms opened wide.

One of the chores around the homestead was to collect firewood and straight branches that could be used to stake the vines. One day I accompanied a couple of men, riding in a trailer hitched to a tractor to Kedong Ranch, a communal Masai farm that spreads for many miles below the slopes of Mt. Longonot. Hudson, a Kamba, was our driver and unofficial guide.

Over the tractor's loud engine, Hudson would shout, *"Twiga!"* and point to a giraffe. He would frequently stop so that I could take pictures of zebra herds galloping across the brown, grassy plains or catch a glimpse of a gazelle darting into the bush. When we stopped for the men to clear away the bush, Hudson warned I should look out for *simba mkubwa*, a big lion. But his smile told me he was only teasing. The ride on the tractor pulling a trailer full of wood was slow and rough across the unpaved trails. At the end of the day, every muscle ached.

I had taken along a small photo album filled with pictures of my family and friends, my home, even my cat. These were a comfort to me but they were also invaluable in my efforts to talk with people. Whenever the lack of a common language rose as a barrier, I'd pull out my book and share the pictures of my parents and grandparents on their farm in North Carolina. In a place where wealth is measured in children, land, and livestock, I had found a common bond. One by one the curious would gather around to look at the pictures, some even to touch, as if tracing the faces within the photographs might bring them to life.

There was one picture that everyone from women in the marketplaces to Masai warriors, to workers in the vineyards held up in surprise. It was a photograph of my grandfather standing in the yard in front of his home dressed in the dark khaki pants and shirts he wore to work in the fields. "He is Kikuyu!" they'd exclaim over and over again. It was spoken definitively and with pride.

During the harvest, the winery was a hub of activity. Every piece of equipment was in use, from the mechanical crusher that destemmed and crushed the grapes as they were brought in from the vineyard to the wine presses that strained every last drop of free-run juice from the grapes. Except for the crusher, imported from Italy, all the equipment, including the fiberglass vats, was manufactured locally following John's design. Even a refrigerated stainless dairy tank was converted for use in the winery. A local artist was asked to design the labels for the wine bottles, and Alfred, a young Kikuyu from a nearby village, was trained to manage all aspects of the winery.

News of the vineyard and winery traveled quickly through the uh, grapevine. John and Elli were hosts to many guests who stopped by on their way to or from safaris, balloon rides over the Rift Valley, or camping trips in the Aberdare Mountains. During my visit, a crew from CNN came to report on the winery. Later, a family who owns a small winery in Bonny Doon, California, spent a few evenings talking shop with John and Elli. Robert Mondavi and his wife discovered Lake Naivasha wine at the Mt. Kenya Safari Club and later made a visit to the winery.

After sampling Kenya's alternative to the domestic papaya wine, it's no wonder visitors found a bottle of Lake Naivasha Sauvignon Blanc, Colombard or Carnelian (a nouveau-style red wine) a coveted souvenir among the *kikapus*, copper bracelets, and brightly colored *kanga* cloths.

Naivasha is famous for its exotic bird life. Blue herons were a familiar sight along the shore, and it was thrilling to watch fish eagles swoop down out of the sky. On Sundays, the family made excursions to nearby game reserves. On picnics at Lake Nakuru, we watched flocks of pink flamingos feeding and bathing on the lake. Just a few miles from the vineyard is Hell's Gate, a national game park and Masai reserve where jagged cliffs open to Lake Naivasha and mists of steam rise from fractures in the Rift Valley floor.

A short rowboat ride took us across Lake Naivasha to Elsamere, the memorial home of Joy Adamson, the author of *Born Free*. If you arrive in time for lunch, a cast of black and white colobus monkeys welcomes you and usually stays around until you share some of your lunch with them. On neighboring Crescent Island, I wandered through abandoned thatched huts and walked among kongoni, gazelle, zebra, and giraffe, all roaming wild and free on this tranquil sanctuary.

*I*n the years following our visit, relaxed import duties flooded the Kenya market with affordable South African wines. This, along with a 67 percent tax on wine sales made it impossible for the winery to survive. A thriving flower business has replaced the winery; field upon field of brilliant flowers now grow where wine grapes once ripened under the heat of the Kenyan sun.

—Barbara Ellis-Van de Water

My walks along the lake were a peaceful respite from the intensity of taking in so many new sights and sounds, from the far-away roars that haunt the night to the giraffes striding with their long-necked gait, to roadside markets crowded with barefoot women, their babies slung in *kangas* across their backs. I cut the walks short, however, whenever I spotted a dark-gray hump in the shallow waters. I remembered Elli's encounter with a hippo and her warnings that despite their size hippos are very fast.

On the morning before our departure, we took one last look at Lake Naivasha from the top of Mt. Longonot. It was a spectacular view. High upon her peaks, we walked along a narrow path that circled dual craters and discovered a densely wooded forest in one, a sprawling green pasture in the other. When we returned to the vineyard, my husband presented Elli and John with a sign he had carved for them. Etched in the wood normally used to support trailing grapevines was a jagged outline of Mt. Longonot leading into a cluster of grapes chiseled into the shape of Africa.

Emma T. Lucas

A Homestay in Namibia

DURING THE SUMMER OF 1995, I TRAVELED TO NAMIBIA AS A MEMBER OF CARLOW College's Fulbright-Hays Group Project. Homestays in Northern Namibia were arranged for each of us so that we could have a firsthand experience of living with a family.

I had read books, looked at travel videos and slide presentations, and chatted extensively with several people who had visited Namibia. And I'd been given information about the home in which I would be a guest. But there was still much I couldn't imagine. I was eager but a bit nervous as well.

Finally the day arrived when we would meet our host families. After lunch in Oshakati, we headed to Tsandi. Although we were two hours late arriving, the welcome committee was still waiting. They took us to the local school where the community received us warmly with speeches and introductions to our host families.

When a member of the welcome committee called my family's name, I looked behind me and saw two smiling faces belonging to the hostess and her niece. Immediately my anxiety began to dissipate. I walked over and greeted them. All three of us were excited; they didn't seem to mind any more than I did that we were communicating only with hugs and smiles. My hostess, MaMa Sunna, was a schoolteacher. Both she and her niece, Loide, who had recently graduated from high school, spoke limited English. We could communicate quite effectively, however, with hand gestures and facial expressions and words that were a mixture of English and Owambo.

It was dusk by the time we left the school yard with about ten people following us; this was my own welcome group. I could see a man just ahead of me carrying my suitcase and could hear lots of chatter and laughter all around me, but I could understand nothing of what they were saying. I followed MaMa Sunna as we took off along a narrow path toward lights that I could see in the foreground. Soon we came to a wide opening with several bottle shops and people sitting and standing around the entrances. We entered one of the shops with difficulty—everyone wanted to shake my hand and welcome me—and MaMa Sunna asked what I would like to drink. I had decided that my liquid intake

I recommend that you take some small items to give as gifts to people who might do little favors for you. Trinkets like key chains, pencils, or pens with the name of your business make nice little tokens of appreciation. I found that not everyone who assisted me was looking for money in return. Many treated me like kin and to accept money would be an insult.

I also learned that some gestures of appreciation that I considered significant were not necessarily so for some of my African friends.

When I was in Ghana, I took a young brother out to dinner to thank him for taking me around his village and teaching me the language. Solomon Mensah had spent a lot of his time with me and I wanted to do something special for him. I thought he would be impressed with dinner at a nice restaurant since he could not afford such a luxury. Throughout dinner Solomon seemed quite subdued. It wasn't that he was ungrateful, it was just that fancy dinners made this village youth uncomfortable.

I didn't know what I could do for him to show my appreciation. When I was preparing to leave the village for America, I no longer had use for the mud-crusted boots I wore as I worked on the farm and on the construction site where we were building a school.

When I unceremoniously gave him those boots he beamed—something to protect his feet as he trudged through the bush and walked miles to carry out his duties was something he could truly use. He was so thrilled with the gift that he wrote me a letter later telling me that he had changed his name to honor me. He is now Solomon Mensah Jones.

—Linda Jones

would be limited because I did not know what the bathroom facilities would be like. We agreed on coke, and she asked for two large liters, indicating that it was all for me.

After a brief visit, we walked toward another bottle shop where a truck was parked. My welcome group ascended on the large pickup truck that would take us home. I was told to sit in the cab and, to my surprise, four of us crowded in. The back of the truck was crowded as well. As the truck pulled off, I realized my knee was against the stick shift and the driver was trying to change gears. My effort to move my leg was in vain; there was no room to move an inch. We rode along a dark narrow path. I could see nothing beyond the range of the truck's headlights. I wondered how the driver knew where he was going but realized that he had traveled these paths so often he knew every curve in the road.

When we finally came to a gate, the truck slowed. Someone in the back jumped down and opened it. The truck pulled through slowly, giving the gate opener time to get back on the truck. In the far distance I could see a flickering light. The truck came to a complete stop when we reached the light and the cab door opened for unloading. Three cheerful children, Tomas, Shigwedah, and Iikila, and a teenager, Christophena, ran toward us. Each small child wanted something to carry, and MaMa Sunna gave them the cokes and her purse.

MaMa Sunna began walking and I followed, unable to see anything except the person in front of me. We passed a fence made of tree branches, several large baskets elevated above the ground, and objects spread around several large huts. We entered a concrete block house and the family proudly showed it off to me: a small room with a table in the center, a cabinet nestled in one corner, benches along the wall, and a cooking area under the window behind the door. The adjoining small room, the bedroom, had two beds jammed against the walls.

Now I was formally introduced to the three boys and two nieces. The children jumped about as I reached to shake their hands and say hello. I listened to MaMa Sunna and a niece conversing while the children looked at me with curious eyes. I asked them their ages, but their looks suggested they did not understand me.

MaMa Sunna removed glasses from the cupboard and with gentle care, dipped one into a bucket of water then filled the glass with coke and offered it to me. I really did not want to drink anything but felt this was a welcome gesture I should not refuse. She then began clearing the small table, brushed a brazen roach to the floor, and placed plates from the cupboard on it. Christophena spread a mat on the floor and placed two pots in the center. One contained goat meat stew and the other, millet. Everyone sat on the floor, and MaMa Sunna beckoned for me to join them. I claimed a spot on the end of the mat, and the food was blessed. I waited to see how MaMa would serve the plates.

Namibia gained independence in 1990 after decades of colonial occupation. South Africa mandated the system of apartheid in Namibia and African people were obliged to live in specially designated areas called "homelands" on the outskirts of towns. The effects of apartheid still exist today for many people of African descent. All aspects of life (education, housing, employment, etc.) are affected. Economic development in Northern Namibia has been slow and some of the nation's poorest citizens live in this region.

—Emma T. Lucas

The boys began picking meat from one pot and were quickly stopped by MaMa who searched in the pot for a piece of meat to give them. She picked up pieces, examined them, and then decided who would get each piece. She picked up a delightful lean piece and put it on my plate. She then instructed me to reach in the second pot of millet, form a ball, and dip it in the stew. The first ball was very gritty, and my face gave away what I was feeling. Everyone laughed at me. MaMa instructed me not to chew the millet, but to swallow the ball whole. This proved difficult to do. I then tried to bite into the meat but found that it was very tough and I could not bite it. The stew, however, was spicy and delicious. After the meal we chatted for an hour before I announced that I was sleepy.

Holding a candle that gave off little light, I followed MaMa Sunna to a small thatched-roof hut. She proudly announced that this was my room, opened the tin door, instructed me to bend down so I would not bump my head, and pulled back the piece of cloth that draped the door. I was pleased with what I saw. The earthen-floor room was very neat, and held a bed and small table. There was one small window with a dainty white piece of lace over it. MaMa placed the candle on the table and told me it was mine, and that I should blow out the flame when I went to bed. The brightly geometric patterned linen on the bed was new. I sat on the edge of the bed for thirty minutes reflecting on my arrival in Tsandi and deciding how I would brush my teeth and change into my night clothes.

The sounds of laughter and conversations floated through the thatched roof and small window. After a while, I heard a woman's voice coming in my direction in the dark of the night. It was MaMa coming to say good night to me. Despite the thick blackness of the night, she traveled about the compound without a lighted candle. I asked about a place to brush my teeth, and she led me past my hut and the concrete house to an open area with a small concrete slab. She told me this was where I could release myself and brush my teeth. I didn't need to worry about privacy because as far as I could see there was darkness. My candle had guided my footsteps and dimly lit this small area. I brushed my teeth using Evian water and relieved myself.

I returned to my hut, blew out the candle, laid my tired body on the bed and covered it with the sweet-smelling linen, and a cozy comfort enveloped me. I lay in the dark, listening to the goats and chickens moving about on the other side of the cloth door. I looked up at the thatched roof and saw sprinklings of the night sky peeking through. Many thoughts raced through my mind. I was in Southern Africa. I was a guest in a family's home. I had never slept in a hut before, but I felt a closeness to this environment. I thought about how warmly I had been welcomed, how generously they had shared their food with me, and realized that poverty is relative. There were so many lessons they had taught me in a brief six-hour period. I began to question my own life priorities.

About 5 a.m. a rooster boldly crowed and the goats bleated: the compound's alarm clock. I wondered if the animals were going to march past the cloth door and honor me with a visit, but they didn't. Around 6 a.m. I could hear movement outside my hut but decided I would listen to the rhythms of the activities and chatter from my bed. Soon I heard someone call my name; it was MaMa who suggested I get up, wash up, and take breakfast so we could leave for school.

I gathered my change of clothing and toiletries and headed to the bath area. I passed Christophena who was cooking the breakfast porridge.

I was feeling very enlightened to have "come home to my roots" when one day during my three week stay, I noticed a bellman at the hotel grinning wryly at me. I asked him, "Lual, why do you grin at me so."

He said it amused him to watch Americans. "You must be so confused."

"Confused?" I replied. "What do you mean confused?"

"Well look at you all. You come over here with your fancy clothes and ways and call yourself African Americans. You don't know what it means to be African. We call you black Americans because you're just Americans with black skins. You don't know anything about being African. If you did, your country wouldn't be in the state it is now."

I felt so still I could hear a pin drop in my brain. I thought about all the kente cloth, "African" rituals and festivals, styles of dress, etc., that we constantly reach out and support. We jump at anything African to identify with. But being African, I was to learn, has little to do with the way you dress, wear your hair, the music you listen to or even events that you celebrate. Being African is a knowledge of self, respect of tradition and acknowledgment of culture.

It's knowing who you are and what your purpose is on this earth. It's knowing what tribe you came from and the customs that are traditional to it. It's respect for your mother and father and respect for all elders. It's knowing the value of religion and faith and the belief in something. It's knowing your history.

The Sudanese think all Americans are rich. By their standards, we certainly are. But the question is, rich with what? Fancy cars? Jewelry? Education? Welfare? Elaborate churches? Modern prisons? Greed?

On the way home from the airport, my husband began to tell me all of what I missed while I was away: someone smashed the window in my car and stole my CD player, an update of the O.J. trial, gory details of the Oklahoma City bombing, $1000 dollars worth of roof repairs at home and that my once college-bound nineteen-year-old year old cousin had given up his college career to work full time at McDonalds.

"Welcome to America," I thought to myself.

—Sylvia Perry, "Khartoum, Sudan"

She stirred the pot over an open hearth with a long stick that didn't look long enough. Her hands appeared to be too close to the high flames. How is it that she was not burned? I asked if the flames hurt her arms and was told that she had to stir the porridge until it was well cooked.

She put another twig on the fire and continued stirring. A large wash basin of warm water awaited me at the bath area. I looked up at the light blue satiny sky. The morning air was crisp; as I washed, the feel of the air against my body energized me, but I hurriedly covered myself for warmth, pulling each piece of clothing one by one from the tree branch fence.

MaMa said that we would have to leave in five minutes, so I hurried to finish my tea and collect my bag from my hut. We started out of the compound, passing the huge millet storage baskets, and Shigwedah and Iikila followed us to the gate. I could now see the road we had driven on the night before and several paths, all of which looked the same. We walked past one compound after another and MaMa identified her relatives that lived in each. I asked about the distance to the school and was told it was not far. What is the meaning of "not far"?

MaMa suddenly indicated that she heard the truck. Within five minutes, a small beige truck pulled up and everyone climbed on the back. I wondered how MaMa could hear the sound of the truck in the far distance. What a keen ear! I also wondered how long it would take to learn directions since the wide-open field had only bushes for markers. The truck stopped to pick up school children until the back was full. Hands waved to the walkers as the truck passed. Students and teachers walk as far as seven miles daily to and from school, year-round. We rode for about five minutes before I saw something that looked familiar: the bottle shops and the school where we had been the night before.

The day was spent mingling with students, taking pictures, and talking. Many of them had questions for me. What is America like? Do I know Michael Jackson? What was my school like? At the end of the school day, MaMa and I walked to the bottle shop we had visited the night before. The beige pickup arrived and we got in. We headed up the road and disembarked in front of a few shops. We went into one, but MaMa could not find what she wanted. We then went in the bottle shop where five people were enjoying beer. MaMa offered me a seat and a coke. We sat and chatted for an hour. Everyone was enjoying their beverage with several drinking very freely. About every ten minutes a beer bottle was emptied and a full one opened.

Eventually, we went to the store across the road. MaMa told me that she wanted to serve spaghetti for dinner. We left our purses with the security guard and walked down the aisles until MaMa chose a box of macaroni and a bottle of catsup. These were the ingredients for my special meal. I thought we would be going home then but no, there was another stop to be made, at the bottle store that we had visited earlier. MaMa and several other women chatted, and a woman helped me give responses in Owambo to the people who were trying to start a conversation with me. Finally we loaded into another truck and started down the road toward the house. The children ran to meet us and open the gate.

MaMa cooked the spaghetti, and, although it was different from what I am used to, it tasted fine; it was my first full meal of the day. The children and nieces and I chatted all evening. What was my daughter's name? How old was she? Where did I live in America? Did I have pictures of my home? The children entertained me by reciting verses and singing songs in broken English. MaMa pulled out the family photo albums, identifying everyone in the pictures, and telling stories of the events they depicted. I learned that her husband (along with many other local men) worked in Windhoek because there was no employment for him in the area. I gave them each a small gift, and the children, especially, were exuberant about them. I took pictures of them with a sharp shooter and the children loved watching the images develop before their eyes. The evening passed quickly and soon it was bedtime.

Before retiring for the night, I again reflected on the day's activities. I valued these people and their humble lives. I understood their happiness and their determination. Listening to the animals, I drifted off to sleep.

The morning came quickly. The routine for my morning wash was now familiar. The nieces were busy heating water and preparing the morning millet. MaMa was in the kitchen preparing our lunch of chicken and boiled eggs. The children were running around. When we left for school, one of the nieces went with us to carry my suitcase. As we walked out of the compound, I realized that I wished I could stay longer.

The children waved to us until they were wee people in the background as we strode through the open field toward school. We walked much farther this morning than we did the morning before. In the distance I heard the truck. I knew that it would carry me away from my Namibian family, which I had grown attached to in a short but memorable stay.

Lucinda Roy

Seeing Things in the Dark

WHEN I WENT TO AFRICA FOR TWO YEARS AS A VOLUNTEER TEACHER, I WAS twenty-one. I was afraid, not of the land itself, but of being without my mother, my best friend. How would I manage to find happiness thousands of miles from her laughter? I was a girl alone, hardly a woman yet. How would I be able to uncover places in the land that knew me? I'd never traveled outside of Europe before. I didn't know the local language. I was afraid of puff adders and malaria, leprosy and crocodiles. Most of all, I was afraid that the people would not like me. For a "colored girl" raised in London, Africa meant going home to my ancestors, but home had been England for twenty-one years. If no one recognized me in Sierra Leone, how would I recognize myself?

Two and a half decades later, having lived now on three continents, I am accustomed to abiding within my own difference. With my Jamaican and British heritage, I am not your typical Brit anyway. And there is something sweet about singularity—something that says I will never have to see the same things others see. But back then, yearning for the familiar stole my breath away and almost made me forget to see that I was being blessed.

It was pouring when I first set foot in Sierra Leone. The heat was like a swaddling cloth, and the darts of rain met the ground as steam. I traveled in the back of a van to the Catholic girls' school in Lunsar where I would be teaching. I sat in the windowless back of the vehicle with a young Sierra Leonean of about eleven who had needed a ride to and from the capital city. Every time the priest who was driving swerved to avoid a pothole, the boy would murmur in terror. I tried to comfort him, but we didn't speak each other's language; even if we had, his terror was beyond words. So great was it, in fact, that it eclipsed my own for a while. Fear didn't surface again until we pulled up to the concrete block, single-story house I would occupy for the next two years. In my bedroom was a bed, a table, and a chair. Outside, the rain came down and hit the tin roof like the wrath of Jehovah. When night came I sprayed the room with Shelltox to kill anything living within ten feet of me, checked my slippers for tarantulas, tucked in the mosquito net around the wafer-thin mattress in a ritual that bordered on paranoia, and listened to the sound of drums coming through the bush. I didn't just taste fear, I feasted on it. Why had I traveled so far? Home, though times had been hard, was more comfortable than this. I wanted a burger. I wanted a television. I wanted to be someone's daughter again.

Each day I walked down the pink dust road to Our Lady of Guadalupe to teach English to girls who came from regions throughout the country and who were taught by the nuns to behave like someone's idea of a "lady." Each day two hundred voices rang out across the playing field as the girls spoke Temne, Mende, Krio, and English, and I sat in the teacher's lounge, wishing for a fan, just one fan, to mitigate the heat. Each morning I found a large mound of ants and soil in the corner of my living room where I had swept the night before, and each evening when I went into the kitchen, a dozen roaches scurried away to hide in the dark. My anger was often directed at the nuns and the priests, may of whom lived as strangers among the people, importing wine and cheese from Italy, and speaking with certainty about truth and redemption. Yet I too lived as a stranger among the local people, waiting for the next food package from my mother, or the next trip to the capital so that I could buy real ketchup and mayonnaise.

At twenty-one I became a teacher of young women who looked at me with hunger, and who dreamed of wearing watches and contact lenses, of traveling to England and America, and of working in the city at a bank or a hotel. A group of Namibian girls, brought to the school by missionaries from the south, sat in the shade during study periods and sang about their families and home. The father of one of them had been hanged for insurrection and the others didn't know how many of their relatives had been killed in the war. Their voices threaded inside of one another until their harmony was as tight as the braids on their heads, and no individual voice could be picked out from the entwined grieving tones. They brought out in me an even deeper yearning for those I'd left behind in England—a yearning I felt guilty about. After all my dreams of making a difference, I had arrived in West Africa with too much baggage to be any good to anyone.

For several months I closed my eyes. I refused to see the beauty of the women as they balanced firewood or huge bowls of water on their heads. I couldn't see the sweetness on the faces of my neighbors' children. I forgot to look at the way the bananas on the tree in my backyard were turning from green to gold. City life had pulled a veil over my eyes. Like many travelers who forget to surrender to the journey, what I saw was a country that occupied the negative space of my vision. In the foreground was London and the familiar roar of urban life. I lived in West Africa, but I wasn't really there. I talked with other volunteers: Peace Corps volunteers from America and CUSO volunteers from Canada. Because they remembered what I had known, we would reminisce like elderly people who have seen the best of times once and want to return to them again.

Living in the small village of Sawaya in Niger, West Africa, reminded me of my hometown of Adel, Georgia. The people all knew each other and everyone was in everybody else's business. For the men, their busy time of work came in seasons. When they were not working, they could be found under a shade tree shootin' the breeze in a language I thought I would never grasp. For the women, their busy time of work also came in seasons: the Hot Season, the Cold Season, the Rainy Season, and the Dry Season.

As a peace corps volunteer in a country where leisure time was as important as work, I had a lot of time for myself. Time to reflect, release, and renew my mind. Time to shift from the nine-to-five world to one free of constraints and time limits. I fell asleep each night under God's starlit canopy and awoke each morning to the sounds of the men praying to Allah. I learned to tell time by watching the sun.

The children became my constant companions and teachers, and in turn my yard became their playground. The women were an unending source of inspiration. Whether they were pounding millet or washing clothes or carrying water on their heads, they did it with grace and finesse. Their hips swinging and their heads held high, they had a natural strut runway models could only wish for. These sisters were bad! Mothers and daughters, grandmothers and widows, they had a confidence which had been passed down through the years.

—Dietrice Carnegia,
"Américane Noire! Américane Noire!"

Then one day I went to collect the mail as usual. The journey to the post office was quicker if I cut through the bush. I greeted the woman who sold sweet potato sandwiches and the man who was stoking his fire ready for meat sticks laced with red hot peppers. *"Kusheh,"* we said to each other. *"Kusheh-ya."* But my greeting was hollow. I had tunnel vision. At the end of the tunnel was a letter from home. The bush ran past me like a scared animal. The blue airmail envelope was the prize I had to have.

At the post office the gray metal mailboxes that lined one side of an outside wall glinted in the glare of the tropical sun. I opened my box with my precious key. Nothing. No letters from home. Although my mother wrote to me every other day, it wasn't enough. I was self-pitying to the point of fury. I turned around to walk back through the bush and almost stepped into the body of a boy. I jerked backward and felt the warm metal mailboxes on my spine.

The boy was closer to me than my shadow. His face was that of an old man, and his eyes were lined with what once must have been expectation but which had now been replaced by a kind of bitterness. He shoved something toward me and I leaped out of the way, backing off as I spoke. It took me a while to realize that what he was trying to shove in my face was his arm. I hadn't recognized it at first because so much of it had been eaten away. Raw pink flesh and yellow pus were having a kind of party on his forearm. In Krio, he demanded money, forced me to look again at his pitiful limb. In his tone was the anger of the poor and the dispossessed. I'd had it in my voice as a child when I had to call out in class, "Yes, I am a free lunch person." I recognized it. It made me sick.

I would like to tell you that I took him in my arms and carried him to the mission hospital to be healed, though the wound looked strangely aged, as though the boy had lived with his suffering for months. But it would be a lie. Instead, a terrible thought came to me before I could censor it. I thought: The colors on his arm clash with each other. And then I backed away because, in spite of my color, I was from the West, and fear was a noose around my neck.

It was only later, when I dared to let myself think of what had happened, that I felt an overwhelming sense of shame. Deeper than the fear that had held me in its grip for months, shame took hold like fire can and made me journey back to the post office for weeks afterward, looking for the child I had turned away. I never found him. But there were others who took his place.

Little by little, the British fog began to rise. I don't recall when it was that I first noticed the haunting beauty in the Muslim call to prayer that echoed through the town in the mornings and the evenings. And I couldn't tell you when it was that I first understood that Eliza and her children who lived across the dusty road were my friends. It is hard to know when I first noticed the diversity in Sierra Leone—its modern city buildings and its carefully crafted mud-and-thatch homes up-country. You would think I would be able to remember when it was that the river we traveled to whenever we could was a ribbon of olive light more beautiful than the Thames could ever be, and more ancient than the sound of breathing, but I can't remember because it was a gradual acclimatization. By the time I recognized what had happened, I had already been living among friends for many months, and we had picked many bunches of bananas from the tree, and the sky had lightened and darkened over the town a hundred times or more, and tragically, it was almost time to go back to where I had come from.

In Africa I learned and relearned myself. On a continent that blind Europeans had called "dark," I began to see how light could reveal itself in a spectrum of intense, unapologetic oranges, reds, and greens. At the risk of sounding foolish, my journey back to a land I'd never visited elevated me to a state of grace. If God exists, I found It there. It was in my shadow when the noonday sun stretched me out along the pink dust road. It was in the mouths of Sierra Leoneans when they laughed with me over *foo foo* and bitter leaf stew. It was in the hands of children scratching out their sweet responses to Macbeth in classrooms exploding with heat and necessary ambition. And it was in the dawns and dusks of a country steeped in unabashed phosphorescence. In Africa, "dark" took on another resonance. It wasn't the dark of Conrad. Instead, "dark" was an intensity of color, complexions I could approximate with my own. Terrified though I had been to leave my mother's home in London, the journey to Africa taught me more than I could ever teach. I learned how to listen to the land and its people—a lesson I have tried to take with me on all my journeys, however challenging they may be.

It has been many years since I was in Africa, and the only way I have found to treasure it is by writing and painting what I saw. I plan to go back next year. This time I will take my own child with me. When he meets strangers-who-will-soon-be-friends over there, I will remind him to listen to what they say even when they are not speaking. Because, if you listen well, their quiet words are housed in the land, and the rain uncovers them, and the sun burns them to a cacophony, and the words rise up to shake our hands. And we are not strangers after all.

There is a collection of stories by Bessie Head, the South African writer, called *The Collector of Treasures.* It is a book I read frequently with my students because in it you can learn how women bless themselves by mining small treasures from the earth: another woman's smile, perhaps, or the touch of a child, or an elderly person's many stories. When I go back to Africa, I will endeavor to collect as many treasures as possible. When I unpack each invisible gift, I will place it around my house next to the photographs of my late mother and father, who still find time, however far away they may be, to speak to me. Abiding with us in our home in Virginia will be the greetings of new friends, a gorgeous African sky, and the glory-darkness of a continent alive with light.

Tahra Edwards

Movements

"KWACHA FOR DOLLARS, RAND FOR DOLLARS—WE CAN EXCHANGE FOR YOU," THEY yelled, some in Portuguese, others in fluent King's English. The Mozambican boys were self-taught money brokers with the ability to outwit any experienced banker. They could recite the exchange rate of the rand, dollar, lira, yen, pound, or the lesser valued Malawi kwacha and compute their profit in seconds. With no formal education, these boys developed minds like calculators, yet never learned to read.

One could say that education was a casualty of war. During the 1980s, South African troops destroyed their schools, hospitals, churches, and water sources. A second, perhaps third, generation of people suffered because other governments disapproved of national efforts toward free health care and education. The countryside was sprinkled with land mines and shredded roads and power lines; the only safety lay in a zone that stretched from Zimbabwe to Malawi, called "the gun run," where money could be made from tourists.

The sun beamed down as we stood in line to go through customs at the border post between Malawi and Mozambique. My skirt stuck to my legs and my back itched from the sand that was everywhere but on the ground. It was scorching, as if all the gunfire and screams of the past several years were collected into one huge ball and it was focused right on us.

The traveling English speakers in line whispered complaints and observations. The Mozambicans milling about occasionally wiped their brows, intent on whatever task had brought them to this spot. I could hear the street vendors thinking: *Either buy something or move quickly so we can get to the next bus.* As transients, we were all alike, either incidental to or an opportunity in the survival of these people who spent their days and nights along the border.

I looked about me, past the mob of vendors. Women with babies on their backs were trying to pump water out of land that had long been dry. Some retied their fabric skirts, waiting with bundles to board the "chicken buses." Others hung intricately crocheted blankets and sweaters on trees to entice passing travelers. Little girls and boys were drinking out of Fanta bottles that travelers had left half full. The glass bottles could be redeemed for change at Coca-Cola kiosks sprinkled along the roadside. This was a safe zone. Living here was a notch or two above being a refugee.

"Ugh. Unnnnnn. Ugh," it said. I didn't know where the sound was coming from but it got louder as I moved closer to the office door. Unfamiliar with the environment, it was difficult for me to discern the sounds that belonged from those that did not.

An elderly Indian woman once suggested to me that when you're stuck somewhere with "nothing to do," concentrate on singularities—a tree, an approaching bus, or the enter/exit form I held in my hot hand. I tried to do this, but couldn't sustain it. My attention drifted to the focal point of choice for most of the travelers: an argument between border officials and a Nigerian man with apparently questionable credentials.

The line moved slowly. The officers were inspecting all bags, cars, and every stamp in every passport. They wanted to know where we had been and where exactly we were going. The sun got hotter, the dust was suffocating, and the heat seemed to be out for vengeance.

My attention drifted back to the odd human sounds. "Ugh. Unnnnnn. Aaah. Ha. Ha. Ugh." Only this time, the "ugh" became a sick grunting then a gurgling laughter. The sounds were coming from someone sitting in the dusty corner of the building. I looked away and my skin felt cold.

I knew that the RENAMO soldiers who were the Mozambican strong arm for South Africa, cut off ears, breasts, feet, limbs, and digits of the Mozambican people. Was I looking at a badly mutilated woman, a starving man, a boy, girl, what, who? I looked again. It was a woman with a keg-shaped torso, a scarred sunken chest, grotesquely twisted legs, and a mouth full of large teeth. "Ha, Ha, Ha. Heeee. He. Ha. Haaaa." The laughter ranged from the highest pitch to short bursts crescendoing up to the borderline of a moan. It somehow seemed to embody the force of the sun but without the hope that tomorrow would be just as bright.

Was I the only one who heard the sounds? The money brokers kept hustling, the women kept pumping and selling their crafts, and the kids scampered about. No one paid attention to the woman banging her head on the concrete wall and laughing hysterically. Why was this broken body with no feet wearing a thick red wool sweater and dirty white shorts? No feet. She couldn't run away. She couldn't run toward…what? Nevertheless, she was surviving, second by second, the hours that add up to a lifetime.

It was the same with the people all around me. They were making loaves of bread out of dust. In my mind, I follow the footsteps of the refugees, swinging with the zephyrs that cross the Transvaal: I am in the diamond deserts, the coal and copper mines, and alongside the posh avenues and boulevards, where they can only gape at what they will never have. I see them arrive in rickety chicken buses from Malawi, dragging their babies on bent backs.

In Harare, Zimbabwe, I lived with a Shona family. I was their foreign exchange student for a semester and I felt like I was really living! Hearing conversations between the gardeners about job insecurity; seeing my host parents go to work and transport their kids to ballet lessons and BMX bike races; watching a young mother calm her toddler, and young adults hanging out in sidewalk cafés, I soaked up everything about life in this middle-class neighborhood. I read up on issues like abortion, birth control, AIDS, literacy, environment, and the touchy dynamic of tradition versus modernity. On the weekends, the clubs were jumping, the *shabeens* overflowing, lovers stealing away, and urban children visiting their grandparents in the countryside.

It wasn't until I reached Durban, South Africa, on a traveling seminar, that I was challenged to move past the limits of my world view. I was walking down Soldier's Way Avenue, past the "sisters of circumstance" who were selling their wares, aggressively trying to persuade tourists to let go of a few rand. But I didn't see them. In my daily struggle between empathy and irritation, they were shadowy figures, not full-blooded humans. I felt impatient when they thrust crocheted shirts in my face and placed wooden statutes in my hands, although I knew it was their means of survival.

"Those women are refugees from Mozambique," Titi Pitso, my escort, said, and I began to see them differently. "They sleep on this street at night, right there where they are working," she continued. "Every night they are raped. So, what they do is sleep lined up. The one on the end, on the corner, is raped repeatedly over the course of the night. Drunks, homeless men, gangs, they all rape. The next night, another woman is on the end. They take turns so the others can sleep."

"What about rape crisis centers or the police?" I asked.

"They don't say anything because they are here illegally. They are ashamed. No one really cares. Okay. That building over there is the addition to the new market square. It holds over one hundred new shops," Titi went on.

A new market square?

I don't really remember much about the rest of the tour. That night, I watched the moon gambol across the Indian Ocean from a hilltop. I heard the sky say "Sebona," and the high-pitched chords of Indian music. The sky was clear and the wind didn't bother but to whisper that it was present.

Around midnight I rode back down Soldier's Way Avenue. The wares were boxed up and the line in place. I saw the body of the woman on the corner, wrapped in a green blanket and scraps of newspaper. I saw a man with a bottle in a brown paper bag stumbling toward her. In the beautiful still of the night, shadowing the silent terror of a sister, I heard like resounding cymbals, a chorus of girl-child screams. I heard nothing at all. For the first time during my stay, I did not hear the "cuckoo cuckoo" of birds praying before sleep nor the same "cuckoo cuckoo" of their daybreak flight.

African women. They carry their babies on their backs and ten-pound bags of meal on their heads. They herd cows and walk miles for water. They are bought, burned, cut, and bound and make it through the next day. They fight revolutions even when they know their concerns will be ignored. They sleep on corners knowing they will be raped. They keep their shoulders square, their backs straight, and their heads up high when their uncles debate their bride price. There is no sunset, no blue-period portrait, no shoreline, or cloud formation more striking than the brief glimpses I had of African women enduring, coping, and struggling to break through oppressive walls.

I heard beautiful sonances in Southern Africa: the singers of Makokoba Township in Bulawayo, the melodies of the *mbira*, the morning prayers coming from Malawian mosques, the chatter of children in the classroom of Soweto's Isaac Morrison High, and the roar of Victoria Falls. But I will never forget the laughter that wasn't laughter at all or the silence that braided a sisterhood. And I learned my first lesson in the inner strength you gain when you choose not to walk among others in luxurious oblivion.

Emma T. Lucas

My Color Follows Me Wherever I Go

OUR DAY'S JOURNEY ACROSS NORTHERN NAMIBIA WOULD TAKE US FROM ETOSHA'S deep bush and vast open plains to Waterberg Plateau Park where threatened game species breed undisturbed and rock paintings and engravings stand beside rare and exotic plants. After a long ride in a cramped *combie* (a fifteen-passenger van), we made a lunch stop in the mining town of Tsumeb. Finally, a chance to stretch our legs and enjoy the freedom to move without encroaching on someone else's space!

MiMi, Jan, and I headed down the street in search of a restaurant. We were eager to have a relaxing lunch, since we would not arrive in Windoek until late in the evening. We stopped in front of a sign that read "wait to be seated" and made eye contact with a waitress who was busy adjusting several dishes on a long buffet table, a gesture which we thought clearly indicated that we had arrived for lunch.

While we were waiting, we noticed a modern air-conditioned motor coach stop in front of the entrance. Soon a group of about fifteen white tourists disembarked and entered the restaurant, speaking animatedly in German. The waitress walked past us without saying anything, greeted them, and escorted them to tables, leaving the three of us standing. We looked at each other at the same time and our faces spoke our thoughts. My instinct was to leave, but MiMi suggested we stay to see what would happen next.

We observed the white tourists serve themselves from the buffet and begin to eat their meal. After an additional five-minute wait, we were finally seated, not inside, in the main room, but outside on the terrace

I belong any place in the universe I want to be.

—Mae Jemison,
the first black woman astronaut

where we were the only diners. While we waited for a waitress to take our order, we took inventory of the terrace and noted the difference in ambiance between the main dining area and the terrace. The inside had bright colored table-cloths and flowers, while the terrace tables were bare. There was nothing particularly pleasant about the terrace; the walls blocked a view of the lovely flowering bushes outside. Ten minutes later, with no waitress in sight, we left. As we passed through the dining room, the coach tourists chatted away, several with plates in front of them that held evidence of the completion of their first course.

We huddled together going over and over the details as we walked down the street covering one block that seemed like ten. There was no doubt that the white tourists had been given preferential treatment. Was it because of our dark skin? Halfway down the long block we fell quiet; we each needed to do some personal reflection.

When we passed a small pastry shop we looked at each other and nodded. We'd already consumed about forty minutes; counter service would give us time to visit the local shops. We scanned the case of scrumptious pastries and the sandwich menu displayed on the wall and placed our orders. Soon Jan and MiMi received what they ordered, and we started to relax. We were not going to let a racist act ruin our day! I stood in front of the counter waiting, assuming I would be served next. I observed the lone crispy brown frankfurter that was left on the grill and imagined it for my lunch.

I kept my eyes on the woman behind the counter who was moving about busily but not toward the grill to retrieve the frankfurter for my sandwich. She walked to the pastry case, selected the pastry I had ordered, placed it on the counter in front of me, and asked the white customer behind me for her order. To my surprise, the customer ordered a frankfurter as well. The woman immediately put the frankfurter in a bun and passed it across the counter to the customer.

"Is there more?" I asked.

"You'll have to order something else," she said.

"I was her before her!" I blurted out with irritation.

"She was here first," was the woman's reply.

Shock went through my body like lightning. I couldn't believe this had happened twice in one hour. I told Jan and MiMi that I would not be eating and stormed out of the shop. I'd lost my appetite.

Years of painfully jolting memories of my childhood and teen years in Meridian, Mississippi, flooded me as I strode down the street. I remembered the Greyhound bus station, its small dingy waiting area with five stools at the snack counter that sat beside the large, brightly lit Whites

Waiting Room sign. I remembered the Kress and Woolworth stores with their separate lunch counters for blacks and whites. I remembered being told to always go to the back of the bus. I thought about James Chaney, my neighbor, murdered by the Ku Klux Klan.

This treatment—referred to as "petty apartheid" in the newly independent Namibia—felt no different than what I had experienced as a black child in Mississippi. Although separateness of the races is now prohibited under Namibia's Constitution, no legislation will change racist thinking and behavior overnight. I knew this only too well. Generations of older whites who are less willing to change will have to pass on before true independence from white rule can occur.

I knew what the blacks of Namibia must feel in a country where they comprise 95 percent of the population, yet whites are the possessors of the money and skills. I knew, too, that reconciliation was critical as blacks and whites forge ahead to build a truly democratic society. I knew that they would gain ground and lose some of it, then go forward again, just as we have done in my lifetime in the U.S.

It had been a long time since I had felt so deeply about the years of pain, death, and fighting that I and other African Americans have suffered, and I felt, at that moment, deeply connected to this place I had come to as a visitor.

Renée Kemp

An Apology in Ghana

DURING PANAFEST, A BIENNIAL CONFERENCE OF TWO THOUSAND AFRICAN AMERI-cans and Caribbeans, held in the hope of bringing the diaspora back to Africa, dozens of us, dressed in African-inspired *gèlès* and robes, went late one night to see the historic slave dungeons at the oceanside city of Cape Coast, Ghana.

As we crowded into the dungeons, we shivered in the cold, damp tombs where millions of slaves had been crammed, sometimes for months, waiting to be taken on a journey of no return. We stood on the floor of the dungeons, now eight inches higher than when they were built due to the tons of compacted excrement and exfoliated skin cells from the bodies of slaves. In the women's chambers, we saw staircases leading to the Dutch and English sailors' quarters, where young African girls were taken. And afterward, as we crossed the yard that led to the male dungeons, we glimpsed the shores that were the last sight of home for Africans who were our forebears.

On entering the male dungeons, a middle-aged woman suddenly col-lapsed, overcome by emotion. Others, holding torches, sat quietly beside her on the dungeon floor. Several of us inclined our heads as if listening for voices. Everyone cried.

The time spent in the dungeons gave new meaning to a ceremony many of us had witnessed the night before. Tribal leaders from chiefdoms across Ghana had gathered at midnight in a clearing just out-side the capital city of Accra to perform a ritual "washing of stools and skins"—the Ghanaian ceremony of apology. The priests and priestesses wore red and black robes, the colors of mourning. They began by asking forgiveness on behalf of their ancestors, those chiefs who reigned centuries ago and accepted guns and promises in exchange for men, women, and children from their villages. The tribal leaders explained to us that the practice of slavery dated back thousands of years on the African continent, where it had been a condition of servitude and not, by tradition, one of cruelty. Now, with proof of the barbaric nature of American slavery, the chiefs wanted to be forgiven.

There was chanting, ceremonial dancing, and the rhythmic beating of drums. Then the Ghanaian chiefs marched in procession through the streets of Accra, spreading herbs and libations on themselves and on those who joined the procession. Soon the chiefs shed their robes of mourning to reveal white robes underneath. The white robes represented a new beginning.

As far as we knew, this was the first time the ceremony of atonement had been performed as an apology to African American and Caribbean people. For all of us who had touched the walls of the slave dungeons and sat holding torches on the impacted floor, it was clear why this ceremony had been necessary. We have always found it difficult to accept that the slave trade could not have flourished without the participation of Africans. But now the issue of African complicity had been addressed in the only way still possible: by the descendants of those who had sent their brothers and sisters in chains to the New World, and by the children of Africa who had returned to heal their ancestors' wounds. And though their atonement was four hundred years in coming, it was as joyous as a wedding, as solemn as a funeral, and as poignant as a long-awaited family reunion.

PART TWO

SISTREN
TRAVELING
THE DIASPORA

Jill Nelson

A Plunge into Adventure

TRAVELING ALONE CAN BE A DREAM COME TRUE OR A NIGHTMARE, DEPENDING ON your expectations, preparation, and attitude. The Caribbean is a good starting point for the first-time solo traveler. I'm convinced that my romance with the Caribbean is due, in addition to the sun and sea, to the startling sense of freedom that comes from being surrounded by people who are the same color I am, people who share the same legacy. I am able to relax, rejoice, and replenish my tired and cold bones.

The hardest part of traveling alone—and the most rewarding—is taking the time to understand the nuances of a country, the way people use language, interact as women and men, reveal social customs, and set up value systems. I try to spend as much time as I can interacting with the people and as little time as possible at the hotel.

Great Expectations

A lot of what happens on your trip has to do with your approach. I've found the best way to travel alone is to be adventurous, yet sensible, and to keep expectations to a minimum. Expect simply to have a restful, good time, and you're likely to have that and more. Expect to encounter true love on the beaches of Negril, and you'll probably end up feeling angry, used, or more than a little bit of a chump.

Preparation is critical to having a successful trip. First, figure out if you know anyone with friends or family in the country you'll be visiting, then call them for contacts in the islands. I've done this every time I've traveled to the Caribbean and invariably depart from the United States with a pocketbook full of phone numbers and addresses of aunts, uncles, and cousins "to call as soon as you get there." If you come recommended by Cousin So-and-So, you're sure to be protected, pampered, and shown a good time.

Second, write or call the embassy in Washington or the office in the United Nations in New York. Usually these offices have handbooks and packets of recent news stories and reports that tell you a great deal more than travel brochures. Tourist offices, most of which are in New York or Miami, are helpful for investigating hotels, packages, and places of interest.

Third, before you leave home, investigate the system of transportation in the country you'll be visiting. Are there public buses, affordable taxi service or cars for rent? Often there are locally organized island tours and day cruises. If you decide to use public transportation, be prepared for something very different from what you're used to. Ask at your hotel how and where to catch a bus and what the fare is. If you drive, have a good, detailed map and a full tank of gas. Should you decide to hire a taxi, be specific about where you want to go, inquire about the driver's knowledge of the island, and set a firm fee. The local tourist office can probably help you secure a car and driver.

Setting the Pace

Visit the island's tourism office at the airport for the most current information when you arrive. Decide from your research and from talking to people which places you want to visit: Bob Marley's birthplace in Jamaica; Coki Point Beach at Coral World in St. Thomas; or, in Martinique, the ruins of St-Pierre, which was destroyed when the volcano Mount Pelé erupted in 1902.

Spend your evening of arrival marking off places on the map that you'd like to visit. I usually begin my trip with walking-distance excursions the first day and build up slowly, so that by my third day I'm packing lunches and making day trips. Remember, too, that what might not interest you at home—a factory, a market, or a meeting of the local government—can be fascinating elsewhere. You give adventure a bad name if you return home having seen nothing but your hotel room, pool, beach, and bar!

Plan so that getting there is as much fun as your destination. Try to travel a route where there are beaches, historical sites, and marketplaces, stopping off whenever the feeling hits you. Since I've often traveled alone as a reporter, I'm usually carrying a notebook—a good device for meeting people and keeping a journal of your trip. Inevitably you'll be asked what you're doing, a great way to strike up conversations and hear people's opinions about where they live.

Always carry a swimming suit and towel so you can stop off at any of the gorgeous beaches you'll find. I always make it a point to leave at sunrise and return to my hotel by dark when I'm traveling, usually sunburnt, exhausted, and deliriously happy.

Setting the Tone

As a woman traveling alone, I've found that modesty is the best policy. I don't swim nude in the Caribbean because, as a rule, local women don't. You may see topless bathers, particularly in the French West Indies, but indigenous women commonly wear one-piece bathing suits, often with T-shirts over them, into the water. Nudity may be interpreted by Caribbean men as a come-on. Unless you mean it as such, it's simpler to wear a bathing suit. When I wear shorts, they're loose and comfortable, not hot pants.

Use your powers of observation to gain a sense of how men and women interact. If you want to know if it's alright to go to a nightclub unescorted, to ask a man to dance, or walk the beaches alone at midnight, watch what the local women do. If that doesn't answer your questions, ask someone. It's a lot better to ask a dumb question than to act like a dumbbell. Keep in mind that you're not in another world, just a different country. If you're tempted to do something you wouldn't feel comfortable doing at home—say going out with a man you just met, going to a house party you haven't been invited to, or diving off a cliff into the ocean—don't do it here. Remember, this is a vacation, not an endurance test or a chance to prove you're Superwoman.

In general, the best way to relate to the men you'll meet is in a casual, friendly fashion. I spent a marvelous day on an island once with a steel-drum player whose initial come-on turned me off. I told him so, with humor, and we ended up spending a wonderful, platonic day on the beach and driving around the island. If you find yourself being aggressively pursued or harassed by a man, first try to discourage him with

Hawaii is the only state in the union where people of color are in the majority. When I jointed a soccer team a few years back, my teammates were from many backgrounds, including Japanese, Filipino, Tongan, Samoan, Guamanian, and Chinese. I was the only African American, but I didn't feel alone because there is an active and thriving African American community here. African Americans have lived in Hawaii for hundreds of years. We are represented on all of the islands and make up about 2.5 percent of the state's population. There are African American teachers, professors, doctors, lawyers, and business professionals, as well as soulful restaurants and nightclubs. A little-known historical fact is that in the 1800s Betsey Stockton, an African American woman, opened and was superintendent of the first public school on Maui.

—Daphne E. Barbee-Wooten, "Come Ashore for African American Adventures" humor. Then get serious. If these approaches don't work, tell him firmly but not rudely that you're not interested and move away. Rejection has an international language, and the average man you'll encounter knows it when he hears it. Treat the men you meet on your trip the same way you do the men you meet on your block, and all should go well.

You might find yourself being hustled by vendors on the beaches and in the marketplaces. Just say no. Be pleasant and polite but firm when you're offered black coral on the beach or woven baskets in the marketplace. If you come across a particularly persistent and obnoxious vendor, remind him or her that you're an African American, as hardworking in your country as he is in his—it has worked for me every time.

Money Manners

Since many people on the islands depend upon tourism for their livelihood, tipping for service in restaurants, hotels, and bars is expected. A good rule is to change some of your U.S. dollars into local currency as soon as you arrive. Pay daily expenses and tips with this. Tips should be about the same amount you pay at home, but if someone has been particularly thoughtful, by all means leave something more than the standard 10 to 15 percent.

If you prepare carefully for your trip (spending as much time studying the history and the culture of the country and deciding what you'd like to do while you're there) as you do on what to pack, you're bound to have a marvelous time. The Caribbean effortlessly provides fabulous weather and gorgeous scenery. For the adventurous African American woman traveler, a trip to the islands is a chance to enrich your mind with the experience of visiting a new place and getting to know its people and culture, and to learn some new things about yourself in the process.

Sheila S. Walker

Sailing My Fantasy

I HAD BEEN INVITED TO A SEMINAR AS PART OF TRINIDAD'S EMANCIPATION CELebration and took my mother along because I thought she'd enjoy the cultural activities. Shortly after my presentation, one of the organizers took the floor.

"I'm sorry to interrupt, but something's going on. We're not quite sure what. Everyone should go straight home. There's nothing to worry about. We still plan to go dancing tonight, so we'll be in touch later. Oh, and don't go through town."

"They said not to go through town," said the man who was driving us to our guest house. "Let's go see what we're not supposed to see," he continued, to my relief.

Flames shot into the air and machine gun fire burst from buildings we'd strolled past yesterday.

"Let's get out of here," he said, less cavalierly, again to my relief.

We found the guests and staff standing in the lobby, watching a blank TV screen with steel band accompaniment. Suddenly an image came on.

"This is not a revolution made by men. This is not a revolution made by guns. This is a revolution made by God," Abubakr said solemnly. "Our foreign visitors have nothing to worry about. You are all welcome here. And," he added after the man standing behind him whispered in his ear, "the soccer match will go on. We will return to tell you more later."

Revolution or no revolution, the Imam of the Muslimeen didn't want to alienate all those soccer fans from Trinidad and its neighbors, who had gathered for the Caribbean cup match. One must have a sense of priorities. A coup d'état is one thing; soccer is another.

"What's going on?" I asked, as the blank screen and its musical background returned.

"Some local Muslimeen have taken over the government. When Abubakr came on before, he had a machine gun. I guess his PR man told him that it didn't present a good image. But we really don't know what's going on," said Jacquie, the manager.

Abubakr didn't come back, but a half hour later a uniformed official, whose hat shaded his face to invisibility announced that a state of emergency had been declared, and a curfew—twenty-four hours in the center of town, where the shooting probably encouraged people to stay off the street anyway, and 6 p.m. to noon elsewhere.

Jacquie immediately sent the staff home except for the two charming barmen who didn't have spouses and kids to tend to. After an improvised dinner, we went to bed with no call from the Emancipation Celebration organizers.

"What do we do now? Lie on the floor?" my mother asked calmly, when close-up machine gun fire startled us awake.

"I don't know."

"I thought you'd done this before."

I was pleased that she estimated my adventure quotient so high.

"Sorry. I haven't been in a coup before," I admitted. "This building is stone and seems pretty solid; our beds are more comfortable than the floor, unless the shots get closer." I tried to sound authoritative.

The next morning we found that another dutiful employee had reported to work: Trotman, the plump, cheery, elderly, hard-of-hearing night watchman, who had gathered a pile of small stones with which to defend us. We thanked him loudly.

About 9 o'clock, someone from the conference committee called to tell us to come to the airport right away for one of the two flights to the States, neglecting either to offer transportation or to suggest how we should get there, given that the curfew didn't lift until noon. It occurred to me that people with influence would want to get on the flights, making our chances slim. Better to be stuck in the congenial guest house than in an airport full of upset people, I decided. After all, Abubakr had said we were welcome. And if we kept our mouths shut, who would know we weren't Trinis? Trinidad was hardly a hostile place. Everyone but the Muslimeen knew that the citizens of the Carnival Capital of the Caribbean would rather fête than fight.

We soon learned that the Muslimeen had captured Red House, the seat of government, and were holding the parliamentarians hostage. They also occupied the Trinidad and Tobago television building. Rumor had it that Caricom troops were coming from Jamaica to help the

Trinidadian soldiers retake the government. I wasn't worried about any Caribbean military. My only fear was that the U.S. Marines would use this as a pretext to show their power by attacking the tiny island, presumably for its own good, as they had done to neighboring Grenada a few years earlier.

At noon Jacquie said she needed to go home to get some clothes, and invited us along. Four blocks away, a military roadblock stopped us.

"What are you doing out here? We have 'shoot to kill' orders," one of the six heavily armed soldiers said in the nicest way someone so equipped could say such words. I was pleased that my mother, my all-time best traveling companion, didn't seem upset. I did, however, wonder how she'd describe this incident to her friends, probably beginning with something like, "Let me tell you what Sheila did to me this time...."

"I manage a guest house," Jacquie said. "These ladies are my guests. I wasn't expecting this coup business. I need to go home to get some clean clothes. You don't want me to smell bad for the clients, do you?" she asked, smiling.

"Of course you shouldn't smell bad. Go get your clothes. But don't be long. And come back by us. This state of emergency is serious."

"I'm going to make some sandwiches and drinks for the soldiers," Jacquie said, after gathering her clothes. "Maybe no one is feeding them. We're not used to coups." The soldiers thanked her profusely for thinking of them.

When we returned we found that the other guests had found flights to their respective islands, leaving my mother and me alone with the staff. The patron/client relationship immediately transformed itself into one of people sharing an unprecedented experience.

The barmen, Cliff and Jerry, who also needed to go home for clothes, took us along. We started by driving downtown to see what was happening. Looting, not shooting, was the trend in the commercial area near the besieged government buildings.

"Getting your Christmas presents early, huh," Jerry shouted encouragingly to some people with a shopping cart full of merchandise. When we got to the modest area where they lived, Jerry told a friend his foot size, and asked him to see if he could find a brand-name sports shoe, which he later showed us on his feet.

We spent some nights at Jacquie's apartment in an affluent area, where some of her neighbors stood guard against potential looters. There we watched the shooting and burning on CNN, and the occasional strained TTT broadcasts of police officials reinforcing the reality of the state of emergency. After a few days the curfew was modified to dusk to dawn, and the Trinidadians began organizing curfew parties. You had to arrive by dusk and couldn't leave until dawn. We visited friends of Jacquie's in the country for dinner, a party, and breakfast.

"Why did the Muslimeen in Red House lose contact with those in TTT?" Jacquie asked at the party.

"Because they wouldn't use ham radios."

I had vowed not to leave Trinidad until I heard some coup jokes. Now we could leave.

We flew to Grenada for the August carnival. After looking up my Grenadian friends, we began carnival properly—with a show of improvisational calypso singers for whom Abubakr was a prominent theme, an all-night dance, and *jouvé*, opening morning, in downtown St. Georges. Floats blared carnival songs and *jab jabs;* men in brief shorts with blackened oil covering their bodies and snakes up to six feet long writhing around their necks, smeared adults and terrified children. In an hour we'd seen enough and were ready for sleep.

"Why do those people have dirt on their bodies?" I heard a voice ask.

What sounded like a deprecatory tone inspired my anthropologist self to answer, while walking away and without looking at the source of the voice. "They're standard carnival characters here and elsewhere in the Caribbean," seemed like enough of an answer.

"And why do people have on raggedy clothes?" the voice continued, again inciting my anthropologist self to respond.

"If you'll look closely," I said, still not looking at the source of the voice, "you'll notice that those aren't rags, but that people have cut patterns into their T-shirts," I said over my shoulder.

"You're from the States, aren't you?" the voice continued.

"Yes. And I hear that you are too," I responded. I had been taught to answer politely when people talked to me, but hadn't come to Grenada to meet Americans.

"What are you doing here?" the relentless voice continued.

"Carnival. And you?" Some rule of polite conversation made me add the reciprocal question.

"Sailing."

"Sailing? Where?" I focused my eyes on the source of the voice and was astounded to see four pleasant-looking African American men. The perceptive reader may begin to perceive a subtle change in attitude .

"The Tobago Keys."

"You can't go to Tobago. There's a state of emergency," I volunteered, in marked contrast to my previously perfunctory responses.

"The Tobago Keys aren't in Tobago. They're in the Grenadines," one of them said.

"The Grenadines! You're sailing to the Grenadines? That's my fantasy! You're doing my fantasy!" I suddenly wasn't tired any more. Nor was I walking away. In fact, we all began walking in the same direction, away from the carnival. Now I was the voice that kept asking questions.

"Why don't you start by visiting us on the boat?" one of them asked.

"I'll come at noon," I offered quickly, before the invitation could be rescinded, not bothering to sound cool.

I was wide awake an hour later. This situation was too serious for sleep. For months I had been doing visualization exercises, the theory being that what you visualized would manifest in your life as a result of mobilizing the energies of the universe. When I had tried visualizing the most beautiful place and activity I could imagine, it was sailing in the Grenadines. I had pondered at length how I could make it happen. Now I'd run into these brothers who were doing it in my stead. The universe wasn't playing fair.

It was time to think creatively. I could offer to write an article about them, I thought. I had had articles published in *Essence* and *Ebony*. And a friend worked for a new, upscale African American magazine for which such an article would be ideal. I would promise to be unobtrusive and speak only when spoken to.

At the dock at 11:45, I waited impatiently for noon to arrive. It came, but they didn't. I worried that they had changed their minds. Finally a dinghy came for me.

At the risk of sounding like a space cadet—though having taught at the University of California at Berkeley for more than a decade made doing so seem not unreasonable—I explained about my visualizing, and that my only recurrent vision had been sailing in the Grenadines. Before mentioning the article idea, I asked their advice about how to make my fantasy come true.

"Look," one of them said. "There's an easy solution. Why don't you just come with us."

"Don't joke. This is too serious."

"I am being serious. Another friend was supposed to come but went to Senegal instead. So we have extra space. Want to see the boat?"

He pointed out the berth that could be mine.

"Well, do you want to come?"

"You really mean it?"

"Of course."

"Ask your friends if it's OK."

They said it was. It was that easy.

My mother and I met them that evening for a dinner of delicious Grenadian specialties at Mamma's Restaurant. The next day I packed a bag with what I thought I'd need for a week on a boat, left my suitcase at the hotel, saw my mother off at the airport, and sailed toward the horizon with the four men I'd met in the street the day before.

I began to seriously regret my decision three hours into the canal between Grenada and Carriacou. The scopolamine patch Gary had stuck behind my ear failed to keep my tuna sandwich from returning to the sea. My only thought was how great it would be to get off the boat I had been so excited to get on, and to terra firma, where I was convinced we would spend the night, conveniently forgetting the berth into which I dared not venture. I was embarrassed to be more conspicuous than intended and in the worst way possible. It was a relief to my feminism when Cliff and Bill both headed for the rail.

We approached Carriacou as day cut quickly to tropical night. Ted, the skipper, started grumbling about having left too late, and how we might not be able to go into the harbor because he couldn't see the red and green channel markers. Suddenly we couldn't see Carriacou either, as a power outage made it blend into the night.

"That's it," Ted said. "We can't find the channel, so we can't go into the harbor. We'll just have to stay out here and float. Keep watch, Gary. I'm going to sleep."

"Wait a minute," I said, violating my anti-conspicuous rule. "What's this all about?"

Bill was lying under the table in the middle of the narrow bridge, and Cliff was stretched out on the bench, not daring to descend into their berths either. Gary and I sat on the other bench, the only place to be.

"Why can't we go into the harbor?" I asked, trying not to sound too unhappy to hear our erstwhile captain snoring below, as the boat bounced like a cork with no land in sight.

"Since we can't see the channel markers, we could hit a reef or rock and tear a hole in the boat," Gary explained. "There's nothing to worry about," he added. "Out here there's nothing to hit. So we'll just float until morning."

"Morning!"

"There's nothing else we can do. Don't worry. You're in good hands."

Yeah, right, seemed too obvious to bother saying.

"Ted knows what he's doing," he continued. "He was the first African American to sail around the world solo."

I guess it occurred to him that in spite of what could be interpreted as my intrepidness (or foolhardiness) that had gotten me where I was, I might be feeling a little uneasy about floating randomly in total darkness with four strangers.

"When did he do that? What's his whole name? How did you meet?" When in doubt, do research.

"1987. Ted Seymour. I took a course with the Annapolis Sailing School, and was real happy to find a brother teaching. Ted was ecstatic to find a brother who wanted to learn to sail. So we got to be friends. He lives on his boat in St. Croix."

"How can you prove that you've sailed around the world alone?" I pursued in my research mode.

"You have to check into each port in each country where you stop. So your ship log is stamped with the place and date, like a passport."

So I now knew the full name and some very interesting information about one of my companions. Being inconspicuous, I certainly couldn't initiate the "and what do you do" routine. About me, they knew my first name, my mother, and my fantasy.

During that night of keeping watch on the small, hard, rocking bench, Gary called Ted once to move the boat from the path of a freighter fast approaching us. The stars came out in full splendor and I knew I was exactly where I belonged.

In the morning we went into Carriacou and explored briefly before sailing off up the Grenadines. We swam, snorkeled, and just were, in the most incredibly beautiful environment I had almost succeeded in imagining. Dolphins occasionally frolicked off the bow, an unexpected extra. The Tobago Keys came fully into focus and the four strangers became friends. (I've since sailed with various combinations of them.)

When I got home, I was so excited, I told my stories to everyone who would listen. Only one friend said, "I wouldn't have done it."

"Huh? You visualize the most beautiful fantasy you can, then you encounter the agents of its realization, and you say, 'No thanks?'"

"Pick up some guys in the street and go off on a boat with them? I wouldn't have done it."

It had never occurred to me, even floating through the night off Carriacou, to think there might be anything dubious about what I was doing. I'm certainly not in the habit of picking up men in the street and sailing off with them. I guess that's what's called intuition. Good traveling depends on it.

Rachel Christmas Derrick

Easy in the Exumas

BY THE TIME THE THIRD MOTORIST PULLED UP TO OFFER ME A RIDE AND A PEDAL biker had volunteered to lend me his spare cycle, I resigned myself to the notion that walking wasn't the exercise I was going to get on Great Exuma. Here in one of the more tranquil parts of the Bahamas, people were just too friendly. It wasn't simply that they thought it would be impolite to let me exert myself while they glided by on wheels. It was that they wanted to chat. "You from the States, ay?" a man with a child in the passenger seat had called to me. "Hey, didn't I see you a few months ago when you were at Club Peace & Plenty?" a familiar-looking woman inquired, poking her head through her car window. "You coming to the party Saturday night?" another driver asked.

Early that morning, I had set out to walk the mile or so from my hotel to George Town. As I strode along, I caught glimpses through the wispy casuarina pines and bushy coconut palms of the startlingly varied and vibrant blues and greens of the sea. The silence was punctured by the squawks of sea gulls, the sudden rustling of lizards in the roadside bushes, and the distant cries of roosters. I was about halfway to town when I succumbed to motorized transport.

Independent from Great Britain since 1973, the Bahamas is made up of about seven hundred islands, islets, and rocky outcroppings. Great Exuma and Little Exuma, joined by a bridge, are the two largest links in a hundred-mile chain comprising some 365 cays (pronounced "keys"). The Exumas are members of the mainly undeveloped group called the Out Islands (or Family Islands). They resemble better-known Nassau (the country's capital), Paradise Island, and Freeport about as closely as a ripe papaya resembles a royal poinciana tree in bloom. Like the tree, the more commercial locales are large, busy, and flamboyant. On the other hand, the Exumas, like the delicately sweet tropical fruit, are smaller, with a subtle yet addictive flavor.

While the busier parts of the Bahamas get plenty of African American tourists, black visitors are less common in the Exumas. So wherever I went, I ran into Bahamians who blurted out right away how pleased they were to see a vacationing sister, or who told me this in their extra-broad smiles, their insistence that I sit and talk, have a drink on them, or accept a juicy slice of mango. In this place where everyone knew every-one else, I felt perfectly comfortable traveling alone. Here I quickly learned that a brother's warm greeting was usually just that—a warm greeting—not necessarily code for "how fast can I get you between the sheets?"

Most of the nearly four thousand residents earn their living by fishing and farming. You won't find glitzy hotels, golf courses, or high-tech nightclubs in the Exumas—at least not yet. The main activities in the Exumas revolve around socializing with locals as well as fellow travel-ers, and spending time on, in, or at the edge of the ocean. Glass-clear turquoise and neon-blue water slaps itself against the stark white beaches, many on uninhabited cays. Blizzards of fish, in all shapes, col-ors, and sizes, dart by undulating purple sea fans and magnificent stands of coral. These islands let loose with some of the Bahamas' best sailing. Many visitors sidle up to shore on their own boats or charter them once they fly in. Scuba diving and snorkeling in eerie, otherworldly grottos are also spectacular.

The Exumas were first settled by Lucayan Indians. But Spanish adven-turers decimated this population during the 1500s and other European explorers began to arrive. By the late 1600s, the islands' salt pans had become a gold mine and many foreigners had turned themselves into permanent residents. Pirates had a field day attacking the ships of salt merchants. Despite this problem, Great Exuma was a great escape for many people from nearby New Providence island, where both rambunc-tious buccaneers and ruthless Spaniards were making life even more miserable.

In 1783, the Exumas also became a refuge for Loyalists who no longer wished to live in the United States after Britain's defeat in the Revolu-tionary War. For a while, cotton production boomed in these islands along with the salt industry. Swelling their wealth with free field labor, English planters brought in large numbers of enslaved men and women from Africa and other parts of the West Indies. Then insects began gob-bling up the cotton. And the far more profitable salt production on neighboring islands left the Exumas in the dust. Most white land owners packed up and returned to whence they had come. Lacking in similar resources, the Africans and their descendants remained in the Exumas and continued to work the land.

One of the first things I noticed is that the surname of almost every other person is Rolle. This is because the once-enslaved, whether or not they were blood relatives of their former masters (as some were), took the last names of their owners, in this case, Lord John Rolle, who enslaved more than three hundred people. Some historians say that Lord Rolle freed those who worked on his plantations, then magnanimously gave them the land. Others believe that after they were emancipated by the United Kingdom in 1834, they simply appropriated the real estate themselves. Whichever way it went, the fertile land of Rolle's plantation has been passed down through the generations and cannot be sold to outsiders.

According to some people, Lord Rolle never actually came to the Exumas; he just sent his agents. As restaurateur–taxi driver–farmer Kermit Rolle told me, "If he'd been here himself and seen the land, he probably wouldn't have given it away." One day I asked him how, with so many people sharing a last name, anyone could be sure whom they could and couldn't marry. "Oh, we know," he answered with a smile, as sunlight clung to the gold edging of two of his teeth. "We keep track of our blood relatives."

I had been to the Exumas before, on assignments for newspapers and magazines. Yet each time I came, I uncovered still another layer of life on these islands. George Town, where most of the few hotels are clustered, hugs Elizabeth Harbour, protected by Stocking Island. This long, narrow strip of land, a brief ferry ride from town, is rimmed with luscious talcum beaches. Club Peace & Plenty, which faces the island and provides the ferry, could be considered the hub of Great Exuma. The two-story pink wings of this hotel were built around the remains of a sponge warehouse and a kitchen dating back to the days of slavery.

During a previous trip, I was enjoying a grouper sandwich at the hotel's restaurant when I saw something I will never forget. There was a sudden commotion outside the sliding glass doors. Everyone was looking up. When I went outside, I saw a rainbow in a perfect circle around the sun. Within the circumference, the sky was a darker blue-gray and jagged clouds created a strange luminous design. Both vacationers and locals were shaking their heads in awe.

Rainbows 'round the sun may be rare, but Club Peace & Plenty's legendary Saturday night party is a regular event. Vacationers and locals pour onto the waterfront pool deck and the energetic band causes many a hip bone to slip. One April evening during the annual Out Island Regatta, I found this hotel so packed with partygoers that I could barely squeeze through the front door.

Of course, the three-day regatta, which draws far-flung Bahamians, foreign yachties, and both local and visiting landlubbers, is really about sailing—well, sort of. From both shore and sea, masses of people watch the locally crafted work sloops, with their tall billowing sails, as they race in Elizabeth Harbour. But, quiet as it's kept, some folks are even more enthusiastic about the accompanying festivities than about the celebrated nautical competition itself.

Vendors at food stalls along the water sell cracked conch (pronounced "konk")—that mollusk in the large pink-lipped shell, served pounded and fried—fresh fish, peas and rice, and other local favorites. Reggae and calypso throb from speakers as long-lost friends get reacquainted with the help of Kalik, the local beer. Men huddled over domino games slap tiles onto card tables with histrionic arcs of their arms. Pulsing down the street to the sound of pounding drums, clanking cowbells, blaring horns, and shrill whistles, a Junkanoo band works the crowd with its indigenous African Bahamian music.

However, during my most recent visit, George Town slumbered. Sunlight poured over white, blue-trimmed St. Andrew's Anglican Church, perched on a rise overlooking sparkling Lake Victoria. I walked up the hill to this handsome building and stood by the gravesites in the back. What a serene and lofty resting place this is.

The rosy, white-columned Government Administration Building was a short stroll away. This impressive waterside edifice houses the post office, police station, and Ministry of Education. Under the ceilinglike branches of enormous shady trees, women were at their usual posts selling T-shirts, a selection of straw goods, and freshly prepared breakfast. I decided I could use some sustenance, but I wanted to sit down, so I went to the Towne Cafe & Bakery.

With its white tile floor, white tables and chairs, white walls, and even a white ceiling fan, this bright dining room is known for its morning meal. I wasn't hungry enough for "boil fish" (cooked with onions and peppers) or chicken souse (a poultry stew), two Bahamian specialties served with grits and mildly sweet johnnycake. I opted for orange juice and a bran muffin instead.

Veronica Marshall, the owner, seemed delighted when I asked about the old corn mill and baskets on display near the counter. She showed me how her grandparents had taught her to pour the dry corn into the funnel, grind it several times to get the right texture, then "riddle" (sift) the grits in a flat round basket. Holding the basket while horizontally circling her arms, torso, and hips, she demonstrated the dancelike motion that proper riddling required.

"Where you from?" a woman called from the doorway of N & D's Fruits & Vegetables after I left the restaurant. When I stopped to answer, she introduced herself as Denzella Rolle Nixon. She invited me to take a seat with her on the bench in front of her market, and offered me some *kineps.* I took the gumball-size green fruit, bit open the brittle skin, then pulled at the tangy pink meat with my teeth. She proudly informed me that Great Exuma grows about 80 percent of the island's fruits and vegetables (unlike many other Bahamian islands that import most of theirs). When I mentioned that in a few days I'd be going to Staniel Cay, an island up north, she made me promise to give her regards to some friends there (more Rolles, of course).

I walked around Lake Victoria to the other side, past chickens in front yards, an ice cream parlor, a few mom-and-pop restaurants, and a couple of tiny churches. At the edge of the water, a table was piled high with shells, their glossy pink interiors gleaming. A sign read "Stone's Fresh Conch." I watched as a man hammered a shell, deftly cut out the dark mollusk, then quickly skinned it, exposing white flesh.

*I*f you're traveling alone to the Caribbean or any beach destination and you'd like to meet people, consider bringing along games that you can play on the beach or by a pool, like Scrabble or a deck of cards. When you whip out one of your games, kids will come running and the grown-ups will soon follow. Games are a great icebreaker.
—Elaine Lee

When he learned that I was American, he told me he had gone to high school in Maryland but was happy to be home. "The onliest way I'd go back to the U.S. is to visit," he said. I was startled when the conchs on the table suddenly began moving, making clunking sounds as they knocked into each other while brown "feet" groped the air in slow motion. A flash of guilt went through me as I remembered the scrumptious cracked conch I had eaten for dinner the night before. "How long do they stay alive out of the water?" I asked. He explained that if he didn't sell his whole catch by the end of a day, he would keep the remaining conchs alive by putting them in the water overnight, after tying them together so they couldn't amble away.

That afternoon I sat on the nearby pier gazing at St. Andrew's church on the bluff across the lake. It was dead quiet, except for the sloshing against the dock and the calls of a few stray birds. Beside me, an old weathered boat was half in the water, half onshore. It had been abandoned so long that mangrove bushes, with their spindly leglike roots, were growing out of it. Looking down, I could see a huge underwater mound of discarded conch shells—testament to how popular this local staple is.

Another day Kermit Rolle helped me introduce Great Exuma and Little Exuma to two sisters I'd run into who were visiting from Detroit. "Send some more of your friends here," Kermit told us, after saying how happy he was to show his island to a trio of black Americans. We set out southeast of George Town, stopping first at Rolle Town. With a crumbling shingle roof and peeling wooden shutters and doors, an old-style Bahamian house stood in sharp contrast to the spiffy modern one next door. Kermit told us that the newer home belonged to the uncle of Esther Rolle, the American television actor whose family came from Exuma. From the road, we could see waters striped with turquoise, aqua, and navy along the island's two parallel coasts. We walked down a wooded path toward a cluster of palms. In a clearing were three stone tombs that had been there since the eighteenth century. The largest was shaped like a double bed with a headboard and footboard. Its marble plaque told us that a twenty-six-year-old woman, the wife of an overseer during slavery, had been buried there in 1792 with her infant child. Kermit pointed out a tamarind tree in the corner ("The fruit makes good jam") along with the limbs that bear bumpy green, similar-looking soursops and sugar apples.

When we reached the end of Great Exuma, he explained that before the long drawbridge was built, people had to help the ferryman haul them and their vehicles across the water on a plank attached to a pulley. "If the wind was strong, it could take half a day," he said. "And don't let the guy be drunk!"

In no time, we were on the other side, at the cluttered home/boutique/museum of Gloria Patience, better known as the Shark Lady of the Exumas. Her front yard flourished with royal poinciana blossoms, cactus, and descendants of the cotton plants brought by Loyalists during the 1700s. The white-haired septuagenarian, whose family came from Ireland and Scotland, had earned her nickname through decades of capturing sharks from her boat. "I use everything," she told us. "The meat is eaten or buried for fertilizer, and I make the jewelry I sell from the spines and teeth."

In Williams Town we saw the sprawling pinkish salt pond that had once been so lucrative. The aroma of warm bread, coconut tarts, and rum cake pulled us into Mom's Bakery. In this house at the edge of the rocky shore, "Mom" took a break to talk with us as we nibbled banana bread and marble muffins. Then we headed back up north, past George Town.

Off a long, exquisite beach, the craggy boulders known as the Three Sisters posed in a row against the horizon. Small homes dressed in time-worn pastels or bold yellows, blues, and greens were shaded by tall palms. An old woman sat in a doorway braiding "straw" (actually dried palmetto fronds). We asked if she had any baskets for sale, but she said she just "plaited" sections, then sent them to Nassau to be sewn into straw goods. In hilly Rolleville, where many enslaved Africans landed, we had cool drinks at Kermit's Hilltop Tavern, the center of August Emancipation Day celebrations. On our way back to George Town, Kermit took us to his farm, where he picked fresh melons for us.

When it was time to fly to Staniel Cay, I boarded a charter plane. Below us, the beach-fringed Exumas were laid out in a seemingly endless line through some of the most brilliantly colored waters imaginable. The whimsical jade, robin's egg, and royal blue swirls could have been part of a giant finger painting.

Almost everything is within walking distance on tiny Staniel Cay, with its peaceful beaches, two hotels, and single village. Hand-lettered signs on trees direct visitors to the "Straw Shop on Your Right, East of Church," the pink supermarket (not to be confused with the blue grocery store), and even a local pilot. Here you are as likely to see a satellite dish as a woman pulling a bucket of water from a community well.

Joe Hocher, the owner of Staniel Cay Yacht Club, took me snorkeling into Thunderball Grotto, in a rocky islet just off shore. As soon as I swam in, I could see why scenes from two James Bond movies and *Splash* had been filmed here. Coming through holes in the high ceiling, columns of sunlight pierced the clear water, illuminating the orange, lime green, and maroon sea life below. Parrot fish, yellowtail snapper, trumpet fish, and queen angels zipped back and forth against backdrops in various versions of blue.

Staniel Cay is a good home base for visiting the Exuma Land and Sea Park, about an hour away by powerboat. Some twenty-two miles long and eight miles wide, this protected region boasts empty beaches, awesome dive sites (including a large stand of rare pillar coral), marked nature trails, and old Loyalist ruins. Large iguanas, tropical birds, hawksbill turtles, and scores of fish are among the varied wildlife.

One morning I hitched a ride with Ray Darville, the park warden, on his daily boat patrol. The highlight for me was a visit to Shroud Cay, where I swam in "Camp Driftwood." The current in this natural whirlpool whipped me around a rocky outcropping to a sandy beach. We found a shovel handle in the water, so we climbed a hill to deposit it on the artfully arranged heap of other items that had washed ashore. When I looked closely at an old telephone, I saw a tiny lizard perched on the receiver. I hoped it hadn't called too many people to tell them about the beauty of the Exumas; I like these undiscovered islands just the way they are.

Jennifer Sanders

A Bahia Story

I AM SIX THOUSAND MILES AWAY FROM HOME AND LOOKING THROUGH THE WINDOW of a yellow bus that cruises like a big, lazy animal down this forest highway toward Salvador da Bahia. Last night when most everyone on the bus was asleep, I sat with my face pressed against the window glass, searching for constellations in these southern skies. My ears filled with music from my headphones; I was happy to be the sole inhabitant of this dark, star-filled kingdom. But this morning the sun is very bright, though it is still early, and it is difficult to pretend that I am the only passenger on this bus. Now I am frustrated that I can't speak with anyone.

I spend my hours gazing, mute, at the countryside outside my window. I see forests slashed and burned to make a clearing for this road. I see cities that look like they were torn from the crust of the earth. Streets are red clay filled with people, and everything is covered with fine red dust. I see blue skies turn to gray and then to red ochre like molten lava, at sunset. I see barren shrubs, brown and brittle like sticks reaching toward the sky asking the clouds to send just a little rain. But the clouds are content to be gold and silver silhouettes against the big sky. This is the Sertão, where it hasn't rained for years. We stop at a roadside stand for food. I point at a bottle of Coke and some pastries filled with meat. I flap my arms to indicate which one I want because I do not know the word for chicken.

My first vision of Bahia was of the early sunlight brightening bits of sky between gray clouds. Beneath the clouds, kisses of orange and red *f*lying through darkened skies, the city below us was completely obscured by thick black clouds. Fleeting breaks in the clouds allowed glimpses of red tile rooftops. "We're coming in on a thunderstorm," my seat mate informed me, his remarks accented by a streak of lightning. I thought it no mere coincidence that on my lap lay a book on Xango, Yoruban god of thunder and lightning. It was a fitting welcome to Salvador, capital of Bahia—a state in Brazil boasting one of the largest African populations outside of Nigeria. Of an approximate two million people, 70 to 75 percent are reportedly of African descent.

—Lula Strickland,
"Africa in the Americas: Travels to Bahia"

rays of light touched the black silhouette of the city. Four hundred years ago Africans had arrived on these shores just like my ancestors had arrived in the United States. In the light of dawn I feel things within me begin to simmer and stir. I can't wait to hear the music of Bahia, which holds the passion and soul of Brazil. I can't wait to see for myself the strong African culture, preserved and held intact through the centuries.

I find my way into a part of town called Graça and a little *pensão* (guest house). The streets here are narrow and filled with many-storied apartment buildings in greens, ivory, and grays. Mango trees and flowers are everywhere—such a stark contrast to the barren, dust-filled Sertão. Near the top of a hill is a fork in the road with a fruit and juice stand. A small brown man sits inside every day with his newspapers and his fruits hanging from the ceiling and covering the counter. He looks at me when I walk by, his face staring from amid the *acerola, caju, laranja,* and *abacaxí* fruits. I look back and smile.

The *dona* of the *pensão* is an kind, older Brasileira who thankfully speaks English. Her husband is thin and white-haired. He seems grandfatherly and smiles warmly. They give me a bed in one of the guest rooms and my own key, and inform me that they serve *cafe de manhã* (breakfast) at 8:30 am.

I awake eager for the day and devour the *cafe com leite,* rich, sweet Brazilian coffee with lots of milk, a plate of fresh-cut fruit slices, orange juice, and bakery rolls with lots of butter and jam.

There are a few other travelers here at the *pousada:* a couple from England, a young man just arrived from Portugal, and a Swiss man who has returned to Bahia for the second or third time. All but the Portuguese speak English, and they've given me a map and explained how to get around the city.

I spend my days walking. I hear people speaking a musical language whose words hold no meaning for me yet. I smell scents in the air that I have never known before. At a beach-side café, a beautiful brown boy of six or seven rushes up to me with his friend. His small hand gently touches my arm. Instinctively, I raise my arm as if to strike. But his touch is a touch of curiosity and affection. This is one of the reasons I've come here: to let go of my fears and distrust, habits born of city life in the United States, and to live in this place with an open mind and heart. The humid tropical air soothes my skin. The strong sun warms and darkens me. My body is beginning to fall into pace with the silent, powerful pulse of this city.

Every Tuesday night in Pelourinho there is a party; not thrown for any particular reason, it is a party "just because." The Swiss man explains this to me as we sit at a small table in the plaza of Terreiro de Jesus, sharing a shot of *caxaça*. Across from us, set up in front of the Museu de Arqueologia, is a large truck with a frame built into its bed that will become the stage for a band. A beautiful Afro-Brazilian man with dreadlocks takes the stage to sing a popular samba-reggae song. Beneath the backup singers are a troop of young men playing drums almost as big as they are. They play deep, rolling bass rhythms and higher, syncopated beats that pound into the bodies of the dancing crowd.

The people around me look like a chocolate rainbow. They are of every color from ivory white chocolate to milk chocolate, semisweet, and rich, dark chocolate. I can see familiar features in their faces. Some have eyes the color of honey with hair in golden-brown ringlets. Others have piercing black-brown eyes with skin to match, high cheekbones, and thick lips. Everyone is beautiful. This is beauty from the sons and daughters of Angola, Nigeria, and Benin, with a little mix of Native South American and Portuguese blended in and seasoned to taste. Of this jambalaya, Brazilian culture was born.

Yes, Africa is in this place. She is in the rhythms of the samba and samba-reggae. She is in the swing of the hips when women walk and in the accent of the Brazilian voices around me. At booths situated along the plaza, older black women sit regally dressed in starched white lace blouses and layered, full white skirts sewn by hand. Upon their heads are beautifully wound and twisted white cloths and kerchiefs rising high like crowns. At their sides are caldrons of *dendê* oil, a red-tinted palm oil used in Brazil as it was in West Africa and used to fry the pounded bean meal that they have rolled and shaped into little balls. The bean fritters

It was here in the early 1500s that Portuguese colonists first brought West Africans as slaves to tote the mineral wealth from the interior of the country. Later the slaves labored on vast sugar cane, tobacco, and cattle plantations and built the imposing baroque style architecture that still stands as a testament to their craftsmanship. Descendants of these Africans populate Bahia today, along with indigenous Indians, European immigrants, and a hearty intermixture of all three races. In the midst of a country where blacks have a reported 30 percent illiteracy rate and where social discrimination based on skin color is practiced, Bahia remains a bastion of African culture.

—Lula Strickland,
"Africa in the Americas: Travels to Bahia"

(*acarajé*), cooked, drained, and still hot to the touch, are sliced in two by roughened brown hands and filled with peppers, shrimp, okra, and other condiments.

As people walk by, I notice that they don't look at me like I am a stranger. The Swiss man has light sunburned skin and blue eyes; he is the stranger. I, with my long brown limbs, brown eyes, and bushy hair, look just like them. That realization gives me a feeling of great pride.

Now I'm bolder. Instead of walking, I get on a bus, not knowing where I will end up, and get off in a place that looks interesting. I go to museums and shops, to the lower city of banks, fishing docks, and big warehouses. I take the Elevador Lacerda up to the upper city to Pelourinho, filled with color and light, *capoeira,* and the smell of *dendê.* I've bought a book of Portuguese grammar and I'm trying to read the signs I see. The *livraria is* where you buy books, but the *papeleria* is where you buy paper and pens to write. I daydream in little cafés where I stop for mid-morning or afternoon *cafezinho.*

When people approach me and speak in Portuguese, I can only pantomime or respond in broken Spanish. Usually, they do not understand. And they do not understand even more why I look like them but cannot speak to them. Some people think I am playing a joke and they repeat their phrases to me louder and more clearly. Others sit down with me and speak very slowly as if this will help me regain knowledge of a language I have never known. The kindness and patience of the people who try to help me make me feel deeply frustrated that I cannot communicate with them.

One day I sit by the sea. There are waves of rolling white foam. I think that if the world had no curve and I could see as far as the horizon of this flat earth, I would see the shores of West Africa. The water and this thought bring me gentle peace. The sand's color and texture is like raw sugar. Under my feet, I think the crushed granules could blend into molasses. There is a silhouette of a large sea vessel in the middle distance. A man walking past eclipses the low, orange light of sunset for just a moment and a warÖ gentle breeze blows through. It fills my clothes and fills the air to the west where the sky is full of the hazy, golden light of late afternoon.

I walk up to the Farol da Barra, a lighthouse at the point where the Bay of Todos os Santos meets the Atlantic Ocean. I climb up a low wall and sit in the breeze and fading light. I speak softly to the ocean, to Iemanjá: Mother of the ocean, I have come all this way. How can I touch the Bahia that I hear in the drums, that I see in the colors of Pelourinho and the laughter of children playing in its streets, that is in the eyes of the *baianas* selling *acarajé?* Mother Ocean coos and comforts me. She wraps me in her arms, which are the warm winds blowing from the sea. She kisses me with kisses that are her warm and salty spray. She tells me to have patience and to love myself. When I have this, she says, my heart will open without fear. All that I see and long for around me, in the laughter of the people, in the smiles of their bright eyes, in the rhythms of the drums, the soul of the city itself, will fill me. She says that the magic of this place is much deeper than I know and that this magic is also within me.

Back at the *pensão* I fall asleep with peaceful dreams.

The next day I am looking for the office of Tatu Tours by way of the local Xerox shop (my guidebook places them on the same street). I pass by, I wander around, up and down stairs to check that the address is correct, but I cannot find the office. The man from the copy shop sees me and gestures for me to come inside. I show him my book and try to explain that the place I am looking for is not here. He knows where Tatu Tours has moved and draws me a map of how to get there. It is not far.

I find my way into Edificio Vitoria Center, Sala 1108, where I find Conor O'Sullivan on the phone. I enter and wait quietly by the door. "Do you speak English?" I finally ask.

"Of course," he answers with an Irish accent, "how can I help you?" Conor had come to Bahia over nine years ago and fallen in love with it. He and his best friend returned about seven years later and started a travel agency whose tours show the proud roots and beauty of Afro-Brazilian culture.

Conor suggests that I stay in an *albergue de juventude* (youth hostel) in Barra, close to the beach. He tells me that Tuesday nights, late at the Africa Café, the premier drumming band of Salvador, Olodum, Olodum, plays. Everyone goes into the courtyard and dances until dawn. He interjects, jokingly, that giving advice on free things to do is not so great for his business, but he feels obliged to help me.

The Albergue de Juventude da Barra used to be the mansion of the owner's grandmother. It is a beautiful place, an old Portuguese-Mediter-

*I*n the Largo do Pelhourina ("the Pillory" in Portuguese), an area in the heart of the Upper City where slaves were once traded, is the Afro-Brazilian Museum which houses an extensive collection of religious iconography of the African-based Candomble faith. Though Catholicism is the official religion of the country, the ancient Yoruban *orixas*, or gods of Africa, rule the population. Certain Candomble sites of worship are open to the general public such as the oldest, Casa Branca. Our Lady of the Rosary of Blacks, a church built in the eighteenth century by Africans not allowed to worship with whites, is still an active parish today. Three-hundred-year-old statues of black saints adorn the altar.

—Lula Strickland,
"Africa in the Americas: Travels to Bahia"

$\mathcal{O}$ne of the highlights of my trip to Bahia was a journey through the breathtaking Bahian countryside to the historic black town of Cachoeria, the first economic capital of sixteenth-century Brazil. Walking along cobblestone streets (stones literally stomped into the ground by black slaves) you see the occasional smiling child riding by on a donkey and craftspeople working in open-air shops.

The city's most revered residents are the Nossa Senhora da Boa Morte, "the Sisterhood of Our Lady of the Good Death," a religious order of African women. Founded in 1823 during Brazil's slavery period, the society originally formed when a group of enslaved African women worked overtime, saved money, and bought their own freedom. Subsequent monies were pooled to purchase the freedom of other women in bondage, particularly women who had been priestesses in Africa.

When the Catholic Church forced them to reunite as an order, ancient African religious rites were wed to Catholic liturgy, giving birth to a unique syncretism. Today the 167-year-old organization is stubbornly considered a part of the church, though the majority of the small group of women are head priestesses of Candomble houses and act as counselors in the community.

As the Sisterhood they are known for their participation in Brazil's Holy Week, beginning in early August, where they co-officiate the Assumption of the Virgin Mary ceremonies through the performance of elaborate rites and syncretized rituals. People the world over travel to Cachoeria during this period to observe. Realizing their importance to all Africans, representatives from Howard University purchased a building in Cachoeria for them so that they may have an independent space not owned by the local parish.

As I left the Sisterhood's small, one-room chapel, I was moved by the departing embraces and generous blessings I was given. I memorized the images of four women standing proud in their white-and-black traditional dress.

—Lula Strickland, "Africa in the Americas: Travels to Bahia"

ranean style stucco house. The outside is salmon colored with accents of dark hardwood in the corners and arches, and in the courtyard. All around the house are almond trees. There is also carved dark wood to complement the white walls inside. I am led up a white stone spiral staircase to a room that has five bunk beds, high white walls, and a high window that opens inward with brown wooden shutters. There is a verandah beyond the brown, heavy doors that are open to keep the room cool. Hooks on the side walls of the verandah are meant to hold a hammock. My new home is on the street Rua Florianopolis in a neighborhood called "Jardim do Brasil," Garden of Brazil.

The large living room has a color TV and comfortable couches. There I make a discovery: TV is an excellent tool for learning a language! I sit down in front of the screen and watch endless commercials, political propaganda shows, and soap operas. In the midst of a political speech, I turn to a Brazilian man sitting across from me and say a word I have just learned, *"Mentiras!"* Lies! He laughs and realizes that even if I don't understand much Portuguese, I can tell a politician when I see one.

There are new and interesting people to meet at the *albergue* every day.

I've met Eric and Sandra from São Paulo, Helen and Alex from Sweden, and I've made a friend from Zaire named Olivier. But I was not at all sure that I liked the woman named Giuliana when I first saw her. She wore her auburn hair long or pulled up into a bun. Her small round glasses against alabaster, freckled skin made her look like an intellectual or a librarian. At the same time, her clothes suggested she was an artist. In any case, I thought her pretentious and made no effort to talk to her, although we shared a room.

One day when I was out, my mother called. Giuliana, who speaks English, French, Italian, Spanish, and Portuguese, spoke with her. Later that night in the kitchen she confronted me.

*F*rom the moment I walked into the compound, I knew I was walking on sacred ground. *"Ore yeye O!,"* a ceremonial greeting to the goddess Osum lettered in gold, sprung from a whitewashed wall to enthrall me, to welcome back Africa's child, especially. I was at Casa Branca in Salvador, the oldest *terreiro* (place of worship) for the ancient African religion, Candomble, a Yoruba-based practice brought to Brazil by enslaved West Africans during the mid-fifteenth century.

Not being allowed to practice their beliefs, the slaves were forced to adopt Catholicism but continued to worship their own gods under the guise of worshiping Catholic saints. Olorun is considered the supreme god. Associate *orixas* include Ogun, god of iron, Yemanja, goddess of the waters, Xango, ruler of thunder and lightning, and a host of others. All interact and serve as conduits linking the spiritual and physical worlds.

Guiding me was an elderly, spry woman who bore a striking resemblance to my great grandmother. Zurica lived on the premises and performed daily rituals required by the gods. During ceremonies, she tends devotees who fall under the influence of "the spirits." Along with other designated women (men are prohibited from even entering the cooking-place), she prepares consecrated food on a charcoal stove (gas is never used). Each *orixa* has his or her own pot.

Casa Branca is laid out in the fashion of a traditional West African village spread out on a steep hillside: Dotted up and down the red-clay enclosure are the stone-faced houses where the *orixas* "reside" and shrines erected in their honor. Pressed tight outside the compound walls are the homes of the three hundred or so worshipers.

The day of my visit, the main sanctuary was festooned in turquoise blue in honor of Oxossi. The high ceiling was completely smothered in soft blue ribbons overlooking a crowned area in the center of the room that was ringed by several chairs reserved for spiritual leaders during services. A statue of the "protector of the forest," dressed in blue, stood near the altar on a pedestal covered in white-laced cloth. Gold bands were painted about his ankles. After tithing at a small shrine to Yemanja as a sign of respect, I bid my farewell. Zurica and I embraced and she touched the top of my head just as my great-grandmother Lula had once done, putting me under the protection of an *orixa*. *"Axe!"* she said, *"Axe!"* (peace, power).

—Lula Strickland, "Casa Branca: Original African Religion Flourishes in Bahia and Brooklyn"

"Are you Jennifer?" she asked, wisps of hair falling onto her face.

Shocked to hear her speak English, I answered, "Yes?"

"Your mother called tonight. Would you like some spaghetti? I've just made some."

Giuliana was born in Italy but moved to Rio de Janeiro with her family when she was two and lived in Rio until her mother died, when she was thirteen. At fifteen, her family, with a new stepmother, moved to Buenos Aires. Giuliana returned to Italy for college, then came back to Brazil to decide what to do with her life and to make peace with events in her past. In the wee hours of the morning, eating spaghetti in the kitchen, I discovered once again the reason I was traveling: to open my heart to the people I encountered.

In Giuliana, I found a kindred spirit. We rambled around the city together, often with our friend Tio, who was from Uruguay. When we three were together, Giuliana had to speak in English to me, translate to Spanish for Tio, and then talk to Brazilians in Portuguese. Once, a woman listening to our multilingual conversations turned to me and asked where my friends were from. As I looked at the woman in puzzlement, Giuliana spoke and explained that she was the native and that I was the foreigner!

At a local night club one evening, I slipped my shoes off under the table, and along with other audience members, joined a local dance troupe on stage, where we danced African freestyle to a chorus of drums, percussion and clapping. Bare-chested and wearing loose-fitting white pants, the brothers from this group demonstrated the exciting *capoeira*, an African martial-arts form of fluid acrobatic proportions. The fierce drum accompaniment and sensuous sounds of the *berimbau*, a one-stringed gourd instrument played with a bow, from Brazil's interior, held me mesmerized.

—Lula Strickland, "Bahia"

We go to the church of Bonfim and children rush up to sell us little ribbons. Each is of a different color, each has a different saint and prayer. Giuliana asks them, in Portuguese, what they are for. The children explain that you tie a ribbon around your wrist or ankle and you make a wish. When the ribbon falls off, your wish will have come true. We go to Praia do Forte to play with the sea turtles and swim in the waves. We found at Imbassaí a stream as warm as bath water. In it we lay down flat and let it carry us to its outlet at the sea. Tio takes a photo of Giuliana and me. We lie next to each other in the sand and see how the white of her sun-drenched skin reflects against the deep brown tones of mine.

Giuliana and I have become sisters. Though I know neither Portuguese, Italian, nor Spanish, and her English is not perfect, we have found an intuitive language without words and in this way we understand everything that is left unsaid. I contemplate how amazing it is that two people raised in such different worlds can become as close as a family. We joke about getting an apartment together in Buenos Aires, (I could teach English and she would go to school). We would stay together as sisters reunited after a lifetime apart. When she leaves I miss her terribly.

I join up with Conor and go to Praia do Forte and walk around the first fortress built in the New World. We drive along the Coconut Highway to Imbassaí, swim in the creek, and walk through the warm sand. He sends me on a tour to Cachoeira, where I see a cacao plantation (where chocolate grows) and meet some of the Sisters of Boa Morte. The Sisterhood of Boa Morte is a religious society of free black women dating back to the time of slavery. We go Saturday night to see Ilê Aiye play drums in the old part of town past the Largo do Carmo at the Fort of Santo Antonio. There are men selling cheese that they roast over hot coals carried around in a tin can. There is a man who drinks kerosene and breathes fire. Ever present are the *baianas* in starched white dresses, selling their *acarajé* until the hour when everyone leaves to go home and sleep.

One night there is an art show for a friend and Conor would like me to go. Maria Adair is an artist and mother of ten children, several of whom are artists as well. She has a café in Pelourinho that is also her workshop. Inside the café there is always music playing. Because Conor is a special friend, Maria invites me on a tour of the whole place. Upstairs is the studio with paints, wood, wire, tools, and brushes everywhere. Downstairs, she offers us coffee and hot chocolate, then tells us to look around. Everything here is painted: the tables and chairs, the walls, and even the refrigerator. From the ceiling hang bicycles she has made of different materials. One is of pieces of wire twisted into wheels and a frame. There are others made of graphite, aluminum, and bamboo. On walls covered with splashes of paint and handwritten script, in blue, gray, and green, are clocks of all types and sizes. "They are painted," Maria says, because her art is the "autobiography of [her] time spent in this time."

We go to sit at a table made of scrap wood and metal. It is black and green with drips and splatters of color—red, yellow, white, and blue. The top of the table is shaped like a bowl and covered with a thick sheet of glass. Through the glass you can read the inscription, *"A arte de viver com arte."* It means: "Art for living with art." She creates art so that she can live in a world of art—and art is a part of everything in her world.

After a month and a half I can understand quite a bit of Portuguese and can speak to people. Every day is a new adventure, with more people to meet and more places to explore. People are starting to recognize me around Pelourinho now. They say, "You're that American girl," and they tell me that even though I'm from another country, I am a sister, not a tourist, to them.

On Christmas Day I am on the beach with friends in Itapuã. That evening we are at a party in Rio Vermelho, dancing and drinking *caipirinhas.* There I meet Lisa, a woman who radiates a quiet power and tranquillity .

We meet in a café the next day, on a balcony overlooking the cobblestone Rua Gregório de Mattos. It is late afternoon and the sky is full of pastel clouds behind the eighteenth-century buildings of Pelourinho. Lisa has been in Salvador for two years. She came here from the States, having decided to leave everything behind: her debts and her assets, her family and her friends, her ideas and her theories about life and living that were shaped by the institutions she had been a part of her whole life. She found a room in a house of Brazilians, and for the next six months she spoke not one word of English. If she saw someone who looked American approaching, she would turn her eyes or cross the street.

Lisa understood how it was to live in silence. She understood the void, the longing, and the loneliness. But she tells me she has walked through to the other side—she has learned a new language and culture, a new way of thinking and being. Lisa has come to know herself profoundly, and she has found love: a love of self, a love of divinity, and all that it has created. She says this love is the magic that colors the soul of Bahia. "How else to explain it?" she exclaims. She closes her eyes and thinks for a moment, then she tells me, "It feels like you have just eaten and you are finally satisfied."

It is New Year's Eve and my last night here. This is the time when all of Brazil, in celebration, gives thanks to Mother Ocean, Iemanjá. In Salvador da Bahia everyone is at the beach dressed in white. In pockets or in bags, they carry presents to give to the sea. I have prepared three white roses, each with a wish and promise for the new year. Timbalada, its forty drummers' bodies painted with polka dots, circles, and stripes of white, plays on a stage near the Farol da Barra.

Into the dark waters we wade, and we wait for the new year to approach. A countdown has begun. We throw little silver-wrapped candies into the water along with coins, candles, and perfume. Each gift is in some way symbolic of the virtues of the patron saint of Bahia and Yoruban goddess of the sea. It is said that when midnight comes, the waves will rise up and swallow our offerings in a great surge of saltwater and white foam. If Iemanjá accepts the gifts, her waves will carry them out to sea. Suddenly there is a hush and then, a great explosion of fireworks on every beach, all along the coast. *"Feliz ano novo,"* everyone yells. I raise my three roses and throw them onto the waves.

Pant legs rolled and white skirts pulled up high, all of Salvador is in the water. A baptism. The washing away of all sins. We cover our faces and heads with this holy water. We embrace and kiss, wishing one another love and happiness. Dripping in my wet clothes, I remember to look out to sea. By the light of the moon, my eye can find three white roses floating away, with the current. "Love," "peace," and "happiness" drift away, and I realize that my three wishes have already come true.

In addition to the Boa Morte festival, Bahia has a wealth of festivities year-round. While Rio is famous for its flamboyant carnival in February, Bahians have their own five-day Mardi Gras that reflects their traditions and culture. Other colorful events include: Our Lady of Conception on December 8, the Festival of Bonfim on the second Thursday in January, the Yemaja festival dedicated to the Yoruban goddess of the seas on February 2, the three-day St. John's Festival in June, and a grand New Year's procession. During these fests you will hear a wide range of Bahian music, including the samba do roda, Candomble drumming, lambada, and ethnic music from all parts of the country.

—Lula Strickland, "Africa in the Americas: Travels to Bahia"

Barbara Ellis-Van de Water

Delivering Sasonoa

YOU LEARN TO TAKE LIFE ON THE WATER LIKE THE EXPRESSION, "GO WITH THE flow." Sailors, when faced with sudden violent squalls, don't run from the fierce winds and rains but embrace the raging fury; they turn their vessels into the storms and ride the turbulent waves like cowboys bucking a wild horse. You can also experience dead calm, and fight to imagine what dying a slow death would be like as your sails hang slack, and you drift on an open ocean miles from nowhere. These are extremes and there is, of course, much in between. But whatever the condition, you must surrender to the elemental forces of nature. That's why I love sailing.

The boat that was to give me my first experience sailing was Sasonoa, a sixty-foot ketch that was leaving her chartering days in the Virgin Islands and sailing off to her new home in the Bay Islands off the coast of Honduras. A delivery crew was being assembled, all of whom would work for no salary—only the price of a one-way ticket back home. But for anyone who enjoyed sailing, these were coveted assignments.

I was looking to escape what had become a routine job aboard a tour boat ferrying cruise ship passengers across Pillsbury Sound to swim and snorkel at Trunk Bay on St. John. I wanted to travel and I wanted to learn to sail. Working a delivery seemed like a good way to do both, though without any experience, I didn't think I had much of a chance of getting hired. It was a big surprise and thrill when Captain Rod agreed to take me along on Sasonoa's final journey.

I joined Alana, a veteran of many deliveries, Kelly a youthful and energetic first mate who crewed a day-sail charter boat on St. Thomas, and

Helle, a student from Denmark who was working and traveling her way around the Caribbean. Helle had sailed to St. Thomas from San Francisco via the Panama Canal aboard a twenty-seven-foot sailboat. Accompanying us on the delivery was David, Sasonoa's captain for all the years she chartered in the Virgin Islands. Rod brought experience as one of the best delivery captains in the Caribbean, but David knew the vessel and was ultimately responsible for delivering Sasonoa to her owners in Honduras.

We left St. Thomas on a bright, sunny day. Once we cleared the harbor, David and Kelly hoisted the main and Captain Rod turned off the engine. We were sailing! Alana took the helm as Captain Rod picked up his guitar and launched into "Sloop John B." We tossed our final sips of champagne over the side in a toast to Neptune, hoping the mythical god of seafarers would favor us with fair weather and strong winds. We expected to arrive in Roatan within a week, maybe less, if we sailed on the strong Caribbean trade winds common during the spring.

Sasonoa drifted lazily toward Puerto Rico on 2 to 4 knots of wind and the crew settled into the long, lazy days ahead. Two hours on; eight hours off. A relatively easy watch detail for a crew of six. Our days took on an easy rhythm like the waves riding under Sasonoa's keel. We rose from restful naps, read, wrote letters, and jotted notes in our journals.

Excerpt from Journal: N.17 19.9 long W.73 45.51 12:00 am

Happy Birthday! I am celebrating my birthday somewhere in the seas between Haiti and Jamaica. It is my first solo watch. Everyone is down below sleeping. Prince is blaring on my Walkman. I'm trying hard to stay awake. There's moonlight on the water and all is peaceful. It's sooo beautiful. I can't believe this is me really doing this.

Today, David caught another bonito, which he quickly tossed back. He keeps hoping to catch dolphin or wahoo. He's trying to give us as much variety in our diet as possible. He cooked many a gourmet meal on Sasonoa during her chartering days, but our delicious meals served underway call for simplicity and easy preparation.

Meals and showers are the big events in our daily routine. Showers are short and frugal—a soap down with Joy (the sailor's choice for its ability to suds even in saltwater) and a tea kettle rinse so named for our daily ration measured from a full tea kettle of freshwater. We're all agreed, it's ice cold beer and a long, cool shower when we get into port!

I was never bored. I was surprised how full the days could be and how quickly they passed. In the close quarters our crew quickly bonded as we shared responsibilities and worked together to perform the most routine tasks. We enjoyed a game of Trivial Pursuit as much as teaching each other to tie a bowline or casting a line off the stern for wahoo.

Your destination may be to one of the most exotic reaches of the world, but for the true sailor it's a journey of the mind, not miles. It is a time of self-reflection. I'd look out at the horizon and think of how far I'd come in my life and what was next for me.

Alone on my night and early morning watches, I sometimes wove the most frightening scenarios of disasters at sea. But the absolute certainty that night becomes day was enough to keep me going. A lone shining star, a cool breeze that blew from nowhere on a hot still night, a dolphin

One of the most wonderful experiences I've ever had was bicycling around Havana, Cuba. We took the back roads at first, through neighborhoods with architecture that told the story of this country's strong affiliation with the Spanish—old stone structures with detailed engravings and statues. On one street every single house was like that and they were beautiful despite the peeling paint and decaying windows. Through the doorways you could see an old lady rocking in her chair or a lone man with a dog in his lap staring into the street. We rode toward Ciboey, an affluent area where the more privileged live, and saw mansions like Tara in *Gone with the Wind*. In Old Havana we walked along the cobblestone streets to the central square, poking our heads in the shops, art galleries, and *paladas,* the recently legalized family restaurants which line the square and serve sumptuous, authentic Cuban food.

I wanted to practice my photography and the light was perfect for it. So we went along the Malecon, that famous strip along the sea where the people of Havana hang out. Facing the sea are tall dilapidated old buildings that illuminate the orange sky and stretch toward the center of town for miles. We had to step over sewage, around underfed dogs and large cracks in the sidewalk to capture the smiling, magical people who passed their time playing dominos, walking hand in hand, kissing along the wall by the sea, or just looking out their windows at the passersby. Cubans are an effusive people, expressing themselves with great passion. You hear it in their music, which is played everywhere, in their language, and certainly in the way the men approach you.

—Sabine, "Letters from Havana"

that adopted me as its playmate and followed for miles dipping and darting across the bow—these were the small comforts and great joys of day-to-day living.

After a week at sea it seemed the brisk trade winds that we had hoped for would continue to elude us. Rod and David reluctantly started Sasonoa's engine. But with an eye on conserving fuel, even the progress made under power was slow and measured. So far, it had been an uneventful journey without even so much as a passing squall, which we would have welcomed for the sudden gust of wind.

But one night, as I began my watch, black clouds crept across the starry midnight sky unleashing a furious storm. Suddenly, Sasonoa was in total darkness with only the raging sounds of the wind and the sea. Rod, David, and Kelly hurried onto the deck to drop the mainsail. At any moment I expected Alana to relieve me on watch. This was no time for a rookie to be at the helm. But Alana stayed below to secure the cabin. Anything that wasn't fastened down would be catapulted across the cabin every time Sasonoa was pitched into the wild sea.

"Steer her into the wind and hold her steady," David shouted as he struggled with Kelly and Rod to strap down the sails. My clothes were soaked. The rain lashed across my body. The wheel was wet and slippery under my grip. But out of fear (or paralysis of will) I held fast to the helm. Finally, David joined me in the cockpit and told me he planned to have me finish my watch. I was as surprised as I was grateful for his confidence in me.

From down below I could hear Rod's wails of laughter. Clearly he was enjoying this storm as much as he would an afternoon surfing at Malibu beach and I found his hilarious howls a reassuring diversion.

When Alana came on deck to begin her watch, the storm was still raging. I went down below and nestled into my bunk. Muscle aches and tensions eased. But sleep would not come. I was restless with excitement, and lay awake listening to my heart beating along with the restless sea. Something had changed in me; I had grown stronger.

The next morning we reached the coastal waters off Honduras. It was gloriously sunny—not a cloud in the sky. We had yet to spy land, but a gathering of local fisherman in dugout canoes was a welcome sight. Sasonoa's female crew sparked a friendly interest. We yelled a few greetings in Spanish and they offered us lobster from their catch. A few stayed with us as we made our way into Roatan to clear customs.

From Roatan we sailed through a ring of alluring islands—each one no more than a brilliant white slither of sand with a cluster of palm tree—to Cayos Cochinos. Nestled in the hillsides were rustic cabins and old Caribbean-style plantation houses. The crystal-clear turquoise waters were a diver's haven, with a labyrinth of caves to explore, coral reefs, and a bountiful assortment of exotic fish. Sasonoa had left one paradise for another.

The crew, having safely delivered Sasonoa, could now relax and enjoy day and night dives and hikes into the lush tropical forest to villages of thatched-roof huts and friendly locals who shared pineapple rum with us. After a few days of rest, I left on another delivery, this time, to Solomon's Island on the Chesapeake.

It was here that my husband and I bought our own sailboat and began sailing around the Caribbean. But delivering Sasonoa was the adventure that led to all others. I will always be grateful for the lessons I learned.

Rosalind Cummings-Yeates

Journey to Yard:
A Jamaican Cultural Experience

Mi born in foreign but mi love yard still.
—"Warning Sign," Born Jamericans

THERE'S A LOT TO BE SAID FOR A BLACK PERSON VISITING A BLACK COUNTRY. THERE'S something that touches the spirit and reconnects what has been lost, stolen, and forgotten. It outlasts photos and souvenirs, burrowing deep within. Jamaica possesses this power; it can weave an unbreakable spell on the most cynical tourist, but it's true essence can only be absorbed by touching the culture—the people, the dialect, the food, the lifestyle.

Soon after my feet first touched Jamaican earth, I was angry. Rolling down the winding road in a bus from the airport to my hotel, I was surrounded by loud, rum-swigging tourists. Their "irie mon" comments and subtly arrogant attitude toward Jamaicans irritated me. As the only black face on the bus, apart from the Jamaican guides, I felt resentful that I had to endure the same narrow attitudes toward people of color that I had just left in the U.S. I had come to relax and work—I was writing a travel article on the Jamaica beyond the beaches and resorts—and I didn't need that kind of aggravation. I journeyed far from the tourist arenas and this was my only encounter with such attitudes.

After I checked in, I rushed to the hotel restaurant for jerk chicken but learned quickly that I wasn't going to get anything authentic as long as I was in a hotel. The chicken was slathered in barbecue sauce and lukewarm, not unlike poultry in your local American chicken shack. The waiter grinned at me and told me about the stall that served the best jerk. "Gal, yuh got to go outside a here," he said. And that's exactly what I did.

> *If you're flying, call ahead, arrive at the airport on time, and check in early. The sooner you know about delays, cancellations, or overbookings, the sooner you can adjust without freaking out and calling people rude names at the airline ticket counter. Remain calm. In a hundred years, who will remember that you arrived a little late?*
>
> —Pearl Cleage, "Reluctant Road Warrior"

Negril has intangible attributes that are just as striking as the turquoise water and white sand beaches. There is a thick, enveloping aura that permeates the town. It feels moist and seamy and it hangs around you, lurking just above the dirt roads. Part of this feeling comes from the fast-paced atmosphere that accompanies tourism: clubs, fast money, and drugs, mixed with the conservative, strongly Christian yet frankly sexual Jamaican sensibility.

Another part of this feeling can be attributed to the aggressively intense manner of many of the men I encountered. I found that despite the stereotype of the well-hung, smooth talking, Jamaican playboy there are many brutally direct, woman-loving, beautiful men. Nevertheless, one must still deal with the smooth-talkers, and I quickly developed my own method. I had been warned by friends who make annual pilgrimages to Negril that there is a "rent-a-dread" market, where single women pay the way for male companions who may incidentally sport dreadlocks. In part, that explains why strolling through Negril alone I drew unwanted comments and offers; it was assumed that I must be looking for a man. To avoid such advances, I dressed in "roots" fashion: long dresses, flowing African garb, and headwraps. This is a style I favor anyway, but I detected a certain level of respect for my attire. Tourists in skimpy shorts and ultra-revealing swimwear usually trigger disdain and catcalls among the townspeople. Jamaican women observed my clothes and I saw them nod in approval. The men smiled but weren't so quick to approach me. It's much easier to get around in conservative Jamaican society dressed conservatively.

It's also easier if you shun behavior based on stereotypes, such as saying "hey mon" and expecting every Jamaican you meet to have a "no problem" attitude, falling over themselves to meet your needs. I found that being respectful and not too familiar with the people I met helped ease cultural barriers and smoothed the way to glimpsing Jamaican life.

For an up-close look at Jamaican life, I looked up Don, a friend of a friend, who knew the streets and people of Negril. We started the day by hopping one of the mini-vans that serve as public transportation. Since most people commute from surrounding towns, it was crammed with folks on their way to work. It was a whirlwind ride, the van lurching down narrow roads, barely stopping to let passengers out. Nobody seemed to mind, though, and it was interesting to see the landscape of coconut trees, cows, marketplaces, merchants, and uniformed schoolchildren as we whizzed by. We paid our fare at the end of the ride and climbed out in front of Negril Craft Market. Noted for unbelievably persistent vendors, the marketplace can be a web of hard-sell frenzy. Both tacky and exquisite jewelry, sculpture, clothing, and paintings fill stalls lined up side by side.

"Come, I give you a spe'shell deal!"

"Just take one look, no pressure! No pressure!"

Proposals and pleas rang out from every crevice, making for an overwhelming experience, although the presence of a native Jamaican did help. Don cautioned vendors to let me decide if I wanted to buy and they backed down. I was able to concentrate on the beautiful craft work and select what I wanted in peace. When I was on my own it was much easier to buy souvenirs from roadside displays or vendors along the beach. Local gift shops usually stock less creative, higher-priced items.

I wanted to sample Jamaican food prepared for Jamaicans, not the watered-down dishes aimed at tourists, so Don steered me to a small eatery that was a local favorite. Furnished with bright curtains and tablecloths, it didn't look like a restaurant, but rather, a kitchen. I had slightly spicy, curried chicken with plantains, which are sweeter cousins of the banana family, and Don had "manish water," or fish-head soup. I drank sour sop juice from the sweet creamy tropical fruit, and Don had Irish moss, a thick beverage made from seaweed. The service was quick and no-nonsense and the atmosphere was relaxed and unpretentious. Since Jamaica is not really an "eating out" society, it's a treat to go to a place that caters to local tastes. The prices are low and the food will usually be well prepared.

On the road back to my hotel, I sampled sugar cane from a roadside vendor. They cut the long stalks and I sucked the sugar cane juice from the pieces. It's very hard and chewy but the pure sugar rush is unlike any you get from mere candy. I also bought a small sampling of local fruits—"pawpaw" (papaya), june plums, sweet sop (even sweeter than sour sop), and mango. Needless to say, they were all bigger and sweeter than anything imported to American supermarkets. The only problem was figuring out exactly how to eat the more exotic fruits. I had to get instructions from the "higglers" (market women) on what to cut with a knife and what to bite.

After a short nap made necessary by the relentless afternoon sun, I met Don at my hotel for a tour of popular nightclubs. My first clash with Negril mores came when I discovered him waiting behind the wooden blockade manned by a hotel employee. "Visitors are not allowed, Miss," I was informed in crisp, British-inflected words. Translated, hotels make it a policy to bar local people from entering, lest the hotel guests be "bothered" by beggars or vendors. When I protested, Don just shrugged it off. "It's a way tings are," he said calmly.

Another thing about the way "tings are" in Negril is that foreigners are recognized on sight and usually treated with condescending wariness until they prove that they deserve otherwise. The looks I caught when I entered the first club were mocking and slightly challenging. I couldn't understand how they knew I wasn't Jamaican just by looking at me, before I opened my mouth. "It's your skin," Don explained. Although I'm the same walnut-brown as Don, my skin didn't have the burnished look that his had from being in the sun.

I heard murmurs of "rent a" across the room. Since I was the only non-Jamaican in the club, they assumed I was paying for Don's escort services. Tourists rarely venture into local clubs for any other reason, he told me. But after they observed that I didn't pay for any of Don's drinks and that I was familiar with the latest Buju Banton records, the attitudes vanished.

The clubs and dance halls of Jamaica have a culture all their own, unseen at hotel bars or beach concerts. They tend to be dark, all the better for the couples "wining" in corners along the walls. (Wining is the Caribbean way of suggestively gyrating your hips to the music's rhythms. It can be done solo or by rubbing up against a partner.) Dancehall tunes with heavy bass lines are usually favored, along with flashy, sexy clothes. Sometimes the music slows down for a show by partially covered strippers, who tend to be plump, in accordance with the taste for "mampy" (extremely voluptuous) women, but they don't do much more than the wining the patrons do themselves. Both men and women performed, and I didn't feel any of the lasciviousness that I would have expected. The spectacle was treated the way most Jamaicans treat sex—as something natural.

I saw more deeply into Jamaica when I traveled down the southern coast. I passed through Savanna-La-Mar, or "Sav-La-Mar," as the locals call it, where a crumbling fort serves as a swimming hole for children. Here you can see agile little bodies bobbing and diving all along the edge of the waterfront, which also boasts a bustling marketplace. You can buy everything from goats to pencils from the efficient vendors, but I preferred just to soak up the sights and sounds of everyday life.

Effortlessly negotiating prices and carrying bushels of produce, the women looked self-possessed and strong, comfortable with who they were. The men were easygoing and masterful. I saw a clear relation to the African sense of community that so many black people around the world struggle to hold on to. These people didn't look like they had many material comforts, but their bearing pointed to emotional and spiritual strength that warmed me with pride.

As I traveled along the coast I marveled at the beauty of the waving sugar cane fields, the lush greenery, and colorful scenes of rural life—a part of Jamaica not seen on T-shirts or tourism ads. Though most of

Jamaican tourism emphasizes Bob Marley memorials, a lesser-known memorial lies in the town of Belmont, on the southeast coast. This tiny fishing village claims to be the resting place of Peter Tosh who was a noted member of the Wailers and a popular solo artist.

Further along the southern coast is the Maroon town of Accompong. The Maroons were escaped slaves who established settlements in the hills, out of reach of the plantation owners. They have retained African culture and some language, due to centuries of isolated self-government. Accompong was established in 1739 and was part of a treaty agreement with the British. Today, it is an autonomous state.

The road to the village is treacherous and narrow, but there has been talk of expanding it for the visitors who come for the January 6 celebration of the Maroon victory over the British. Accompong carries an aura of battles and hard-won survival, and I saw this in the strong Ashanti faces of its people. Visitors must first obtain permission from the colonel, who is the elected leader. I visited the monument to Cudjoe, the Ghanaian-born leader of the Maroon War of 1729, which lasted ten years and won the Maroons the freedom to govern themselves. I also saw the Peace Cave, where the 1738 treaty for Accompong was signed, and the three-hundred-year-old *abeng*, or horn, used to warn Cudjoe's warriors of approaching British attacks. I found visiting Accompong to be a deeply moving experience. Witnessing the unbroken legacy of the strong African spirit of resistance should be an essential part of any visit to Jamaica.

The tranquil town of Mandeville boasts sprawling, mountaintop houses and gentle, upright, people. The town is the center for "community tourism," a philosophy that promotes connecting tourists with the people of Jamaica. Visitors may stay with families or simply have lunch with locals to get an understanding of Jamaican life. A magnet for retirees, Mandeville exhibits more flower shows and golf greens than it does tourist attractions and peddlers. For souvenirs, I visited the SWA Craft Centre, which is a workshop for unemployed women who create clothes, toys, and crochet work, and I purchased a handmade "Banana Patch" doll, complete with passport and dreadlocks.

My hotel, one of only two in Mandeville, was only slightly bigger than a bed and breakfast, and had fruit baskets displaying homegrown orantinques (a cross between oranges, tangerines, and grapefruits), and home-cooked meals featuring callaloo, a cousin of the spinach family, *bammy*, which is pounded cassava, and thick Jamaican hard-dough bread. The friendly young staff reflected Mandeville's international allure, with members from France, Germany, and Canada.

The staff took me for a night on the town, Mandeville style. Our first stop was a private party at a country club. The first thing I noticed was the reserve of the dancers. Reggae and soul music were playing, but there was no wining or suggestive dancing. The patrons were basically just swaying to the music or slow dancing in couples. "They're well-brought up ya' know," it was explained to me. I detected a smirk behind that explanation and I soon discovered that, like the U.S., there are variations and divisions within Jamaican society.

Next, we went to the local disco, which provided indoor and outdoor dancing to the latest reggae, Latin, and calypso tunes. Here, dancers wined and did the lambada and merengue along with the latest American dances. We left there for a local hot spot in the neighboring town of Porus. This nightclub was packed with young people from all of the surrounding small towns, and they were bursting with energy. The floor shook as the patrons wined, pranced in conga lines, and swayed to old and new reggae and R&B. The revelers dressed in crisp, formal clothes, from silk shirts and khaki pants to flowing dresses and miniskirt suits. The dancing lasted until 3:00, by which time I was thoroughly overwhelmed.

My last night in Jamaica, I returned to Negril for a huge outdoor reggae concert. These concerts are usually out of the price range of the locals, but this particular show included Jamaican favorites that aren't well known to tourists, such as Junior Tucker and Tony Rebel, so the price and the show were more accessible. Not only did Jamaicans outnumber tourists—a rare occurrence at large events in Negril—but the Jamaican appreciation for a wide range of music was well displayed.

American music, from country to hip hop, fills Jamaican radio airwaves, and you could hear its influence in the ingenious cover songs with reggae stylings. Reggae evolved from the melding of American R&B and early jazz or swing with Caribbean calypso and samba music. This myriad of influences float through current dancehall and roots reggae songs. Singing in a mix of patois and standard English, the performers embodied the richness of Jamaican culture. Junior Tucker crooned with a melting smoothness and Tony Rebel "toasted," or rapped, with all the thunder of a man aware of his heritage. Freddie MacGreggor lilted through calypso and country-inspired tunes, and Judy Mowatt sang the message-oriented reggae made famous when she backed Bob Marley with the I-Threes. It was a fitting finale for my journey into Jamaican culture.

Marianne Ilaw

Oh, Oh, Those West Indian Men!

REMEMBER THAT WICKEDLY FUNNY ROUTINE EDDIE MURPHY DID A FEW YEARS AGO? Don't let your woman visit the Caribbean alone, he warned. Because she's gonna run into "Dexter St. Jacques," the island playboy, who will purr, "I want to make love to you endlessleeeee!"

Sisters who vacation in the Caribbean shrieked in recognition when they saw that number, for anyone who has ever stepped foot on West Indian soil knows that "Dexter St. Jacques" is ubiquitous throughout the region. He's tall, often lean and long-legged, cocoa brown, with a luxurious mustache fringing his full kissable lips. Or else he's very fair skinned (known as "clear," "red", or "bright" in the islands) with wavy blondish-brown hair, green or hazel eyes, and a penchant for bragging about how his "granfodder" was a pureblood Englishman. (The Puerto Rican variation on this theme is, "My grandparents came from Spain.") Whichever West Indian model you choose—and both are plentiful—he's likely to be named "Trevor," "Fitzroy," "Winston," "Neville," "Denroy," "Basil," "Godfrey," or "Junior." He has a lilting accent, and when he addresses you as "me darlin'," you're ready to sell your Chicago condo, resign from your job in human resources, and make plans to open up a beachside café ("Chez Wanda") on his island.

Girlfriend, get a grip! West Indian men are great—they're sexy, sweet, charming, and attentive. They're a lovely diversion for sisters fed up with self-absorbed buppies and commitment-phobic boyfriends. And there is no man shortage in the Caribbean.

Now, don't get me wrong—all island men are not playboys or gigolos.

There are just as many hard-working family men who are faithful to their wives, churchgoing, dignified brothers, and studious young guys who would rather prepare for the future than fritter away their hours badgering tourist women to buy them a shot of Mount Gay. However, if you are a single black woman traveling without male companionship, the men you're going to meet will be the ones who are looking for babes like you—cute, sassy, with discretionary income and no husband lurking in the background.

But remember it's only an island fantasy. If you keep a clear head and remember that your Caribbean fling is just that, you'll enjoy yourself. And remember, too, you don't have to have sex with an island man to enjoy his stellar rap. Kissing and midnight walks on the beach will give you that nice tingly feeling without having to worry about the consequences of pregnancy or disease. And, if you're an exhibitionist, you can get your jollies by simply doing a "wicked wine" to a steamy *soca* tune on the dance floor.

Keep a cool head, and don't get hung up on that muscular bartender who serves you a frosty "Bahama Mama." He's had plenty of practice, and he knows just what to say: "What! A beautiful woman like you and no husband?" "I've never felt dis way before, for real." "Of course, I'll wait for you to come back next year. There'll be no odder woman!" Trust me, they'll be cruising the arrivals terminal the minute your Delta flight takes off.

But don't take my word for it—listen to my good buddy Rhona A., who was born in Dominica and raised on St. Croix: "West Indian men are oversexed, girl!" she says, laughing. When Rhona and I and another pal went to St. Martin some years ago, she was not impressed with the antics of the local men and yawned as I gaped, wide-eyed, at the sexy, loose-hipped, chocolate-skinned brothers who were crawling all over us. (She sniffed, "You yellow gals go for these 'hard-core' nasty men. Not me. I want someone quiet, with a small face—not these twenty-five-pound-head guys.")

These dudes literally hid in the bushes behind our cottage, grabbed our ankles as we splashed in the ocean, and even hung over the roof of our unit one morning and peered in the bathroom window, hoping to catch one of us showering. Happily married to a soft-spoken Southern-bred brother, Rhona says, "Yeah, I liked West Indian men, but they have to have a lot of women: a wife, a girlfriend, and some stuff on the side. And you know what—they love fat women! Sure, they're romantic, but that's because they've had a lot of practice!" (But they're so irresistible, like the gallant Bermudian admirer who told me, as we strolled through a fragrant garden during a tropical shower: "Oh, sweet lady, the island is crying because you're leaving tomorrow.")

Desmond B., a West Indian–born bachelor who now works in New York City, reluctantly agrees with Rhona. "Yes, there is some truth to this," he sighs. "There are some West Indian men who love to philander. They just don't have any restraint. Now, if an American man could get away with this , he would! But American men understand the consequences—West Indian men let the urge overpower them and they just go for it."

Yes, I know West Indian men and how they work. I live in New York City, a magnet for island immigrants. Many of my suitors here have been of Caribbean or Latino ancestry. (And I also have island blood in my own veins, so I know how mangoes, curry, and rum can enliven one's temperament.) However, after years of being exposed to rap music, BMWs, Armani suits, and the hype over the black man shortage, the transplants have adopted the "cool" façade of American brothers. They don't have to work for the boots. The indigenous Caribbean man, on the other hand, is earnest, anxious, and "in your face." (It's kind of like the difference between powdered ginger in a jar and the fresh, pungent root—both are spicy, but the unadulterated stuff has the biggest, nose-opening kick.) And for a black woman who is weary of men who are too selfish to cater to her, Caribbean men are a sweet treat.

For fifteen years now, I have been fulfilling my college dream of traveling widely throughout the Caribbean. I often go alone, since I'm a freelance travel writer and I don't want to be encumbered by companions who prefer to spend their days at the beach and their nights at the casino. ("Girl, let's check out that $8.99 buffet over at the Tropicana!") No, I seek out adventures, talk to everyone from cabinet ministers to barefoot crackheads. I've been to nearly every island, from sprawling Jamaica and Barbados to tiny Bequia and Nevis. I've danced barefoot at the Friday night "jump-up" in Gros Islet, St. Lucia; got into a heated discussion on male-female relations ("de problem wit' American men is dat dey rodder buy a foncy cyar den take care o' dey woman") in a smokey bar in Tortola; and ventured alone, my thirty-five-year-old body poured into a scandalous orange miniskirt, into a packed disco on Grand Cayman, where I had nineteen-year-old studs panting to "wine" with me.

Traveling alone has many advantages: You can make your own itinerary each day, without worrying about the friend who wants to price crystal and perfume; you can eat when and where you choose (some of my best meals have been takeout curry chicken and homemade ginger beer consumed on my balcony at sunset) and you have a greater opportunity to meet local folks, including men.

Some Caribbean men think black American women act "hard to get." Once I was in a nightclub in Freeport, dancing with a guy who sported a gold tooth and pink polyester pants. He asked, "Are you Italian?" "Spanish?" (I'm beige with that "Is that a weave?" kinda hair.) When I replied, "No, I'm a black American," he left me standing on the dance floor. Damn, right in the middle of "Caribbean Queen!" I asked his homeboy what was going on, and he replied, "Oh, you know, black American women don't give it up and they sure don't spend their money on you, so he thought he was wasting his time. He wants a girl who will give him sex and greenbacks."

I didn't know whether to be flattered or pissed off, and when I later asked the fire-eater (who wore a jheri curl with enough grease to fry five chickens) to explain what had happened, he said, "White women want these black island men. You sistahs have black men at home, so you expect more from us. It's not enough that we be big and black. For a blonde chick we're a novelty. So it's easier to score with them." If it's any consolation, I was later propositioned by the portly, balding contortionist—in his civilian garb of a black felt "Superfly" hat and orange and yellow satin cape—who whispered, "Wanna see me scoot naked across de floor like a crab?" I passed.

In St. Croix, I met a man who had six jobs. (Yeah, just like the Headleys on the show, *In Living Color.*) Foxton was a photographer, a waiter, a bodyguard, an illustrator, a security guard, and a paramedic. He used to joke and say, "Me so black, I gotta smile for you to find me face at night." He thought he could win my favor by inviting me to his house to view videos of fatal car crashes. "Yah, you should see dis one partikalar video. It was brutal. De mon, he bloody head roll out on de ground!"

In Grenada a ruffian followed me along the beach for about ten minutes. I thought he was trying to get a rap, but, actually, he was trying to steal my bag. He insisted that he was a member of the secret police and wanted to search me for drugs and contraband. I shrieked a string of curses, New York–style, and a security guard came a running. He ordered the suspect to "sit on de beach until de police come!" Surprise— he did! The constable took the ne'er-do-well into custody and assured me, "We don't really have crime in Grenada. The only reason this guy tried to rob you is because he used to live in New York." Gee, thanks, pal. The following day, the arresting officer paid me a call at my hotel, and questioned me for about, uh, forty-five minutes as I was sprawled on a chaise lounge in an eye-popping pink bikini. He asked in earnest if I needed a bodyguard for the remainder of my trip.

He wasn't the only one who offered his services. After word got around about my unfortunate experience, all manner of local men were volunteering to squire me around. Humphrey tried to impress me with his brute strength by bragging, "You know I killed 'tree people with a machete." I yawned. "It was I alone who killed dem." Yawn plus a shrug. He leaned forward and whispered, "Dey wuz 'tree *white* people, woman!" I later learned from Virgil, a beachside crafts vendor who claimed to be a former cop, that Humphrey fabricated stories to impress women. "Dat bwoy kunna kill a damn mosquito if it land on him nose!" Virgil offered to protect me by spending the night in my hotel room. "I promise, I sleep on de floor and stay awake all night to guard you!" With his eyes trained on my overflowing tank top and his breathing raspy and labored, I declined.

Some of these island guys are too bold to be believed. I was minding my business on a beach in the Bahamas, eyes closed, Walkman snugly attached, when I felt a dog licking my foot. I reached down to stroke him, but when I opened my eyes, I discovered it was a young man. Sunglasses lowered, my neck popping, I demanded an explanation. He shrugged sheepishly "I was just removing the sand from your toes." (Feet must be popular in the Caribbean. In a beach bar in Barbados, a man I had never see before pulled off my sandal and put it in his mouth. "These shoes have walked on the streets of Manhattan!" I shrieked. And in St. Thomas, a handsome local dinner date dropped his car keys, dove under the table to retrieve them, and gave my bare tootsies a quick slurp.)

On the ferry from St. Vincent to Bequia in the Grenadines, I was ogled by a hygienically challenged dude with bare rusty feet housing toenails so long and strong they could open up a bottle of ginger beer. He winked his bloodshot eyes at me and ambled over. "Hi dere," he nodded, wafting breath that smelled as if a monkey had slept in his mouth. "You wan' company?" "No, thanks," I declined. He clucked his white-coated tongue and peeled a scab off his arm. "You gwine be sorry you turned dis down, sister!"

Despite some crude knuckleheads, for the most part I have felt cherished, respected, and admired, even if I was being handed a truckload of fertilizer. And I did meet a bunch of men who were absolute gentlemen and were appalled at the behavior I described. "Dey 'ave no home trainin'," one cab driver clucked.

The fellas in St. Lucia were pretty smooth; well, you know, those Creole cultures have that extra little continental twist. I met men who would bow at the waist and kiss my hand, a guy who crooned to me in French under a palm tree one evening, and a bunch of mannerly teenage boys who plucked hibiscus blossoms and fresh coconuts for my approval. Why, even a local crackhead was a bucket of charm. As I explained the penalties for narcotics possession in New York, he fashioned a cricket and a beach hat out of palm fronds for me.

I was the only patron in a charming seaside restaurant one night off-season. The elderly owner was courtly and attentive, and as the cooks prepared my fresh dolphin, and the bartender concocted a special drink just for me, the proprietor spun me around the establishment's concrete floor as an infectious calypso tune poured from ceiling speakers. Just the two of us, twirling around the empty room.

Startling or sweet, I have great island memories:

—Walking past a soccer field at dusk in Barbados, clad in a black, ruffled off-the-shoulder dress with a giant hibiscus blossom tucked behind my ear. The game stopped and the players gave me a rousing round of applause.

—Being given a tour of Antigua by an earnest young business man who suddenly stops the car, leaps over a roadside fence and plucks a fat, juicy mango to present to me.

—Strolling along downtown Nassau, minding my own business, when this dude jumps off a moving bus and rushes up to me. Startled, I asked him what was up, and he kissed my hand and said, "You just so pretty, I had to say hello to you." He pointed to the sky-high water tower behind us and said, "Men would jump off dat tower for a girl like you." (Even if it was a crock, I sure ain't never had no brothers in New York jump off a speeding subway train to rap to me.)

—Hanging out with two of my girls at a hot nightclub in Bermuda, basking in the male attention. We all get up to dance, and when we return to our table, there are twelve—count 'em—twelve pastel-colored drinks in front of us, courtesy of several admirers.

—Chuckling while I overheard two waiters arguing over who was going to serve me at my hotel's restaurant in Aruba. Alright, alright, so the only other customers were a group of middle-aged German men.

—Lying on a deserted beach in St. Kitts, hearing giggles floating from behind a sand dune. When I turned my head to check it out, I saw two young boys whispering and pushing each other. "Hi there," I waved. One of them waved timidly and said, "When we grow up, we gonna look for a girlfriend just like you, Miss!" (They start young, don't they?)

If you've never been to the islands, you're in for an unrivaled experience. Whether you're sixteen or sixty, slim or stout, sophisticated or shy, you'll return from your trip agreeing that if Caribbean men could bottle and sell their charm, their finesse, and their sex appeal, the region's sluggish economy would soar. Be safe, and don't take it seriously.

Aya de León

Catching a Glimpse

THE UPHOLSTERY OF THE BUS SEAT WAS FALLING APART, AND THE METAL BENEATH it dug into my behind. The bumpy road didn't help either, and I tried to stay squashed into my corner so as not to knock Gigi off the seat we were sharing. She has a tall, svelte figure, but is by no means thin. I'm a size-able woman, myself, and our hips were barely contained by the single passenger seat.

We ate our *platanitos* in silence, watching the lush green Dominican landscape out of the dusty window. Behind us, the young Kansas City Missionary Baptists chatted. Gigi, the driver, and I were the only brown faces on the bus.

I had met Gigi on the way to the beach a few days before. She was a chocolate-skinned young woman with a super straight pressed bob like the sisters back home. I had wondered if she might be African American. I missed the cadences of home: "wassup?" and "haaaay!" and "hiyadoin' baby?"

Gigi turned out to be Haitian. However, she had spent her junior year of high school in New England and spoke enough English so that we could communicate across the lapses in my Spanish, which were frequent, unpredictable, and very frustrating to this third-generation Puerto Rican/African American raised in Aztlan, California.

Gigi was trying to move back to the States. She had a fiancée in New York, and she was working on getting a visa to join him there.

She was twenty-two to his thirty-something. "I prefer an older man," she told me later. "Not these *boys* like my brothers. They have kids and no plans to get married. They still live at home. I'm the oldest girl, so I help my mother cook, clean up, and watch my little brothers and sisters. My brothers do nothing to help."

Gigi also did service for the church, including translating for the missionaries. Their church back in Kansas City sponsored Gigi's church, the Haitian Missionary Baptist Church, which ministered to the abundant needs of the Haitian community in the Dominican Republic, particularly those in the *bateyes*.

Bateyes are labor camps. These small villages without water or electricity are exclusively for the Haitian immigrants who work in the cane fields—work that few Dominicans want to do, yet many are resentful of the powerful, unabashedly African presence of the Haitian people in their country. Do they think that if all these Haitian people didn't come across the border, the cane would maybe cut itself?

As the bus came around a curve, the road turned and we could see mountains in the distance, and the cane. To the left and to the right were fields of it. The cane that makes sugar for coffee, coca cola, cake, cookies, candy.

The fields of cane stretched all the way to the horizon. An ocean of cane, with gentle waves in the afternoon breeze. The bus went up a hill and I caught a glimpse of a path of red earth parting the sea of cane—an empty path because it was Sunday, the only day the laborers didn't have to work.

When we went up the next hill, I could see there were two little black girls on the path. Black like the night sky, like the color waiting for me behind my eyelids when I sleep. Black angels walking down the red road in yellow and white dresses under a blue sky through a green sea of cane. The bus went around the next curve and they disappeared.

We drove twenty minutes more and arrived at the first *batey*. People came out of their houses made of cane stalks and palm leaves, and for the fortunate ones, bowed wood. All the houses had dirt floors and folks had bare feet and ragged clothes. I said, "*Saludos,*" which means "greetings," then felt suddenly tongue-tied. What could I say? That I was enraged that they had to live without running water, without health services? That the old woman in the worn dress reminded me of my grandmother? That the tiny girl with the big eyes reminded me of my little sister, who is a twin but the other one had died? That I am furious that they earn in a month what I can make in a day?

Many of the babies had hair that was dark auburn at the roots, but honey blond at the tips. It seemed strange to see such dark children with such light hair. I asked Gigi about it, and she said it was malnutrition.

The white teenage missionaries smiled as they handed out pens and gum. The dark children mobbed them, jumping up and down, reaching for their very own Bic or Paper Mate or Dentyne or Doublemint. The missionaries were so blasé, as if they were on a field trip to a museum or the zoo. As if we were not looking into the faces of children who were starving and adults who were being worked to death.

Those same adults in the *batey* watched, tolerating these young white strangers who could descend on their community and woo their children with empty calories, consenting to put their children's desire and enthusiasm on display. These same children might be sick one day, and they might need to wait all day or all week to see the one doctor, financed by the few dollars that came from the church of these young white people. But I could see their swallowed rage, and I moved away, wanting to disassociate myself from the scene.

I wandered to the edge of the *batey*, where the fields began. The cane was alive with hens and their chicks, alarmed by the presence of a foreigner.

I knelt down to pray: Please God, have mercy upon all of my Caribbean people that they may have justice and peace and dignity and work that does not break their bodies or their spirits. I am an African daughter of the Americas with roots in Puerto Rico and St. Kitts and Nevis and South Carolina. Because the ships that carried slaves from up and down the west coast of Africa delivered them at random to islands throughout the Caribbean, and to the U.S., and throughout Central and South America, I claim the Haitian and the Dominican people as my people, too.

I caught a glimpse of my ancestral past that day. This is how African Americans lived not so long ago—in slave quarters, as sharecroppers. And I shed naive and luxurious tears into the same soil that they had to work six days a week under an unforgiving sun.

Gigi came up behind me and led me to the little green church. It was wooden and held together with barbed wire. There were several pews on the concrete floor, and in the front was an altar with a white cloth, artificial flowers, and three small, worn chairs. The ceiling was of corrugated metal, and although it was the most durably constructed building in the *batey*, it leaned precariously to one side.

A group of children came in. They were spindly six- and seven-year-olds, all with long arms and legs, and dancing eyes. Led by a bold girl, the tallest of them, they asked what had I brought for them.

Nothing.

Where was my gum? Where were my pens?

I didn't have enough Spanish to explain myself to them, to justify my opulent empty-handedness. And would they have understood me in Spanish? Here in the *bateyes*, children didn't go to school, did not learn the language of the country, were not trained to integrate into the larger society, were not expected to.

The second *batey* was smaller. I went into the church, which was little more than a hut, but it had a drum in the corner. I stepped back outside to find Gigi talking in Creole to an elderly woman with sharp eyes, and weathered, red-brown skin. She had a naked baby on her hip, and was smoking a cigar. Through the open door of her tiny house, I could see a double bed, which took up almost all of the space inside. I nodded to her in acknowledgment.

The missionaries were hot, and they pulled out a cooler from the back of the bus full of Coca Cola and 7up in those old-style bottles with caps that don't twist off. Gigi popped the tops off on the edge of the metal track on the sliding bus windows. She gave one to the sharp-eyed woman, and poured some of it into a cup for the baby.

I watched as Gigi went about her business, this young Haitian woman, living in the Dominican Republic, translating for the missionaries from Kansas City, befriending the African American Puerto Rican writer, inviting me to church, pouring cola into the earth by the house of a sharp-eyed Haitian woman smoking a cigar.

On the way back, I wanted to dismember the casual chatter of the two guys sitting behind me on the bus. I wanted to make the girl with the sandy hair swallow her laugh. I wanted to walk up and down the aisle, and slap all the missionaries for being white Americans. I could have slapped myself while I was at it. I avoided Gigi's eyes and stared out the dusty window.

About ten minutes after we hit the road, I saw the two little girls, one dressed in white, the other in yellow, walking out of the bright green cane. It was at least an hour since the first time I had seen them walking, surrounded by nothing but cane and sky and road. How long had they been walking before that? Gigi said they walked all that way just to go to the church.

There was hope in the determined stride of those girls, and their hope affected me powerfully. It reminded me that freedom is not dictated by circumstances. Freedom is waiting inside the drum in the corner of that church. Freedom is pouring cola into the earth for our ancestors because we know we need their loving presence. Freedom is me confronting God about the conditions under which my folks are allowed to live, instead of taking my rage out on the missionaries. Freedom is two little black girls daring to have faith in the midst of great obstacles. Freedom is me, avoiding the traps of indifference and guilt to face the vastness of black peoples' oppression with open and compassionate eyes.

Daphne E. Barbee-Wooten

Visiting Nannytown

I think we should live up in the hills.
—Burning Spear

TO GET AWAY FROM THE HECTIC PRESSURES OF BEING A TRIAL LAWYER IN HAWAII, I travel yearly to Port Antonio, Jamaica. I have been doing this for sixteen years and I have no plans to stop. I love Jamaica. Every time I visit, there is a new place to explore, something to learn, and the realization that there is more to life than arguing, fighting, jostling, and figuring out where "justice" is hiding.

During a recent trip, I traveled to Mooretown, a small village high up in the lush, tropical mountains of Jamaica. My husband and I drove on a windy dirt road from the coast upward through villages, farms, and fields of pimento, mango, coconut, allspice, bananas, and sugar cane. Near the top of the blue mountains, where you can go no further, is a single lane road leading downward into a valley. There is only one way in and one way out.

In this valley, surrounded by giant pyramid-shaped mountains, is Mooretown, named after the Maroons, the fierce African warriors who were runaway slaves during the early 1700s. (The term *marrón* means wild, untamable, in Spanish.) The Maroons ran into the hills and established their own villages where the African language was spoken and African culture was alive in the spicy food and stories told by one generation to the next. Drumming was used to send messages to people in faraway enclaves. One of these villages, which no longer exists, was called Nannytown, after their leader, "Nanny of the Maroons," who was mother, healer, political leader, and advisor of the Port Antonio Windward Maroons, a woman whose strength and courage are legendary.

The Maroons were not content to obtain their own freedom; they raided slave owners' plantations and freed other slaves. These raids were so successful that the slave owners requested a peace treaty with the Maroons. They offered them freedom if they would agree to return escaped slaves, promising that every time a Maroon returned an escaped slave, they would be paid. Nanny's position on this "peace treaty" was an emphatic *no*. (When Nanny said no to slavery for herself, she said no to slavery for all people.) She spoke eloquently and persuasively, convincing the Maroons not to sell their freedom for another's enslavement. As a result of the Maroons' continued efforts to free slaves in the plantations, the slave owners eventually raided Nannytown in a bloody battle, but Nanny was never captured. Eventually, Nanny reluctantly agreed to the peace treaty, which was entered into with the British in 1739. Maroon descendants to this day enjoy the benefits of that treaty, including perpetual tax-free lands.

I knew this history and was thrilled to be going to the place where the Maroons had made their home. I thought about them, and especially about Nanny, during the two-hour drive up the bumpy dirt road in our rented pickup truck. As we entered Mooretown, we drove past an old green wooden church and came across a plaque on which was written: "Nanny of the Maroons, National Heroine

of Jamaica. Beneath this place known as Bump Grave lies the body of Nanny, indomitable and skilled chieftainess of the Windward Maroons who founded this town." I paid my respects to the memory of Nanny. This is what I had come here for. I felt a kind of exhilaration at the connection—with Nanny and with my history as a black woman.

As we made our way back down the dirt road, avoiding the potholes and roaming cattle, I knew that this had been an important pilgrimage. Of course, as a woman of African American ancestry, it is rewarding to travel to a place where an African woman's battle against slavery is honored. But this was more than a transitory feeling of pride. Something happened to me there that gave me a new sense of what we, as descendants of African slaves, could accomplish.

Nanny is as present in the lives of the Windward Maroons as if she had lived yesterday. Mooretown is rumored to be protected by the spirit of Nanny and other Maroon ancestors who abide in the form of the white "watchbirds" that wing about the lush, mountainous area.

—Linda Cousins, "Grandy Nanny"

The next day at the post office in Port Antonio I overheard a family, visitors from Florida, discussing "the Right Honorable Excellent Nanny." Overcoming my nonlawyerlike shyness, I asked if they had visited Mooretown and if they knew about the shrine in Nanny's honor. To my great surprise, they introduced themselves as descendants of Nanny. I thought to myself, I, too, am a descendant of Nanny, but then I realized that they were *direct* descendants! They showed me photographs of their relatives and their recent visit to Mooretown. The father picked up his wallet and produced a $500 Jamaican bill with pride. On this bill was a picture of Nanny of the Maroons, his great great great-grandmother.

When I returned to Honolulu, I began to search for a house in the hills overlooking the city. I thought of Nanny and her courage and I felt sure that living high in the hills is a good place for fighting spirits and free souls. Here, overlooking the Pacific Ocean, I await the day an African American freedom fighter such as Harriet Tubman or Sojourner Truth is depicted on American currency, and I try, in my own way, to carry on the work that Nanny began four hundred years ago.

Linda Villarosa

In Search of Black Peru: Christmas in El Carmen

MOST OF THE MANY TRAVELERS WHO PASS THROUGH PERU ARE THERE TO MAKE A pilgrimage to Machu Picchu, the legendary Lost City of the Incas constructed more than five centuries ago. I was traveling with several Peruvian friends, and of course we did that, too, flying to Cuzco, the mountain town that is the base for tourists headed for the ruins, where artists and craftspeople sold items ranging from wool blankets to jewelry.

After a day of shopping, we rode the train to Aguas Calientes, the town at the foot of Machu Picchu. The train itself was an experience: We opted for the local, or "Indian," train, packed mostly with women who cheerfully sold fruit and vegetables out the windows at each stop. Once we arrived at Aguas Calientes, we dumped our stuff in a youth hostel and then took the rugged hike two hours uphill to the ruins. Machu Picchu is breathtaking. The history of this complex stone city is still subject to debate, but it wonderfully reflects Incan ingenuity, like the intricate terraces that allowed crops to grow on the rocky mountainside. Signs of temples, fortresses, homes, and even an observatory remain intact.

When we were sitting around back home, planning our trip, dreaming of *ceviche* (an appetizer of raw fish and shellfish marinated in lime juice, onions, peppers and spices) and street vendors selling *chuelo con queso,* (corn on the cob with a hunk of cheese) and tamales, I had turned to my friends and asked, "What exactly does your country have to offer me as an African American?" (Even as I asked, I felt disingenuous. With a Spanish surname like Villarosa, I would have enough of a cultural homecoming.) But to my surprise the group said in unison, "Vamos pa Chincha familia."

To Peruvians, this familiar refrain, which loosely translates as "Let's go home to Chincha," refers to a region about a hundred miles south of Lima, the nation's capital and largest city. Chincha is the area that houses the country's largest concentration of blacks. Within Chincha, the village of El Carmen is considered the Afro-Peruvian cultural center and is best known for two festivals that combine Peruvian music, dance, food, and drink with the African influence of the black people who live there.

Over the Christmas holiday, the townspeople put on a four-day celebration culminating in the Day of the Virgin of El Carmen—an all-night, all-day gala that pays tribute to their town's patron saint. In February, El Carmen and neighboring communities reconvene for La Yunza, a musical street party that roughly resembles Mardi Gras. Each of these celebrations draws hundreds of tourists to the usually sleepy village.

In order to see El Carmen for ourselves, my friends and I headed south from Lima by car on Christmas Eve. Rather than staying in El Carmen, we rented a house in the nearby coastal town of Paracas. Best known for a natural game reserve, Paracas is one of Peru's favorite tourist spots. Some people think of it as a poor man's Galapagos Islands.

After spending some time in the morning seeing the beach and wildlife in Paracas, we set out for El Carmen. Driving through the dark countryside, our car knocked and bumped over a deserted dirt road, and I began to wonder if El Carmen was really such a big deal. As we neared the town, however, we passed a sign that read El Carmen: Peru's Capital of Black Folklore, and we could see lights and hear music.

The town square was jammed with people ready to kick off the festivities in celebration of both Christmas and the Virgin of El Carmen. Some brightly dressed folks were spilling out of church, following the Christmas Eve mass, while others were hanging out, listening to groups of children sing and dance, and eating *anticuchos* (beef hearts roasted on a stick) and french fries dipped in spicy salsa. Many were also drinking a potent homebrew called *tutuma*, made from wine, *pisco* (grape liquor), and the root of the *tutuma*, a gourdlike plant that grows in the area. Standing in the midst of the rowdy crowd, I was struck by the diversity of the townspeople. Some were clearly of African extraction, while others had straight hair and brown skin. The rest were of various shades and hair textures in between—the products of hundreds of years of intermarrying among the three races.

In 1532, when Spanish conquistadors arrived to seize Peru from the Incan people, African slaves accompanied them. The country's black population began to increase markedly several decades later, when Africans from the Bantu regions were captured by Spaniards and brought forcibly to Peru as slaves. By 1570, census takers counted more blacks than Spaniards in coastal Peru. Even as late as the mid-1700s, some historians believe that half of the population of Lima was of African origin.

After slavery was abolished in 1854, Incan and Aymarian peoples from the mountain regions flooded the cities in search of work and became part of the workforce and the official census count. Over time this influx of indigenous peoples, as well as race mixing and the effects of disease and wars, reduced the population of "pure" blacks to what it is today: less than 3 percent of the population of twenty-two million.

Amador Ballumbrosio, a singer and master violinist who has lived in El Carmen all his life, has made sure that black Peruvian traditions survive and thrive in his community. Though he considers himself 100 percent Peruvian and isn't sure about his ancestors' path from Africa to coastal Peru, the music and dance that his father taught him clearly recall the sounds and rhythms of West Africa. Dark-skinned with gray hair, don Amador holds his violin low, tucked under his armpit. When he plays he looks like Chicken George of *Roots* fame.

The African influence was in full swing on December 26. We arrived in time to follow a group of young boys, mostly black, dressed in white shirts and dark pants with brightly colored, handmade sashes around their shoulders. Led by don Amador on the violin, the group paraded through town, stopping in various houses to dance and sing in tribute to the Virgin of El Carmen. The boys sang folk songs in Spanish and performed a lively line dance that looked like a fraternity step show. The procession ended at the Ballumbrosio's modest dirt-floor home. There the *tutuma* was flowing as the older brothers settled behind their *cajones*, a popular Peruvian drum made from a simple wooden box. I sat there transfixed, listening to the soulful rhythms and watching the children tear up the dance floor.

Throughout the rest of the trip I saw signs of the black Peruvian legacy. Black singers, dancers, and musicians were very popular throughout the country, especially in Lima. *Musica negra* or *musica criolla* could be heard in small, crowded nightclubs, and black dance troupes performed concerts in local outdoor gatherings. It was at once eerie and empowering to realize the far-reaching and enduring strength of our collective African ancestry.

Loretta Henry

Before I Was a Bajan

"Yuh goin' down now?" she said. Another friend insisted, "Are you kidding girl, yuh should wait for Crop Over." But I was on a serious mission that had nothing to do with carnival, bacchanal, or jumpin' on de congaline. Make no mistake, I am a *soca*-loving dancin' fool, and until then, the Labor Day Parade on Brooklyn's Eastern Parkway was the only Caribbean carnival I had ever been to, so I was long overdue for a genu-ine West Indian Carnival. But never mind, I had work to do.

My work began back in January of 1978, the year Alex Haley had the nation, and eventually the world, spellbound by the telecast of *Roots* for two consecutive weeks. From that point on, like thousands of others, I caught "Roots fever." Diligently, I tried to shake down whatever family information I could get, grilling my mother, father, uncles, cousins, and anyone else I could manage to get to, but despite my rigorous interrogations, very few of them could recall facts from fifty years ago. Nevertheless, I continued on with my modest gleanings.

By the fall of 1990, I had reached a frenzied level of curiosity in my quest for family knowledge. I had grown envious of coworkers casually blabbing how they are French on their mother's side, German on their father's side, and a quarter Irish. I even met someone who claimed to be a descendant of Ole King Cole. Well I don't know about that, but I do know that life for our Caribbean ancestors started long before Columbus and company set sail. I know that before I was a Bajan, or "West Indian," I was an African and this is what I wanted to learn about. Then, late one night, while flipping through a book on how to trace your family tree, I discovered something truly unfathomable: The Mormon Family History Center.

Less than an hour after my first visit to the center, the excitement became so intense that I feared I would lose my lunch right then and there at the computer terminal. Fortunately, I was able to calm my nerves and continue to feed the computer the names that had become ingrained in my memory: Augustus, Ambrozine, poor Jane who drowned at the age of eleven. Never in my wildest dreams could I have imagined that I'd be sitting across the street from Lincoln Center in Manhattan reviewing baptismal records of my grandmother's aunts and uncles. But, by sheer chance, I had discovered this repository of thousands of genealogies from countries all over the world.

I was enraptured the moment I found out that the small Caribbean nation of Barbados, of which I am a daughter, was extremely well represented in the West Indies collection. Unlikely as it seemed, the Mormon Family History Center had become the saving grace in my ongoing quest.

Take a personal tapeplayer and pair of sunglasses on the plane with you if you're not big on bonding with strangers just because they happen to be seated next to you on a cross-country flight. These simple measures allow you your privacy without being rude.

—Pearl Cleage, "Reluctant Road Warrior"

It should be no surprise then, that on my first full day in Barbados, I didn't hit the beach, the shops, the sights, or even the cousins, strange and familiar, who I had heard about for as long as I can remember. I took a bus to the long, winding path that leads to the National Archives building (formerly the Lazaretta) in Black Rock, St. Michael. The archives staff, friendly and trained research professionals, went the extra mile to help me. After a few visits, I found the will of my great-grandfather Henry Hope, which eventually led me to the will to *his* father, Matthew Hope. And what a gold mine it turned out to be. It listed everyone in the Hope family, including two adult married sisters of great-grandpa that even Dad and cousin Tom didn't know about.

And yes, eventually I did get down for Crop Over, and after attending my first calypso tent I was a certified Crop Over addict. The comedians and their taunting jokes about all the Bajan Yankees, Brits, and Canadians in the house made me laugh out loud at myself. And the cleverly worded calypsos sticking it to one politician or another were rib tickling examples of classic calypso in its truest form. In no time at all, I was casually tossing around Crop Over phrases like *Ring Bang* and *Kadooment,* as well as giving my opinion on who should win for Road March and Monarch. I even became a semiregular at Eddie's Supertent,

*A*ruba is the ideal spot for African American women to vacation as ethnicity and gender are not obstacles. You can stroll along the beach in the late evening and enjoy the ocean breeze as it beats against your body without any fear of being bothered. If shopping is your pleasure, you can patronize any jewelry shop or clothing boutique, regardless of how posh, and whether you browse or buy you'll be treated with the same respect and dignity afforded to others.

Dining in the various restaurants scattered throughout the island was always an adventure. Establishments that were not pleasing to the eye from the outside were actually quite charming on the inside, and the food was often superb. The staff made me feel as if their primary goal in life was to cater to my every need and desire. I felt truly welcomed, not only into their restaurants but into their lives.

After a couple of days of being treated with such respect, I began to feel as if a heavy burden had been lifted from my heart. I realized that the defenses I have built up over the years as a means of protection and survival were painful aches and wounds that were now being healed.

My spirit was renewed, along with my sense of pride and appreciation for myself as an African American woman. I was able to view the world with new eyes. I arose each morning to greet the day and watch the sun rise in all its splendor. The sky and the water were the most vivid and vibrant shade of blue I had ever witnessed.

—Laura Joseph, "Aruba, a Spiritual Haven"

a huge roadside disco that was open all night, every night. I felt as if Barbados and I were two old friends who lost contact thirty years ago and were just catching up on old times.

I will continue my search to fill in the blanks on my family tree and to discover which of the many languages of West Africa my ancestors spoke before they were separated or worse. It's anyone's guess whether my family name would be Dansoko, Ba, or Ademako, or any other, since slavery forever distorted the course of my family's story. I still long for the privilege of boasting about how I'm a quarter this and an eighth that, but I have become resigned to the fact that, as a member of the African Diaspora, that may never happen. Nevertheless, I am proud that I can rattle off the names and birthplaces of all eight of my great-grandparents and most of *their* grandparents. It means a lot to me that almost every time I meet an African, they tell me that I look like a Bambara (Mandingo) or Fulani from Mali or Guinea. I know that I was called to do this work for a reason and remain hopeful that one day I may find the answers to the mysteries that my African soul longs to know.

Linda Cousins

Culture-Rich Carriacou

THERE ARE ONLY TWO SAVING GRACES TO LEAVING AN ISLAND AS LOVELY AND CUL-turally blessed as Grenada. The first is the pleasure of that intense desire to return for another visit as soon as possible, and the second is the excitement of heading toward yet another magnificent cultural adventure—this time to Grenada's largest sister island, charismatic Carriacou.

Grenadian friends had emphasized that Carriacou was quite different from Grenada—much smaller, much quieter, and quite a bit more rustic. These were welcome words of introduction to the island, as I enjoy visiting a lively, upscale island and then topping off the vacation entree with a "dessert" of a refreshing, meditative getaway to a serenely placid spot where I can contemplate, commune with nature, and totally relax mind, body, and spirit.

I would have preferred taking the leisurely boat ride to Carriacou, but my remaining days in the Caribbean were limited, so I opted for a flight that took only a few minutes rather than a few hours. I had hardly taken my eyes from Grenada's retreating shores before we were ready to disembark in culture-rich Carriacou. So here you are, I thought, as I gathered up my possessions. I have heard so much about you, Carriacou. Now we finally get to meet each other "face to face."

My first acquaintanceship with the diminutive island had come through reading *Praisesong for the Widow* by one of my favorite authors, Paule Marshall. In the novel, a middle-aged, conservative African American traveler, Avey Johnson, becomes reconnected with her long-lost African heritage partially through visiting Carriacou and experiencing the African Nations Dance performed there. We learn through the novel that many Carriacouans actually know the African nation from which they are descended and pay homage to their ancestors through a number of traditions, including the African Nations Dance, also known as the Big Drum Dance. From the moment of reading *Praisesong*, I longed to learn more about these rituals.

My wish was granted through meeting the Carriacouan historian, poet, and educator, Christine David, who amply describes the Big Drum Dance and other African-derived rituals of Carriacou in her work, *The Folklore of Carriacou*. In an effort to keep the Big Drum Dance tradition alive, David formed a dance company in the 1970s called the Carriacou Carib Organization. The company consists of not only the youth who are interested in learning about and celebrating their heritage but also of skilled elder dancers like Ms. Lucian Duncan. (David's poem, "Drum Echoes," is featured in my Caribbean cultural travel guide, *Caribbean Bound!—Culture Roots, Places, and People* and a photo of the beautiful elder Big Drum dancer became the inspiration for the book's cover artwork).

Christine is delighted to meet those who appreciate the richness of the island culture and especially those who appreciate the significance of the African traditions. She is disappointed, though, by those who have come to the island to videotape or film the performances, promising to send back copies. Unfortunately, she's never heard from most of those people again. I mentally determine to send copies to Christine of everything I write about her work. She is a global treasure and a valuable resource person engaged in the important work of both recording and promoting one of our great ancestral traditions.

Christine visited me one rainy island day. Stepping across the puddle in front of my door we sat on the terrace as the rain slowed itself to a drizzle and discussed her work in spreading the word on the

> The slaves, usually taciturn, came alive when they assembled in a "Ring," symbolizing unity, solidarity, and continuity. They found escape in their traditional rituals. The drum beat, blending with their rich voices and tribal dances, rang out a tradition of resistance to oppression—and hope. The music healed their physical and mental anguish. Their performance depicted their dreams and visions of survival, a longing to identify with their original home and country. This transplanted race felt trapped with too few words to express their pent-up emotions. Feeling lost with a new name, a new language, a peculiar way of life, they found their tongues in the drum beat as they enacted their ancient tribal customs, rebelliousness, and visions of a new day.
>
> —Christine David, "The History and Tradition of Carriacou's Big Drum Dance"

Big Drum ritual and teaching the tradition to the Carriacouan youth. As we sat chatting, I recalled my many readings and rereadings of her work, *The Folklore of Carriacou.*

In the book she discusses the *saracas,* or tombstone feasts. Although there is an elaborate parting ritual for the deceased, as in the motherland, the most significant of the activities around an islander's transition is the setting of the tombstone, which Christine explained can be delayed for as long as ten to twenty years. The entire community takes part, even those who have moved abroad; they often send contributions and arrange, if feasible, to return home. Food is prepared, which is shared by guests at the home of the departed as well as at the cemetery where the tombstone is being laid. (The tombstone is first brought to the home of the deceased, placed in the bed under a white sheet, and spoken to by family members who also sprinkle rum and water over it.)

During the *saraca* feast, a "parents' plate" is placed on a table with a candle for the ancestors. The "Big Time" is subsequently marked with an African Nations Dance complete with drumming and singing. The homemade goatskin drums consist of two side drums (called *bulas*) and a middle drum called the *cot* drum, which is made of female goatskin as compared to male goatskin for the *bula* drums. The side drums provide the foundation rhythm, while the *cot* drum explores more creative, intricate beats inspired by the movements of the dancers

The dancers, garbed in wide, colorful skirts, frilly blouses, and stately headwraps, perform the dances of the varied African nations who were brought to Carriacou during the slavery era; they included the Kromantis, Ibos, Arradah, the Yorubas, Hausas, Mokos, Temnes, Mandingos, Bandas, and Chambas. As artfully described in Marshall's *Praisesong,* the opening dance (the "Beg Pardon"), inviting the ancestors' presence and participation, is performed in honor of the Kromantis (or Akan) people of Ghana. They are so honored for they were the most rebellious, courageous, and determined in fighting and led battles against enslavement not only in Carriacou but across the world. After the Akans are honored, then the other African nations are honored in turn with their specific dances. Meeting and chatting with Christine became the highlight of my visit to this lovely little island. She is a great Caribbean woman who has not only immersed herself in the history and culture of her ancestors but has endeavored to pass it on globally.

> *The* dance's authenticity and uniqueness make it significant culturally as well as popular with the islanders. The drum beat, the song, and the dance serve to perpetuate the link between ancestors and descendants. The drum ritual regenerates itself, lending each generation an understanding of the past—and an appreciation of the present.
>
> —Christine David, "The History and Tradition of Carriacou's Big Drum Dance"

An *Islands* magazine article had introduced me to the work of Winston Fleary. I had been meaning to look him up, when I ran into him sitting on the terrace of the Plymouth bar enjoying the island atmosphere. We were introduced and I spent the next hour or so listening to his enthralling account of the African history of the island. Originally from Haiti, he mentioned that he is descended from the Fleary who fought with Touissaint L'Ouverture during the Haitian Revolution. He explained how he has written about and carried the Big Drum performances to varied parts of the world, viewing this as a part of his life's mission. Those fearless Haitian ancestors must be very proud that one of their sons is carrying on their work in his own special way.

On my last day, Carriacou was bountifully graced by the sun once more but was still a bit muddy. The annual Carriacou Regatta, held in August, was right around the corner. The islanders were busily preparing for the large annual influx of fun-loving visitors and kinfolk returning home from across the world, and getting ready for the Big Drum Dance, which is performed at most of the major festivities, particularly the boat launchings. They wondered how I could be leaving just before the Regatta. (I explained that I enjoyed viewing the island in its quiet, laid-back period but would definitely come back one day for the colorful, nonstop "lively up yourself" time.)

I slipped and slid down the steep hill to the black sand beaches, where fishing boats were being given the final touches for the upcoming races and chose a huge, eye-catching conch shell from the sizable mound of seashells near the side of one of the fishing vessels. As I listened to the ocean roar in the shell, I thought about the immense cultural treasures safeguarded on this tiny island of humble fishing villages. And I marveled at the tributes paid to the Akan and other African ancestors I am descended from. I think perhaps it is these ancestors who have brought me here to link with and celebrate our great African heritage.

Audre Lorde

Is Your Hair Still Political?

MY FIRST TRIP TO VIRGIN GORDA EARLIER THIS YEAR HAD BEEN AN ENJOYABLE, RE-laxing time. After coping with the devastations of Hurricane Hugo, three friends and I decided to meet somewhere in the Caribbean for a Christmas vacation. Based on my personal and professional travels, Virgin Gorda, less than an hour's flight from my home in St. Croix, seemed to be the ideal spot.

One friend and I deplaned in Tortola to clear British Virgin Islands immigration at the Beef Island Airport. I was happy to be a tourist for a change, looking forward to a wonderful holiday, posthurricane problems left behind for a few days. The morning was brilliant and sunny, and in our bags was a frozen turkey, along with decorations for the rented house.

The black woman in a smartly pressed uniform behind the Immigration Control desk was younger than I, with heavily processed hair, flawlessly styled. I handed her my completed entry card. She looked up at me, took the card with a smile and asked, "Who does your hair?"

My friend and I were the only passengers going on to Virgin Gorda. As a black woman writer who travels widely, I have been asked that question many times. Thinking we were about to embark on one of those conversations about hairstyle that black women so often have in passing on supermarket lines, on buses and in laundromats, I told her that I had done it myself. Upon her further questioning, I described how.

I was not at all prepared when, still smiling, she suddenly said, "Well, you can't come in here with your hair like that, you know." And reaching over she stamped "no admittance" across my visitor's card.

"Oh, I didn't know." I said. "Then I'll cover it." And I pulled out my kerchief.

"That won't make any difference," she said. "The next plane back to St. Croix is 5 o'clock this evening." By this time my friend, who wears her hair in braided extensions, was trying to come to my aid. "What's wrong with her hair?" she asked the woman. "And what about mine?"

"Yours is all right," she was told. "That's just a hairstyle."

"But mine is just a hairstyle, too," I protested, still not believing this was happening to me. I had traveled freely all over the world; now, in a Caribbean country, a black woman was telling me I could not enter her land because of how I wore my hair?

"There is a law on our books," she said. "You can't come in here looking *like that*."

I touched my natural locks, of which I was so proud. A year ago I had decided to stop cutting my hair and to grow locks as a personal style statement, in much the same way I had worn a natural Afro for most of my adult life. I remembered an *Essence* story in the early 1980s that had inspired the line "Is your hair still political?" in "A Question of Essence," one of my most popular poems.

"You can't be serious," I said. "Then why didn't I know about this before? Where is it written in any of your tourist information that black women are only allowed to wear our hair in certain styles in your country? And why do we have to?"

Her smile was gone by now. "It's been a law for more than five years," she snapped. And I realized she was very serious when I saw our bags being taken off the plane—and it preparing to go on without us.

"How was I supposed to know that?" I protested with visions of our holiday feast defrosting on the tarmac, our friends from New York wondering where we were, our hostess at the airport waiting in vain to drive us to our rented house by the sea.

"I've read I can't bring drugs into the British Virgin Islands; I've read I can't seek employment in the British Virgin Islands; I've read about everything else I can't do in the British Virgin Islands—but how are black tourists supposed to know we can't wear locks if we visit the British Virgin Islands? Or don't you want black tourists?"

By now I was outraged. Even with the hot sun outside and the dark face before me. I was confused for a moment as to where I was. Nazi Germany? Fascist Spain? Racist South Africa? One of those places where for so many decades white people had excluded black people because of how they *looked*? But no, it was a black woman in the Caribbean telling me I wasn't acceptable as a tourist in her country—not because of what I do, not even because of who I am, but because of how I wear my hair. I felt chilled to the bone.

By this time the young white pilot had come in to see why the flight was being delayed. "What do you mean, because of her *hair?*" he said. Finally an immigration supervisor came, asking me to fill out another entry card.

"Why can't I go on to Virgin Gorda?" I began. "I've been there before. And what's wrong with my hair? It's not unhealthy, it's not unsanitary, it's not immoral, and it certainly is not unnatural!"

The supervisor looked at my well-groomed, ear-length locks. "Are you a Rasta?" he asked. And then it finally dawned on me what this was all about: religious and social intolerance.

He didn't ask me if I was a murderer. He didn't ask me if I was a drug dealer or a racist or if I was a member of the Ku Klux Klan. Instead he asked me if I was a follower of the Rastifarian religion. Some see locks and they see revolution. Because Rastifarians smoke marijuana as a religious rite, they see drug peddlers. But the people who are pushing drugs in the Caribbean don't wear locks; they wear three-piece suits and carry diplomatic pouches.

I stared at this earnest young black man for a moment. Suddenly my hair became very political. Waves of horror washed over me.

How many forms of religious persecution are we now going to visit upon one another as black people in the name of our public safety? And suppose I *was* a Rastafarian? What then? Why did that automatically mean I could not vacation in Virgin Gorda? Did it make my tourist dollars unusable?

What if he had asked me if I was a Jew? A Quaker? A Protestant? A Catholic? How little have we learned from the bloody pages of history, and are we really doomed to repeat these mistakes?

There was an ache in my heart. I wanted to say, "What does it matter if I am a Rasta or not?" But I saw our bags sitting out in the sun and the pilot walking slowly back to his plane. Deep in my heart I thought, *It is always the same question: Where do we begin to take a stand?* But I turned away.

"No, I'm not a Rastafarian," I said. And true, I am not. But deep inside me I felt I was being asked to deny some piece of myself, and I felt a solidarity with my Rastifarian brothers and sisters I had never been conscious of before.

Is your hair still political?

Tell me when it starts to burn.

My immigration card was stamped "admit," our bags were put back on the plane, and we continued our journey, twenty minutes overdue. As the plane taxied to the end of the runway, I looked back at the Beef Island Airport.

On this tiny island, I had found another example of black people being used to testify against other black people, using our enemies' weapons against each other, judging each other by the color of our skin, the cut of our clothes, the styling of our hair. How long will we allow ourselves to be used as instruments of oppression against one another?

On a black Caribbean island, one black woman had looked into another black woman's face and found her unacceptable. Not because of what she did, not because of who she was, not even because of what she believed. But because of how she looked. What does it mean, black people practicing this kind of self-hatred against one another?

The sun was still shining, but somehow the day seemed less bright.

Linda Cousins

Gan Gan Sarah

TO MY DELIGHT, I WAS SENT BY A MAGAZINE I WRITE FOR TO COVER THE TOBAGO Heritage Festival. After experiencing the music, dance, song, and delectable foods of that exquisite island during this festive period, I returned to my hotel room late every night; I was on a working vacation and was having a magnificent time doing what I love best—networking in a rich island culture.

One morning, after going to sleep in the wee hours, I woke up at 4 a.m. with the feeling that a blanket of ominous foreboding and overwhelming darkness covered the room. It was too dark to be simply the darkened morning hours. I sat straight up in the bed and fumbled for the light switch but couldn't find it for the life of me. It felt like the room had rearranged itself while I was sleeping. When I finally got the light on, I sat there for a moment wondering, as the elders in the South would say, What in the John Brown is going on? My mind was beset with questions.

Then I remembered that this was the site of a former plantation. I wondered if perhaps the ancestors were not at rest here. Maybe a lot of brutality had taken place here. I had stayed at other former-plantations-turned-hotels in the Caribbean and had never had an experience like this one. There had been brutality on *all* plantations, whether physical, mental, or emotional. Just holding an individual in bondage is brutality in and of itself. So what could have caused these strange feelings in the room this morning?

Puzzled, I showered and dressed while pondering the unnerving experience. Later, while I relished my island breakfast as the morning light chased the last vestiges of darkness from the room, I picked up a travel guide and looked through it. After turning a few pages, my eye was caught by the mention of a gravesite of an early ancestor named Gan Gan Sarah. Although I knew nothing of this woman (after all my years of research on the islands!), I was offended by the reference to her resting place as a "witch's grave." Instinctively, I felt that this derogatory description was not the truth, and I determined to find out the real deal on Gan Gan Sarah before leaving Tobago.

Later in the day, as I was being further introduced to the beauty, cul-

---

I always believe that the angels are smiling on me. After thinking that I would leave Cuba without having learned anything about Santeria, a Cuban friend took us to the home of Enrique Hernandez Armenteros, a prominent Santeria priest, who lives just outside Havana. Driving there, I thought of what a privilege it was to have this experience and I didn't want to embarrass myself or our host by approaching it purely as an intellectual exercise. So it was with humility that I entered his home. We were welcomed in true Cuban fashion with warmth and affection. I spoke with the priest in Spanish punctuating every sentence with a *lentament* because he spoke too fast for my rudimentary understanding of the language. Santeria, which the slaves brought with them from Africa, is based on rituals where offerings are placed to deities such as Oshun, the goddess of love, female sensuality, and rivers.

Señor Hernandez Armenteros led us to a room in the back of his house. This sacred room was filled with offerings to the gods—glasses of water, plastic dolls, and statuettes of Catholic saints which are corresponding images to their African gods. There, he gave each of us a small glass of Havana Club rum and asked us to take a mouthful and spit it out on the shrine. I must admit, we had to do this about three of four times before we got it right. It was a bit comical because the whole idea was to spit so it would spray all over the offerings to the gods. Instead, it got all over our shoes and blouses. We all had a good laugh.

—Sabine, "Letters from Havana"

---

ture, and history of the island, I asked the tourist board guide if he knew anything about Gan Gan Sarah. He told me that she was reputed to be a healer who had flown in on her own power from Africa. He also told me that she had died after the slavery era, trying to fly back after having lost this power. He took me to see the huge, mysterious-looking cottonwood tree from which Gan Gan Sarah had attempted to make her ill-fated flight. The tree had a very mystical aura about it.

I told the guide of the troubling experience I had had earlier in the morning and that I had awakened thinking, What was this place? Something had gone on here that I needed to find out about. And he told me that my intuition was correct. My hotel had been built on the site of an Amerindian burial ground, and many artifacts and a skeleton had been found there. These things, including the skeleton, were now at the museum in Ft. Frederick where we were headed. I recalled the disturbing of the Negro Burial Ground in the Wall Street district back at home. Déjà vu on a global level.

When we reached the museum, I found that it looked like many others I'd visited throughout the Caribbean, with its displays of Amerindian artifacts and other remnants from that decimated early population. Its chief difference lay in its scenic perch atop one of the highest areas in the island. As I entered the museum, my eye was immediately pulled to the Amerindian skeleton the guide had mentioned earlier. It lay encased under glass. I felt sick that this early indigenous settler's remains had been disturbed and removed from its resting place to be put on public display.

Before closely inspecting the other contents of the museum, I was led into the back office where Mr. Hernandez and an assistant were working. He was a warm-spirited, amiable Tobagonian, and when he learned of my interest in the island's history and folklore, he brought out a portfolio of his wonderful pen and ink drawings. They had been part of an exhibit called "Passages," and there among the illustrations was a depiction of the Gan Gan Sarah tree with her spirit eerily embodied in it.

He answered my eager questions about this island ancestor, telling me that she was said to have flown to Tobago during slavery days in search of a brother who was in bondage on an island plantation. While in Tobago she used her healing powers to minister to the slaves, but once slavery was over, she felt that having done as much as she could for her people here, she would fly back home to the motherland. She climbed the tree on which she had initially landed to make her homeward flight but fell to a tragic death instead. She had forgotten that while she was on the island she had eaten salt, which had robbed her of the power of flight.

While pondering the life of the great Gan Gan Sarah, I thought of all the other women of the past who had been healers—and who had not only been falsely labeled but also robbed of their lives because of horrid lies and mass hysteria. I recalled Tituba, the African from Barbados who narrowly escaped with her life during the Salem trials and whose life was depicted so beautifully in *I, Tituba* by the Guadeloupean author, Maryse Conde.

Gan Gan Sarah, I vindicate and celebrate you, and the next time I visit Tobago I will place some of the island's beautiful tropical flowers on your resting place there in Golden Lane. Thank you for your services, African mother.

Charisse Jones

My Carnival Journey

GROWING UP IN CALIFORNIA, MY WEST INDIAN ROOTS WERE OFTEN MISUNDER-stood. No matter how often I told my friends that my mother was from Guyana and my father was from Mississippi, they always insisted that both of my parents must be from Jamaica. It was inconceivable to them that a black American had married a black person from another culture. And it was impossible for them to understand that black people with accents came from somewhere other than Africa or the Caribbean island that gave birth to reggae. My childhood was a melange of delta blues and calypso, pepper pot and collard greens. And there was always an intangible link to the islands of the Caribbean. We had relatives in Barbados, vacationed in Montego Bay, and danced the high life to the Mighty Sparrow. Come Easter, when some people spoke of Fat Tuesday in New Orleans, and a Brazilian bacchanal, I thought only of Carnival in Trinidad.

I was a grown woman when I finally made the sojourn. An editor thought it would be interesting for me to travel to Trinidad with immigrants who were leaving New York in the dead of winter to go home and celebrate their most joyous tradition. I traveled down with two fellows and hooked up with a woman who was to be the third subject of my story.

Most of my family had long ago left Guyana. The one time I visited, I was a young girl. So my trips to the West Indies were usually like those of other tourists. I would stay in hotels, venturing to town only from time to time. But it was a narrow, distant glimpse of a culture that was actually my own. My mother and several Trinidadians tried their best to school me before I boarded the plane. My ignorance was profound. In my mind, *mas* was a Catholic church service. I had never heard of *winin'*, had no idea what a *pan yard* was, and had to be told a dozen times how to spell *jour o'vert*.

This trip was different from previous ones. This time, I stayed with the people with whom I spent my days. We slept late, ate curried crab, and visited *mas* camps, where we gazed at the costumes that would fill the streets on Dimanche Gras—the headdresses made of sequins and gold lamé flashing in the sun, and the elaborate masks crafted from crepe and cloth that would transform schoolboys into dragons, bus drivers into eagles, and housekeepers into angels.

In the competition for Carnival King, men strapped themselves into steel harnesses that rolled on wheels, allowing them to wear and manipulate contraptions that towered in the air—huge structures, months in the making, that took on the forms of samurai warriors, giant birds of prey, even a rolling thunderstorm complete with lightning and rain. And then there were the "moko jumbies," the giant boogie men of Trinidad, brought to life during Carnival by young people shimmying and prancing on stilts, ten feet high.

In the evenings, parties began under a pastel sky. Nowadays, though calypso's taunting lyrics and rhythms are still a Carnival staple, the music that moves revelers through the streets is *soca* or soul calypso. I was vaguely familiar with the music but not with the moves that seemed to be the national dance of Carnival—winin'. To wine required me to release my stateside inhibitions and relax (something that was hard to do in the midst of reporting a story that I would have to file on a tight deadline). To wine is to move your hips as though they turn on a swivel, with a man standing in back of you, melding with your rhythm. On Carnival Monday and Tuesday people wine and walk at the same time. Even I eventually got the hang of it, after I had filed my story and rejoiced in being liberated.

By then, the people with whom I had come to Trinidad had gone from being the subjects of my story to friends. Melvin, a New York City transit dispatcher, had moved to New York with his mother in 1969. He had married a woman there, fallen in love with the music of James Brown, and raised five children. But he always longed for Trinidad, hoping one day to live there again. For now Carnival had to do, his annual sojourn a welcome respite from the stresses and winter chill of New York. Once there, he slipped easily into the island's rhythm, spending time with friends and with his mother, who one year had packed her bags and moved back to Trinidad for good.

Roxanne had been a young beauty and aspiring dancer when she moved to the United States twenty-four years ago. The mother of three children, she too returned to the island as often as she could, visiting her oldest daughter and parents who still lived there. She held on fiercely to her island lilt, declaring that she didn't want to "talk like no Yankee." She felt I was too "plain" and so she dressed me up in some of her jewelry. We ate *channa,* visited the pan yards, and gazed in store windows together, like girlfriends.

We'd tire at dawn, then drive to Smoky and Bunty's to drink Caribs under a new day's sun. Hours later, the celebrating would start all over again, the darkness broken by the tin riffs that echoed from the pan yards. By week's end, I could almost hum "Lara" in my sleep. Everywhere we went, islanders were caught up in the merriment and revelry that is Carnival. The chicken curry, and *souse,* the *roti* and *bakes* were the foods of my mother's kitchen. At last I was surrounded by people who knew and loved those food as I did.

I didn't plan to play *mas,* the Trinidadian term for masquerading. I figured I would just stand on the sidelines and watch. But my friends wouldn't let me. So on Jour O'vert morning, I rose while it was still dark, doused myself in baby oil (so later the paint would wash off more easily), and prepared to join the throngs. This was the part of Carnival without the pomp and glitter. Instead of fancy costumes and beautiful makeup, people wear costumes made of rags and smear their faces with oil, mud, and paint.

The men and women who played pan stood in rows behind their steel drums, practicing throughout the night. During the celebration they stood in moving flatbed trucks, their tinny renditions of calypso classics and American pop tunes echoing through the streets.

—Charisse Jones

I took the tube of yellow paint my friends had bought and lathered it on my face and arms. I'd been told the more you put on the better, because if you look too clean, the others in the street will come over and dab you until you are dirty. We put on our costumes and drove to the *mas* camp, the place where members of our masquerade group would gather. After drinking sodas and rum, it was time to start the Carnival. We got behind a truck blasting the most popular *soca* jams and shuffled and wined our way through Port of Spain.

A mother carried her baby in her arms, elderly people found spring in their step, and we all again were mesmerized by the rhythm of thousands of shuffling feet, sauntering through the streets of Port of Spain. I could not imagine any place in the U.S. where people could gather in darkness and drink and dance to a pounding beat without the threat of trouble.

> *Carnival was a much more spiritual experience than I had expected. The drums and shuffling of feet felt like a heartbeat, ancient and familiar.*
>
> —Charisse Jones

There is a beauty in a country filled with black people. I'm not naive. I realized that I was in Trinidad during a joyful time, and so I wasn't feeling the frustrations that probably come with seeing a country run by your own that doesn't work as well as it should. But all I had to go on was how I felt at the time. Walking in the darkness and daylight, surrounded by strangers, I felt embraced. It didn't matter that those around me had no names. It didn't matter that my hair was pulled back or that my makeup was melting under a searing sun. I was beautiful, and black, and one with thousands of West Indians.

The night we left Trinidad, there was fish soup and champagne. I knew I would miss the island. But I figured I would not long for the *soca* songs that thumped in my head like a heartbeat. I had danced to them so many nights, jumped to their rhythm so many days, I thought I would never want to hear any of them again. But when I returned to New York City, a friend put the songs of Carnival on a cassette, and I played the tape until it broke. I went to the store to buy David Rudder's CD, and I reveled in the music because it reminded me of Trinidad.

I plan to go again, to partake in the revelry of Carnival and jump till dawn. I want to hold hands with my culture, to taste my mother's past, and spend time with friends who have now become family. Recently, I played my newly fixed Carnival tape for the first time in a long while. I wined around my living room and jumped up by my lonesome. When I went to bed, I hummed "Lara" in my sleep.

Jill Nelson

At Home on an Island

I WAKE UP AT DAWN IN BOOK-TOUR PANIC. WHAT CITY AM I IN? WHAT TIME IS IT? Have I slept through a major media market, left a zillion book buyers hanging—finally, after two months on the road, blown it? Lying here, I try to unscramble a tired brain before opening exhausted eyes. The acrid-sweet scent of salt drifts into my nostrils, the seductive back and forth of waves stroking sand curls into my ears, and even before I open my eyes I know I am home at last, on Martha's Vineyard.

(…)

Here I know who I am. Here I am first myself, my mother's daughter, my daughter's mother, and then everything else. It is as it has been for thirty-eight years: a homecoming. Growing up in New York City, we lived in apartments and moved as often as upward mobility allowed. In the city, home was a temporary shelter until something bigger and better came along. Knowing that we could not dig our roots into the earth, we wrapped them around ourselves and each other and waited until summer came.

My parents first came to the Vineyard in 1956, when I was three. My mother tells the story of how they rented a ramshackle house in the Highlands, the twisting hill community above the harbor, part of the town of Oak Bluffs where black people first formed a summer community in the early part of the century.

Oak Bluffs is like a fun-house mirror of the black middle class. Here the images expand, multiply, into a world. The children of lawyers, doctors, school teachers, engineers, Ph.D.s, business people, and dentists are the rule, not the exception. No one ever chants, "I am somebody." That goes without saying. If you weren't, you couldn't hang.

Affirmation comes from many places, one of which is seeing yourself reflected in the world around you, in a sense of commonality, in the very unspecialness of knowing there are thousands of other folks pretty much like you within hollering distance. Nine months of the year I lived in a world where this was not the case. Where being black, bourgeois, going to private school, and having parents who were hardworking professionals was perceived as aberrant. Positive, but aberrant nonetheless.

It is lonely growing up as one of a few dozen black students in a school of hundreds, or the only black people in a building of thousands, living on Manhattan island in a city of seven million people, where there is no certain place, no piece of land where middle-class black people own land, live in houses, put down their roots.

"It rained all week long," my mother will say of our first visit here, laughing. "But we fell in love with the island."

Me, I remember splashing around in the rain with my brothers and sister, free, safe, muddy, and not having to ask permission to go outside or having to ride down in an elevator, an absence of all the fearful things city kids must know about. But these memories may be more elaborations on a tale oft heard than what was. I know what my parents fell in love with. The neat shingled houses with elaborate ornamentation on porches and eaves, the tiny, intricate, gingerbread cottages in the Campgrounds, a world all its own until Illumination Night, when each house is festooned with colored lanterns and lights and it seems the whole island wanders through, awestruck.

The red, gray, and ochre cliffs of Gay Head, which we used to scramble down as children on our way to long days spent on the beach and cookouts with driftwood fires late into the night. The cliffs are now off-limits, protected, as they should be, from human erosion. But the water remains icy sparkling, somehow magical, the mussels pulled from submerged rocks as fat and sweet as ever. Now, in deference to the land, we no longer cook on the beach. Instead, we go to the Aquinnah Shop, founded in the early 1940s by Napoleon Madison, a member of the Wampanoag Tribe, the island's original inhabitants. There we eat blackened bluefish burgers, washed down with a slice of superlative strawberry rhubarb pie baked by Luther Madison, Napoleon's son and the chief medicine man of the Wampanoag.

We came to the Vineyard every summer. As children, the four of us would prepare for the long car trip judiciously, hoarding bags of penny candy and comic books. By the time we were, at best, a few hours out of the city, the candy was gone, comics were read, and the squabbling was in full swing. We fought about whatever: who was hogging the space in the backseat, who ate the last half-sandwich, what radio station to listen to, who was the better group, the Temptations or the Marvelettes.

Now I think the bickering was merely a prelude to entering nirvana, interstate purgatory before boarding the ferry to heaven. All summer long we rode bikes, swam in the ocean every day, went fishing, crabbing, had cookouts on the beach, picked wild blueberries, occasionally got poison ivy. We were free against the backdrop, the beauty of the island itself: winding roads, surprising views, a multitude of beaches, each with its own particular smell, taste, surf.

The Vineyard. The Vineyard. The Vineyard. It's like some geospiritual mantra chanted nine months of the year for nearly a lifetime; a lifetime. If I have a home, it is here, off Cape Cod, in the town of Oak Bluffs, in the house my parents bought thirty years ago.

I have lived many lives here. As a child with pigtails, my mother taught me to swim at the beach across the street from our house. "Stroke, down, breathe. Stroke, down, breathe," she chanted. I thought I would never get it, sinking, and then suddenly I was skimming through the water, forever. I rode the Flying Horses carousel until I could snatch eight rings with one finger.

Here I was a plump adolescent who one summer insisted on wearing a beige, waterproof, knee-length trench coat everywhere, including the beach. I had my first kiss here, at a yard party strung with Japanese lanterns, bestowed wetly by a young man whose name is irrelevant but whose appropriate nickname, Chubby Lips, is unforgettable. I went sailing and learned to dive for mussels, to boil perfect lobster, and to scale, gut, and fillet fish. When big changes came—when I had my daughter, had a broken heart, decided to quit my job at *The Washington Post*, finally sold my book—I came here to get sane.

I lie in bed, smiling, looking at the ancient wallpaper of entwined roses. Here familiarity breeds contentment. I climb out of bed and walk through my mother's silent house, where everything has both a place and meaning. I search for pictures, a vase from Grenada, a sweater always left hanging, my daughter's clogs by the staircase. I find them all. I sit on the wicker porch swing and watch the ocean, wave occasionally as friends, parents of friends, stride by on their morning constitutional. I check the flower and vegetable gardens, note weeding to be done. Finally I go for an early morning dip, swim in the path the sun makes along the cold, salty water.

That first morning, I walk through the town of Oak Bluffs, searching for and finding the familiar. The houses of the Finleys, Overtons, Thornes, Thomases, Smiths. The tennis and basketball courts. Waban Park, where as children we chased my father's golf balls, four for a penny. The Oak Bluff Public Library on the corner of Circuit Avenue, the main street, where I have borrowed hundreds of books and now people borrow mine. Unfortunately, it is too early to get a peppermint stick ice cream cone from Cozy's, or succulent clams from the Clam Bar, or whatever's cooking at Lobster in the Bluffs. I settle for doughnuts from the Old Stone Bakery, happily munch my way past the gazebo where the island band plays on summer Sundays, toward home.

Entering, the screen door slams behind me and my mother calls from the kitchen, "Star? Is that you?" It is a nickname earned this summer, since my book was published. It is said lovingly, teasingly. It does not connote any change in family status. No one ever says, "Star, can I fetch you something?" or "Star, shall I peel you a grape?" Instead, it's the same old same old. "Star, would you do the dishes? Go to the grocery? Weed the garden?" This is as it should be.

The wonderful thing about the Vineyard is that most everyone believes you're going to do well, though sometimes they're not quite sure in what or when, or maybe it is that they don't care. It's what is expected, what everyone before you did and after you will do. If the black summer community on Martha's Vineyard forms its own world, it is a world absent the assumptions of inferiority rife elsewhere. It is, I think, the absence of burden, of carrying around both the negative assumptions of others, and my own. On the Vineyard, as the old spiritual goes, I can lay my burdens down.

Here there is no feeling of unearned, condescending specialness so often bestowed on successful African Americans by others, that "Golly, you're not like most black people. You're different."

Here, fourth and fifth generations of college graduates, advisers to presidents, writers, politicians, and artists tend neat shingled houses, plant tomatoes, swim early each morning with the rest of the Polar Bears, mow lawns, have cocktail parties, play cards and tennis, and talk politics and stuff. Just like everybody else. The phenomenon is that there is no phenomenon. Quiet as it's kept, this is nothing new. I'm just a link in the chain.

On August 14, in the yard of my mother's house, we celebrated her seventy-fifth birthday. We pitched a tent, hung balloons, and, since seven in the morning, made trays of canapés. By twilight the lawn was filled with laughing, talking people, champagne glasses in hand. My mother held forth, a diminutive diva in black and silver. Miles Davis's "So What" floated through the particular air of twilight.

We waited until dark to pass out sparklers, lighting them on cue. My niece, Olivia, and the other children raced around the yard, squealing as white sparks flew, delighting in that remembered time when the adults, slightly high and talking intently, forgot all about them. The faces of friends and family, ages three to eighty-three, glowed and became children as sparklers sprouted from fingertips, lighting up the night and their peaceful faces. Whirling our torches in the air, we sang "Happy Birthday," cradled by the ocean on one side, the island on the other.

Someone called out, "And many more," and I smiled, knowing that there will be. We are here, we have roots. We are not Halley's Comet, visible only once every seventy-five years.

Toni Eubanks

A Sea Island Legacy

DRIVING ALONG THE DIRT ROADS OFF THE BEATEN PATH, I WAS OVERTAKEN BY THE natural beauty of the Sea Islands. The ancient majesty of great live oaks seemed to hold secrets of years long past. The heavy, moss-covered branches that met over dusty roads, masking the sun and transforming the roads into long, gray tunnels of mysterious shadows; the musty aroma of ocean air and nearby marshes—all stirred my senses keenly.

I had come with a group of elderly New Yorkers who were born and raised on the islands (and still owned property there) to attend the annual Heritage Week festivities: a symposium of scholarly research, storytelling, an old-fashion craft fair, including sweetgrass baskets and handmade fishing nets, a community sing out, a fish fry and oyster roast, low country tours, music and dance. Through these former Sea Islanders' eyes I could see islanders of generations past walking down these dirt roads to prayer services, toting heavy baskets on their heads, or steering oxen carts loaded with goods.

The Sea Islands (including James, Johns, Wadmalaw, Kiawah, Edisto, St. Helena, Hilton Head, and Daufuski) appear on a map as a series of dots along the east coast of South Carolina and Georgia. They are bounded on one side by the ocean, and on the other by salt marshes and lagoons created as the tidal streams bring in salt water and carry it back out to sea. These tidal streams drain the shallow, marsh-filled lagoons in an intricate system that separates the islands from the mainland, and from each other.

The secluded lagoons in the salt marshes once facilitated illegal slave traffic long after states prohibited slave importation. It was in one of these lagoons that legend tells of a slave ship that landed secretly with a shipload of African prisoners. In one version the courageous men, women, and children drowned themselves rather than submit to slavery; in another version, they walked on the water back to Africa.

Early in the Civil War, federal troops seized control of the islands. White plantation owners abandoned thousands of acres of rice fields, which were eventually sold by the government to men and women newly freed from slavery. St. Helena became part of the Port Royal Experiment, a program developed to help its ten thousand slaves make their transition to freedom.

Charlotte Forten became the island's first African American teacher. She came to St. Helena in 1862, but her poor health caused her to leave the island two years later. While I was there I read about her experiences in *The Journals of Charlotte Forten Grimke*, edited by Brenda Stevenson. Two women sent by the Freedmen's Association of Philadelphia to educate the black population, Laura M. Towne and Ellen Murray, taught on the island until their deaths in 1901 and 1908. The Penn School, where these women taught, was the first school in the South for African Americans. The elderly people with whom I was traveling told me they had to walk three or four miles to attend school (after pumping water for the household, gathering wood for the cook stove, cleaning the kerosene lamps, and feeding the cow). In 1905, courses offered included carpentry, blacksmithing, wheelwrighting, basket weaving, harness making, cobbling, mechanics, and agriculture. I wandered around the old school buildings and cottages, musing on all that had gone on there.

I can hear the ancestors singing as they welcome me home. Their voices whisper through the Spanish moss that hangs on the oak trees they planted long ago. The beat that they play on the spiritual drum hits my heart as each wave hits the shores that surround me.

—Marquetta L. Goodwine,
"Traveling the Trails of the Ancestors"

Then I visited Brick Church, a sturdy edifice built in 1855 by the hands of men and women in slavery, and spent a quiet hour in the adjoining graveyard reading the headstones. The church is still in use and has a balcony where, during pre–Civil War days, black people were permitted to worship. In her letters, Laura Towne described the seeing "oddly dressed Negroes" crowding into the church, the women in head kerchiefs or small braids and the men in carpet suits or calico trousers. My traveling companions explained that in order to be accepted into the church, young people had to study with a spiritual guide and in isolation until they had an important vision or dream. The elders would meet to determine if the vision was significant enough, or if further study and prayer were needed.

The York W. Bailey Museum houses a permanent exhibition on the Penn School and Sea Island cultural heritage. There, I spent hours looking through frayed photograph books at pictures of Sea Islanders living their daily lives during the 1920s and 30s, reading their first-person narratives and reflecting on how life was for them. They were property owners who lived off the land and sea; they knew the habits of local wild animals, and understood the ebb and flow of the tides.

I'm thinking about the rice that was grown from this rich soil when a refreshing salt breeze comes in from the marsh, just like the ones that assisted my mother, her mother, my father's mother, and all their foremothers to separate the rice and the husk while standing in the yard with children at their knees and sweetgrass fanners in their hands.

—Marquetta L. Goodwine,
"Traveling the Trails of the Ancestors"

While exploring a wooded area on Daufuski Island, I recalled that it was a Gullah tradition to bury the dead there. Sea Islanders believed the woods were sacred because they contained the spirits of their departed loved ones. Graves were decorated with whatever items the deceased used last—combs, cups, mirrors.; the pieces of glass and mirrors were believed to capture the spirit of the deceased. Relatives might collect soil from the grave of a loved one, placing it in a pouch that they carried everywhere because they believed the soil contained the spirit of the loved one buried there.

On St. Helena, I visited one of the few remaining praise houses tucked in the woods where slaves went to worship in their own manner, this one restored and still in use. An elderly deacon allowed me to enter, and I noticed the long, narrow wooden benches that gave worshipers the freedom of movement they need for their style of worship. I was able to witness the traditional call-and-response style of worship. The minister called out and the congregation repeated his call in rhythmic replies. People jerked their bodies in the "shout" and "get happy" movements found in other black churches, the "shout" accompanied by spiritual singing and hand clapping. As in many black congregations, a Sea Island minister is judged on how well he or she uses rhetorical skills to excite the congregation.

Across St. Helena Island, I met a woman who told me her mother would bleach the printing out of ten-pound grits bags and use them to make underwear, and I visited the island's oldest remaining house, built at the end of the eighteenth century. It is called the Tombee house for its builder, Thomas B. Chaplin, Sr. As I looked out from the house at the vast, well-cut lawn, my mind played tricks on me and transformed the lawn into the cotton plantation it once was. I could see men and women stooped over in the unyielding sun, the women in head rags, painfully picking cotton with sore, bleeding fingers.

Until the first bridges were built in the 1930s, connecting the islands to the mainland, the Sea Island populations of Gullah- or Geechee-speaking people lived in isolation and were thereby able to preserve the language and culture derived from their West African heritage, along with were many superstitions. They painted their door and window frames blue from the residue skimmed from indigo pots to keep out ghosts or "hants." Some of these faded blue frames can be found on island homes today. Ghost tales were told around a campfire or fireplace at night. One popular tale was about "the hag," who sat on people's faces at night while they slept in order to terrorize and confuse the victim. To stop a hag they would keep an open bible on the night table because hags must stop and read the entire bible backward before the sun rises. Similarly, many people lined their walls with newspapers because each line must be read by mischievous beings before they could cause harm. At funerals, families would pass the baby over the casket of its deceased mother to prevent it from being haunted by the mother's spirit.

The abundant palmetto trees on the Sea Islands, with their fan-shaped leaves that rattle like dry bones in the wind, are also the subject of legends and ghost stories. And there is the story about a "Magic Hoe," which was widespread in Hausa and Ashanti folklore before it was brought to America. It concerns a hoe that could work the fields by itself, but the owner had to know how to talk to it.

In the 1930s, the Penn Center on St. Helena Island became a major retreat for civil rights groups. It was the only facility in South Carolina where multiracial groups could meet during the 1950s and early 60s. Dr. Martin Luther King, Jr., met there often with his staff, and partly planned the historic March on Washington, D.C., on Penn Center's campus.

Now, with increased accessibility (all the islands except Daufuski can be reached by car) development threatens to cover the Sea Islands with golf courses and tennis courts. Already, Hilton Head is a resort area for the wealthy. In the 1950s almost all of the residents of Hilton Head were black. Thirty years later, black residents were greatly outnumbered by whites. As the demand for beachfront property increased, many African Americans who had owned their land for generations either elected to sell or were forced to sell because of rising taxes. More than a few black residents became landless and these proud, independent people began working in the low-paying, resort-industry service jobs.

But despite encroaching development, the Sea Islands remain a place of great significance to African Americans and I return over and over to experience the mystery and quiet beauty of the land and sea, and to reflect on the lives of these extraordinary people.

Sharony Andrews Green

Miss Sippi

ON THE LAST DAY OF THE YEAR, I WOKE UP AND GOT BUSY WASHING CLOTHES. I looked in every nook and cranny for dirty clothes: the hallway hamper, the bedroom floor, the towel hook behind the bathroom door. My husband just stared at me, grinning. He finally said, "You can tell country people. Y'all don't wanna bring in the new year with no dirty clothes."

I had to stop and think about what he said. I knew the superstition that bringing in the new year with old dirt could cause problems for the soul—I remember kinfolk scurrying around to gather soiled laundry on New Year's Day—but I hadn't given it any thought as I gathered my own laundry. I looked down at the clothes on the laundry room floor and realized: Some things you just can't get away from.

It made me want to go home to Mississippi.

I say "home" because that's what my mama's people call it. M-I-SS-I-SS-I-PP-I. Writing it is harder than saying it. Most locals don't catch all those S's and I's. They just say Miss Sippi like they talking 'bout some lady.

I arranged for my grandparents to meet me in Indianola, my grandfather's hometown and the birthplace of blues singer B.B. King. My grandaddy Richard Earvin says he used to play marbles with B.B. down on the Klondike plantation. Now my grandma Lillie Mae Golden Earvin was born in Belzoni, the so-called "Catfish Capital of the World." Belzoni and Indianola are both in what is called the Mississippi Delta, best known for miles and miles of hot, flat, sterile land.

My grandparents were among the many blacks who followed the crops all over the South in the 1940s and 50s. If it was time to pick cabbage in South Carolina, that's where they went. If it was time to pick peaches in Georgia, well, that's where they headed. And when it was time to pick oranges, tomatoes, and pole beans in Florida, that was the next stop. One year they got down to Florida and got to liking that sun so much they decided to stay. Grandma did day work most of her life; my grandaddy did some of everything, but he was mostly a carpenter.

My mama and grandma had long been talking about my granddaddy wanting to go home "one more time." I never liked it when they said it like this because I feared that once he made it back to Mississippi, he might just keel over and die. I wanted to make that trip "home" happen for him so he could pick up his suitcase and go back to Miami. Then both he and I could tell them "toldja so." Sometimes people just want to see where they've been to make peace with where they're going.

"You like catfish?"

This is what my Cousin Push asked me on the phone when I was still at the airport in Detroit where I live. Push was the cook at a catfish farm in Mississippi, and she was married to Cousin Tommy Lee. I had no memories of loving or hating catfish so I said, "Sure."

"Good! I'm agon' make you some catfish tonight!" Cousin Push said.

I told the shuttle bus driver who took me to get my rental car that I was meeting my grandma and granddaddy. Even had four dead frozen birds in one of my bags for them. He turned around and looked at my bags. "Pheasants?" he said.

I nodded.

"Ooh, they're gonna love you!" he said.

Now this city girl knows nothing about pheasants. And I had real problems walking into that poultry shop on Russell Street to buy them. The smell hit me long before I got near the building. The day I went, people were handpicking their Thanksgiving turkeys. These birds would just be gobble-gobblin' around and you'd point out the one you wanted and some man would reach in and snatch one—didn't even care if they snapped the poor fella's wing—and take it to a back room, and before long that bird would be all skinned in a bag, ready for your oven.

Made me want to be vegetarian. Made me really want to be vegetarian when the poultry shop man asked me if I wanted to keep the head and the feet of my four birds. My face told him more than my mouth could.

◦ ◦ ◦

"I'll just give you the feet," he said. "You say they're for your grand-parents down South? Yeah, they'd like it if you brought the feet. They'd like the feet."

I was losing my sunlight, and I thought back to what my grandma had told me about the time when no black person in her right mind would consider riding alone on any back road of Mississippi, day or night. I made a few hooks and turns and got lost, ending up on a bridge named after some woman named Mae. I knew I was sho 'nuff in the South if I was seeing bridges named Mae.

I like the name Mae. One year a girlfriend and I were at a women journalists' retreat in Jacksonhole, Wyoming, trying to count all the Maes in our family. She had a Hessie Mae, a Flossie Mae, a Jessie Mae, and a Hester Mae. My grandma was a Lillie Mae. I had an aunt Lottie Mae. And the woman who named me was my aunt Willie Mae. We marveled at how Mae had managed to fit real snug next to all of those names. Like poetry. Many of those women faced the worst conditions but still lived to the next morning to tell the world about it. They did it because their very names gave permission. Mae or May. Mae-be. Or Maybe. Maybe they could be still and know everything was going to be all right.

Remembering the Maes, I stilled my heart.

I was just four the last and only other time I had been to Mississippi. I mostly remember her smells, particularly the smell of the truck of pigs on one highway.

"Ooh, you pooted!" I remember telling my brother, who was a year older than me.

"Un-huh, you did!" my brother said.

Grandma and Granddaddy pointed to the pigs in the truck next to us. And we city-babies looked out the car window and did our "oohs" and "ahhs." And then there was the clean smell of pressed wood in the trailers where many of our relatives lived. Long, narrow trailers out on empty land. On stilts. High enough for a four-year-old to look under.

And the dust. Lots of it. Shortly after we arrived, our little cousins grabbed my brother's hand and raced down a sandy path into a field behind their trailer home, leaving dust in their tracks. I remember running behind them to keep up, but I became afraid that I'd get lost in all those trees. And all that tall grass. No streets. No sidewalks. No streetlights to take me back home if it got dark. I ran back the other way and began to cry. The faster my little feet ran, the more I cried. Dust mixed with my wet face. I got so upset, I ran off the path and got lost. When I finally made it back my cousins were waiting, laughing. "Scaredy-cat ran the other way and got lost anyway," they sang.

In time, I learned not to be afraid to go anywhere. Now I can get on a plane and just go. By myself. Anywhere. Alone. Once I went to Vermont in December. My friends thought I was crazy. "Vermont winters are just dreadful!" they said. And "Girl, there are no black people in Vermont! What are you thinking about?"

I went anyway. Stayed in a hostel in Burlington. The woman who ran it took me to a country club where they had a thing going on for Miss Vermont, who happened to be black that year. I smiled. I met her and the other blacks in the state. All ten of 'em, okay? Six were college professors. Three were students from Africa. Miss Vermont. And me.

When I rolled into Indianola shortly after sunset, Cousin Push and Tommy Lee were at the end of the highway that led into town waiting for me. Make myself at home is what they told me. Their home was nice, with four bedrooms. Real cozylike. Cousin Push had trimmed the kitchen walls with wallpaper covered with little ducks. They had nice china and dishes, but it felt more like home drinking soda out of mason jars. And that's what we did. While Push got busy making her fried catfish dinner, Tommy Lee and I went to pick up my grandparents, who had spent a few days with Cousin Isabel. Cousin Isabel wasn't really a cousin—just like Push and Tommy Lee weren't cousins—her first mama was my great-granddaddy's first wife. But when you get so far away and much older, all them great uncles and aunts and second cousins and grandma's sister's daughter get lumped into one fine cousin.

When I got to Cousin Isabel's, Grandma and Granddaddy rose to hug me. "I looove my grandchildren," Grandma said over her shoulder to Cousin Isabel. Grandma was a big woman, near 'bout five foot ten, so

The Black Flight Attendants of America (BFAOA) was founded in Los Angeles in 1974 by Jacqueline Jacquet-Williams and Saundra Tyler. Then it consisted primarily of Los Angeles–based Continental flight attendants. The flight attendants worked diligently to promote aviation in the minority community by presenting career day and mentor programs in inner-city schools. BFAOA first received national recognition when members participated in the Inaugural Martin Luther King Jr. March in 1986.

The idea of giving information and serving as role models in inner-city schools continued to grow. In October 1992, a chapter was founded in Atlanta by then-President Eden Kassa. With the organization of this chapter it became clear that a national organization would be the next step.

On January 12, 1993, the "Inaugural Reception—A Convention of Black Flight Attendants of America" was hosted by the Atlanta chapter. The middle of January has continued to be the annual meeting time so the group can participate in the Martin Luther King Jr. March.

We look forward to welcoming new members from other cities and organizing additional chapters across the nation.

—Black Flight Attendants of America

her hug was tight. Granddaddy, who was much shorter with a round belly, hugged me, too. He was in his mid-seventies now and moved a lot slower than Grandma, who was about ten years younger. "Still a baby," I tell her often. "Glad you know it!" she always laughed back.

They couldn't wait to tell me about their trip on the train from Miami. I had gotten them a sleeper car and they liked it, they told me. They ate three big meals a day, they said. "Nice big steaks and big baked potatas," Grandma said, adding that those steaks and potatoes "were 'bout the only big thing on that train, too." It seemed Grandma and Granddaddy's well-endowed bodies could barely fit into those small seats in the dining car. But they still had a good time. They even played bingo, and my grandma tells me the young white girls on the train flirted with Granddaddy the whole way up.

Cousin Isabel told them to hush. "Y'all know this chile hungry," she said. "Y'all g'on and get ready."

While they were packing, she took me to her kitchen, where I learned the first rule about Southern hospitality: You never turn down food lest people think you lack home-training.

"You must be tired. Hungry. Come and have something to eat," she said.

"No, I'll pass. Cousin Push is making catfish," I said, smiling.

"But it'll be a while. Have a seat and I'm going to fix you something," she said again.

My grandma poked her head into the living room and gave me a look that said I better take that seat. While Cousin Isabel busied herself in the kitchen, heating up some pork chops, rice, and peas, I surveyed her home and took in things that were immediately familiar: "Good" sofas and chairs covered with sheets. Leafy plants in pots wrapped at the bottom with plastic grocery bags to catch the water. Outside was another familiar: the "church" car. Everybody in Miss Sippi had a car to go to work in and another finer car to go to Sunday meeting, it seemed.

Cousin Isabel pointed out the pictures of all her kids and grandkids. More people to tag "cousin." One was working on her doctorate in Memphis. Another was a television news reporter. Then she asked me to step outside and see her green patch. Here I learned another constant about Miss Sippi: greens. Everybody had them in their yards. Collards, mustards, and turnips. Cousin Isabel took me to the side of her house and proudly showed me her mustards. "They fine, ain't dey?" I nodded and smiled. They were indeed.

Cousin Push had a spread that was light and easy: fried catfish with potato salad, tossed green salad, and warm dinner rolls. It was too good. After dinner, Grandaddy and Cousin Tommy Lee left to watch the game in the den, while I got busy getting to know Cousin Push.

Push—named by a relative who saw her as an especially frisky child who loved to wiggle, pull, and well, push—lit a cigarette as my grandma updated her on all my business since I was a baby. How I got my job as a newspaper reporter. And how I met my husband, who was a chef. And, humph, that blazer from Barney's New York I paid $370 for.

I noticed how Push would look over at my hair every now and then. Grandma finally reached over and patted down my long, nappy locks and laughed, "Girl, don't you know they got chemicals now for this problem?"

I laughed, too. There weren't too many dreadlocks in Miss Sippi. I knew this because the passengers of every car I passed on my way here, black or white, would spin around and do a double-take.

"I was all up in my rear-view mirror lookin' back, too," I told Cousin Push and Grandma. Cousin Push was particularly tickled and fell over laughing. The ice had broken.

"What choo like to eat, Cuz?" Push asked, taking out another cigarette. She was a big-boned woman with a hefty laugh and a beautiful smile. She read a poem during announcements at church every Sunday.

"Everything you do," I said. "Shrimp, cornbread—no lima beans—collard greens, mustards, neck bones, um, some chitlins...."

The chitlins did it. "You do!?" Push said. She smiled. The ice had melted sho'nuff. "Well, I'm gon' make you some chitlins, too, Cuz!"

We arrived in Belzoni, where my great-grandma Louella Halbert had given birth to my grandma, and were greeted by a Confederate flag on the town's main drag. Most of the stores were closed or boarded up. One storekeeper said the older folks had died off and their kids had mostly left for the big cities. Not too much left but catfish farmworkers and some "dope heads," he said.

Lou, as we called her, had been a foxy little woman with a tiny waist, who loved to work in bars because she made plenty of tips, my granddaddy had told me more than once. She used to talk all the time about going down to Biloxi on the gulf, where she could really make some money.

"But she never went," my granddaddy said, stepping outside to join me, wearing a sporty cap and a jean jacket with matching jeans. "She was too afraid of them hurricanes."

Lou was the daughter of an Indian. (Black folks like to claim Indian blood. It's one way of placing our cheekbones.) Her father was a medicine man who used to make herbs for sex diseases for people too shamed to go to the doctor. He was also a jack-leg preacher. He'd go from church to church in back-road towns and preach on the real pastor's Sunday off. When it came time to take up the offering, the real pastor kept the paper money but gave the jack-leg preacher the money that jingled. Lou was really close to her father, but one day while still a teenager she met an older man and had three babies by him.

"My mama is only fourteen years older than my ol'est brother," my grandma always said.

I never heard much about this man she had her babies by, but I knew his name was Allan Golden and that he died in the late 1980s. So we went looking for some Goldens and found an Ollie Golden working at the nursing home up the street. My grandma looked at her and smiled and said, "Do you know Allan Golden?"

The woman, a tall, brown-skinned sister who couldn't have been more than thirty-five said, "Why yes, he was my stepfather."

"He was my father," my grandma said. They embraced and quickly caught up on each other's lives.

She also asked her if she knew anything about what had happened to Albert Golden. Albert had been part of a group of black agriculture experts from the South who went to Soviet Central Asia in the 1930s to teach the Russians about farming. He was a black Communist who married a Polish Jewish woman. Because of the racism in the States, they decided to make their life in Russia and never came back.

Ollie had heard nothing about Albert. We all hugged and promised to stay in touch.

We then headed to the little town of Isola ten minutes away, where my great-grandma Lou's childhood friend lived. My grandparents argued, trying to recall which house the lady stayed in. Nobody wanted to get out of the car to knock. When my grandma finally did, some lady let her in and hugged her. They talked for a bit. It wasn't until about five minutes later that they realized Grandma was at the wrong house. Age works the memory.

"I thought Ida was dead but figured maybe miracles happened when you walked up cuz y'all sho do favor," the lady said, escorting Grandma to the door.

We went to another house around the corner, but I wasn't going to go inside until relations were confirmed sho' nuff. While my grandparents knocked, I took out my camera and walked across the street to a cemetery. The first tombstone I came upon was for a woman named Mattie Mae and I took a picture of it.

Grandma's voice stirred me from my reverie. "See them cotton fields over there? Why don't you take a picture of them?" she said. So I walked over and took in the rows and rows of brown sticks and white puffs. I stooped down to pick up a piece of cotton. It was soft and nappy like my hair. I thought about all of the people who had gone before me. And my grandparents. Those who had toiled in those fields. I snapped two pictures and went back to the house. My grandparents watched me coming, both laughing about how cotton picking was one of the most painful pickin' they'd ever done.

As it turns out, they were finally at the right house, but Great-Grandma Lou's friend had died. Her daughter, Rosie, invited us in, though she was busy preparing plate dinners to sell to the catfish farmworkers in the area. I hadn't realized that those occasional perfectly squared-off "lakes" we had passed on the highway were actually catfish farms. While some workers headed for local restaurants, many went to people's homes, where plate dinners are served. I suspected it was a successful underground economy. About a quarter to noon, the first worker, wearing a powder blue paper hair net, came in Rosie's side door. And then another. And then two more. Her menu was standard soul food fare with bread pudding or pound cake for dessert. And a can of soda. All for $4.75. She told us she sometimes got fifty orders a day.

We began the next day with a trip to Greenville to the Boat, a riverboat casino on the Mississippi. We did the slot machines. I played $5; made $50. Grandma played $200; broke even. Granddaddy didn't play. He just took a seat next to a white man who was winning. Every now and then, when he won some money, this white man would toss Granddaddy a few tokens. And that's what Granddaddy gambled. Not his own money—just the white man's. It tickled me.

Uncle Sam Loyd, Great-Grandma Lou's half-brother, lived in a rickety house across the street from about two hundred acres of land he owned. Mississippi's black population, along with South Dakota Native Americans, were the poorest statewide demographic group in the country, with an average income of about $11,000. But while there was much poverty there were many fellas like Uncle Sam Loyd who had worked an honest living and saved up money even though appearances insisted otherwise. His weather-beaten door was covered with plastic to keep out the cold, and a wood stove sat in the middle of the living room.

We took a seat and his wife, Isabel, came out to meet us. Though she had aged considerably and had Alzheimer's, one could tell she had been a fox in her day, too. And she loved her Sam. Had more than a few kids by him. My grandma use to babysit them.

"Lord, I use to say, 'Bel, when you gon' stop havin' all these babies?'" my grandma laughed. Isabel brought her hands together in a single clap, shook her head, and grinned. She rocked on the edge of the sofa. Isabel had the sweetest gray eyes.

When we rose to leave, Uncle Sam admonished us with: "Don't y'all go without taking some of those greens." Granddaddy took a brown paper bag and picked a few. Then Uncle Sam told my grandparents to come back by before they went home to Miami. He had a "package" for them. Granddaddy smiled. He knew it was some Miss Sippi moonshine.

o o o

On the way to Moorhead, pecan trees waved at us along the road. Granddaddy pointed at the piece of land that used to hold the house where my mama was born. Grandma pointed to a plantation where she and Granddaddy ran a jook joint for the field hands.

"We sold plenty of hot dogs, had a lil' jukebox, lotta fun," Grandma said. Then we pulled into what was left of the town. More boarded up windows.

"Make me depressed. Look at how this place has gone down," my grandma said, looking out the window at all the closed storefronts. "In that spot right there is where that one fella killed the Chinaman. It's a shame how this place went down, and with a university nearby! How could they?"

We sat in silence outside the little wooden house she and my granddaddy had purchased soon after they had married. It was barely standing, but someone managed to live inside.

Slowly we walked to a house on the next block to visit Miss Mary

I did not know until after my grandfather's death that the reason he never spent the night after taking me to school was that he did not like to have to eat out. He recalled all too vividly the times when he or his family members would be embarrassed when told "we don't serve coloreds." And I once dated a pilot who told me that one of his saddest trips involved an elderly black couple who refused to eat during a long transcontinental flight. As it turned out, they thought they would have to pay extra for the food.

And there are still echoes of that racism today. I'll never forget the time some girlfriends and I caught cabs, subways, and a bus to get to a new restaurant in New York City. We had read about it in *Essence* and seen it on television. We got to the place both excited and ravenous. The hostess treated us like trash and had us wait twenty minutes for a table even though the place was virtually empty. Fortunately, this experience was balanced by our eating breakfast one morning at Sylvia's in Harlem. We had been away from our Southern roots almost a week so this was like coming home. There were biscuits and salmon croquettes and even grits! We had to wait a while to shop for clothes.

It should come as no surprise that you can usually find good food anywhere there is a high ethnic representation. Of course, as far as our community is concerned, cities like Chicago, Atlanta, Memphis, New Orleans, and even Paris have an abundance of restaurants geared to our tastes. Some places, such as Atlanta, even have several health food or vegetarian restaurants, one appropriately named Soul Vegetarian. The best references are usually the real people who live and work in a town. Ask the postal worker, the construction worker, the business-person. If you're staying in a hotel, you'll generally fare better asking the doorman rather than the concierge.

—Rita L. Stotts, "Eating on the Road"

Parker, another friend of my great-grandma Lou. Miss Parker used to run the general store next door to her house. Now it was all boarded up with crates of old soda bottles stacked up outside.

Grandma told me that Miss Mary also used to do hair in her house. I looked over in one corner and saw a red-leather beauty parlor chair next to a beauty parlor sink and a table with a hot comb heater, some straightening combs, a jar of combs and brushes, and some Royal Crown hair grease. Looked like she was still in business.

She was a cranky old woman with long, pretty hair. "Cuss like a sailor," Grandma said about Miss Mary to her face.

Miss Mary turned around and grinned, "Now, Lillie...," and then stumbled. Underfoot was a little brown puppy. A pet to keep her company. Maybe even kept her alive.

"The lil' shit gon' be the death of me," she said. "Chunky, sit yo' ass down," Miss Mary told the puppy.

But the puppy didn't pay her any mind. Just went to biting her ankles. I couldn't help but notice the contrast between the puppy, full of energy and with its whole life ahead of it, and Miss Mary, with the long-gone years on her face and her hands. And her now slow, lumbering walk. Doorways and furniture were her crutches. She'd stop every now and then to lean on one or the other. Miss Mary's step used to have plenty more pep.

"Sometimes she used to run from the house where she was doing hair to the store to help a customer, to the bedroom to tend to her sick husband," my grandma said. "Miss Mary, you a saint."

We sat down in her living room, which was cluttered with furniture and pictures. In each corner stood tall, thin stalks of cactus. The cactus near 'bout reached to the ceiling. She saw me looking.

"Boss Lady got it from Africa. Gave me just a lil' bit of stalk when she died. It grew like crazy. Some white woman from the nursery came over here and bought a piece from me for $40. They say it's rare. I'll give you a piece before you leave, baby."

Noticing a piano against one wall, I asked Miss Mary if she played. She didn't answer me. She just slowly got up from her seat at the dining room table and waddled over to the bench and sat down to play.

"I do alright when this 'thritis ain't actin' up," she finally said. And then began to play like we were at Sunday service in some nice Methodist church. "I'm a God-fearing woman ready to meet Jesus!" Miss Parker howled after she finished playing the last note. "And I must rest now."

She took a pair of beautician's scissors out of her dress pocket and cut two stalks from one of the four towering cactuses as Chunky went over to bite at her ankles again.

"Lord, this damn dog!" she said. "Deliver me!"

Grandma and I fell over laughing. We pulled out of her driveway before she called out, "Hey, y'all want some greens?!"

Push had started on the chitlins she'd promised, but Grandma shooed her out of the kitchen. She was jealous of other folks feeding me.

"You ain't leaving here till you have some of my cookin'," she said. She quickly picked her greens, soaked them, and placed them in a big pot of water already heating some smoked turkey bones. She patted some chicken down with flour and other seasonings. I went to bed happy, my belly full.

As I fell asleep, my young-girl memories were vivid. Of Pa-Pa, as we called him when we were younger, taking my brother and me to the horse and dog track on Family Day. How we loved to see how fast that plastic rabbit could run. And to the airport to watch planes take off and land. We'd hurry along the fence bordering the runways, trying to out-run them.

Grandma used to take us fishing up at Lake Okeechobee in central Florida. Dare us to make too much noise lest we scare away her bite. She'd bathe us—and the baby sister who would come later—in her big, claw-foot tub, and then pile us into her bed and slip a Gladys Knight and the Pips album on the hi-fi. "Cuz you're the best thing that ever hap-pened to me," Grandma would sing. "One, two, three," she'd add, plac-ing a single finger on each of our noses.

Before I left, I got a quick lesson on how two people could be married for forty-eight years and still be in love.

"Richit (she never called my granddaddy Richard), wake up and say goodbye to this girl," Grandma said, shaking him. He barely stirred. So she reached for a black knit cap and put it on her head.

"Richit. Richit Earvin," she said, shaking him again. "Who am I?"

He slowly opened his eyes and mumbled, "I don't know."

"Who am I, Richit Earvin?!" she asked again, this time louder.

"Why you...why you Johnnie Cochran," my grandfather said, recog-nizing the classic scene in the O.J. Simpson trial's closing arguments for the defense that she was acting out.

My grandma took the knit cap and pulled it down over her face. "And who am I now, Richit Earvin?" she said, hands still on her hips.

He peered harder and declared, "Why you still Johnnie Cochran!"

I was in stitches, laughing. They were as silly as schoolkids. We said our goodbyes and Cousin Push crawled out of bed to lead me back to the highway.

My visit to Mississippi was brief, but I had spent some time with the people I loved and who loved me even if I had funny, nappy hair and sometimes talked like dem white people. I'd been safe. At home. With my own.

Brenda Joyce Patterson

The Kindness of Strangers

"I DON'T REMEMBER THE TRAIL BEING THAT ROUGH BEFORE," I OVERHEARD ONE OF the hikers say, while shaking his head in disbelief. My eyes followed his group as they walked toward the parking lot. Great, I thought as I bought my tram ticket. The Tucson guidebook rated the hike to Seven Falls as "easy to moderate." Why in the world did I pick this for my first hike? Taking a deep breath, I decided to stick to my plan and headed for the tram to the trailhead. I wanted to see what it looked like. After all, I'd only lose three dollars if I didn't try the hike and I hadn't come from Florida to Arizona just to stop at this point.

My decision to visit Arizona surprised my friends and family. And why not? After twenty-eight years, I had never flown on a plane, never been farther away than eight hours from home, alone, and never been farther west than New Orleans. Yet I found myself on the phone making plane, rental car, and bed-and-breakfast reservations, outwardly sounding as if this was all old hat. I refused to give in to the inner voice that had squelched most of my previous adventuresome impulses. I made my plans in secret, shoring up my courage for the inevitable, well-meaning third degree:

"Where are you going?"

"You're going where? Isn't that where they voted against the Martin Luther King, Jr., holiday?"

"Do you know anybody out there?"

"Is someone going to meet you?"

"Where are you going to stay?"

"Do your bed-and-breakfast hosts know you're black?"

"Aren't you afraid of going by yourself?"

I answered everybody's questions calmly, assuring them that I had planned my trip well. But now, as I stood looking at the mountains, fear nibbled at the edges of my courage. I felt small and very much alone. My mind filled with a newspaper headline, "Stupid Black Woman Found Dead in Sabino Canyon after Days of Searching." Television close-ups of my friends and family saying over and over that they warned me not to go to Tucson alone.

Wandering into the visitors' center to wait thirty minutes until the tram returned, I wandered around the gift shop looking at all the tourist knickknacks and take-a-hike T-shirts. Let's stop all this hiking nonsense, my inner voice said. Just let it go before something bad happens and you get hurt. The voice sounded like a cross between my mother and Mrs. Wright, my first-grade teacher. I silenced it by asking the gift shop employee, an older woman around sixty-five, about the difficulty of the Seven Falls hike.

"Oh, you won't have any problems with that hike." she said, "I made the hike just last week. If I can make it, you can."

"Thanks. Do you think I have enough water?" I held up my bottle of water for her to check. She made the hike, I gloated to my inner voice. I'm young; I'm learning TaeKwonDo. I can do it."

"That's more than enough." She looked at my clothing, my boots. "You'll be fine, but I suggest that you change your shorts for long pants. It's easy to get scratched up while you're climbing."

I started out of the gift shop to go to my car for a quick change of pants. "Your shorts are fine," said a woman's voice behind me before I could reach the door. I turned toward her. She was wearing a turquoise tank top and denim shorts. She had heard my questions and assured me that she had hiked to the falls while wearing shorts and had had no problems. After learning that she was going to Seven Falls on the next tram, I hesitantly asked if I could trail her party on the way up. She agreed and introduced herself as Pennie.

I followed her to the tram to meet Larry and Sean, her husband and son, and Tom and Donna, her relatives. My quick, desperate prayer had been answered, I wouldn't be totally alone making my way. I envisioned myself as a little brown duckling trailing her group, keeping them in sight. Yet when we reached the trailhead, they insisted that I hike with them. We started on the two-and-a-quarter-mile hike with me in the middle. We made small talk along the way. I found out that Pennie and Larry were both teachers; Tom and Donna were visiting from Indiana; and this was eleven-year-old Sean's first time leading the way to the falls. When they learned that this was a trip of firsts for me, they asked the same questions my friends and family had asked: Did I know someone in Tucson? Did someone meet me? Wasn't I afraid to travel alone? I felt right at home.

On either side of us were walls of rock covered in pale green cacti, dark green trees, brown grasses, and an occasional yellow or red flower. The sun was high in the sky and the light formed a yellow corona around the camera lens as I snapped photos.

It took an hour and a half to get to the falls. One and a half hours in dry ninety-degree heat with no shade and the sand reflecting the sun back into our faces. It was so different from the muggy Florida heat I was used to. There, our first steps would have drenched us in sweat. Here, the only signs of the heat were our moisture-darkened waistbands, and the wet circles under our arms.

We climbed over rocks, across boulders, and around

Two years ago, when I told people my husband and I were going to tour some of the great national parks of the West for our honeymoon, they looked at me as if I were crazy. "Don't you want to go someplace like Bermuda or the Bahamas?" they'd ask. I have to admit that initially, I thought the same myself. I've never been outdoorsy, and the idea of lying on the beach was so much more attractive to me than tromping through the woods.

But the trip out West turned out to be the best vacation I've ever had. It may sound corny, but I gained a deeper appreciation of the physical majesty of our country hiking through nature's beauty—and I had a lot of fun.

I was saddened, though not surprised, by how few other African Americans I saw on our trip. Many of us live in urban areas, and we are never introduced to the simple pleasure of walking outdoors in a beautiful setting. But we cheat ourselves by staying away from these treasures. As African people, living in harmony with nature is an integral and important part of our heritage. We owe it to ourselves and our children to give them an awareness and an appreciation of the natural world. America's great national parks are a wonderful place to start.

—Martha Southgate, "Walk on the Wild Side"

trees growing almost horizontally away from the side of the canyon. We traveled single file. At certain points, the trail was only wide enough for one foot, with rock on one side and a cactus-filled drop to the canyon floor on the other. To my novice eyes there was no trail. No markers, nothing to point you in the right direction. Nonetheless, Sean's lead never wavered.

Seven Falls was worth the hike. The bare gray rock and the pools of water all around the falls made the sun a spotlight. Water cascaded onto seven lips of rock from the top of the canyon wall to collect in a series of pools before falling over the mesa's edge into the canyon below. The only thing that stood between me and my destination was a last hair-raisingly minute shelf of rock and the canyon floor four to five stories below. The trail stopped, merging into the canyon wall. We looked across the chasm to a few intrepid hikers splashing in the pools below. I asked how we were going to get over and down to the falls. Sean pointed to the canyon wall a few feet in front of us, where two hikers were climbing toward us. They looked like human spiders, finding nonexistent foot- and hand-holds.

The hikers reached the trail, smiling and telling us the water was perfect. Then, without any discernible fear, Sean began to climb across and down the canyon wall. Pennie and Larry followed. I groaned, fear drying the last saliva left in my mouth. Tom and Donna echoed me with their own sounds of distress. I wanted to cry uncle and not move another step, but the fear of being left alone galvanized me.

Pennie called out encouragement as I began to climb down, and told me where to put my feet and hands. Halfway across, I peeked between my feet. There was nothing immediately below me except a few protruding pieces of rock and the sound of water splashing far below. Pennie advised me to not look down. Too late. But the sounds of Donna and Tom climbing across behind forced me to continue.

I jumped the last few feet to the bare rock of the falls, Donna and Tom following. Pennie congratulated us on making it across. The air was cool and damp and smelled of minerals. I was astounded that I, Brenda Joyce Patterson, was actually sitting in a canyon, in Arizona, and not merely dreaming about it.

The water from the falls was ice cold. Everyone took off their boots and dipped aching, blistered feet in the pools. Pennie's group began to unpack their backpack. I used the diversion to sit a little away to give them a chance to be together. I listened to their voices divvying up food and drink behind me, conscious for the first time that I had left my food in the trunk of my rental car. One and a half hours and a canyon away, writing in my journal, I tried to act nonchalant while my stomach gurgled.

Good going, Sherlock. You get this far and now you realize you left the food in the car. My pesky inner voice chided me about the forgotten food my hosts had generously given to me that morning. Sean joined me on my shelf of rock. He asked questions about Florida and my hometown, Lakeland. Donna came up and, sitting on my other side, asked Sean if he wanted some bread and cheese. I concentrated on writing, hoping they wouldn't hear my stomach growl.

"B.J., would you like something to eat?" Donna asked, handing Sean a hunk of bread and some cheese. "We've got bread, cheese, apples...."

"Hmm, sure. I'll have an apple. Thanks." I abandoned my journal writing for the moment.

We sat in silence eating. Donna insisted on giving me bread and cheese when I finished the apple. Tom called over to me, offering a piece of chicken. I declined. They waved my offers of money away and even included me in their photos. After an hour or so, we worked our way back through the canyon to the tram stop. After exchanging addresses for the photos, we said our goodbyes.

As I drove away from Sabino Canyon, I burst into laughter. Thumbing my nose at my inner voice, I thought about my fears concerning this trip. Fears that I would never make the trip, that I would get lost, fear of the unknown. I also thought about the generosity shown by Pennie and her family and by my bed-and-breakfast hosts, Sheila and Tom. Each morning they gave me tips on getting around Tucson and gave me extra food for lunch without charge. Each evening they asked me about my day and listened with interest as I enthusiastically told them about driving in the desert and about my forays into the surrounding cities.

I had prepared for the bad, prayed for the good, and found that I can rely on the kindness of strangers.

Dale Grenier

Homegirl on the Range

I AM A FRESHLY SELF-DISCOVERED PAGAN. MY SANITY DEPENDS ON SPENDING TIME in places where I can be alone with nature. I've been this way all my life, but I never knew what it was called until recently, when I read Alice Walker's *The Same River Twice* and came across this passage: "Pagans are people whose primary spiritual relationship is with nature and the earth...." When I read that it was like coming home. I never did have much time for organized religion, but plenty of time for mountaintops, trees, and sunsets.

I vacation in rural, remote areas of the United States, places with deserted meadows, forgotten river banks, and range land traversed by county roads—deep blue ribbons stretched taut and clear out to the horizon. No humans in sight for miles and miles. Humanity and civilization are what I seek to escape when I take my trips. I do escape for a time. But, no matter how remote the terrain, I eventually have to enter a town—for supplies, or simply because it sits along the road between where I happen to be and where I want to go.

Tuesday

White travelers will never understand the complex dynamics that affect the travel experiences of their black brothers and sisters. Why? Because most white people can move about this land freely without anyone batting an eye or questioning (with a look, an action, or a remark) their right to be in any place at any time. Blacks, even those with daring natures, proceed with caution before going where no one black has gone before. I'm not even talking about anything as dramatic as violent encounters. The discomfort that I'm referring to is the all too common situation that many blacks experience of being made to feel just so very damned conspicuous.

For example, here I am, once again, the center of unwanted attention in a small town. Most of the folks are friendly—at least the ones working in shops where tourists are their bread and butter. "May I help you?" Smiles, mixed with obvious curiosity. I get the feeling that some of these local greeters just want to talk to their first black person. (Not many opportunities to do that living here.) It will make good conversation for months, maybe years. Perhaps I'll become a reference point etched into local folklore. Summer of '95—hottest one on record. The year of the Town Hall fire, the Miller boy's wife had twins, and that black gal went through town.

Negotiating narrow grocery store aisles, I am greeted by clerks and even an occasional patron. "Good afternoon." "Find everything you

---

*S*even Steps to Appreciating the Great Outdoors

1. **PLAN AHEAD.** There's a ton of information available. If you don't know exactly where you want to go, write or call Public Inquiries, National Park Service, P.O. Box 37127, Washington D.C. 20013-7127 (202/208-4747). And once you get to the park of your choice, drop in at the visitors' center.

2. **GET SOME GUIDANCE.** There are guides aplenty to direct you to the virtues of various parks.

3. **INVOLVE THE KIDS.** Children will enjoy any vacation more if they're invited to help plan it. All of the parks offer activities for youngsters.

4. **GET GOOD GEAR.** You may remember hiking boots as big, clunky leather things, but no more. At between $30 and $85 a pair, sturdy, lightweight day-hiking boots will make walking easier. Your local outdoor store will get you outfitted right if you tell them what kind of trip you have planned.

5. **FLY GOLDEN EAGLE.** If you plan to visit at least five parks over the course of a year, a Golden Eagle pass issued by the National Park Service could be a real money saver. For $25, it will grant entry for an entire year to you and your brood. You can pick one up at any park or order it by mail from the National Park Service (above).

6. **GET OUT OF THE CAR.** I was appalled at the number of people who would jump out of their cars, videotape the scenery, then jump back in and speed away. Get out and walk around as much as possible—you may never see anything this beautiful again. And you don't have to be a diehard jock; all the parks have short hikes and easy walks if you prefer to take things slowly.

7. **GET TO KNOW THE RANGERS.** Friendly and informative, they can provide a great introduction to the park's greenery and animal life.

—Martha Southgate, "Walk on the Wild Side"

want?" Quizzical natures, but restrained enough so as not to be rude. Genuine. Their words are delivered without the snitty suspicious edge that was so prevalent during my time back East. Nearly every day there I confronted some ham-handed store security goon for acting as if I were planning to put the store on a flatbed and just drive it home.

I prefer friendly, curious locals over the kind that cuts their eyes and foams at the mouth. Still, it would be nice to just blend in once in a while. Not that I want to lose my color. But I would prefer that it not be an issue all the time. That's what whites will never understand—that I never have and never will blend into most places within my own native country.

Some of the folks in this town have been looking directly at my arms. My arms are toned, muscular (and brown, of course). I work out in a gym, but nothing approaching bodybuilding stature or stare-evoking distinction. Perhaps they're looking at the color of my skin against the white T-shirt. So many whites seem to have this obsession with tanning their own skin, along with a fascination for the real thing. A white landlady once said to me, upon seeing me in shorts for the first time "Ooohhh, your legs are so brown!" The mixture of envy and surprise in her voice was bare-ass unmistakable. Since my face is the same brown shade, and she had certainly seen that before, I couldn't imagine why she thought my legs would be any different in tone. She didn't catch on to the stupidity of her remark even after she had said it! It was meant as a compliment, but I was stunned speechless.

Friday

Lots of giant tires with trucks attached driving up and down the main drag of this dusty place. Cousins of the vehicles that do battle at monster truck rallies. The darkened windows and mammoth size set me on edge. Who are their faceless occupants? What crazy reason have they found today for being pissed at every brown person on earth and dying to kick some pigmented butt? Have I finally gone off the deep end or is this a good time to remember that paranoia equals self-preservation?

Time stands still when I'm out on the range. But when I finally get into a town, I feel like I'm on fast forward—especially when I go into stores. People in this town move a little slower than what I'm used to, even out here. The gas station/convenience store is particularly Twilight Zonish. The manager and clerk seem a little befuddled by the cash register, soda dispenser, and gasoline meter. It's as if this store just dropped out of the sky last night while they slept. Come morning, the locals found this completely stocked establishment with a note attached, "Staff it and sell stuff."

I exchange a slice of life story with someone every once in a while during these trips of mine. Today I talked with the grocery store owner, a sixtyish white woman who told me of losing one of her two sons in a logging accident just last year. A horrible death. Yesterday she received word that her other son, a distance trucker and her only surviving child, broke his ankle in the middle of nowhere by stepping out of his truck onto an uneven piece of pavement. Shattered the bones all to hell.

No doctors or medical facilities for hundreds of miles. So he called his folks from his cellular and they started driving the five hundred miles to meet him. To cut the time he drove himself toward them, God knows how with his foot hanging off. Man! Mom took Junior home in the car while Dad followed behind in the truck. Last and only child is now recovering at home, much to Mom's relief.

For a moment, this woman and I connected. She trusted me, a stranger, with her most intimate emotions. I have no children, but it was not difficult to imagine her fear and anxiety for her son. It is a concern for loved ones that we all share, no matter our color or culture. I was glad that her son was okay, and cringe even now thinking about his injury and pain. People contact like this on the road does happen from time to time, and it ain't bad.

Wednesday

I take these trips to become intoxicated by landscapes, light, and clouds. I love traveling the remote areas of our country—despite some moments of uneasiness. As a little girl, I always wanted to visit national parks and other geological wonders of the American "outback" regions. The local PBS, along with slides of my fifth-grade teacher's summer vacations in her RV, set the stage for a wanderlust that has never left me.

Dad would never take us on these outdoor adventures that I begged for every summer. Why not? Combination of lack of money, raggedy-assed car, and scared stiff that some crazy white people might hurt us out there. I understood the money part as a child. But it's only as an adult that I figured out the extent of his fear about these unknown, uncharted-to-us territories. He wanted to protect his family from physical and psychological injury that could come in God knows what form—unexpected, cruel, possibly deadly.

I understand the reluctance. Who enjoys feeling the need to be so careful all the time? On guard, even on vacation. Not to mention dealing with the wariness of other blacks who think you might be just a little too weird or somehow low-ranking on the Blackness Meter for engaging in this behavior. If the call of the wild weren't so strong within me, I too would avoid this type of leisure, like most other people of color. But it's a shame that more of us don't visit the wide open spaces. This is our country too. The beauty is for our eyes as well as everyone else who visits.

My sister once visited a friend in his native Great Britain. She stayed for a week in the tiny hamlet where her friend had grown up. She told me of her experiences shopping, going about town, and visiting the local pub. My sister has a very distinct presence, a combination of royal dignity and sensuality. Now, London would be one thing. But the image of my brown sister going about this tiny English village intrigued me. I had to ask the obvious: Did the villagers drop their jaws when they saw you coming? Did they stare at you when you entered the pub? "Not as much as the locals did in Salt Lake City when I attended that conference last fall," was her reply. Since this was a phone conversation I'm not sure if she was grinning, frowning, or nonchalantly filing her nails while she revealed this tidbit. But I know my sister, and one thing is certain—she was not kidding.

And I wasn't too surprised. On my first venture to Europe—France, Germany, and Switzerland—I saw no gaping mouths, no fish-faced looks, no double takes. I was astonished to discover that most of the Europeans I encountered viewed me first and foremost as an American. Not a black person. Not even a black American. As far as they were concerned, any differences between us were due to my American culture, not my color. I had never experienced that perception before—certainly not in my own country, where my color is the first thing that most people notice about me (and I of them).

Sunday

Why do I continue to travel the "outback"? Because I love rugged country. I feel close to the truth and close to God in these places. I love how small and insignificant it makes me feel. As humans, our true state is small and insignificant. We conveniently, foolishly delude ourselves daily about our own importance.

Another reason I travel the wildlands is to feed my fascination with places where you are on your own in an emergency. You have to be prepared and resourceful enough to hunker down in case you can't move for a while due to weather, floods, or other natural disasters. Nature is clearly in control.

I learned to crave this when I lived in Maine. (Am I the only real-live black woman who lived and loved living in Maine? If so, I don't care who knows it!) You had better have a change of clothes, blankets, boots, hat, gloves, and food in your car during the winters there, unless, of course, you live in Portland or Bangor and never travel outside city limits. Break down far enough out of town and they will find your frozen ass during the spring thaw.

I am sure that I would love Alaska for the same reasons. It's even more outrageous there. That edge of danger, letting you know that your very life is on the line if you mess up. The reality that nature has the upper hand and will smack you down hard if you forget it! During quiet moments in these unspoiled places I hear voices of the First People who respected and understood this land the way no others have since. I feel these spirits, their anger, love, and tears out here on the range.

I travel these wild places because I crave to understand myself and the purpose of my life—as small as that might be. My need gives rise to a never-ending journey through this vast universe, which begins, for me, on the open plains.

PART THREE

TRIPPIN'
ALL OVER
THE WORLD

Faith Adiele

The Encroaching Forest: Southeast Asian Memories

Plants and Houses *(Chiang Mai, Thailand)*

A few months after I come to live in the house, I begin to realize that nothing in the compound exists without effort or purpose. The lush, tangled gardens surrounding us serve as constant reminder that until only recently the neighborhood belonged to the encroaching forest. The house, a perfect cube with glass walls and a frame and floors of solid, polished teak, is just big enough for Khun Ma and Khun Pa, my host parents, their daughter Nuan-wan, and me. Gleaming and new, the house sits unobtrusively in the space it has claimed for itself. With all the glass louvers open, it is as if there are no walls at all and we are living in the midst of tropical wilderness.

It takes a while before I notice things—that the family never buys medicine, that the lemony-smelling bushes hedging the house repel mosquitoes. I attribute it to sheer luck that the trees droop heavily with red finger bananas, fat pomegranates, and softening, sugary guavas whenever I'm hungry, that randomly grabbed twigs are always flavorful, that a rambutan, with its rubbery red and green antennae resembling sea life, slipped inside somebody's sheets, never fails to elicit a terrified shriek. I do not question the things I notice any more than I question the fact that every morning I awake to the fragrance of mango, orange, and fig trees ripening in the sun outside my glass walls.

Once she sees my interest, however, Khun Ma spends hours trying to teach me about the surroundings she has created. I trail her through the gardens, a basket looped over my arm, as she pinches annatto seeds and sniffs galangal root. "I planned *every* plant you see in this compound," she tells me, handing me a stalk of lemongrass to test. Its clean, hot bite sears my mouth, and she nods briskly. "As a developing nation, we need to know our environment," she explains. "In order to liberate ourselves."

At the dinner table she is continually fishing one plant or another out of the soup. Brandishing it aloft, she announces: "This prevents sore throat!" or perhaps, "This one is clearing your sinuses!"

Attentive, I nod at the dripping leaf, which—no matter how hard I stare—looks to me like a weed, indistinguishable from any other.

The house has three different cooking / eating areas, each with a different name and function, each of which translates into English as simply, *kitchen*. The first, a sleek room with Western appliances, is where we take our meals. Here, thanks to the maid, *Phi* (Older Sister) New, a steady supply of hot drinks and chilled fruits appears almost magically to replenish itself all day long. The second kitchen, located behind the house in the same small concrete building that contains *Phi* New's quarters and the laundry, is used to store bulk foods and a baking oven—quite rare in the tropics. The last cooking area, my favorite, is merely an open clearing in the garden where a slab of concrete has been poured on the ground. The wok and gas burner stand on one side, the chopping board and mortar and pestle on the other. This is the real kitchen.

There are two sounds I associate with this last kitchen: The metallic staccato of *Phi* New's heavy Chinese knife against the worn chopping board—a solid cross-section of tamarind tree—and the steady, hollow *thwap* of the wooden pestle against the side of the mortar as she pounds chili peppers, the seeds spraying into the air and tears streaming down her face.

I sit for hours on the warm concrete at her feet, half asleep from the soothing rhythm of her chopping and pounding. Giant flies hover just out of reach, driven wild by the stench of warm meat. I close my eyes and pretend that the noises are those of trees being cleared in the nearby jungle.

One evening early in my stay, a sudden wave of heat sweeps through the house during dinner, followed by an unprecedented chill. Immediately the kitchen is flooded with the overpowering perfume of nightblooming jasmine. There follows a deafening crack, as if all the glass panels in the house have shattered simultaneously, and it begins to rain.

"First rain!" someone cries, and the entire family leaps up from the table, shouting directions to each other in Pasat Nua, the local dialect I don't speak. They seem excited but not upset, so I try to stay out of the way. Each person grabs a basket and rushes outside. No one thinks to direct me, and I am too surprised and too new to the household to demand an explanation.

Once they all leave, I run to the glass louvers and peer out. I can hear the family laughing and calling to each other in the rain, but the wind blows their words away. Blind outside the glass perimeter of light, I chart their progress from inside the house, following the sounds from room to room. They move along the outside corners of the house, keeping low to the ground. After twenty minutes, family members begin to straggle in, flushed and triumphant. Nuan-wan extends a basket crawling with plump black beetles for my inspection.

"Good thing we remembered!" Khun Ma says, rejoicing. "The first rain last season we forgot all about them!" She turns to me and promises, "I'll roast them for your breakfast tomorrow!"

I grin weakly.

The next morning I find a basket of small bugs awaiting me. The almost weightless creatures are still intact, their tiny legs permanently curled in the air above them. As I stir them with my finger, wondering how to begin, the dry bodies make a faint rustling sound.

On one of her trips from one kitchen to another, *Phi* Niew shows me how to peel off the head casing and dip the body in chili sauce. The crisp insect pops on my tongue, a rich, oily taste like nuts or fried meat flooding my mouth. Relieved, I smile, and just then Khun Ma comes in. Surveying the scene, she beams. "And *twice* the protein of meat!" she crows.

Another morning I accompany Khun Ma to a Buddhist temple. At the front entrance we pass two nuns dressed in white, their heads and eyebrows shaved. They stand outside the door to the sanctum, clutching meager posies in the folds of their robes, their faces shining as brightly as their polished heads. I linger to smile at them, while Khun Ma looks on, a strange expression on her face.

When we're out of earshot she leans close to me. "See how they sell flowers to support themselves?" she whispers. "They can't even take the vow not to touch money!" She explains that, though circumstance forces nuns to support themselves, using money relegates them to a lower spiritual plane. While monks receive food, clothing, and shelter from both the church and devout lay people, nuns are no one's concern.

Inside the sanctum, we prostrate ourselves before the altar three times and light three sticks of incense. Like Christianity, Thai Buddhism is based on a trinity: the Buddha, his teachings, and the community of monks. The importance of the number three runs strong throughout Thai society, even secular life. Everything must be constructed, articulated, allocated in threes, Khun Ma explains.

When we leave the temple compound, the nuns look up to say goodbye. Once again I linger, trying to imagine what makes these hungry women smile so. We walk slowly to the parking lot, and at the car door I turn to find one of them hurrying after us. As she nears us, I see that she is holding out one of her flowers. Reaching me, she tucks the golden blossom into my palm in a single, smooth movement.

"For you," she says, her face aglow. And then, with one last smile, she is gone, her bare feet crunching over the gravel of the parking lot as she returns to her vigil at the temple entrance.

Stunned, I stare at the gift in my hand, and even Khun Ma looks surprised. The flower is so delicate, its veined, buttery-colored petals so thin, that it looks made of paper. I turn it over and over in my hand to convince myself that it is real.

Inside the car, I put the flower on the dashboard and immediately, a full, heady perfume fills the sunny car. If I close my eyes, the fragrance reminds me of summers as a child, when I would ease my way through a cloud of bees to reach the trumpets on the honeysuckle vine, break off an orange blossom, and suck the nectar from the warm neck.

When I feel the car pulling into the compound, I open my eyes to find that the flower has disappeared. The papery petals have burned up in the sun, leaving nothing but a scattering of pale, scented ashes across the dashboard like the residue of incense.

In the early evening I like to emerge into the quiet cool and ride my moped around the neighborhood. I pedal down narrow roads overhung with giant wild banana and coconut palms, leaving a cloud of red dirt behind me. Dwarfed, I feel on the verge of discovery.

I pass young housemaids with smooth, shy faces who look up from their laundry to smile at the first black woman they have ever seen, children sprawled asleep on porches, their mouths open, still wearing their school uniforms. The faint rasp of their snores is like the distant buzz of drowsy bees. Occasionally a new cluster of houses surprises me, almost hidden in the underbrush: modern glass-and-stucco bungalows, all pastel whimsy and odd geometry; traditional wooden houses on stilts, simple except for handmade lace curtains behind scrolled window grilles.

One evening as the sun is fading, I turn a corner and come upon a middle-aged woman in a clearing. Dressed in a white bra and faded print *sarong*, she rakes weeds into a roaring bonfire. She works furiously, never once looking up. Just as the sky turns to night, the thick black smoke of the fire billows up around her and she disappears before my eyes—first her bare feet, then the *sarong*, the gleaming bra, the brown of her shoulders, and finally her head. I am left alone in the dark clearing.

Turning the moped around, I start pedaling for home as fast as I can. I think about the first time I took out my contact lenses. My entire host family stopped talking and watched me, their eyes round. After a few weeks, we devised a system where each morning before breakfast I wash and rinse my contacts, then place them on the counter near the back door. *Phi* Niew boils the case for ten minutes along with Khun Pa's eggs and brings it to me in a little cut-glass bowl, still steaming. She walks slowly, the dish clutched in her hand, her eyes trained on the sterilized case rolling around inside.

This particular evening when I approach the compound gate, I notice for the first time the tall concrete walls surrounding the house, the tops glittering with barbed wire and crushed glass.

Besides the glass house, there are two other houses in the compound. The old house stands cool and dim in the back, everything about it worn smooth with years. It is quiet with sleeping children and women. Khun Ma's mother lives there with her teenage daughter-in-law, the daughter-in-law's two children and the maid, Nong. Hidden in the garden between the two homes is the family shrine, a miniature house with the traditional three-tiered roof of a Thai temple. Every morning *Phi* Niew and Nong pass between the houses, delivering the food they have prepared. With each trip they pause at the shrine to leave offerings for the ancestors—balls of sweet rice, waxy jasmine blossoms, tiny cups of green tea.

One morning at breakfast *Phi* Niew looks distracted. She watches Nong carefully, worrying a cold sore at the corner of her own mouth. I help clear the table, and she tells me that years ago Khun Ma took in a foster child—a teenage boy who had been orphaned when two car accidents within one year claimed first his mother and siblings, and then his father and the father's mistress. When the boy himself was twenty years old, a truck hit the motorcycle he was driving, and he was killed.

Because it was a violent death, Khun Ma engaged a spirit medium to hold a special ceremony that would recall the soul from its exile on the side of the road and grant it peace. According to *Phi* Niew, the medium went into a trance, selected the boy's favorite clothes from a large pile in

*H*appiness is determined by expectations. I see families in Thailand who have little material wealth living with bamboo huts, no plumbing, and little food, yet they are full of a joy I rarely see back home. They expect little, get little, and seem mostly satisfied. The problem starts when they come in contact with people that have so much more. The poor in America live their lives in the shadow of incredible wealth flaunted in front of them by the media. High expectations, low return equals frustration, unhappiness, and rage.

—Sylvia Harris Woodard, "Postcards from the Global Village"

front of her, and put them on. Speaking in a young male voice, she demanded foods that had been the boy's favorites. After eating and answering a number of questions to establish the authenticity of the spirit, the medium said the boy wanted to confess to murdering his father's mistress. The second car crash had not been accidental, the voice said. Everyone in the room was stunned.

The medium then bowed before Khun Ma and begged forgiveness for destroying her motorcycle and leaving this world. At the end of the session, the boy's spirit moved to a tree above the shrine between the houses and refused to be born again.

A year or so later the maid Nong, who passed the tree regularly on her way to and from the two houses, fell ill. She had a high fever, and large blisters covered her face and body. Khun Ma took her to doctor after doctor, but no one could cure her or explain her illness. Finally they went to another spirit medium who claimed that the spirit of the orphan boy was lonely. He had looked down and seen Nong passing through the bushes. He was trying to kill her, the medium explained, so that her spirit could join him in the tree. Khun Ma and the medium made offerings at the shrine beneath the tree, and Nong recovered that night. *Phi* Niew ends the story with a shy smile. "It is nothing," she assures me, touching the sore at the side of her mouth. "Perhaps a reminder."

Nong says nothing. Hoisting a load of dishes, she disappears into the vegetation between the two homes. It is difficult to see her—though the walls of the house are glass—but I can smell the plants she brushes against. Long after she is gone, a fading trail of lemon grass and ripening persimmon marks her path.

Later, as I wheel my moped out from behind the house, I think about the boy whose spirit has climbed a tree and refuses to come down, about how even death could not destroy his ravenous loneliness. I wonder how offerings of orange sections and sticks of incense are supposed help him. So far, no food, no scent, has helped fill that hungry space in me. Only movement.

I leave the compound and ride toward town. This time along the road I recognize meaning in things I previously could not even see. Nearly every few miles there is a cluster of white flags and string, with chalk lines etched in the dirt. The highway is crowded with them. They are not, as I had always assumed, traffic markings, but sites where spirit mediums have lain the souls of countless transit victims to rest.

I now understand why the third home is crucial to the compound. It serves to remind us that death drives along the side of the road with us, eating the same food we do. The thin white string and chalk lines not only bind the spirit's essence to earth but show how slender is the boundary between the two worlds.

I see why Khun Ma works so hard to make ancestral offerings and engage spirit mediums: It is, after all, a full-time job helping those who have suffered violence, those who are lonely, those of us in trees who refuse to be born again. Sometimes the work is not so much saving those who have left their souls at the side of the road, as it is keeping the survivors alive.

Love Tourists *(Pattaya, Southern Thailand)*

It is a neon night in the sex resort, the balmy air weightless against our tanned faces. Thatched-roof bars strung with bright paper lanterns and girlie calendars line both sides of the town's only road. This is not what we expected.

Things have changed since we were here last. Then it was a cheap student vacation. We slept on the beach and bought fresh crab and coconuts from the native islanders. No one paid attention to us, two friends from school. This row of bamboo bars, looking like something from the set of a South Pacific movie, did not exist.

Now the entire city dedicates itself continually to sex. Packs of men on "love tours" swagger the Strip, undressing all brown women with their eyes. Arab men, American men, Australian men, German men, Japanese men. We learn to walk with Scott's proprietary white hand on my brown arm.

Local teenagers crowd the free discos. Flamboyant, heavily made-up mixtures of fashion and race, they do the latest dances from London and New York, next to tourists who could be their unknown fathers. Their younger siblings haunt the streets and bars, draped in chains of jasmine, selling packs of Lucky Strikes. The police maintain paradise by rounding up beggars, revolutionaries, the deformed, anyone who ruins the ambiance.

As foreigners fluent in the native tongue, we attract attention. Countless child vendors approach just to hear us speak. We paw through basket after basket in hopes of discovering some halfway useful trinket to buy. At last I come across a find. "Look, Scott," I cry, holding up a flat yellow box.

He looks up from his basket to smile. "No way!" he shouts. "Chiclets! I can't believe it!" We buy the gum and keep moving.

Grinning pimps swarm everywhere, pressing business cards against us that advertise the skills of their sisters and daughters. Scott pushes away their advances, shaking his head *no*, holding up his hands to ward them off.

There is a flurry, two men shouting, a brief scuffle, then somebody flees and a fan of cards falls to the street. The squares of paper lay face up in the mud, boasting *Live live American-style show! See pussy eating banana! See pussy to blow out candle!*

We ignore the offending cards like road kill, stepping over them to enter the safety of a quiet, open-air bar. On rattan stools, we order drinks and giant saffron prawns. The drinks—local rot-gut whiskey distilled from rice—are dressed up with pastel paper umbrellas. As I take a sip of the harsh fermented rice, I feel a softness at my knees and look down to find a child gripping my leg. It is a young boy. He beams up at me, one tiny hand steadying himself, the other clutching a wire loop strung with plastic bags of pink shrimp crackers. His huge eyes meet mine easily. His unselfconscious touch in this place of pimps almost makes me cry.

As if pulled by strings, Scott and I both bend forward on our stools to reach him. The boy stands bravely between us, beautiful and so very, very small. He wears a scruffy yellow sweater over a powder blue safari

I have traveled over the years to many places—the beaches of Hawaii, Mexico, and the Caribbean, the ruins of Machu Picchu, Peru, and the Mayan ruins of Tulum and Chichen Itza, Mexico, the ski slopes of Canada and the Colorado Rockies, Windsor Castle and London Bridge, the Eiffel Tower and Notre Dame Cathedral. I've seen the Mona Lisa in the Louvre, Michelangelo's David in Florence, the Leaning Tower of Pisa, the canals of Venice, the Vatican and Coliseum of Rome, and the beautiful blue Danube in Budapest. I've traveled to the islands of Fiji, Tahiti, and French Polynesia, Australia and New Zealand. In all my travels, whether alone or with family and friends, I am always aware of my color and automatically notice if other blacks are at the resort, on the cruise, or on the tour. I am not saying that this is good or bad, it is simply automatic. I think it comes from a desire to feel comfortable. In most instances, I enjoy the special attention I have received for being "different."

The one trip where I felt these "rules" did not apply was a recent trip to Thailand, a remarkable land of many peoples where I did not perceive racial tensions. I traveled with a racially mixed group of travel professionals. We saw the Grand Palace and the Emerald Buddha, the fabulous beaches of Phuket, James Bond Island, and the Muslim Village of Koh Pannyi, built entirely on wooden stilts. We went to the River Kwai where the famous bridge was built and visited a World War II POW memorial camp. We shopped at a floating market, toured the Golden Triangle area where one can stand and see the Thai, Laotian and Myanmar (Burma) borders meet. We visited an elephant working camp and actually rode the elephants during a rare eclipse of the sun. I was amazed to realize periodically that I was not particularly conscious of race.

—Stephanie Spears, "A Career in Travel"

suit. I reach out and cup the point of his chin loosely in my hand, half-afraid of leaving a stain on his translucent skin. He flushes and ducks his head deeper into my palm. Scott asks his name at the same time I ask his age.

"Thum," he replies, too young to be surprised that we speak Pasat Thai. "I am five." He is the size of a three-year-old American child. He braces himself sturdily against our barrage of questions and answers each with great seriousness. Yes, he has already eaten. No, he doesn't go to school yet. Six, he has six brothers and sisters. At the mention of his siblings, his face blooms into smile. We ask him what time he goes home, but he is either unable to understand or unwilling to answer. Already it is after ten o'clock.

I ask the price of the shrimp crackers and Scott bolts upright, smacking his forehead with the ball of his hand. "Oh no!" he groans. "I *hate* those things!" Thum hoists the wire loop up to show that someone has carefully drawn the number *three* in red marker on each bag. Three *baht*. About ten cents. I hold up one finger. One bag. Thum gnaws his lower lip as his tiny fingers wrestle to pull a bag off the wire loop. After great effort, he hands me the crackers in exchange for three coins.

Instinctively, I reach for the box of Chiclets and Scott begins to laugh. He shakes his head. "God, you're a pushover!" he says. I hold the gum out to Thum, who immediately sets down his wares and pads his palms together, tiny fingers splayed. He bows to me, bringing his hands up to his forehead in a *wai*, a sign of respect and thanks. He is a child, so instead of returning the gesture as I would with an adult, I hold out my hand to receive it. As he brings his hands down into mine, I feel the faintest brush of his fingers across my palm. Only then does he accept the box. In perhaps just another year he will learn to put away such gifts to sell to the next tourist, but tonight he is still a child.

Again he chews his bottom lip until he succeeds in extracting a piece of gum and puts it in his mouth. Again his face flowers into a smile. He then labors to find his shirt pocket under his sweater, managing after several tries to slip in the box.

"I can't believe you're giving him all our Chiclets," Scott moans in mock distress. "*All* our Chiclets!"

At that exact instant someone takes Thum by his left arm. We look up to protest. A teenage girl stands in the street behind him. She starts to pull Thum away, the resolve in her expression silencing us. A split second later a policeman takes his right arm. The policeman's grasp is gentle but determined. The girl looks at the policeman. She does not let go of the boy. The policeman returns her look. He gives his head a single, firm shake, and then Thum is gone, our empty hands around the space where he used to be, our silent mouths still open.

° ° °

A few moments later a dark *Nissan* police truck creeps by, clearly on a sweep. Half a dozen child vendors lounge in the open pickup bed, their eyes at half-mast. The studied boredom on their faces resembles that of their sisters, the painted bar girls who throng the street, looking on with only the vaguest of interest.

The policeman tosses the boy's shaking body into the back of the truck, and Thum crouches where he lands. A second later, his face crumples and he begins to scream, his body shuddering with the force of his cries. I barely recognize him, the intensity of his unhappiness almost unreconcilable with the soft child of five minutes before.

The girl flutters, distressed, near the back of the truck, the flesh of her palm still warm from holding him. She says nothing. None of the other children move. Thum is by far the smallest and the youngest among them. The truck moves on. Minutes later, though the truck is gone, Thum's shrieks still hang on the warm night air.

Long after life in the street has resumed, long after we have finished two plates of prawns in silence and several drinks each, we still do not look at each other. Though we don't know it, we are already checking out, we are already getting ready to leave. A few days later, in the final incident that prompts our departure, one of the posh international hotels burns to the ground, and the remains of at least five native women are found chained to beds. But tonight we dream of children.

"No," Scott finally says, shaking his head curtly and once again holding up his hands. *No.*

He may be saying *no* to what happened, *no* to what will happen, *no* to this place of pimps. Perhaps he is saying *no* to action, or to responsibility. But this time innocence is not so easy. It is not as simple as walking away from the obscenity of business cards. We are here, and though perhaps we can never save five women or even one five-year-old boy, we are somehow responsible. Even if we never speak of this again, we have already by our presence said *yes.*

The Splendor of Fruit *(Rangoon, Burma)*

It is dusk in Rangoon. I sit smoking in my room at the famed Strand Hotel. I am alone and feel as though I am the hotel's sole occupant. Since my arrival I've seen no evidence of any other guests. Because of delays in Bangkok I missed the friends I was supposed to meet. I am pleased at the way things have turned out, pleased to have been left behind. Closed to the West since the forties, Burma is a country that has been left behind. Solitude seems somehow fitting in this place.

After the harsh, modern reality of Jakarta and Bangkok, Rangoon feels like an abandoned movie set. I can picture the dramas that took place:

mysterious foreigners with strange appetites lounging downstairs in the smoky lobby; opium smugglers vanishing into the murky lighting of the black market; colonial wives escaping the capital to summer in the cool hills of Maymo. Dressed in tennis whites, they sit fanning themselves on the verandah. Below, native servants crouch in the garden, transplanting imported strawberries by hand.

The postwar flight of the British must have been similar to the departure of a film crew—the fantasy cut short; the elaborate, impractical structures beginning to crumble into disuse. Today, rotting colonial mansions house small cities of the homeless. Families squat in the echoing halls of deserted ministries. Outside, the sons of military officials rumble through the streets in the country's few cars—antique fin-tailed Cadillacs, their radios smuggled over the border from Thailand.

Listless, I do nothing. At seven in the evening, the city is no cooler than at noon. A book of stories by Somerset Maugham lies abandoned on the dresser next to a half-empty bottle of beer. The warm, root smell of malt clings to the open mouth. Mandalay Beer is notorious among travelers on the Asia circuit. Perhaps its foul taste is due to a missing ingredient that can't be imported from the West. Perhaps it is simply a matter of local preference. Either way, the result is a dark, yeasty concoction, served warm in a country without ice. It is still fermenting as it touches the tongue.

The hand-drawn label on the bottle depicts a famous pagoda not in Mandalay at all but in Pagan, miles to the north. Pagan, where my friends are. Burma's ancient capital. Village of a hundred temples. Favorite among the four cities to which each closely guarded phalanx of tourists is rushed. I think I understand the marketing strategy: Mandalay is the country's most famous city, Pagan's temples its most recognizable image.

The Strand Hotel used to be the center of colonial society, and being here is like stepping into someone's faded memory. I close my eyes to fix the scene: the bed covered with soft chenille nubs; the fragile,

You can fly to Europe or Asia for as little as $150 round-trip if you're willing to be an air courier and can manage with only carry-on luggage. Courier companies offer overnight delivery of air freight for businesses—mostly legal documents, small machinery and videotapes; the exact contents are listed and given to you. Someone from the courier company meets you at the airport at each end. Most courier flights depart from major U.S. cities for major European and Asian cities. Two agencies are: Now Voyager, 212/431-1616, ($50 registration fee, payable when you book your first flight) and International Association of Air Travel Couriers, 561/582-8320; email: iaatc@courier.org, ($45 registration fee).

—Elaine Lee

yellowing lamp shade that coughs like an old drum at my touch. Draped over the rattan whatnot, my freshly washed underwear drips slightly like someone perspiring. The carpet is indistinct; years ago it may have been red or violet but can no longer remember.

I open my eyes, and Maugham stares out. As reflected in the dresser mirror, the room makes an old photograph, stained and curling at the edges. Something about the reflection is wrong: me, a black woman holding a cigarette. When did I take up smoking? It is difficult to isolate my own memory. Originally I must have been dreaming of menthol and thought that cigarettes would keep me cool, but Burmese cigarettes are made of cloves. Their warm, cloying scent hangs over the entire country. There is no escaping the fragrance.

Suddenly it is an hour later—eight o'clock. The ceiling fan whines, languidly revolving its arms. Even on high speed it is virtually useless. It swirls cloves and malt into the thick atmosphere, unbreathed in years. Sporadically the air shifts like a musty animal, placing a damp, scented hand on my shoulder, the back of my neck.

In search of anything cool, I leave my suite. The hallway is as wide as the street outside. My bare feet slap against the cool marble, and I am tempted to lie down on the unswept floor. I pass through anterooms and parlors and sitting rooms crowded with dark furniture: settees and writing desks, dusty ebony and teak. There is no sign, no sound of anyone else. At the end of the dimly lit corridor, the communal bathroom gleams white.

I enter and sit on the edge of the claw-footed bathtub. The room is easily five degrees cooler. Everything in the long, narrow space is white: Glittering white tile walls and floor. Oversized white ceramic fixtures. Stubbly white towels. The only spot of color is the pale orange toilet tissue that feels made of corrugated cardboard. Envisaging a long, cool bath, I twist the bathtub knob, and a ribbon of rust sputters out. I remember that there is also a soap shortage.

I climb into the tub and mop up the rusty water with toilet paper. The tissue is the exact color as the water. Once the tub is dry, I take off my shirt and lie on my stomach. Pressing my face and chest against the cool, hard porcelain, I dream. Of ice cream. Cold beer. Lemonade.

It is nine-thirty when I awake, blue light streaming across my body. The light comes from the open window above. If I stand up and climb onto the edge of the bathtub, I can just squeeze my head through the narrow opening. The window faces a shanty town behind the hotel, leaning on the verge of collapse: wormy planks patched together with scraps of cloth and cardboard; the eerie glow of battery-run blue lights after curfew. Noise and light spill out of every crack of the structure: Michael Jackson on black-market cassette. Voices raised in laughter and anger. The cries of children and dogs. In contrast, the dark street is utterly barren, as hushed as the hotel corridor. I am protected and yet trapped.

In my best Gloria Swanson imitation, I sweep down the grand staircase to the hotel lobby. Two white-gloved attendants in frayed uniforms spring up, leaving their conversations behind. They usher me through a stately set of glass doors and I enter another series of empty formal rooms, pale blue walls stretching to twenty-foot ceilings. I wander, already having forgotten why I came. Finally, something feels out of place: An English-language newspaper strewn on the floor; an abandoned slab of papaya growing soft on a plate. Only a hotel guest would be allowed to do this—someone else has recently been here. I hurry ahead.

The dining room, an elegant, Old World affair with ornately carved ceilings, is nevertheless empty. Everything stands ready: tables swathed in snowy linen, set with china, crystal and silver; wicker screens curving inward to isolate private conversations. A young waiter, his face dramatically scarred by pockmarks, rushes toward me from his post.

Leading me to a chair, he suggests that, "Madame is wanting a nice bottle of Mandalay beer?"

"No," I respond, staring hungrily at his hands. His manicured nails are the color of raspberry sherbet. "I want fruit," I declare. "Lots of fruit. Any fruit. All the fruit you have." Anything to relieve this thirst.

In what seems like only seconds, the waiter returns with a large silver tray. He begins to pile dishes and dishes of fruit atop the table until every inch of cloth is covered. He works quickly, silently. I gape at the staggering still life, at the splendor of fruit. The musky perfume of mango and pineapple. The whimsy of rambutan with its red and green tentacles. Plum-colored mangosteen. Huge juiceless pomelos, tinted rust. With a flourish the waiter places before me a cut-glass bowl set inside a larger dish of chipped ice. "Chilled strawberries," he announces proudly at my startled look. "Just brought down from Maymo hills!"

As I pick up a heavy silver spoon, I begin to understand the colonial aesthetic—the addiction to privilege—the seduction of creating a role and starring in one's own fantasy. What then if the hand holding the spoon is brown?

Dorothy Lazard

Finding Myself in the World

The world is a great book, of which they who never stir from home read only one page. —St. Augustine, 354-430 A.D.

GEOGRAPHY WAS ONE OF MY FAVORITE SUBJECTS IN SCHOOL. FROM MY EARLIEST days, I have been mesmerized by maps, but I knew that no map—relief, topographic, or contour—could capture the richness, the sublime beauty, the smells, and variety of this earth. Even as a little girl, I was sure of that.

Books baited me even more. After reading about moors and mountain-top villages, igloos and trout-choked streams, I wanted to go out and see this world. Deciding to be a writer at ten cinched it; I believed it was my destiny to travel. A personal and professional imperative. Yet the more I learned about other countries and other peoples, the more overwhelming it felt. How can I understand it, if it is so big and mysterious? And so far away?

I wanted to travel to make the world more comprehensible, more familiar. I wanted to learn the dances the real Watusis did. I wanted to see if the Eiffel Tower was as tall as my father said. I wanted to go to sleep on a train and awake in another country.

I was a dreamer.

Fresh out of graduate school, I took my first vacation when I was twenty-four. It seemed incredibly decadent. In my family, we vacationed only to relatives' houses, which we reached by car, or, occasionally, by train. I went to London to spend Christmas with my sister Sarah who was a Peace Corps volunteer stationed in Gaborone, Botswana. Neither one of us could afford to get to the other, so we settled on London, an intriguing halfway point. Sarah's Botswana neighbors had recently moved to London and offered to put us up for the week.

Having never been out of the country before I was thrilled. I felt vulnerable and exhilarated at the same time. But our attempts at group sightseeing felt like someone had thrown a wet blanket over my expectations for a great adventure. Each trip out was marked by a litany of monologues about imperialism and the obsolescence of British royalty. I was obliged to agree but felt London was too old, too full of history—granted, much of it bloody—for me to look on it as completely worthless.

Back at our hosts' apartment I listened to all-night political discussions about the situation in South Africa, their lives as immigrants, British yuppies, and the doomed fate of America as a world power. Being a political naif, their talk of apartheid swarmed above my head like bees. But I listened, as isolating as it was, because I was learning something new in that crowded council flat. I learned I had to open up if I wanted to be a world traveler. Shyness had no place there; only honest and forthright participation was valued.

They proved to me that one could be political, even radical, and still love music and art and all the things that make life beautiful. They argued as fiercely about who made the best blues album as they did about world political systems. My hosts were not as dour as my first impressions would have me believe. That trip taught me that I had a place in the world. A voice in the world. Sometimes personal, sometimes political.

Traveling, they taught me, means giving up personal ego and nationalistic arrogance. My hosts referred to me as the "American." I had to accept the fact that, as quiet as it's kept here in my own country, I am an American. Yet nothing in my experience had allowed me to think of myself in that way. At best I was a hyphenate: an African-American. Some derivative of the "real" thing. In London I was a different type of "other," standing outside of another norm.

I am an American.

After that first experience in London, I began traveling in earnest, both in and out of the country, with friends and alone. More than anything, I like the solo trips I made. Alone I operated at a heightened state of awareness. Being out of my element, being totally dependent upon my own wits was a little scary, and a little exciting. I came to realize that travel was frightening in the best sort of way. And for a time I got hooked on living for that feeling of being out in unknown territory and making my way back home safely. It was like leaving a warm house to step out in the snow. Your eyes and skin and breathing have to adjust to the new climate. But, after a while, everything normalizes. You adapt.

When I travel I try to dissolve into my environment. Being designated a tourist, I find, distances one from the most interesting people—namely the people who live there. My main incentive to travel is to observe how people in other places act, dress, communicate, and entertain themselves. Back in London, for example, I wanted to talk with black folks. Plays at the Africa Centre, lectures at bookshops, and a few pleasantries exchanged at the vegetable market in Hackney gave me insight into the Afro-Anglo experience. I had discovered part of the diaspora, and in doing so, stretched my notion of what "black" can mean in the world. True, their

On the crowded platform of a train rumbling through France, a French man kept smiling at me and saying repeatedly, "You are beautiful." This infuriated a stout, rough, unpleasant French woman. "Don't talk to her!" she shouted angrily. "She's from America. They hate black people! Nobody there respects her kind."

"No! I don't believe you," he said. Then asked me gently, "Is that true?"

He was smiling, she was glaring, others were staring. I decided to play dumb. I smiled back at him. He asked again. I smiled again. "Oh," he said sadly, "she doesn't understand." Then he added, *"Mademoiselle, vous êtes noire, mais très jolie."* (Young lady, you are black, but very pretty.)

Several years later, I told the story to one of my sisters and my then-husband.

"That man was calling you 'Blue Bell,' not *beautiful,* and you thought it was a compliment," he sneered.

"He must have thought your hair was natural," my sister chirped.

"It *was* natural," I replied. "I'd been in France a long time. My hair wasn't straightened anymore. It had gone back." Her face fell in surprise and disappointment.

It was the 1960s and blacks were widely proclaiming our physical beauty. Black is Beautiful, we sang, rapped, and shouted. It was a sad reminder that the metal chains and shackles once used to hold our ancestors captive still had to power to cripple our thinking and lock our minds.

—Marian E. Barnes with B.J. Taylor

blues was like mine, but not completely. It was influenced by another culture, another process. I had to rethink the effects of slavery and colonialism on Africa's children.

I am a displaced African.

Awareness of other cultures has brought along with it an uncomfortable awareness of my own marginalization. I have been several places and run into incredulous stares and comments about black women vacationing. I am frequently asked, "Are you visiting relatives?" or "Do you work here?" As if they can't believe a black woman would have the money, time, or interest to leave her home.

This phenomenon, if I may call it that, first struck me about eleven years ago when I was in Paris for the first time. Traveling as I often do, without an exposed map or camera, I was approached by a white American couple, clad in Florida State University T-shirts. They consulted each other for a moment before the wife came over to me. Speaking very carefully and loudly she asked for directions to the nearest metro station. Having just come from that station a few hours before, I answered her question and headed on my way. But before I was out of earshot, I heard her say to her husband how amazing it was that "they" speak English so well. Something in her sense of possibilities would not allow her to see me as a traveling black American.

Limitations and stereotypes abound, but not enough to keep me at home. I was once on a Greyhound bus riding east to Washington, D.C., for the first time. Sitting behind the driver and across the aisle from an older black woman, I dozed through the flatness of Indiana. I felt a tap on my shoulder and looked up to see a middle-aged white man standing

*S*ince earliest childhood, Scotland has loomed large in my imagination. I pictured a land dotted with ruins of castles, lonely lochs, and rushing rivers. I also felt a kinship with the Scottish people, believing that they would like me, that they would look at me and see someone more than a descendant of a slave. So I was thrilled when I was awarded the Hawthornden Castle International Fellowship for Writers and got to live in Scotland in a real castle, for a month.

Hawthornden Castle was built in the Middle Ages and purchased by the American heiress Drue Heinz centuries later, who converted it to a writers' retreat. Perched on the edge of a sharp cliff, with the river Esk a rushing torrent two hundred feet below, it was everything I'd imagined a castle would be, with its thick stone walls, massive doors, and narrow spiral staircases. There was even a dungeon! On my first night at the castle I could have sworn I heard the lonely cry of wolves howling in the moonlight. And it was impossible on those cold nights, as the castle's walls creaked and moaned, not to conjure up ghosts.

The landscape was as remarkable as I'd pictured in my child's mind's eye: towering mountains, deep ravines, winding rivers. The heather wasn't in bloom, but still a faint hue of purple clung to the hillsides. When I arrived, autumn was at its breathtaking peak, and I relished every day the view of the forest from my window: a multicolored palette of every shade of yellow, gold, russet, and crimson. A fire in my fireplace dispelled the chill of the wet October days and I wrote. It was a time of calm introspection for me.

Over time I began to see that Scotland is not all lochs and rushing rivers. Like all post-industrial societies, Scotland has its share of crime, unemployment, and social unrest. In recent years, there has been an increase in neo-Nazi activity, including assaults against people of color. But I was not disappointed by the Scottish people I met. They were as eager to speak with me as I was to speak with them. Their pride and determination reminded me of black people back home. And there was nothing arrogant about them. Rather, they seemed certain on a deeply personal level of their intrinsic self-worth, and this I found comforting and inspiring.

—Viki Radden, "My Scotland Lies over the Ocean"

over me. He smiled and said, "It's getting pretty quiet on the bus. Could you and the other nigra lady sing some spirituals?" What does one say to that out in the middle of an endless Indiana highway?

I am a survivor.

Walk the laundry-draped streets of Paris's brown and black neighborhoods and feel the strong psychic tug of déjà vu. Fall into conversation about dating with a sister at a Liverpool nightclub and feel right at home. Eavesdrop on a young black diva at a chic Monte Carlo eatery and discover that flirting is flirting is flirting, the world over. I've come to realize that black women are all over the world, doing what I am doing: working, loving, laughing, struggling, bonding. My dreams require proof that I can live anywhere in the world.

I recognize the opportunity to travel as a great gift, a gift of imagination and seized opportunity. My mother, addled by epilepsy, never set foot on an airplane, a hydrofoil, or a ferry. Her life was extremely limited not only by illness but poverty and its attendant ignorance. When I travel, I carry her as securely as I carry my luggage, wondering how she would perceive the things I have encountered. What would she think of Arlesian lace, or the huckleberries that grow wild in Washington's forests? What pies they would make! I travel to collect all the experiences she was denied in her short life. Like a patchwork quilt, I mentally piece these images and sensations together and share them with family and friends. I encourage my niece and all younger women I know to expand their horizons by grabbing a bag and taking off on the open road. We have loads to find out about ourselves and each other. My "quilt" of memories is my legacy to them.

I am an envoy.

I still strive to make the world less frightening. Whenever I can afford the time and the ticket, I hop on a plane. At least two vacations away from home per year. Nonnegotiable. In a myriad of incarnations and settings, I have found interesting people, beautiful places, opportunities to practice my still-pedestrian French, and places that satisfy my love for art and architecture. When I travel I go looking for a universality of spirit and sensibilities. I go looking for myself. I am here and everywhere.

I am a traveler.

Rosemary Blake

Magic in Alice Springs

THE LAND WAS A HOT, DUSTY, PALE YELLOW WITH A FEW HILLS HALF-HEARTEDLY rising from the earth and feebly reaching toward the sky. The poetic vision of the desert I'd expected was missing. Instead, a bright, stark reality greeted me as the plane arrived in Alice Springs. I was unprepared. A friend who had traveled around Australia for four months on a motor bike urged me to forget about the cities and go straight to the Center, a magical place, that is literally in the middle of the continent. Despite her advice, I lingered in Sydney for four days, reveling in the taste and feel of that lovely cosmopolitan city. It had chic stores and restaurants, beautiful parks and beaches, and smiling, friendly people. The city-girl side of me had been reluctant to move on to the adventure of tenting, treks at dawn, and heaven only knew what else the two-week camping trip would entail, but a sense of excitement had been stirred as I remembered my friend's descriptions of the area.

So, there I was in Alice Springs, feeling not one iota of magic, just disappointment and a tinge of trepidation. The flight from Sydney had been a short one. But what I was feeling was more than could be accounted for by the shift from the city canyons to the desert's expansive skies. The air was heavy with the late morning heat and something else. It was there with the people: tight faces, neither eye contact nor smiles from those who assisted the passengers at the airport.

On the drive to the hotel, the only folk I saw on the streets were native Australians—the Aborigines—and they walked with downcast eyes and shuffling gaits. There was something very uninviting about this place and my usual impulse to go exploring as soon as I arrived was stifled. Instead, I holed up in my room seeking refuge from the noonday heat and the sights that I was uncertain I wanted to see.

It was remarkably quiet as I sauntered toward downtown Alice Springs later that afternoon. The wide, tree-lined street was free of traffic. There was an absence of sounds. There was no breeze to rustle the leaves nor were birds singing, and although I could see children playing, the sounds they made barely reached me. It was peculiar, as if someone had placed a bell jar over the city and I was on the outside watching. Again, I encountered only Aborigines on my stroll. They continued with their quiet conversations without a glance my way, as if African American women walk down their streets every day. There was none of the usual curiosity, none of the finger pointing and whispering as I passed by.

I had been traveling alone for nearly a year. I'd spent time in Europe, Africa, India, and Southeast Asia, and had gotten used to the flurry of attention I caused. In fact, I rather enjoyed it. "Is she African? Is she American?" "What is she?" I'd heard this exchange in countless tongues and discovered that the body language of curiosity is universal. Often I ignored the comments. Sometimes I playfully responded. But here in Alice Springs there was nothing. This was a new one. I was both surprised and puzzled. Didn't they see me? I began to wonder if I was invisible.

I pondered this as I basked in the warmth of the late afternoon sun and enjoyed the quiet sky that seemed to surround me. Soon my attention was drawn to a woman and two men—a couple in their early thirties and an older man who walked apart from the pair—approaching on my side of the boulevard. By the way they wove their way along the sidewalk and spilled onto the street, I could tell they were drunk. And drunks are to be avoided, whether they're on the streets of Manhattan or in a remote desert city halfway around the world.

I had managed these eleven months of solo travel without an unpleasant incident, a fact I attributed to my New York City street smarts. Those smarts were telling me to cross the street or move over to the nearest store and pretend to window shop. And yet, there was this curious invisibility I seemed to possess, so maybe there was nothing to do. I debated which course to take as I walked along.

When I first noticed them they were a full block away. My strategizing could not have taken more than a minute or so, but before I knew it and could act, they were upon me.

There was no gracious way to avoid them at that point so I continued walking. I inhaled sharply as I encountered the foul cloud of liquor that preceded them. I held my breath and determined not to inhale again until I was safely past. A few more steps, that was all I needed. Thank goodness my sheath of invisibility seemed to be intact. They were ignoring me just as everyone else had been doing. I was just about to congratulate myself and breathe a sigh of relief, to say nothing of fresh air, when it happened.

The old man was closest to me. He stopped at the instant that our next step would have propelled us past one another. With dazzling speed and before I could discern his intention, he reached out, grasped my left hand tightly with his, brought our entwined fingers up to face level, and engulfed me in an intent, focused gaze.

I was completely flabbergasted, frozen solidly in the moment. Our eyes locked for what seemed like an eternity. I was calmly lost somewhere in his bright, black/brown eyes. Although my eyes never wavered from his, I was aware of the contours of the craggy face so close to mine; the pinkish wash tinting the whites of his eyes, his deep brown skin dulled by a coat of Alice Springs dust, the gray-streaked bushy eyebrows precariously perched on a prominent brow ridge, the smooth skin of his broad nostrils, the wide, shapely mouth, his curly, dusty, disheveled hair that a part of me longed to touch and the brown pants and red checkered shirt in disarray. Every detail of him was crystal clear. I was not alarmed at this strange turn of events; I was simply there experiencing it.

Finally my mind kicked into gear and what did I do? Did I jerk my hand away and cry out indignantly, "What the hell do you think you're doing?" Did I push him away? No. With amazement, I felt myself smile and in the sweetest voice greet him with a musical hello. He grunted, released my hand and continued on his way without a backward glance. I know because I stood there watching until he and his companions were out of sight.

The instant he disappeared from view, my calm was replaced with incredulity and a torrent of wild mental activity. What in the world was that all about? Why did he do that? What did he do? Why did I react that way? What happened to my apprehension of this drunken man? How could he have gotten from the corner to me so quickly? My thoughts tumbled out in a pile, as if unrestrained by a door that had been abruptly jerked open. I had all the questions but no answers, so I uprooted myself from that spot and continued into town.

As I walked, the questions that swirled in my head gradually settled down along with the dust disturbed by my footsteps. I let them drift away, in fact, I was relieved that they did. I have learned to put aside questions that do not evoke an instant answer, to trust that the answers will come in their own time.

As I refocused on my surroundings I noticed that something had shifted. The Aborigine faces I saw were turned in my direction, some blank, some with smiles, others evincing mild curiosity. Their conversations drifted out to me from the windows and doorways in a normal tone. I heard a baby's cry. Heads turned as I went by. There was a woman with a child on her lap who nodded a greeting! The bell jar had been lifted and the curtain of anonymity had disappeared. I was in the realm of the visible.

It was a realm that widened and expanded as I explored the Center. Wherever I went I was accepted by the people as if I were a member of the skin group—Nabanati—that I would have belonged to had I been born a native Australian. (In addition to tribes, Aborigines classify themselves by skin group and there is a complex set of kinship rules that go with the system.) I met native artists, greatly admired their art and artifacts and discovered that to be Aborigine is to define yourself as artist. I walked the land, slept under the stars in canyons, visited sacred sites, and the one time that fear was present I heard the spirits whisper, "No harm will come to you in this place."

Much later a thought came to mind that gave me some insight into my encounter on the street the day I arrived. One of my favorite science fiction series describes the impression ceremony that marks the start of a special relationship between a human and a dragon. There is a moment when the eyes of the two creatures meet and they become one, forever bonded in mind and spirit. I have always been moved by the beauty of that moment. It evokes the essence of falling in love; the instant when we open to our oneness with another being.

I did not fall in love that afternoon in Alice Springs, at least not with the dusty old man. I doubt that I'd even recognize him were I to see him again. But I think that he recognized something in me and communicated what he saw to others in the Aborigine manner. It seemed that in that curious exchange when our eyes met he touched a part of me that had been long forgotten but was patiently waiting to be remembered. Perhaps all he sought and found was our sameness, our oneness. Two people of color, meeting on a boulevard in Alice Springs, Australia. I'll never know.

I do know that I fell in love with the Center, that breathtaking land, and that I recognized a kinship with the Aborigines. And I discovered my connection to those mystics who have been faithful keepers of the land of magic for over forty-thousand years.

Lydia A. Nayo

A Sharecropper's Daughter Goes to Paris

I AM LESS THAN FIVE DAYS FROM MY FIRST TRIP BEYOND THE CONTINENTAL UNITED States to someplace where I will know no one other than the person I am traveling with. I will not know the language, I will be unfamiliar with the customs, and I will have no idea how to express a need for allergy relief medicine. It is thrilling. It is not something I have ever done before.

I am a utilitarian traveler, the daughter of poverty. My family travels with objectives, to places that somebody else in the family has settled, away from the hard claims of the past. I go only where I must or only to where I know people.

This is not to suggest that I have been no place significant. Since my native Philadelphia, I have lived in three different states, in five different cities, at fourteen different addresses. I ventured forth, at age twenty, with a toddler on one hip, two thousand dollars literally pinned to my underwear, and all my belongings in drayage, to live in San Francisco. My objective was to hunt down and claim an identity. I was in search of the me that was not somebody else's younger sister, or a young woman with one child who was at risk of becoming an unwed mother statistic, or worse yet (I thought at the time), my parents.

I have gone over the country of my birth at least three times in each direction. But over is not through. I have never seen Mount Rushmore, the Grand Canyon, or a field of wheat. I have not trod the streets of the City of Big Shoulders or heard the beat of the nation's heartland. To the extent that I saw Charm City or the Big Easy or counted the number of streets, byways, and boulevards named Peachtree, there was a purpose underpinning my being there. Somebody I knew lived in Baltimore, New Orleans, and Atlanta.

Former sharecroppers do not teach their children to travel for pleasure. It is not that I blame my parents for their reticence to just up and go someplace. If, in my youth, travel had been fraught with the peril of the wrath of casual racism, I cannot imagine that I would have been quick to encourage my children to go someplace just because it existed on a map. Usually, we went back to see my father's remaining family in South Carolina. We always traveled by car, and that car was hotel and diner through the minefield of Southern states between Pennsylvania and our destination.

My priority, when I left my father's house twenty-five years ago, was to overcome the legacy of suspicion and angry fear that was his method of parenting. After finding a self to be on the left coast—an effort that took a dozen years, and included getting a college degree and finding a life partner—I went back across the country to go to law school in Washington, D.C. Ever practical, I chose Georgetown Law School because my father had been diagnosed with terminal cancer, and it was close enough to Philadelphia so that I could regularly visit but far enough away that I would not be swallowed whole by all that I had run from.

The utilitarian travel habit kicked right in. My sister and I would go together to Philadelphia to spell my mother at home, to be there as my father died by degrees and, ultimately, to help put him away and see my mother into widowhood. We drove past, but never stopped in, cities large and small, hell-bent for Thirty-second Street. I never saw a town named Rising Sun, or learned what South East was southeast of. On those trips toward my father's death, we sped past Baltimore and White Marsh, only saw the names of Christiana, Dover, and Wilmington. There was no reason to stop. They were merely markers of how much longer it would be before we reached my mother. There was an uncomfortable limbo on the road; during drive time, my father could die, without us there.

And he did, on a Thursday in August, in his sleep.

Later, there was more travel by necessity: delivering my daughter to Spelman College and then visiting her there on family weekends; visiting with my husband's aging grandparents in a little hamlet outside Baton Rouge, Louisiana, and the ritual holiday trips to Philadelphia. Once, we drove to Saratoga for the annual jazz festival. Of course, I was willing because someone my husband knew invited us to join their party. But never, ever, to the criminally close Caribbean, or to any point south of Atlanta, for that matter. My mother's daughter, the soul of caution, I did not go where there was no one to visit, no specific reason to be there.

Practicality, in the form of a new job, dictated that I return to California, this time to Los Angeles. A teaching position beckoned, fairly screaming my name. Once again, I traveled by air, knowing what I passed over only to the extent the pilot pointed it out, sotto voce. Utilitarian travelers do not see sights, do not take several days to make trips that can be completed in several hours. The travel-risk-adverse do not follow Route 66, or take up the lyrical invitation to spend the night in Gallup, New Mexico.

I have always been a woman who gets from one place to another for a purpose: switching gears in my career, giving my daughter the dream of college life, finding out what I was made of in the first place. But now I have finished financing my daughter's education. The demons of poverty, if not overcome, have been wrestled to submission. I have completed as much formal education as I need to get the kinds of jobs that will redeem the hard lives of my parents. And I have moved along my current career continuum enough to feel certain that a life as a bag lady is not eminent. I have connected with my self, and I am comfortable with the woman that I am.

Finally, I am free to take a

*A*s an African American living abroad, I often find myself—willing or not—a spokesperson for blacks in America. Black folks from the States are a rarity in Bordeaux; because of the sizable African population here, most people assume that I am French West Indian or African. After they get over the initial shock of meeting a real *"noire américaine,"* I am almost always asked, "Does racism still exist in America?" Of course, my answer is a resounding *yes,* but I have found that people here have such a warped sense of who we are that I am often obligated to elaborate.

Have you ever tried to explain who *we* are to someone who has only glimpsed pieces of our world: the cover of *Ebony,* or *Public Enemy* (shown here on TV), Rudy on *The Cosby Show,* or the cosmetic surgery of Michael Jackson? My people, it ain't easy! I make an effort to be honest and forthright, but how do you convey the complexity of the African American community over a twenty-minute cup of coffee?

I tell them that we are survivors. That we are the children of the strongest of the strong; that we survived the middle passage, slavery, forty acres and a mule, lynching, sharecropping, the new deal, segregation, integration, assimilation, and the trickle down theory. We will survive crack, gangs, the disintegration of the black family, and AIDS. That we are governors, mayors, drug addicts (sometimes at the same time), teen mothers, generals, gang members, supreme court judges (good and bad), Uncle Toms, revolutionaries, Negroes, colored folks, people of color, blacks, African Americans, bus drivers, postal workers, police officers, school teachers, astronauts, engineers, filmmakers, folks who want to uplift the race and others who don't give a damn. That we are at a point in our history, in the United States, where we are producing some of the most talented spirits the world has ever seen and at the same time some of the most downtrodden disenfranchised souls since slavery.

—Carol McGruder, "Observations of an African American Gypsy" trip to a place just because it is there, although I can do no more than greet and thank the native population for its assistance. Maybe Paris will open the door to the rest of the world. Maybe I am ready to go.

Gwendolyn Brooks

Black Woman in Russia

We must tell each other as much as possible about each other.
—Professor Alexander I. Ovcharenko, Soviet-American Writers' Conference, 1982

I WENT INTO RUSSIA ARMED WITH MENTAL PICTURES OF MARCHING MEN, WIDE PEAS-ant women in shapeless skirts and long-sleeved flannel toppers tied with string. I expected to see dark babushkas galore. I expected to experience flavorless cabbage, greasy borscht; a grim landscape, grim babies, grim mothers and fathers. Russia. Land of the cold heart, the regimented mien.

It was the summer of 1982.

No, I didn't "read up" on the country before I went there. I wanted fresh impressions, fresh assaults on a chiefly unschooled consciousness.

I was invited by Harrison Salisbury (dead now) to attend the Sixth Annual Soviet-American Writers' Conference. The travelers included Charlotte Salisbury, Mr. and Mrs. Arthur Schlesinger, Jr., Mr. and Mrs. Irving Stone, Studs and Ida Terkel, Pepperdine University Chancellor Norvel Young and Mrs. Young, Pepperdine Dean and Mrs. Olaf Tegner, authors Robert Bly, Erica Jong, Susan Sontag.

Harrison Salisbury was, in addition to being the former assistant managing editor and associate editor of the *New York Times,* a specialist in Soviet affairs. He had traveled to many parts of the Soviet Union and had written several books. I knew I was fortunate to have as a guide the author of *The Nine Hundred Days: The Siege of Leningrad.*

We were to spend four days in the Ukraine, in clean Kiev, exchanging views with writers Nikolai Fedorenko, Grigol Abashidze, Chinghiz Aitmatov, Mikhail Alexeyev, Genrikh Borovik, Oles Gonchar, Mikhail Dudin, Pavlo Zagrebelny, Yasen Zasursky, Mstislav Kozmin, Vitaly

Korotich. Then we were to spend several days in Leningrad, and several days in Moscow.

The American writers, coming from their several parts of the country, met July 20 at Kennedy Airport, Scandinavian Air Lines Lounge. We boarded a plane for Copenhagen. Ideal flight, proud pilots. When we reached Copenhagen one of them announced, "We can now tell you that there were three pilots in this cockpit and for this landing not a one of us touched the instruments. You have just had an absolutely perfect automatic landing!" We shivered, not with delight.

From my notes: "We check in at the Royal Hotel, after a *long* airport hike and a bus ride. I have a lovely *private* room, which is what I hoped for. All of us "singles" have private rooms. I'm to meet Studs and Ida Terkel for dinner, after I have a nap. In 1014, I have a two-hour nap, and I iron my clothes, and I take a bath. Fruit is sent in by the hotel management. With the Terkels, poet Robert Bly, and Vera Dunham (born in Russia, with much information to provide, about Russian literary personalities—who's "good," who's "bad," who "writes well," who *doesn't* "write well," etc.)—dinner at the Belle Terrace in the Tivoli, a Riverviewish enclosure across the street from the Royal Hotel. After dinner we see a circus act outdoors: a family of red-covered acrobats, standing on each other or silently jumping off heads and high-flung chairs. I tell Robert Bly the story I have heard about his three-or-four hour readings, and how, at one of them, there being no door to use without disturbing the entire assemblage, the students began to leave, one by one and two by two, out of the back windows. Whether Robert is happy to have this bit of information or is *not* happy to have this bit of information I cannot tell. His face is stiff. Back to the hotel.

Flight SU-222 to Moscow, for an introductory Soviet blessing. We are met by smiling welcomers, given flowers and refreshments, and Russian money for "spending change." Chief among our guides is "Michael," Mikhail Kusmenko, twenty-one, who looks quite like the sensitive-faced actor Michael York, or as York looked in *Cabaret*. This Michael (Misha) is warmly solicitous, busily helpful to us all, *very* proud of his excellent English. Michael is everybody's favorite. He travels with us to Kiev and smilingly helps escort us throughout our stay.

Each of the three hotels is beautiful, well-furnished, cheerfully serviced. Sovetskaya Hotel in Moscow, Kiev Hotel in Kiev, Hotel Europeiskaja in Leningrad.

In Kiev, the writers, Soviet and American, meet in a large yellow building, handsome, with great rooms, magnificent staircases, shining floors, high ceilings. The rooms are rich with decoration and planting. Guards are anxious to help, to answer any questions. The atmosphere: a dignified but excitingly pregnant quiet.

In one particularly long, particularly noble room, are two "opposing" tables, for the two "opposing" representations, American and Soviet. (At one point during our proceedings, the second day I believe it was, Studs Terkel, briskly cheery, urged a shuffling: *Why* should all Russians be sitting at a table together?—*why* should all the Americans be sitting at a table together?—*that* was the trouble in the world today! Let's mix it up a bit!—let's be really *together!* Nice little murmurings from the Russian side. Nice little murmurings from the American side. There is an immediate result, a rustle, an excited rustle; a charitable change. And for the duration of our get-together Studs Terkel is at the Soviet table with Russians. The rest of us remain in our appointed places.) There is simultaneous translation. Everyone feels comfortable enough to speak freely, and does. Arthur Schlesinger is dryly analytical, dryly critical. Harrison Salisbury is universal. Erica Jong wants to know: "Where are the women writers? *Where* are the *women* writers?" She is informed, rather sheepishly, that they are all on vacation. "Out in the country." This is not the last time that Erica is to ask her irritating question. The Russian writers know (somehow) that Erica (long-haired, shapely, and always beautifully dressed, having brought oodles of expensive clothes), has written sexy books, and I have the impression that they are prepared to make light of her. At first they trade rascally quips with her. They are surprised and discomfited when her major speech at the table turns out to be brilliant, informed, managed, sane.

Robert Bly and I are invited to read our poetry. Robert—Fedorenko loves calling him that, with every letter in the name magically distinct—accompanies himself on the mandolin (I think that is what it is) and in the high emotion of the moment leaps up and strides toward the center of the room, thus, of course, losing the labor of his translating equipment. "R-O-B-E-R-T!" shouts Fedorenko. "Don't get excited, R-O-B-E-R-T! Take i'*teasy!* Sit down! Take i'*teasy.*"

Among the poems I offer is my longish "The Life of Lincoln West," detailing the traumas of a little black boy who, in a roundabout way, begins to recognize and value his identity. Fedorenko is enthralled. Missing my point entirely, he rhapsodizes over little Lincoln. He tells us all, and at length, about a dear little black boy who had wandered into the midst of heretofore dense folk (including himself). This little boy everyone found *touchable* and absolutely *darling* "with his nice white teeth and nice rough hair. Everyone *loved* to pat his nice rough hair." Afterward, away from the congratulatory tables, Russian and American, everybody is *pleased* with me. I ponder on this, and I begin to get very angry. I get angrier and angrier. And I am sorrowful. Two meetings later I request attention. ("PLEASE call on me, Mr. Salisbury!") And I read the following to the congregation:

"I agree with Mr. Aitmatov—a nuclear blast would abolish everything, *including* all aspects of ethnic concern for ethnic bliss. Nevertheless, I am going to call attention to *blackness,* a matter no one else here feels any *reason* to cite." (I am, of course, the only black in the room and often, it seems to me, the only black in the whole of Russia, although that is not true: sometimes I see a young black male student in the street—and shortly before lunch on this very day I have seen a whole cluster of young African basketball players from, as I recall, Zaire, and run to semi-kiss them. During my three weeks away, entire, I am to see not one other black woman, although I've been told by Russia-traveling friends that there is an "ample" contingent of black women living in Russia. No Russian wants to talk about this, however. I'm looked at strangely, when I'm inclined to mention it, am abruptly left alone in the middle of the floor!) But to resume. To continue with my statement:

"No one *else* here feels any *reason* to cite blackness because on the Soviet side there is very little association with blacks. Soviets *see* very few. And on the *American* side there is as little association with blacks as can comfortably be managed, although there is great opportunity in the United States of America, where there are many many many many many MANY blacks. Well, all of you must understand that the planet is swarming with *dark* people. The other day Nikolai Fedorenko, droll, dry, and when he's right AND when he's wrong, a strangely fascinating personality, out of the kindness of his heart (and I received it as such) 'comforted me' with a tale of a *dear* little black boy whom everyone found *touchable,* and absolutely darling with his nice white teeth.... Then Mr. Fedorenko said something *very large:* "WE NEVER PAID ANY ATTENTION *AT ALL* TO THE FACT THAT HE WAS NEGRO."!!!!!!!!! Well, I *have* to reply to this. *Essential* blacks—by that I mean blacks who are *not* trying desperately to be white—are happy to have you notice that they do not look like you. *Essential* blacks don't *want* to look like you. *You're* OK, *they're* OK. We essential blacks do *not* think it would be a blessing if everyone was of the same hue. Personally, I like the idea of a garden rich with varieties of flowers. Although I like roses, I like other flowers too. So please DO, Mr. Nikolai Fedorenko, go right ahead and *notice* that blacks really look and *are* quite different from yourself. Go right ahead and PAY ATTENTION to that FACT!!!"

Well-covered middle-aged women clean the streets of Kiev, paying an almost affectionate attention to their work.

Seeing the Russian people in the street—watching them adjust their little girls' BIG floppy bow-ribbons which adorn the tops of the neatly groomed heads—watching them adjust the behavior of frisky little boys—watching them converse with each other, smiling, clutching fondly their inevitable collections of two, three, four or more flowers which, work-time over, they are taking home—I decide that these swarms of human-faced people do not *want* to be blown to bits. They want to go on making those little dough pies with blueberry or cherry sauce. They want to go on patting into position their daughters' enormous bow-ribbons. They want to go on taking flowers home.

Chekhov had a warm involvement with the *details* of Russian personality. It is easy to feel I am observing the source of much Chekhovian copy. Much Tolstoyan copy, much Dostoievskian copy.

St. Cyril's Church, Kiev: plastered with religious paintings. One of them in particular seizes me: a thin, coal-black *devil*, with protruding teeth (you just know the artist considered this blackness the essence of evil "incarnate"!) seemingly scolding a plump, paunchy nude white man, sitting, doctor's-patient-wise, with a towel over his knees....

Before we leave clean Kiev for Leningrad (we are told that Kiev is irresistible in *all* seasons, but best in May, when the chestnut trees are in bloom), we go short distances to special features of Soviet history. Visits to a sixteenth-century poor man's cottage and a nineteenth-century *rich* man's cottage. Equally rustic. Well, not quite. A boat ride down the Dnieper River to Kanev—pronounced *Kahn*-yev. The water of the Dnieper River is the cleanest, clearest river water I have ever seen. On the good-looking, well-equipped boat we are fed generously: good dark bread with cheese, coffee, tea, salami, candy, fruit. In Kanev, we visit the memorial to the loved poet Taras Schevchenko, and the Schevchenko Museum.

I go with some of the others to a beautiful festival of folk songs and dances; such innocent joyfulness; we sit in the grass, before a stage full of these colorfully costumed people—and are transported.

Babiy Yar. Near Kiev's city limits. Not until I go there do I understand, fully, what Yevgeny Yevtushenko did for us in writing that poem, long since a classic. What used to be a high-banked deep ravine, with a water bottom in which children once played, is now an arranged green with a look of deceitful peace. Because no one can be peaceful in this presence. Ninety-thousand Jewish people, young and old, were herded here, beaten and shot to death by German soldiers, and buried here, in three days of September 1941. The trees outside the bitter circle look vaguely indignant and reproachful.

In Russia I didn't see anybody who was scrawny or hunger-bellied, although the only *nonglorious* housing I was taken into was the hazardous apartment of the impulsive and rousing poet Bella Akhmadulina, who gave us an impromptu party. I certainly saw in the streets swarms of unedited Russian people. These looked, for the most part, healthy, energetic, well-fed. In the town streets are many, many galloping young women wearing smart little suits, ornate hair, stylish high heels.... After a Writers' Union meeting, a grim Babiy Yar film—bulldozers rolling tons of the dead—little children and young girls and their elders of all ages stripping to be shot, burned or bitten....

On July 29, departure for Leningrad, by Aeroflot. (Grim-looking plane, with seats close and uncomfortable.) Leningrad, "cradle of the Revolution".... Sobering visit to cemetery containing thousands of Leningrad dead, German-killed; the steady mourning-music, insistent, pressuring, distressing.... On July 30—through the Winter Palace to get to the Hermitage: The Rembrandts are proudly cited by our guide—there are paintings, paintings! Paintings galore; and there are treasures of jewelry, jewel boxes, jewel-encrusted swords, capes red and jewel-encrusted, gold rings, gold necklaces, gold bracelets, all richly wondrous....

St. Isaac's Cathedral: All these cathedrals we are to see are high-vaulted beauties sumptuously decorated, with impressive, large works of art throughout, and magnificent huge, engraved, intimidating inner doors.... A drive through country scenes with nonlush grass (a frequent Russian sight) to Peter the Great's Summer Palace....

Part of *my* visit's spectacle is our company's Susan Sontag, whose statuesque dark Jewish beauty strides through Russia, always in slacks: always with one frontal white streak in the otherwise black hair: determinedly intellectual. She is not like Erica, who brought heavy suitcases of dresses, shoes, makeup. Susan at lunch: "Why are the *wives* here?" (meaning the American wives Mrs. Irving Stone, Mrs. Harrison Salisbury, Mrs. Arthur Schlesinger, all of whom are writers of distinction, and the wives of the dean and chancellor of Pepperdine University). It was fascinating sitting behind Susan on the whizzing Intourist bus: "I have *two* books on him.... I have *four* books on him.... I have *four* translations on him.... I have *that* author in SIX translations...." Her companion: "Oh! One of the most beautiful bridges!" Susan: "Yes. I've seen *pictures* of it." Her companion: *"That's a—"* Susan immediately: "Yes, I read about it long before I came here."

Susan got very mad at me in Leningrad. Her back had been listening, as we waited for a palace admission, to Freda Lurye, an editor of *Foreign Literature*, the highly respected Russian magazine, who was questioning me, as she had been doing for days, relentlessly: What Does It Mean to Be Black? Susan begins to inform her. I burn. I address Freda. I say (approximately) "Why do you turn from me to her with this question? Obviously, being black, I know more about What It Means to Be Black than does *she*." Susan (approximately): "How *dare* you assume such Nonsense," (her rage capitalizes the word) etc. etc. etc., in agitated spew. By now we are entering this palace and are proceeding to the little anteroom where we must remove our shoes, for the Russians are lovingly protective of their palace floors. Susan is screaming. My outrageous fancy that I know more about Being Black than *she* knows has pushed her to wild-eyed frenzy. We are sitting beside each other on the low wooden bench provided for shoe-removing. She continues to scream. Finally, she utters an unforgettable sentence—which I can report exactly, because I wrote it down immediately: "I TURN MY BACK UPON YOU." And she does. She carries out this awesome threat. She turns her Back upon me, with a gr-r-eat shake of her bottom to appall me.

I am ass—uredly impressed.

Of course, S.S. had every right to resent my jumping into her Possession of a conversation. I was guilty of a breach of etiquette. So were the hosts of the Boston Tea Party.

At a concert, with merry singing and variety acts, and dainty little dances, it occurred to me that there is a certain Innocence about the Russian people. It's a puzzle. Or at least it is puzzling to *us*, the American "sophisticates," so used to dirt, disarray, degradation. Young Russian people (great cigarette smokers, incidentally) claim to know nothing of drugs or drug running. They claim to know nothing of really *violent* crime. Their stage shows may have advanced to increased flesh revelation, but the meticulous little dancers never *really* let themselves go. I haven't seen EVERYBODY, of course, but I would venture to say there are no Tina Turners over here. No Richard Pryors. No Eddie Murphys. No porno shows....(?)

The Leningrad Writers' Union: At each of our arrivals we have been *met* with flowers and handshakes from smiling Writers' Union people. Here in Leningrad at the Writers' Union special meeting we are afforded buttered bread with caviar, coffee, vodka, and other amenities. Erica Jong stands up and mourns the absence of "the women writers." (Again.) We are told by a jesting director, stout and businessman-looking, that the men have ser·t their writing wives off to summer resort, it being summer, yok-yok. But before Erica J.'s assault, Harrison Salisbury has called on me to lead the self-"explanations." I say to this Leningrad contingent, "My name is Gwendolyn Brooks. I'm a black poet—you can see that. And I want to say how much I appreciate this opportunity to meet Russian people, and how much I appreciate their welcoming kindness." Later, I read my poem for Michael, to wild applause (these people, these Russian people, are warmly serious about poetry, they *feel* and love poetry). The poem is translated, a bit, by cold-voiced, imperious Marina, one of our Leningrad guides, then it is taken over by Sasha (Alexander), who claims the right "because-I-have-seen-this-poem." A major announcement. "I *know* this poem." Michael—Mikhail Kusmenko—("Misha") is merrily disgruntled by the translation, saying to me, "My eyes now are not 'quick' and 'smart', but 'beautiful'!!!!! I say, "That's OK, Michael, they are beautiful too!!!!" I'm having fun with nice little Sasha's twist of my language—but Michael says with serious shyness, "Thank you."

Dostoievsky. The Apartment. His last apartment. Round-top black hat in the little entrance hall (his hat). Umbrellas (not his but typical of the time). Clusters of family pictures on the papered walls. Dining room—no carpet now nor formerly the guide assures us—with handsome heavy furniture; on the dark table a samovar, large, heavily flourishing, ready for tea; a buffet with comely dishes and cups. The Study!—where D. wrote. The ponderous, wide, red-pattern upholstered sofa, on which he died, and which is right behind the heavy, large desk, on which we see his last half glass of tea—supposedly!! "I won't drink the tea," promises Irving Stone (now dead) when he requests permission to sit in D.'s chair and to hold D.'s pen. ("Now that you've let me hold the pen, may I hold it again, and have my wife take a picture"—which is done, to the music of incredulous gasps by myself and the Terkels.) We see the nursery, with a map on the wall, a doll, picture books, a rocking horse. Then we are taken by Ganna, the delightful, giggly, prettily plump, dark-haired little curator of this Dostoievsky Museum, to the narrow room that, she tells us, once served as a kitchen—two large Dostoievsky family portraits have been introduced to a wall. Here, at a round table, Ganna, her quietly efficient assistant helping her, serves us tea, delicious tea, with Lorna Doone-ish cookies; and those little chocolate candies twisted in colorful manipulations of that waxy paper you have encountered before in Russia. Minor biographical details from Ganna Bograd, who gives us, also, a little book she has written about D., and descriptive materials partly in English. How pleasant! Possibly the most purely pleasant and charming half hour I am to spend in Russia. Downstairs we find the Terkels (the Terkels had gone downstairs before tea, Studs pleading weariness). Studs is enjoying mightily what we hear, in our clearer state, a semi-drunkenly offered piece. The singer is a very flirtatious "Anatoly."

August 2, 1982—Last day in Leningrad; we go to one last palace, with glittery, much-decorated rooms. Here, Harrison Salisbury speaks in affectionate Russian to a tiny woman serving as a door attendant. She lights up when she hears this American using her own beloved language. He asks if she has lost someone in the siege of Leningrad. She has. She is reluctant to say goodbye to him.... Pushkin's school. I see his first school-written lines.... The Salisburys and I visit the neat, light apartment of Alexandr Blok.... Nice train to Moscow at 11:55 P.M., arriving in Moscow at 8:30 A.M. (after a tasty breakfast with hot tea, served us in our attractive compartments). It's the Sovetskaya Hotel.... We visit one of Tolstoy's houses, a mighty house in the country. In a large case, his bicycle, two pairs of boots he made for friends. His office holds a big desk, a sofa, quite like the imposing sofa on which Dostoievsky died. To the right of the desk, against the wall, is a large writing or drawing stand. In this office Tolstoy wrote one hundred works. Quite dark, this office....

◦ ◦ ◦

Old old women within the protecting walls of cathedrals. Some with winter coats (on August fourth).... No matter how shabby or decrepit a house, presence of the customary flowers or flower! Gracing windows. On the streets, always, both men and women, carrying flowers home. Just a few, wrapped in skimpy paper, or not wrapped.... The woods are quiet and beautiful and reaching—and there are many: but in Moscow, I observe, *almost* all green areas are weedy. Sometimes you see old women in babushkas, wide dresses, and worn heavy shoes, weeding the green. Some of these weeders' dresses are thinned-out cotton, over which there may be worn sad blue or green or dust-pink sweaters, listlessly buttoned over wide square bodies or *other* bodies with billowing bellies.... Afternoons: plump women sitting, not on their porches, but in front of their fences.... These substantial women may be seen, also, in bus stalls, at bus lines, stalls provided with benches painted over with red and yellow, or stripes.... Interiors: many interiors, seen from the street—just a sneak's eye view—reveal themselves as drear, drab, sad.... Wet clothes hang here, as in the States...hang from windows—from clotheslines—over lines of fence. Familiar itemata: I am repeatedly impressed by the numbers of old women...here is a woman praying, behind a locked cathedral door, making her Catholic signs. Then she strides her short, enhanced self down the rocky road...Father Paul, at the Zagorsk seminary, and the Zagorsk cathedral.... Then another cathedral where, when people, any people, any private people, are moved to commemorate a family member or loved friend, they come in groups to sing in beautiful rich Russian voices.... Question: How are the songs chosen?—for the choices should suit everyone.

Moscow. We're snug in the Sovetskaya. Elegant staircases, sedate halls, fine furnishings, fine dining room, fine food. (Throughout this Russian trip we've had delicious food. Nonslimy borscht! Rich dark bread. Tomatoes and cucumbers galore. Shishkebab, fruits, ice cream. And, outdoors, excellent ice cream cones, much loved by the populace. Apple tarts. Veal, lamb, beef, pork, chicken, fish. Guava preserves. Potatoes in various arrangements. Heavy soups. The popular little dough pies also, but I refuse to eat dough.)

The trip to Zagorsk, for more tours through more museums and distinguished churches, with their leaders in conscious regalia.... A visit to the Kremlin—but we are treated to very little of it, and that little we are whisked through rapidly. Such a whirlwind exterior tour leaves me with no clear impression. On the fast trip to Zagorsk, I see—with difficulty— open doorways that afford views of gloomy, ragged, desperate interiors. Guide Marina does not want to answer any questions about these. She is, in fact, getting quite sick of my days-long questions about houses. "May we see some of the houses?" Answers are vague or vacuous. Eventually, in reference to an isolated nongrand but nonhorrible square,

Marina barks angrily, *"There's* a house, Gwen-do-lyn. You wanted to see *houses."*

In the packed downtown streets of Moscow, the Russian people seem to be walking all in a single parade, a compact parade. The tempo is similar, at least on the neat top, to that of United States downtowners.

Before we leave Moscow we are guests at Ambassador Hartman's mansion. Sumptuous. An open, modern, sophisticated splendor. The ambassador's wife greets me warmly, because she has known and, she says, loved my poetry for many years. Bella Akhmadulina is there. As you read her poetry you feel that you've got a nervous little worm in 'possession'—a bright, twisty, unexpectedly wise little worm; and meeting her personally, you feel exactly that! It is on this occasion that Bella carts some of us off, post-reception, to the rinky-dink apartment she shares with her present husband, who paints, sculpts, creates set designs. Bella was once married to Yevtushenko. You reach the wild, pouty apartment via a tiny, rickety elevator, which can take only five of us at a rising. We rise by fives, and are returned by fives to the vast cold spirit of the first floor. Escape.

What else is Moscow to me? What further "knowledges" of Moscow do I gather to bring home? The beautiful information that it is safe to walk anywhere in Moscow, day or night. The appealing fact that so very many of the citizenry go home from work carrying flowers—a bunch of them, or a few. It is not true that Russians are "rude." I encountered curiosity here and there, that translated into puzzlement that a black woman was walking their streets, but chiefly I encountered pleasantness, smiling or unsmiling "tolerance," or downright cheery welcoming. An author's wife, after our forty minutes or so of casual conversation, hugged me fiercely, exclaiming loudly, "We like you!".... Such a serious appreciation of poetry. One poet asks me the size of a customary edition of poetry in the United States. I reply that, if a poet in the United States sells an edition of five thousand copies, he or she is "doing well." My questioner is amazed, and declares that in Russia an edition of a *hundred* thousand copies is perfectly ordinary. Listening, I remember that Yevtushenko and Voznesensky have recited, often, to audiences of fourteen thousand or more. And I remember what celebration enveloped me because I wrote a poem about Michael!.... It is not true that Moscow audiences sit dull-eyed through theater or opera performances. I see the same smiles and shining eyes, hear the same gasps, giggles, and happy frequent applause as I find in Chicago, New York, San Francisco, and Peoria.... Here plump stomachs are OK! I see hundreds and hundreds of them!—male and female stomachs out-thrust and nonapologetic!—I *do* glimpse *some* cozy little houses, behind fences.... I love seeing the babies in the strollers, pushed by young mothers in neat red sweaters, blue sweaters, print dresses.... It is *not* true that all Russians feel pounded....

It *is* true that the loved children are spectacularly well-behaved.... Good-looking modern clothes are the norm, not the exception.... I meet Moscow people who explain Soviet uneasiness by pointing to a symbol such as the siege of Leningrad—a million and a half deaths in nine hundred days. In short, "all we" are watchful because when we have not been watchful we have been assailed, and assailed, and assailed.... (Forgot to record that, in a Leningrad park, we saw a famous statue of the highly respected black poet Alexander Pushkin. Susan Sontag got as close as she could, spread her arms wide and shrieked, "My Pushkin! My Pushkin!" I wish I had a picture of that.)

Another of my knowledges: Certainly those who have not visited this part of the world are ineligible to vote on what it is or is not.

When I disembark at Copenhagen's airport I observe instantly that what Jean Stone, Irving's wife, had said to me is true: "You'll notice brightness. You notice a difference *immediately,* sharply!" I do, I do. First of all, there is an unmistakable, feelable presence of hope in the air, noticeable on this second "experience" of Copenhagen as, logically, it had not been on the first. This is not to counter-suggest that the Russians looked miserable, but hope was not what I saw as their aura; what I saw as their aura was sanction.

In the Copenhagen airport: abundance. Abundant wares. Cheeses and sausages and candies and games and jewelry and clothing.

In New York: cough drops. And lots and lots of beautiful blackness all around me.

I want to close with that poem I wrote for Michael. It says what I think of the essential spirit of youth in Russia.

MICHAEL, YOUNG RUSSIA

To Mikhail Kusmenko, twenty-one years old.
From a black woman born in America—whose origin is Afrika.

Michael, I see you!
In the Russian winter.
The lights in your quick, smart eyes
are dancing with snow-sparkle.
You ski; you skate over the ice.
In your heart you shout
"I *breathe!* I am *alive!*
My body is moving!
My body knows life is good and my body responds!
I am a straight response, a Reverence!
And I love all the people in the world!"

Michael—
I see you in the woods of Moscow and Kiev,
affectionate with deer and branch and flower.

Young Russia!
You are an affectionate spirit,
with arms stretched out to
life and love and truth and Celebration,
with arms stretched out to
what is clean and kind.

Thursday, July 29, 1982, Kiev
(With sincere respect and admiration
for one of the finest young men I ever met.)

From Michael, Christmas, 1982—a beautiful card showing St. Basil's with Santa Claus in a sleigh before it:

Dear Gwendolyn:

I hope very much that you haven't forgotten me. I want to wish you and yours the best of everything for 1983. I treasure evergreen memories of our meeting and your poem. I'll be happy to meet you again some day. Meanwhile, my warmest regards and friendly love.

Always, Misha

Wuanda M. T. Walls

The Mid-Morning Crowd

HOURS BEFORE I REACHED THE BEACH-FRONT CAFÉ, I KNEW I WANTED SOLITUDE. My vacation was coming to an end, and I needed to savor the final hours alone. I placed my paraphernalia on top of the smooth mahogany table and into the chairs to send a clear signal to the charming, fast-talking, beach Casanovas, now clearly aware of my presence, caballing and throwing me kisses. I made myself comfortable and began writing my last postcards as the sound of rhythmic *cumbia* music nudged my fingers.

My first trip to South America had surpassed all my expectations. If I had listened to a few nay-sayers I would never have experienced the magnificence of the Andes, the beautiful and historic coastal cities endowed with African heritage, the overwhelming hospitality of the people, and the sense of peace, freedom, and empowerment I had found as a black woman traveling alone.

I had come to Santa Marta, Colombia, because a shopkeeper in Cartagena told me the city was fringed by deep-water bays, coves, and fjords with a spectacular backdrop graced by the snow-covered peaks of the Sierra Nevada. "In addition," she said proudly, "it is the oldest city on South American soil."

The waiter pulled himself away from the men and took my order. Fifteen minutes later, when I saw him approaching with my juice—my only request—I repressed my impulse to look at my watch. "Ah, life in the tropics," I murmured as he walked away. I sipped, delighting in the taste of my favorite tropical drink, tamarind juice.

Then, just as I had expected, I heard, *"Con permiso, Señorita."* I refused to look up, determined to hold claim to my private table, although I knew that that is an American value, and here available public seating is for everyone. Before he had time to speak again, I breathed deeply. Slowly, I removed my packages and newspapers from the chairs and looked into the kind, limpid eyes of an elderly gentleman. Tall, lean, unshaven, and somewhat weary looking, he carried a sack tied to a walking stick. In his tattered cutoff trousers, faded shirt, and old leather sandals, he didn't look much like Don Juan poised to romance me. The old gent graciously extended his hand as he sat down across from me and said, *"Gracias."*

Lowering my eyes beneath the hold of his calm gaze, I wondered if he was homeless, a vagabond, or a lonely beachcomber prompted by curiosity to disturb me. The situation was awkward. I really didn't know whether to politely move to another table or just remain silent. I glanced at the waiter who was on guard, ready to shoo the old fellow away. Amused, the other men waited for my plea but my face assumed a no-rescue expression.

We sat in silence for several minutes. I stared at the shimmering sea, then glanced at him trying to see behind his shabby appearance. While I was observing him I heard the voices of my ancestors, my elders, my grandparents. "Never judge a book by its cover." "Do unto others as you would have them do unto you." "Be kind to your elders."

He stood as if to leave and I felt shamed. I knew he had read my first, selfish thoughts. He begged my pardon and headed for the restroom. When he returned looking vivified and hopeful, I smiled genuinely, for my heart had opened to accept him.

"You're a tourist," he said offhandedly as he looked at my postcards.

"Sí," I replied.

He continued speaking in English. "Where are you from, *Señorita?"*

I deliberately ignored his question, and asked, "Where did you learn English?"

"I learned English as a result of my travels around the world, first as a student, then as a revolutionary, merchant seaman, gypsy, and seeker of knowledge."

Quite a character, I thought. His travels made my trips to a few far-flung places seem namby-pamby. His countenance enlivened and the sparkle in his eye conveyed an aristocratic distinction. Although he was sixty or perhaps seventy, his body was virile, and his skin bronzed and healthy, and now that I looked more closely, I could see that his face was vibrant, almost handsome.

Señor Raul admitted that he had at first thought I was from Jamaica but was hoping I was from the States because he had deep respect for Dr. King and the plight of African Americans. He spoke about how the civil rights movement impacted the political consciousness of people of African descent in Latin America.

When the waiter reappeared, Señor Raul asked if I was ready for lunch. He didn't give me time to answer but turned to the waiter and ordered all my favorite things: tamarind juice, crab patties served with fluffy rice cooked in coconut milk, fried plantains, and a salad topped with beets. Astonished, I rocked in my chair in disbelief, thinking he must be a psychic. The ice was definitely broken. Señor Raul seemed to delight in my company, and I found in his, a kindness and wisdom without any pretense.

Our conversation begin to flow effortlessly. When he asked why I chose to visit South America, I told him my story. "For the past several years my dear friends, Joan and David, along with their three children, spent their Christmas holidays in Venezuela and Colombia. Their tales about the wonderful people, the food, the music, and the beauty of the land intrigued me. Being of African ancestry they were captivated by the culture. Their fascination sparked my desire to visit. After I saved enough money, I made my reservations." Smiling like a cherub, I sat back in the rocker, touched by the sincerity of his interest.

> *O*nce I heard an African American woman who had not seen much more than her hometown ask my mother (who would leave the country any chance she got, even if it was just for a weekend in Canada): "How is it that you can afford so many trips?" My mother answered, "That leather you are wearing from head to toe could have bought you three trips; you just have to prioritize." My mother, being of the bourgeoisie in Haiti, did not settle for just wearing anything herself. However, if she had to choose between adding another Gucci bag to her collection, or a trip to Belgium, she would pick Belgium, just as I would.
>
> —Sandrine Desamours, "To Travel Is to Live"

"Tell me, what are your impressions? Do you find this to be a poor, dangerous country?"

Without thinking, I answered, "No, I feel very safe here. There is poverty in every place I have visited, including my own country, reputed to be the richest in the world. For me, the beauty here lies in the ancient land and the rich and complex history of the people, which is very similar to that of my own country. Just as in the U.S., the indigenous peoples were here first, then the Europeans came, conquering and bringing the Africans.

"Everyone I have met here has embraced me with open arms. I have been accepted as a fellow human being. I've loved that no one has been concerned with my status. No one has asked what I do for a living, what type of car I drive, or what schools I attended. None of that superficial stuff. They have been concerned only with my happiness and welfare and have gone out of their way to help me to understand their culture and language and to make me feel at home in their country."

I paused, reflecting for a moment, and ended with, "I definitely believe I've been here before. It is a comforting feeling. I'm really so thankful for this experience."

Señor Raul was pleased. "How insightful you are. How courageous and beautiful," he said, smiling broadly.

At that moment, strikingly beautiful women the color of dark sweet chocolate passed by, laughing. They were balancing large baskets on their heads filled with a cornucopia of delights. Warmed by the heat of the Latin sun the fruit exuded pungent, intoxicating aromas. The scene took hold and led me to recall my first encounter with Colombia's tropical scents, which blended exotic fruits (*pomarrosa, nispero, maracuya, mamey,* and *curuba*) with fragrant flowering trees and flowers. Enthralled, I allowed my reverie to continue with memories of my culinary adventures: *Sancocho,* the national dish (a stew filled with potatoes, *yuca, ñame,* chunks of corn on the cob, plantains, and pieces of meat and seafood); delicious street fare, from corn griddlecakes called *arepas* to chitlins—yes indeed, fried pork rinds called *chicarrones*—and incredible mouth-watering pastries.

Señor Raul remained silent, watching the men play dominoes, aware that they were keeping their glances and comments in check. When my thoughts returned to the present I quizzed him about his life. His words tumbled out. He was born in Peru to middle-class parents in a secure and happy home. As a teenager he traveled throughout Central and South America, then on to Europe to attend a university in Spain. Later, he lived in France and South Africa, and traveled back to South America by way of the Indian Ocean to India and Asia. He spoke many languages, including some I had never heard of. Intrigued, I let him chatter.

He didn't mention a wife or children, and I wondered if that meant that he had refused to allow a family to complicate his life or if he had suffered countless heartbreaks. I immediately thought about my own life and my yearning for travel. I knew that travel provided me with opportunities to embrace new faces and breathtaking landscapes/seascapes, and to escape from the mundane responsibilities and commitments of daily life. And that was a blessing. And then, of course, there were the romantic escapades: a successful Colombian businessman who attracted me with his wit, generosity, elegant style, and sensitivity, and the scion of a publishing house with heart-rending tales and audacious schemes.

The sound of his rocker broke my thought. "The world never sees behind appearances," Señor Raul commented casually, looking at me. When he said, *cric,* I knew it was storytelling time and replied, *crac.*

"Once upon a time there was," said Señor Raul, pausing to check my interest level, "a fisherman who lived in a village not far from this town. Nothing could keep him from the sea. Everyday before dawn he prepared his nets, and he always returned with enough fish for everyone in his village.

"One day a businessman from town was waiting for him when he returned with his catch. He greeted him, then asked, 'Do you fish every day?'

"Beaming, the fisherman exclaimed, 'Yes, I'm a fisherman. This is my life!'

"Hardly impressed, the businessman inspected his bounty. 'What do you do with all the fish?'

"The fisherman answered promptly, 'I give the fish to the sick, those who work in town and don't have time to fish, such as yourself, and at times to the lazy ones.'

"The businessman shook his head in disbelief. 'Why don't you sell your fish in town at the market?'

"Puzzled, the fisherman said, 'Why should I do that?'

"By this time, the businessman was frustrated but kept his cool. 'Because you could make lots of money and do wonders for your family.'

"Listening without listening, the fisherman whistled as he separated his catch. Finally, he asked flatly, 'What do you mean?'

"Happy with his question, the businessman squatted near his boat. 'For starters, you could leave this village, build your family a nice home with electricity, running water, all the conveniences of the modern world, and send your children to school. In other words, you could really live like a king.'

"Frowning, the fisherman looked directly into the eyes of the businessman and said, 'After I have done all those things, tell me *Señor*, what else would be left to do?'

"Not wanting to sound impatient and not wanting to offend the fisherman, the businessman joked, 'Oh, don't be foolish. You could do whatever you want.'

"The fisherman sat down, touched by his blind persistence. But he felt sorry for the man, knowing he had not convinced him. 'Tell me what,' demanded the fisherman, teasing.

"'You could travel, see the world, buy a Mercedes, buy a villa,' the businessman blurted.

"As he gathered his nets the fisherman remained aloof and amused. Miffed by his attitude the businessman kicked at the sand, and said, 'Listen, after you have done everything for your wife and children, traveled and enjoyed life's pleasures you could do whatever you want; take it easy, live it up, or fish all day.'

"With a glint in his eye, the fisherman chuckled and said, '*Señor*, that's just what I'm doing now!'"

I laughed as I watched Señor Raul full of vigor and whimsy observe the revelation that was blossoming on my face. Moments later he expounded, "So, you see, insightful one, people here are basically content with life, they enjoy the simple things, behold the beauty, accept the sorrows, and revel in the grandeur of it all. Like the businessman, I believe people in your country oftentimes are too busy to enjoy life, grasping for more ephemeral things. Looking for utopia, they go around the barn to get back to where we are."

I nodded in agreement, but was tickled because I thought the moral of the story was "never judge a book by its cover."

Constance García-Barrio

A Homegirl Hits Beijing

"Take a solo trip like that," my girlfriend said, "and you'll never come back."

"Drug dealers work the corner a block from my house," I said. "I could catch a bullet from a deal gone sour and never come back from the grocery store."

"You're crazy."

"Insanity and seventeen-hundred dollars will get me to Beijing."

I cooked austerity meals to save the seventeen-hundred dollars. The insanity came ready-made. In 1991 my son, then sixteen, had me on an adrenaline seesaw. His grades rollercoastered. Our fights, when he stayed out late, topped ten on the Richter scale. Beijing was as far as I could get from him without leaving the planet. My husband, calmer about our son's antics, agreed that I needed a break.

Truth to tell, there was more to it than that. I teach Spanish at West Chester University, twenty miles from my Philadelphia home. Eager to learn a non-Western language, I studied Mandarin at West Chester—three years' worth. The time had come to take the plunge. The Beijing Languages Institute (BLI) offered a month-long intensive course during the month of June. I graded my students' finals and hopped the plane.

After twenty-six hours in transit, I reached Beijing. I'd written to BLI, asking to be picked up at the airport. Other passengers from my Air China flight jostled me as I craned my neck, looking for someone holding a sign with my name on it. After much searching, I gave up. It was nearly midnight. I had no Chinese money. Everything was in characters, and I understood every fourth or fifth one. I didn't know a soul in the place. I was dead-tired and a little scared. Would people understand me when I spoke? Had my teacher urged me to make this trip too soon?

I found one currency exchange booth still open. When I told the women there that I wanted to change a hundred dollars, she understood me with no trouble. Emboldened by this success, I asked what a fair price was for a cab ride from the airport to BLI. She told me twenty dollars, and a pack of American cigarettes as a tip, if the service was good. I'd been advised to take a couple of cartons of Marlboros and some jars of instant coffee, so I was ready.

The ride from the airport took me headlong into one of China's greatest political dilemmas. "Why are the police stopping cars?" I asked the cab driver as he slowed down at a checkpoint.

"Today is June first," he said. "The anniversary of Tiananmen Square is coming up. The government doesn't want trouble."

"It was awful those students were killed."

"Yes. A very sad thing."

After fifty minutes and one more checkpoint, we reached BLI. Despite the strange bed, I slept like a rock. I awoke the next morning to the voice of a *tai qi* teacher outside my window. From my dorm room, I saw about sixty Chinese people of all ages doing the slow, graceful movements of this exercise. I dressed and went downstairs to watch.

The Chinese fascinated me from the start, and so did BLI's four-hundred-plus students. They came from all over the world. One of my classmates, an Italian girl, was learning Mandarin for a career in diplomacy. A Nigerian man wanted enough Mandarin to study traditional Chinese medicine at Beijing University.

I lived in Building Ten, a four-floor concrete box. Everyone got clean sheets and a roll of toilet paper every ten days. We had hot water four evenings a week. For eighty-nine dollars a month, I couldn't kick. Classes ran from eight in the morning until noon. Teacher Ma, a plump, lively man, had us sing Mandarin tones each morning. "Bring a thermos of green tea," he said, "to soothe your throat." He spoke nothing but Mandarin, wrote nothing but characters. For me, memorizing characters exacts flesh and blood. Between classes, homework, and private tutoring (two dollars for ninety minutes), I studied nine hours daily.

The cafeteria served Chinese and Western food, but I hadn't come to China for cheeseburgers. Most mornings I paid ten cents for a *youbingr*, a large, flat, circular bread with a light texture and doughnutlike taste. Two more cents got me a tablespoon of hawthorn preserves. A glass of green tea cost one cent. Sometimes I went to the Muslim dining room upstairs. It served no pork. There I got a quiet meal and an inside view of Middle Eastern politics.

The infirmary, too, offered both Eastern and Western options. I'd sprained my ankle before leaving home. When I reached BLI my ankle was slightly swollen. The second day, it had ballooned. The third day, I saw blood under the skin. Dr. Tang took an X-ray. "It's the muscle," he said. "You don't need medication."

"Then what?"

"Massages."

"For how much?"

Dr. Tang charged fifteen *kuai*, about three dollars, for thirty-minute deep-muscle massages. After a week of them, my ankle was fine.

Located on Beijing's outskirts, BLI is a suburban island complete with stores, tennis courts, a track, a bank, a post office, and a pool. All you could need. But I felt marooned there, distanced from China's people. I decided to hit the road.

A hard-seat train ticket in China gets you a wooden seat, a cheap fare, and pore-to-pore contact with the Chinese. On a 220-mile ride from Beijing to Cheng De, I saw farm wives open huge bundles of food. People took out tin cups for the green tea served free in hard-seat coaches. Vendors hawked snacks. People threw garbage on the floor. A voice on the loudspeaker asked people not to let their children urinate on the floor.

Halfway to Cheng De, I became the car's main attraction when a twenty-year-old medical student sat beside me.

"How old are you?" she asked.

"Forty-four."

"Not bad for forty-four," said the woman across the isle.

The medical student felt my Afro and giggled. People stood up and peeked at me.

"You have long legs," she said.

"It runs in my family. My father was six foot, six inches."

A collective gasp came from overhead. Other passengers had gathered for a narrated close-up of a rare sight: a black American woman riding hard-seat. The Far East was meeting West Philly. After that ride, Cheng De's exquisite temples seemed anticlimactic.

I met my Waterloo the next weekend. I'd taken a train to Tian Jin, an hour south of Beijing. I'd heard of the city's famous Culture Street and Food Street. I browsed in the Culture Street's bookstores and handicraft shops then, hungry, went to the Food Street. It had restaurants both swank and shabby. I went in a decent-looking one. When they saw me, the two hundred people who'd been lunching, put down their chopsticks and stared at me. They seemed neither hostile nor condescending but, rather, eager to inspect the novelty that had wandered into their midst. Still, as the object of such intense interest, I wanted to evaporate. Finally, a young couple invited me to sit with them and their eight-month-old baby.

"Are you from Africa?" the man asked me.

"The U.S."

"What are you doing in China?"

"Studying at BLI," I said, giving him the short version of the answer. I didn't have the vocabulary, or the inclination, to explain that I was getting a breather from home, and opening another window on the world for myself by learning a language spoken by a billion people. I could have added that I wanted to see if, in middle age, I could come to the edge of the cliff and leap.

Toward the end of June, I cut class and took a six-day solo trip southeast to Shanghai, Suzhou, and Hangzhou. Shanghai, with its traffic and pickpockets, could have been Mexico City or Manhattan. Suzhou held surprises. After an argument with the manager at a nice, new hotel, I wound up in a six-dollar-a-night room whose amenities included a spittoon, a small black-and-white TV, and three large squares of toilet paper. Like other guests, I didn't have a room key. Whenever I returned from shopping or sightseeing, I asked the staff person on my floor to let me in. Still, give the devil his due. I was the only foreigner in the hotel, and the staff bent over backward for me.

En route to a famous temple the next day, I saw the many canals for which Suzhou is called the Venice of China. Barges hauled everything from coal to produce. Wandering one temple's gardens, I saw barefoot Chinese tourists stepping up and down on pebbles embedded in the ground.

"Why are they doing that?" I asked the group leader.

"It's like getting a massage," he said, massaging my left shoulder a moment to be sure I understood.

"I see."

The trim, twenty-something tour guide looked around, saw no foreigners near me, and asked, "Are you alone?"

"Yes."

"Would you like to join us?" When the tour ended, I had tea in a private garden with the others.

I doubt I would have had such invitations if I hadn't been alone. I liked the flexibility and surprises that traveling alone brought me, though I had to stay vigilant. I never changed money on the street despite the attractive rates. (I could end up with counterfeit money, BLI students had warned me.) I'm sure I paid more than the Chinese would have for clothes and fruit in marketplaces, but that was a small price to pay for my independence.

On the other hand, I never feared for my safety in China. I felt as if I had an angel with me. Still, I paid great attention not only to what people said, but also to their gestures. I scrutinized body language because I didn't understand every word of the spoken language; sometimes the hours of alertness

In Tibet I visited the Dalai Lama's palace, the Potala, by far the most amazing architectural wonder I have ever seen. Built from 700 to 1700 it rivals any castle in Europe. It's the quintessential vision of Shangri-La. It broke my heart to see the Chinese government making money on tourism here while the Dalai Lama is in exile in India. The people miss him and keep the faith through wearing traditional clothes, the main symbol of resistance. Yet in the courtyard of the holiest places, young Tibetan boys perform break dancing routines to Chinese pop music. And high upon the desolate Tibetan plane a few miles from the highest mountains in the world I ran into a Japanese traveler wearing a Malcolm X hat.

—Sylvia Harris Woodard,
"Postcards from the Global Village"

wore me out. In my travels, I found that foreigners, black and white, greeted me warmly—we were all outsiders for the Chinese. You rated with BLI students and faculty if you had enough Chinese to travel on your own. I loved that taste of equality.

On the last day of class, we received certificates. I was pleased, but I valued the trip's intangibles more. I'd jumped in, talked with people, had bizarre, exhilarating excursions. When I returned to Philadelphia, my son looked at me with new respect. Not a bad solo trip a for someone my age, he said. He'd enjoyed telling people, "Could you call back? My mom's in China." He's matured since my trip. I've mellowed, too. The last time I talked about China over dinner, I surprised myself by asking him, "How about us doing China together?"

Dawn Comer

A Black Broad Abroad

My friends thought I was crazy. An African American woman going to Italy alone, to spend Carnival in Venice. "Oh, the Italian men are horrible. They'll chase you down the street and pinch your butt," warned one friend. "They kidnap women traveling alone and sell them into prostitution rings. Black women are considered exotic, so be careful," another cautioned. Taking their warnings with a grain of salt, I packed my bags and boarded a plane for Italy.

I hadn't traveled alone since college, but I fondly remembered my last solo trip—the freedom to go where I pleased, when I pleased, the ease at meeting other solo travelers, and the daily feelings of accomplishment over the little things, like successfully navigating the streets or conquering a dinner menu written in a foreign tongue. I couldn't wait to explore Italy on my own.

I don't speak Italian, and I had no hotel reservations other than for my first few nights in Venice. After that, I wanted to travel at will, making reservations as I went. I knew I wanted to see Rome, and as a college theater major, I remembered reading about Verona, Padua, and Mantua in Shakespeare, so I thought I might tour those cities as well. With my thirty-second birthday rapidly approaching, and being single, childless, and between jobs, I was sure that this would be the only time in the next couple of years that I could travel extensively on my own. It was an opportunity I was not going to miss.

As a result of late planes, stopovers, and lost luggage, I arrived in Venice thirty-three hours after leaving Los Angeles. I was so exhausted—my body in time zone hell—that my eyes watered from the moment I landed until the next day. But when I stepped off the *vaporetto* (the Venetian version of a city bus, except it's a boat) at the Piazza San Marco, the festivities were in full swing, and I could feel my body thrill to the sights, sounds and smells.

Carnival in Venice, I was to discover, is very different from Mardi Gras in New Orleans or Carnival in Brazil. Pushing crowds, drunkenness, and rowdy behavior are the exception, not the norm. It was like an elegant pageant where locals and tourists alike dress in elaborate costumes and masks, parade through the city, and pose for photographers, entertaining the crowds. I took seventy-five photos my first day. The costumes range from Renaissance characters in hoop skirts and white wigs to representations from Greek mythology or Italian folklore. Historically, the masks were worn by nobility so that they could walk the streets unrecognized, behaving in ways that were otherwise unacceptable in the proper society of their time. Most of the costumes were magnificent. Only one young man, a white American, was tasteless enough to dress as his idea of an African native, complete with black face, Afro wig, and a white plastic bone piercing his nose.

I saw three Senegalese street vendors and many Japanese people in large tour groups, but as far as I could tell, I was the only African American woman in Venice, and I stood out in the crowds. As I walked the foot paths and bridges of the city, Venetians would approach me and in either Italian or broken English, say, "I saw you on the Rialto Bridge yesterday," or "You were by the

A bad hair day that I was determined to straighten out led to the ship fire. I had left the U.S. with my hair in croquignole curls, the ubiquitous hair style worn by African American women in those years, the 1950s. The hair was pressed straight with a heated metal comb, then tiny, tight curls were inserted all over the head with a hot curling iron. If you wanted your hair to remain straightened longer than the usual two weeks, the curls were left untouched. Otherwise, they were brushed out and the hair was styled.

I had let my curls "set" and they lasted a long while. But eventually sweltering heat, ocean spray, and time took their toll. My hair "went back." However, with my straightening comb and a can of Sterno, I was prepared. On a cruise ship sailing from Venice to Egypt, I lit the Sterno can, stuck the comb in the flame, and began straightening my hair. When the fuel—largely alcohol—ran low, I added booze to the can. With the first drop, a long tongue of fire exploded up and out from the can, starting plum-sized fires all over the place—the walls, the mirror, the sink, the counter, even the ceiling! I gasped, horrified, then ran around the cabin smothering fires with my hand, a towel, whatever it took. God was with me and those unsuspecting travelers aboard that ocean liner that day.

—Marian E. Barnes with B.J. Taylor

Church of San Polo this morning, do you remember me?" It was easy for them to remember me, I was the only black woman in town. Often, they assumed I was Brazilian, Mexican, or from Great Britain. When I corrected them, they'd give me a surprised look and say, "Welcome to Carnival!"

Despite my friends' warnings, my encounters with Italian men were delightfully charming. Not once was I the recipient of a rude cat call or butt grabbing. I admit that when I started the trip, I made a point of dressing down, wearing no make up and putting on my New York face, ("Don't mess with me, I'm serious"). I wanted to appear strong, independent, capable of handling anything. Men ignored me. But the tough-cookie act is tiring, and after a few days, I lowered my guard. One night, I dressed in fancy duds, did my hair, put on lipstick, and suddenly, things changed. Men smiled as I passed on the street. They gave friendly waves from passing gondolas. I liked the attention. I began to realize that I could take care of myself, be independent and capable, and still interact and enjoy being on my own in Italy. When I went to the world famous Harry's Bar for a taste of their fabled drink, the Bellini (champagne and fresh peaches blended together), it seemed as if all of the waiters in the restaurant were waiting on my table. They rushed to help me with my coat, and when I left, one followed me out and said, "My compliments, you are very beautiful."

Other times, drinks would arrive at my dinner table. A sparkling wine called Brachetto was sent several times by waiters. A tumbler of Grappa (an after-dinner liqueur) was sent by an admiring customer at another table. Never did these men follow up their offerings with an attempt to join me at my table or talk to me. They would just raise their glass in salute, smile, nod, or blow a kiss. They wanted nothing more than to be kind to a stranger abroad. At one restaurant, after several free glasses of Bruchetto had been consumed, I spent the evening talking Latin music and American action movies with the waiters as they cleaned up.

My last night in Venice, I became overwhelmed by the crowds in San Marco Square, so I walked down to the waterfront to be alone. Venice has about a hundred thousand people living there, no cars, bikes, or other vehicles, and violent crime is almost nonexistent except for an occasional crime of passion. So at night, I felt safe walking through the narrow paths and back alleys of the city alone. As I stood on the dark dock and looked across the lagoon at the Lido, (an island across from Venice and the setting for Thomas Mann's book, *Death in Venice*), a peaceful calm came over me. I'm glad I came alone to Italy, I thought to myself. Just as a child is excited every time she learns a new task, at this time in my life, I needed that same sense of accomplishment at being able to do something new. I needed to take this trip on my own. However, when I looked up and saw ten figures wearing costumes and masks surrounding me, my friends' warnings screamed in my ears. I was certain I'd be mugged, kidnapped, or worse. I clung to my purse. I tried to back away, but they were on three sides and my back was to the canal. As they were closing in, I thought about jumping in the water. I started to panic as they reached for my arms, my shoulders, my waist, until I heard them start to giggle. One of them pulled out a camera. They wanted me to pose with them for a photograph. I started to laugh. The masked man snapped his camera. Then I gave him mine to take another picture.

Yes, the world *can* be dangerous. We all read the papers, live in the neighborhoods. We see and hear about tragedy every day. But for me, the tragedy would be in not going out and exploring the world. Traveling to Italy alone reinforced my belief in my own ability to make my way through life. And if I hadn't been alone, I never would have been ambushed by Carnival revelers in search of a picture with a black broad abroad.

*O*ne of the great benefits of being one of the relatively few soul sisters in this part of the world is being able to see and party with many of the African American groups that come abroad. Thus far in my career as an international groupette, I've seen the Pointer Sisters, the Commodores, M.C. Hammer, Maze, McCoy Tyner, Ornette Coleman, the Dazz Band (remember them?), Taj Mahal, and the Chicago Blues Festival. The best thing about these wonderful concerts, aside from their being free, is that the artists are usually as happy to see me as I am to see them. Everybody gets lonely out on the road and being in a foreign country intensifies that need to see a familiar face from home. Many times I am the only personal guest for the whole band. My friends in France are always surprised at the solidarity and the feeling of being a part of the same family that most blacks feel. I am always welcomed and made to feel a part of the group and usually—no matter how big a star or how well traveled—they are impressed and proud of me, proud that I'm out here more or less on my own following my dreams.

I've said many an early-morning teary-eyed goodbye. Hurried hugs and promises (that usually go unkept) to keep in touch with people who felt almost like family for an all too brief twenty-four to forty-eight hours. After hot nights out on the town like these, returning back to my normally quiet and unglamorous life isn't easy. One night in Paris, a few years back, after having eaten at a wonderful restaurant with some of the Commodores, we went onto the Keur Samba, one of the most chic discos in Paris. After dancing the night away, my girlfriend and I headed on back to her place, which was a six-story walkup. How we laughed and laughed as we huffed and puffed at first walking and then practically crawling up those stairs. We laughed so hard that we had to stop and rest several times. And as we stretched out our long tired bodies on her tiny little twin bed, we literally howled with delight at the thought of them seeing us like that. What a life!!

—Carol McGruder, "Too Legit"

Viki Radden

Japan in My Dreams

I'M OBSESSED WITH JAPAN. IT STARTED WHEN, AS A CHILD, MY FATHER TOLD ME thrilling stories about the three years he lived there as a medic in a segregated unit in the United States Occupation Army. When he spoke of Japan, love and longing resonated in his voice. I loved these stories, most of which were about how the Japanese people treated him kindly.

What I learned as an adult, however, about Japanese people's dislike for blacks, did not jibe with my father's stories of loving kindness. I had to go to Japan and find out for myself. Of course, I also needed to see the place I'd heard so much about and that had occupied such an important place in my childhood imagination. I ended up living in Japan for more than three years, and I still dream of returning.

My first home in Japan was Yanai, a small town on the Pacific Coast about two hours west of Hiroshima, where I visited Japanese junior high schools, assisting the Japanese teachers of English. Most of the schools were on small islands, lush with the scenery that covered so much of the Japanese countryside: forests of bamboo and pine, laced with oak and cherry. There were rice paddies everywhere. In autumn, when the leaves turned, and in the spring, at cherry blossom time, the forest was particularly beautiful. I grew accustomed to the sight of mountains (85 percent of Japan's land is mountainous) dotted with Shinto shrines and Buddhist temples, some hundreds of years old, and many perched on daunting hillsides or nestled near waterfalls.

The islanders grew *mikan*, mandarin oranges, a delicacy I often received as a thank you gift from a school. Most of the people I met had been born and raised on their islands and few had ventured far from there. The children went fishing, biking, or checked their octopus traps when they got home from school, unlike in the big cities where children played video games when they got home from school. The islanders were amazed when I told them I'd been to Tokyo. They told me they were afraid to go to there, afraid they'd get lost trying to negotiate abominations like subways and trains.

However, young people are flocking to the big cities and many islands are being left with few inhabitants but the elderly. I felt sad and a bit awed to realize that I was witnessing the last of a way of life. At one school I visited, there were only three students in a classroom of once-occupied desks.

> *T*he world is full of so many wonderful places for us to discover, don't waste time! Don't sit around and wait. Be bold! Be adventurous, even if you have to go alone. I've traveled all over the world alone, and loved it. Whatever you do, don't ever think you're too young or too old or that you don't have enough money.
>
> —Sandrine Desamours,
> "To Travel Is to Live"

And kindness, exactly what I remembered so well from my father's stories, was what I found here. Even at the demoralized three-student-school, everyone, from the principal, to the janitor, to the last student, welcomed me warmly. They hosted a special lunch for me at the local inn (where I enjoyed the freshest fish I'd ever tasted) and gave me gifts. Once I boarded the ship back to Yanai, they stood at the shore and waved until I could no longer see their faces.

On another island, Iwaishima, on a blustery rainy day, the school principal rushed down the hill to the inn where I was staying before my boat sailed for home. The seas were rough; he wanted me to have a special seasick medicine.

Often as a farewell, school children would sing me songs as they waved goodbye. After I had stayed on an island several times, the islanders would grow comfortable with me. We'd eat mandarin oranges and talk in my room. I'd read their tarot cards. When I left, they gave me gifts they had made by hand: dolls and woven straw sandals.

In my second home, Kobe, a cosmopolitan city of one and a half million on the outskirts of Osaka, I found Japanese people who were just as kind. The people in my apartment complex worried about me and looked out for me. When my kitchen sink clogged, a panic ensued; my frantic neighbors scurried up and down the stairs, banging on apartment doors, searching for a plunger. When I had a horrible case of bronchitis in the suffocating heat of August, my upstairs neighbor, who had a lovely organic garden on the steep hillside next to our building, helped nurse me back to health. She brought me iced *somen* noodles, herb tea for my cough, and an ice pack for my throbbing head.

Nevertheless, the racism I was expecting was just as easy to find. Soon after I arrived, a justice minister compared black Americans to Shinjuku's (Tokyo's foremost red light district) prostitutes, saying how blacks had forced "good" (meaning white) people from their homes and neighborhoods, just as prostitutes were forcing the "good" businesses out of Shinjuku. And during much of the time I was there, Japan was absorbed in a fascination with "Little Black Sambo." Red-lipped Sambos greeted me everywhere, on T-shirts, key chains, and in coffee shop windows.

I was furious and deeply hurt whenever I rubbed up against Japanese racism. I'd left America, where blacks are thought of as criminals and blights on society, and there, in Japan, was the same attitude. I had the feeling that much of Japan's racism could be traced to the growing influence of U.S. culture there, especially through television and movies.

At first, when people stared at me and children pointed and laughed, I interpreted their behavior as an expression of racism. *What you got to stare at, huh?* It was a knee-jerk reaction, based on what staring meant at home. With time, however, I was able to see the situation in its complexity. This was not the U.S.; it was a country that I knew very little about and, therefore, my assumptions were not always correct. As I learned more about Japan and woke up to the fact that I was a foreigner there, I stopped lumping everything disagreeable that happened to me into the category of racism (while still able to see clearly the racism that *did* exist). Japan is a very homogenous country and many people, I eventually learned, particularly in the islands, had never before seen a black woman. This understanding put my expectation to be treated like "one of the girls" in perspective.

One Sunday morning, after I'd been living in Japan for almost a year, I was shopping in Yanai's largest department store. I was browsing the aisles leisurely, when I happened upon a full-length mirror and caught a glimpse of myself. I gasped aloud. Standing there, taking in my own reflection, I realized why I elicited stares. A large black woman, I looked like a person from someplace the Japanese couldn't even imagine going.

"Viki," I said to myself in the mirror, "no wonder people stare at you. If I saw you walking down the street, I'd stare at you too!" Later, I began to notice that, especially in the countryside, giggling, pointing, and the like, was directed at other foreigners as well. And as I grew to understand the culture better, I understood that it was not an expression of antagonism.

I loved traveling around Japan, catching glimpses that were breathtaking in their beauty: a Shinto priest in black robes, performing a baby blessing ceremony at the local shrine; young women in ornate silk kimonos on Coming of Age day; the faithful, chanting prayers and burning incense at Kuramedera temple in the mountains of Kyoto; blood-red maple leaves in autumn; farmers in straw hats, threshing rice in August; white egrets, standing as if on stilts in green rice paddies.

But the trip that's remained most vividly alive in my memory was an ordinary boat ride. I go back to those two days often in my memory because they gave me the special gift that traveling can offer: a heightened sense of each waking hour.

I was en route from Kyushu, southern Japan, to Tokyo. The deck hands charged up the machines that hoist the giant anchors, the flag of Japan rippled in the wind and, precisely on time, we set off for Tokyo. There were only three other passengers—a young couple who were holding hands (a very unusual sight in Japan) and a very attractive young Japanese man, about twenty-two, wearing a pair of tight Levis and black motorcycle boots—and we all stood on deck taking in the blissfully warm evening.

The ship rocked on the water like a baby's bassinet and soon the gentleness of the waves enticed me into a catnap. I was traveling "*tatami class*,"—the cheapest section—one huge room divided into sleeping areas for eight with large carpeted areas raised off the floor in lieu of beds. I rented two blankets, one for underneath me and one for on top, and I lay down, alone in my section. Solitude is rare in this overcrowded country; I desperately needed it and I experienced it like a blessing. I fell asleep within minutes.

I woke refreshed and walked on deck with an excited feeling of expectation: I knew there would be a full moon. I don't know if the moon shines so brightly over all of Asia, but I could see the two great land masses we were traveling between: off the port, the western shores of the island of Shikoku; to the starboard side the island of Kyushu. The water was still and black. The sparkling surface of the water, as far as I could see, glistened in the moonlight. There were no waves. I stood mesmerized, watching the crease in the water our ship made, the path of white foam in its wake eventually disappearing, leaving the sea as calm as before. The warm air was heavy with the smell of the sea.

I sat on the deck, bathed in moonlight, until the ship's gentle rhythm again made me sleepy, and I headed back inside to my makeshift bed. On the way in I noticed the young couple, sleeping close together, fully clothed, huddled under a single blanket. I was startled and touched by their innocence and tenderness. Two people in love is a wonderful sight anywhere, but especially in Japan, where men and women are hardly seen in each other's company, much less locked in an embrace.

The sun woke me early and I read for hours, wishing I could read all day, this day and every day. Later, I walked around and sat for a while on the lower deck in the bright sunlight. I could see almost the entire ship, including the upper deck, where the young man with the tight jeans and motorcycle boots was sitting. He looked relaxed; he must not be from Tokyo, I thought to myself. He smiled and waved at me. Soon he was sitting beside me on the bench, looking directly at me.

"Hello," he said. "Aren't you lonely?"

His question threw me off balance but I answered honestly.

"Yes," I told him. "I am lonely."

"May I sit here and talk with you?" he asked politely.

"Please."

"I have wanted to talk to you since I first saw you yesterday night. But I was afraid because my English is not so good."

"Your English is very good." I told him. "Thank you for coming up and talking to me. I'm glad to have someone to talk with."

His name was Jun; he was twenty-one, a law student, and he was beautiful. He was from Kyushu, and this was only the third time he'd been to Tokyo. He had no hesitancy telling me how much he disliked it. "In Tokyo, people walk too fast," he explained.

> If you travel alone, you learn to have faith in your ability to deal with obstacles.
>
> —Tonya Pendleton, "Wanderlust"

Jun's eyes were very dark and they sparkled. He looked right at me when he talked. He sighed when I told him I was from San Francisco.

"I want to visit America very much, but I am afraid I don't speak English well enough and I will get lost. This is the first time I can speak English with real American."

Jun had no idea how attractive he was, or how much I was flustered by talking to him. He told me about his family, about his life in small-town Kyushu. He had years left in school, but he hoped he could travel after he graduated. How must it be to feel so driven to find a job, as most young Japanese men are? Jun went to the school they call "Todai," which had the reputation of being the best school in Japan. I couldn't imagine the pressure he had to go through to get there. If he had scars, they didn't show. He looked young and unjaded.

We talked all afternoon, then went upstairs to the restaurant. Neither of us had much money but we were both hungry and tired of cold sandwiches.

I asked Jun what the small breaded items were. "Is it fish?" I said, pointing at the plastic display plate.

He smiled and scratched his head. "It is not fish, but it is from the sea." It turned out to be scallops, typical cafeteria food, and not particularly tasty, but our meal was as enchanted—enlivened with our getting to know each other—as if we were eating on the fanciest cruise ship.

I had wanted to take a *sento*. Jun knew where the baths were and after dinner he took me to the huge pink-tiled tub filled with steaming water.

It was wonderfully, gloriously empty. I soaped myself and rinsed while the ship rocked gently back and forth. I lay still as the hot water washed around me, coming high up on my neck, then receding, then washing over me again.

It was another beautiful night on deck, bright with moonlight, as I drifted back to my bed and fell asleep. In the early morning I awoke to Jun whispering my name.

"Viki," he said softly, "come outside. It is now possible to see Mt. Fuji in the moonlight."

I got up, slipped on my shoes and stepped outside into the night. The clouds were silver against the black of the night sky; the moon was nearly full over the east. There in the distance, clearly visible between a blanket of clouds was Fuji-san, a perfect cone outlined in snow. It was the first time I'd seen the famous peak (it's usually covered by clouds). We stood gazing at the mountain until the sky was streaked with brilliant red.

I said goodbye to Jun and left the boat, happy in a way I had never felt before. I boarded the bus to the subway where the trains were bulging with schoolchildren in uniform, salary men, and office girls. I made three attempts to pile into a crowded car, but they were so jammed, I gave up and waited while white-gloved conductors shoved people inside until they were sausaged in enough for the doors to shut.

Finally, a train arrived that had room enough for a large American woman with a large red bag, and I loaded myself on. As I watched the whir of giant blue and white *kanji* painted on the walls of every subway station zoom past, then slow into focus, I knew that I was larger in spirit from that perfect slice of time.

Kristin M. Jefferson

Genesis of the Traveling Spirit

I STARTED TRAVELING EARLY. I WAS JUST TWO WHEN MY MOTHER, BROTHER, AND I boarded an ocean liner to join my father, who was stationed in Japan. My memories of Japan are meager, but I remember vividly the housekeepers provided to us because my father was a ranking officer. They were Japanese students trying to improve their English, learn about the U.S., and earn money while going to school. My parents answered innumerable questions for them about life back home. Their questions and my parents' answers helped to shape my interest in the many different ways that people choose to live.

Back in the U.S., I was enrolled in a tiny private school in Chicago. The bulk of the students were Jewish, but there were Anglo-Saxons and more than a sprinkling of Asian, African, and Latin Americans as well. Francis W. Parker's motto was, "A school should be a model home, a complete community, and an embryonic democracy."

I plunged into the third-grade project: to design an ideal community. We developed language, numbers, medicines, and magic. We learned to redistribute goods by trading so everyone would have all the things they would need, and to establish the value of a product or service according to its availability and necessity. We created a currency. We created sacred and secular rites of passage, music, dance, stories, and myths to pass on what we had learned. On and on we went, discovering problems and creating the solutions necessary to live in our ideal community.

My job was ambassador. I was armed with pictures and stories that described life in our fantasy city and was sent out into the school to try to establish rapport with non-third-graders and incorporate their ideas and values into our community. I'm sure it was then that I was launched into a life of travel.

My first experience traveling alone was en route to enrolling in Bard College. I had booked myself into one of those cramped but private sleeper cabins they have on trains. Once installed, I experienced, for the first time, a state of being I've since come to associate not only with riding on trains but with travel in general. It was as if I were journeying in the womb of the possible, beyond the constraints of identity, no longer who I used to be but not yet who I was to become. I rode into the future, amusing myself during the trip by imagining "as if" realities suggested by the fleeting scenarios passing outside my window. I could be whomever I wanted to be. It was exhilarating.

The motion of the train awoke me at dawn. "Next stop, Philadelphia, City of Brotherly Love," a melodic voice intoned outside my compartment door. I swear I could hear the tongue of the Liberty Bell sounding in Independence Hall. In response to the freedoms the imagined strokes of the bell called up in me, a refrain of shivers fluttered through my body as I savored what was left of this intermission between lives.

The student body was primarily upper-middle-class, somewhat bohemian, and mostly white. These were the circumstances in which I'd always gone to school, but now, isolated from a self-image mirrored and reinforced by my family, I experienced consciously, for the first time, the existential questions that would motivate my travels: "Who am I?" and "Where do I fit in?"

I graduated from Bard as the sixties were coming to an end and headed West. I moved into an apartment down the street from the radical Berkeley campus and just below an apartment used by the Black Panther Party for distributing pamphlets and food. The night I moved in there were violent riots just outside my door and a curfew was imposed. The police, unaffectionately called "pigs," had their guns trained on the apartment above throughout the night. It was thrilling! My life of travel and adventure had at last begun.

My first trip overseas without my family took in Europe and Northern Africa. The huge taxis in London, the Left Bank in Paris, the running of the bulls in Spain, and the Casbah in Morocco were all part of my firsthand exploration of the multiplicity of cultures out there in the world. I was fascinated by all that I saw and totally amazed by people's curiosity about me. They were entranced with my hair, the color of my skin, my speech, and the way I moved.

It was a startling type of attention, so different from the charged emotional attitudes that a person of color in the U.S. comes to expect. I was taken off guard. Yet there was something liberating about this attention. It took me a while to figure out that this feeling of liberation came from being viewed particularly rather than categorically and it was most likely to occur when I was far from America. It was this feeling that I came to seek from travel and that allowed me to develop a sense of myself that was nondefensive and organically grown. It was a feeling I grew to crave.

I secured a job as a professor at the City University of New York, but it was not long before I was traveling again, this time accompanying a group of black American students on their first trip overseas. Our destination was West Africa, from which our ancestors had all presumably come. I remember the excitement on the plane as the students anticipated landing in a country where all the people would look like them and the

The ship moved swiftly through the Atlantic Ocean, parting the water like a gigantic knife. The pulsating, musical hum of the engines was hypnotic. This was my first voyage to Europe. I was single, thirty, and excited about the prospect of new experiences. Every so often a sailor's voice tolled the depth of the ocean below the ship. With each announcement the water was deeper. I leaned over the rail entranced by the murky water, humming engines, and the unemotional voice announcing ever-increasing fathoms of water beneath the ship. At last, the voice said mechanically, "No bottom here."

As the words fell woodenly, time stood still. Miles beneath the swirling water into which I was staring, there was an ocean floor, a bottom. But this ship had no instrument that could measure the vast distance. Suddenly, the majesty, mystery, and wonder of God washed over me in a way that I had never experienced. All the world was a cathedral! Everything and everyone in it were creations that testified to the magnificence and glory of the Creator!

Gradually the overwhelming euphoria faded. I was on the ship again, looking over the side. Out of nowhere, two young people appeared and introduced themselves. They were boyfriend and girlfriend. I sensed they had been watching me and decided to join me because I looked lonely. Now they snuggled close on either side of me, sharing their love, laughter and energy. A fitting "amen" to a spiritual milestone.

—Marian E. Barnes with B.J. Taylor

joy and welcome they expected to feel upon returning to their ancestral home. I had come to expect some measure of self-revelation while traveling, but, like the students, I was surprised by what occurred when we arrived in Ghana.

The students got off the plane looking more African than the Africans. While not in Western garb, the Africans were far more subdued sartorially than the students, who, as a form of homage, had adorned themselves with every Africanism they'd ever read about or seen. The Africans greeted their fashion exuberance with detachment. They seemed to make little distinction between visiting white Americans and black Americans trying to reclaim their heritage. We were all foreigners.

Traveling, up until now, had taught me a lot about who I was; now it

In researching the life of legendary Harlem Renaissance sculptor Richmond Barthe, I traveled from New York to New Orleans, Jamaica, to his birthplace in Bay St. Louis, Mississippi, and to four countries in Europe.

In Switzerland I took the train to St. Prex. I had a letter with the name of a Dr. Forel, with whom Barthe had stayed, but there was no street address. I found a phone booth and attempted to look up the address in the phone book but the "F" pages were missing, so I stopped for breakfast at a small restaurant. Over tea and a croissant (with Tina Turner singing "What's Love Got To Do With It" blaring from the jukebox) the proprietor told me that Dr. Forel was deceased, but she directed me to his house.

As I followed the directions and walked toward the lake, I saw a black woman walking down the street going in the opposite direction. She was the first person of color I'd seen since leaving Geneva. I walked down the hill and around the curve, and took a deep breath. Set against the deep blue water was a profusion of beautiful flowers of all colors—lavender, yellow, pink, white, peach, deep purple, and red— neatly lining the road with wooden park benches placed intermittently. Carefully pruned trees faced the still lake. My senses were totally astounded and uplifted by the beauty I saw.

While looking for the house, I saw three young people and asked for their help. They laughed and said, "Sure, sure, we know you're here looking for Michael Jackson." (They saw my camera and tape recorder; Michael had left the U.S. after being accused of molesting a young boy in California, and rumors were that he was in Switzerland. I found out later that he was in the next town.)

When I found the house I saw that it was like a castle with heavy wooden doors. I knocked, but no one was home. I went through an open door into the courtyard and gazed at the view Barthe loved. I could imagine myself sitting on one of those benches for hours while peacefully, restfully, daydreaming of days gone by and days yet to come. Three recently deceased friends flashed through my mind as I took in the beauty. I could hear one of them say, "Barthe really knew how to live well—way to go Barthe!" One would have loved the flowers. He would have tried to name each while smelling their distinct aromas. One would have fallen into a trance while sitting by the water and looking at the incredible view. I suddenly felt deeply grateful for this moment. If life is composed of peaks and valleys, this was definitely a peak.

—Barbara A. Hudson, "Travel Diary of a Research Trip"

was teaching me who I was *not*. The students' surprise and disappointment was palpable and grew more so throughout the trip as the Africans continued to treat us cordially but as strangers, with no particular relationship to themselves. In Africa, a common skin coloring was apparently not enough to establish kinship, while back in the States a difference in skin coloring was more than sufficient to negate kinship. This realization had a profound impact on the students. They didn't talk much about it, but I could see it in the way they began to complain—the toilet paper was too harsh, the bugs too big, and there was no ice. And I could see it in the growing enthusiasm for returning "home."

As a result of my African trip, I was asked to participate in a project that kept me traveling for the next four years. I assisted a professor who had been hired by the Smithsonian to do field research in all of the countries that had contributed significant immigrant populations to the United States. The idea was to determine which parts of American culture were cultural retentions from other parts of the world.

For the next four years we traveled throughout the African Diaspora— to every country to which slaves were sent or to which Africans had fled—isolating the African retentions from the Asian, American Indian, and European mix, and making documentaries of our findings in the field.

But while we were studying the native populations, they were studying us. It seemed that most had had some exposure to white missionaries and anthropologists, but in many sites they'd never seen black people from Western cultures. In Surinam, for example, the Bush Negroes could not understand my refusal to go about bare-breasted as they did. Convinced of my ignorance of all normal behavior, they would follow me around, watching as I slept, ate, and, much to my discomfort, even when I went to the bathroom in the "bush." When I got the behavior right, according to their standards, they would clap with delight. What a way to understand the staggering similarities and defining differences among peoples throughout the world! What a way to come to know myself!

Returning to teaching without the constant travel was a bit of a let down, but the teaching job didn't last. New York was undergoing a financial crisis and had to drastically trim its budget. The City University began to lay people off: the last hired were the first to go. Soon I was pounding the pavement with a résumé that people found extraordinary but which failed to fit any traditional jobs.

One afternoon, walking home from an unsuccessful interview at the Metropolitan Museum, I happened to pass a small gallery window that was filled with tribal art. Having nothing else to do, I entered the gallery and began to talk with the owner. He was amazed that I knew so much about so obscure an art form, and in short order asked me to manage the gallery for him. And so, with serendipity, the next chapter of traveling in my life began.

My work brought me in contact with the American and European curators, dealers, and collectors in the field. Within a year, one of the European dealers offered to set me up in business. I was flown to Brussels and from his huge inventory of tribal art objects I was allowed to take anything I thought I could sell. The art was priced to me at just twenty percent above what he'd purchased it for and I wasn't to pay him until I made a sale. I was suddenly in business for myself, with an inventory of museum-quality art.

I had a knack for the business and quickly placed most of the pieces in major private and/or museum collections. I started traveling back and forth to Europe, becoming a regular at the galleries and auction houses in New York, Brussels, London, and Paris. Soon I developed even more far-flung clients and friends, which allowed me to travel to Asia, Africa, Latin America, and the Pacific Islands, in addition to Europe. Although in this phase of my traveling life bathrooms were not the bush but tiled with marble and equipped with bidets, the lessons were no less profound.

Being an art dealer has proven to be an exciting but precarious job—one never knows from where the next sale, art object, or personal insight will come—but it has allowed me to travel the world, to journey in the womb of the possible, beyond the constraints of identity, no longer who I used to be but not yet who I will become.

Alice Walker

Ubud, Bali

This journal entry, which first appeared in *Living by the Word: Selected Writings, 1973–1987*, is part of this writer's map "to find [her] old planet."

February 12, 1987

Another rainy night. I am in bed, where I've been for several hours, after a long walk through Ubud to the monkey forest and then for lunch at the Lotus Café—entirely inhabited by Europeans and Americans and one stray very dark and pretty Indian girl in a vivid red dress. Then the walk home, stopping in a local shop—where the woman proprietor is sweet and sells wonderful flowing cool and colorful pants. (Rebecca, on seeing them hanging near the street, immediately exclaimed, "Miss Celie's pants!") Anyway, the pants I liked, knee length, with the flowing grace of a sarong, she no longer had, but she urged me to try a kind of flowered jumpsuit, very long—before she showed me how to adjust it to my shape—and Western-influenced Balinese. It looked great, so I bought it.

But the rain threatens to get me down. In the mornings there is a little sun—nothing direct; in the afternoons there are quite heavy showers, which, even if they are warm and we can walk right through them, I find a little overwhelming after the third or fourth day. Also feeling down because I've drunk so much beer, since the water is considered unsafe except here at the house. And, Robert says, this is the week before my period!

Anyway, *very* out of sorts, for me. It's true I overheard the housekeeper (who travels everywhere with an umbrella against rain and sun) tell Rebecca she "don't like black," as Rebecca was saying how much she wants to "brown"; and I resent always being perceived as just another "rich" American tourist and importuned to buy at every turn when we are walking and even here at the house. But Ubud is beautiful! I've never seen anything like it. The green rice paddies, the soft bluish-gray skies, the people who've created the landscape, and themselves, graceful, friendly, amazingly mellow.

So much so it is a shock to realize that as recently as 1965 more than 100,000 of them killed each other after an attempted Communist coup in Jakarta.

Bali makes me think of Uganda. The same gentle countryside and gentle people; the same massacres and blood baths.

Robert wondered aloud why you don't see middle-aged people, only the young and the old. A lot of them would have been among the 100,000.

I have many bites! The ones on my feet are especially maddening. In my gloomier moments this morning I thought: If it's going to rain all the time and I have to suffer mosquitoes as well, I might as well be in Mendocino. (Not knowing that Northern California was experiencing the worst flooding in thirty years!) I felt very homesick, which Rebecca found astonishing. She has taken to Bali—the people, the landscape, the food—like the trouper she is. She is one of those old, old transparent souls the Universe radiates through without impediment, and so, wherever we go, within a week everyone seems aware of her presence. She walks in the rain as it if is sun.

Have been reading *Dancing in the Light,* by Shirley MacLaine; much of it is true, as I have experienced life, and a lot is straight Edgar Cayce. But it is sad to see her spirituality limited by her racialism. Indians and Africans have a hard time; especially Africans who, in one of her incarnations, frustrate her because they're not as advanced as she is! It is amusing to contemplate what the Africans must have thought of her.

But I don't care about any of this. In the kitchen, Ketut is making dinner, chicken satay. Rebecca and Robert are at a fire dance, to which I declined to go—pleading aching joints, footwear erosion, and mildew of the brain. The rain is coming down in torrents. Lightning is flashing. The house we've rented is spectacular: it faces a terraced hillside of rice paddies, two waterfalls, and coconut trees, and is built in Balinese style but is huge by Balinese standards, I think. Two large bedrooms downstairs and an open-air one upstairs, with another great wooden hand-carved antique Balinese bed at one end. The roof is thickly thatched.

Two days ago I celebrated my forty-second birthday here, with the two people I love most in the world; we talked about my visit, before we left home, to a very beautiful Indian woman guru, who spoke of the condition of "judness." A time of spiritual inertia, of feeling thick, heavy, devoid of light. Yet a good time, too, because, well, judness, too, is a part of life; and it is life itself that is good and holy. Not just the "dancing" times. Nor even the light.

Thinking of this, hoping my loved ones are dry, and smelling dinner, I look up straight into the eye of a giant red hibiscus flower Ketut just placed—with a pat on my head—by the bed. It says: Just *be*, Alice. Being is sufficient. Being is All. The cheerful, sunny self you are missing will return, as it always does, but only *being* will bring it back.

Gwen Shervington

Land of the Morning Calm

IT WAS WITH SOME TREPIDATION THAT I ARRIVED IN SOUTH KOREA TO BEGIN A year's contract teaching English at a private language institute. The months before leaving the U.S. were filled with expectation but also uncertainty. I had absolutely no idea what to expect. To add to my anxiety, a few European-Americans felt it necessary to warn me about the racism in Asia. The Japanese are racist. The Taiwanese are racist. The Koreans are racist. Nevertheless, never having been the target of U.S. racism, they couldn't compare it to the Asian variety. I was annoyed; I live with racism every day and didn't need any warnings.

I was fully aware that I might undergo some hardships because of my African heritage, but I was more concerned about having dreadlocks than I was about having brown skin. I've had almost forty years' experience dealing with racial prejudice but only about ten dealing with the occasional negative reaction to my locks. I was worried about how to respond to negative reactions to my hair in Korea. I went so far as to go to a wig store but couldn't find one that fit comfortably. There was also the impracticality of wearing a wig during Korea's hot and humid summer.

Although there is an African American presence in Seoul (because of the U.S. Army bases there), my school was in Taejon, two hours south of Seoul, an area where there are few black people. I was greeted upon my arrival in Taejon with the only racism I faced in Korea: The apartment contract that was arranged for me was canceled when the owner found out I was black, and I had to spend my first night in a hotel. My employer found another apartment for me the next day. He was very supportive, showing genuine concern for my comfort.

He did not, however, explain the situation to me directly; he had one of his managers do it in a very careful way so as not to offend or embarrass me. Korean culture is a very old and traditional one. Although Western values are seeping into the Korean lifestyle, Confucian notions are still important aspects of human relations. Proper etiquette includes avoiding direct mention of delicate topics that may cause embarrassment or loss of dignity and respect.

I wondered briefly if I had made a mistake coming to Korea. Later, as I settled into my sweet, (tiny) efficiency apartment, I decided not to let this one incident overshadow the positive interactions I was having. My students were friendly, people smiled at me in the street, others waved as they passed on their mopeds. I would keep an open mind.

> *I*n Florence, Italy, while walking through the market, I was stopped by a young Italian man in his early twenties who wanted to practice his English. He complimented me on my eyes, and asked if I was afraid living in my neighborhood at home. I told him no. He seemed puzzled and again repeated his question. He wanted to know if the slums and drugs bothered me. I assured him that I do not live in a slum neighborhood with drugs. Based on what he has seen on television, he thinks that all black people in the States live in drug-infested slum neighborhoods. The power of the media to shape what people think of us and how they react to us is awesome and scary.
>
> —Barbara A. Hudson,
> "Travel Diary of a Research Trip"

And I'm glad I did, because from then on, I had only good interactions. I lived in a three-story apartment building on the first floor. My next-door neighbor was a college student in her twenties. She often kept her door open and chatted with me in broken English whenever I passed by. One evening she invited me in to meet her friends, seven young men and women sitting on the floor around the small room. I sat down and was introduced to everyone. I only stayed a short while because, after introductions, our conversation was extremely limited due to the language barrier. Nonetheless, I appreciated the inclusive gesture. The children in my building got a kick out of greeting me and always laughed when I returned the greeting *anyo haseyo* to them.

Despite my exhausting work schedule, I did have a social life. Initially, I spent a lot of time with the other English teachers, but after a while I got tired of the many complaints and put-downs of Korean culture, so I focused on one or two like-minded friends. I also socialized with my students, who were all adult learners. One day, my housewife class took me to one of their homes and waited on me hand and foot as they made lunch. One of my evening classes took me to a coffeehouse instead of having class. The class that I taught to workers in an electronics company took me out for dog meat soup.

The time that I spent with students outside of class was invaluable to me in acquiring the basic information that I needed to live in Taejon. Where do I get water? What bus do I take to get downtown? Where do I do my laundry? Where is the supermarket? Is it safe to be out at night? Is tipping expected? They also wanted to ask me questions, but on a more personal level. Where are you from? Are you married? Why not? How old are you? Do you have a boyfriend? Why not? Why did you come to Korea? Do you have children? Why not? What do you eat? Being asked the same questions repeatedly (sometimes by strangers in the street or cab drivers) was tiresome. Although I knew they were sincerely inquisitive because of their limited contact with foreigners, I found this type of questioning offensive. I consequently developed a lesson plan comparing acceptable and unacceptable questioning in Korean and American cultures.

Kyeryong (Chicken Dragon) Mountain was a twenty-minute bus ride from my apartment. On my first excursion out of Taejon, I went there to visit Tonghak temple, one of the few in the country run by women monks. I wasn't sure whether I should enter the courtyard because there were no other people around besides the monks. I stood at the gate looking in, trying to decide what to do, when a monk in training (I knew she was in training because she had hair) gestured that I was welcome and gave me a very low bow. I returned the bow and ascended the stairs to the temple, removing my shoes before I entered. I took a deep breath when I saw the altars, then stood motionless again to gaze at the intricate artwork on the ceiling. Eventually, I sat alone for a long time, absorbing a feeling of peacefulness. After a while the monk in training approached me and, speaking in Korean, motioned that I follow her movements. She taught me the proper way to kneel and pay respect to the altars. She did it perfectly smoothly, but my knees clunked on the floor every time. When she left the room I put a donation in the box then headed for the door. Just as I got there, she returned with a bag of candy for me. I left feeling oddly blessed and returned frequently.

Dozens of people in Taejon told me they had never seen a real-live black person. I was startled one day when my employer said, "I've never hired a black person before. Their pronunciation is bad, but you are different. Your pronunciation is good. If things go well, I will continue to hire black people." A credit to my race?

My locks, it turned out, were not the first thing people noticed; my Africanness was. Both children and adults stared at me, and at first it made me very uncomfortable, although it didn't feel like the staring I've gotten in the U.S. from European Americans. (Those stares emit hatred and are often followed by some type of racial insult or attack.) In Korea, it felt different; I didn't feel hatred. I couldn't understand what was being said, but it seemed that they were more curious than hateful. Nonetheless, I stayed in readiness for insults, which thankfully never came.

After I had made friends who could translate for me, I learned that the starers were often saying wonderful things. They were admiring my hair, admiring my Africanness, saying I was beautiful. Being admired by strangers for being black was a new experience for me. I had a hard time accepting and believing it, and continued to be mistrustful of the staring. I simply could not let go of a lifetime of conditioning. I never got completely comfortable with people staring at me, but after about six or seven months I did stop expecting insults. I even let the market women touch my hair. (They wanted to know if it was a wig or a perm.)

Living in an environment where I was not constantly bombarded with racism helped me see how this social illness has damaged me. It's required me to walk through the world tense, with armor to shield me from hatred, instead of being open and relaxed. I am grateful that Taejon gave me a chance to experience a different way of being in the world. Now when the nonsense of the U.S. gets to be too much for me, I seek refuge in other countries, knowing that escaping the intractable racism I grew up with allows me to gain new insights into myself.

Dawn Comer

A Chilly Reception in Innsbruck

I DON'T SPEAK GERMAN, BUT I KNOW WHAT *SCHWARTZA* MEANS, AND, IN ANY LAN-guage, being called "nigger" hurts. I came to Austria to meet my brother Brian at the National Brotherhood of Skiers Convention. The convention is a great excuse to travel to some exotic place and party with a bunch of black folks from all over the U.S. who like to ski. And going to Innsbruck, Austria, sounded like fun. But when we walked into a local bar after a hard day of skiing and heard the word *schwartza* thrown at us, the party was over. Patsy, a scrappy little attorney, wanted to take all of her five foot, four inches, one hundred and ten pounds of African American womanhood and mix it up with the towering Austrian who taunted us. The man, blond with chiseled, Nordic features, kicked back a shot of schnapps and glared at us. Except for the strains of "Staying Alive" coming from the loudspeakers, the bar grew silent. Brian and Marcus, a child psychiatrist from California, dragged Patsy out of the bar.

"Girl, we don't want to have to call the U.S. embassy to get your natural black ass out of an Austrian jail."

That was the first of many incidents during our week there, which reminded me that no matter how far you travel from home, you can still encounter the same old absence of racial harmony and understanding.

The United States has done an excellent job of exporting our culture abroad. So much so, that several times I heard the Austrian locals refer to black music as "their music." They watch reruns of *The Cosby Show* dubbed in German, listen to Whitney Houston, Michael Jackson, and

TLC, and their clubs jam to the beat of house music, reggae, and rap. However, when twelve-hundred-plus African American skiers descended on the city, it was as if an alien invasion had occurred.

On registration day, the hotel lobby was filled with black skiers just off fourteen-hour flights from the States. We were greeting old friends and making new ones, when an Austrian man entered and surveyed the scene. Startled by all the black faces, he thought it would be funny to parade through the lobby doing the Nazi goose step and salute. On the streets, our presence often stopped traffic. Passersby on sidewalks turned and stared. Storekeepers followed us from aisle to aisle and made sure to tell us how expensive what we were looking at was. The message was clear. The Austrians loved black culture but not black people.

> Mine was the only black face I saw in Vienna, Austria, for the three days I was there, except for the African waiter who served breakfast in my hotel, and to whom each morning I would nod in greeting. He in turn would nod and smile at me and offer me extra toast, but he spoke no English so we could not communicate. I marveled at his ability to survive in that very white city.
>
> —Opal Palmer Adisa, "Spreading My Wings and Embracing the World"

Several other incidents confirmed these feelings. One day, I got lost following street signs through a mountain village. I approached a man, Berlitz guide in hand, to ask directions to a ski shop. Before I could open my mouth, he put up his hands and ducked his head, trying to avoid eye contact with me. He muttered a few words in English, "Can't help you, leave me alone, go away...."

That scene was repeated several times over until finally I found the ski shop with the help of an Austrian actress who had studied in New York City. When I told her about the bizarre behavior, she explained, "Here, oftentimes, the only people of color we see are Gypsies who try to rob you. So, we see a dark person and assume you're a thief. We Austrians, I'm afraid, aren't always as tolerant as we should be. We see someone different and we are scared." It saddened me to think that despite slavery, the Holocaust, tribal warfare in Rwanda, ethnic cleansing in Bosnia, we still haven't learned. We continue to instinctively fear and hate those who appear different from us.

Of course, I cannot generalize about all Austrians. Like the actress, there were others who warmed the chill of the racially tense climate. Some people went out of their way to make us feel welcome. I got lost after skiing off a cross-country trail and ended up far from town. I took off my skis and started walking back, when an Austrian man in a car pulled over and offered to drive me. Another time, a shopkeeper working on her English questioned me about life in America. Finally she said, "I think of myself as Austrian, Tyrolean (a region of Austria), of that I am proud. And in America, are you Southern, Western—what are you?"

I said, "I'm African American." She smiled and said, "Of that you should be proud."

Later that night, I returned to my hotel, and instead of handing me the room key, the desk clerk, whose English was limited mostly to "hello" and "what want?" eagerly handed me a clipping from the local newspaper. It showed four black skiers on a chairlift. He pointed excitedly at the photo and said, "Your people!"

At first, I was unsure how to take his comment. Then I looked at the grin on his face—clearly he was happy to have made the connection. I smiled back and said, "African Americans ski, just like Austrians ski."

He nodded and said, "We just alike, *jah!*"

Hold Sapphire back. If you are in a difficult situation and someone chooses to reject all your acts of diplomacy...use your common sense to try to diffuse the situation, but make Sapphire your last resort.

—Torrie Nunnally,
"Handling Racism on the Road"

Barbara Chase-Riboud

Why Paris?

I HAVE LIVED IN PARIS HALF MY LIFE. FRESH FROM UNIVERSITY, NOT A FRANCOPHILE, and with no knowledge of the language, I came to Paris from London for a weekend. I never did catch my plane out, and in time found myself with a husband, children, and a French family so enormous that if two generations held a reunion at the same time, we ran into the hundreds. Not only did I have to come to grips quickly with the French on a sentimental level, but I also had to take a crash course in the French method of dealing with everything.

Paris can be unpredictable and infuriating one minute, and irresistible, serene, liberating and generous the next. She can be the height of civilized living and the depth of gratuitous rudeness. She is full of beauty and perfect places to live. Paris offers the best reason to spend a day doing nothing if you feel like it, without ever feeling alone. Every *quartier* of Paris is a little village. Old, young, rich, poor, Left Bank intellectual to River Bank yuppie, everyone meets at the baker's for their daily baguette. Fashions may change in Paris, but never Paris, its splendor eternal and unparalleled. It is a city whose magic is bestowed on both visitor and native.

Here, we can still recall the lives of all those who have come from other countries. From my house, I love to cross the Luxembourg Gardens, with its palace built by a homesick Italian queen, go past a replica of the Statue of Liberty and down the rue Tournon, where there is a plaque on the house where John Paul Jones lived and another on the house where Casanova lived. I can walk past a bookstore filled with the white-jacketed books with only a title and no illustration that Countee Cullen loved so much, or an outdoor café where Richard Wright wrote.

France, perhaps more than any other country in Europe, has valued its black citizens and welcomed black Americans. More than a hundred years ago, Paris recognized the genius of its great historical novelist, the immensely popular black French writer Alexandre Dumas (1802–1870), famous for *The Three Musketeers* and *The Count of Monte Cristo*. For more than a century, black Americans have expatriated to Paris for political, economic, artistic, and racial reasons. The African American painter Henry Ossawa Tanner, son of a Philadelphia pastor and member of the black bourgeoisie, lived and exhibited in Paris between 1891 and 1900, and was acclaimed and richly rewarded by the Parisians. But it was during the First World War, when more than two hundred thousand black soldiers fought on European soil, that the first real immigration of blacks occurred. Although they found themselves segregated in the American army, they were welcomed—and were even considered "American" rather than "black"—by the French.

Not only did the French appear to be color blind, but they were also intrigued by a new American art form: jazz. They loved the 369th Infantry Regiment, known as the Harlem Hell Fighters Band, which captivated French audiences everywhere with its ragtime, its military tunes, its blues, and all that jazz. After the war, a jazz band was formed by members of the Hell Fighters who, along with thousands of other black veterans, remained in Paris. This was the beginning of the love affair between the French people and American jazz that survives to this day.

This passion reached fever pitch when musician Sidney Bechet and dancer-singer Josephine Baker came to Paris with La Revue Négre in 1925. Although it was Sidney Bechet who was the genius, it was Baker who the French took to their hearts. She became the symbol of all the beauty, verve, and energy of the Americans, and between the two world wars she became a legend. Baker strode up the Champs Elysées with a pair of leopards and sang of her two loves: "my country and Paris." During World War II she fought simultaneously for the Free French and against racism in the United States. For her courage and her humanity, the French decorated her with the medal of the Legion of Honor, which was buried with her in a state funeral when she died in 1975. Americans, however, ostracized her for her extravagant, flamboyant style for years, and she never really worked in the American theater again.

Between the two wars, all the great names of the Harlem Renaissance passed through Paris, some of them remaining for years, like the poets Countee Cullen and Claude McKay, both of whom lived here in the 1920s. Literary talents as diverse as Richard Wright, Chester Himes, James Baldwin, William Gardner Smith, and John A. Williams, as well as dozens of theatrical people, including the actor Gordon Heath and the singer Jimmy "Lover Man" Davis, established themselves on the Left Bank of Paris.

These black Americans fled the United States to escape racial tension, discrimination and lynching, and a wave of conservatism brought on by Prohibition that was very similar to today's atmosphere in America. Their purpose in coming to Paris was to define and consolidate their own Americanness outside of racial stereotypes and to have it changed by a European point of view. But, in truth, most of these Americans returned home as steadfastly American in outlook and culture as when they left.

African Americans have held a special place in their hearts for Paris. When the great African American poet Langston Hughes decided to make his home in Paris, his friend Arna Bontemps wrote to him, saying that someone who had reached the stage in his career that Hughes had—when he could contemplate his past and read the biographies being written about him—had earned the right to live in Paris before living in paradise.

The eighties brought high-powered black corporate executives and lawyers, state department officials and stunning photographers' models to the Paris scene. Black Broadway musicals such as *Ain't Misbehavin'*, *Bubbling Brown Sugar, Dreamgirls, Porgy and Bess*, and *Black and Blue* have all had long runs in Parisian theaters. The Alvin Ailey American Dance Theater is always sold out on its annual tour here. *The Jeffersons*, the television sitcom, is one of the most popular shows in France. Singer-dancer Vivian Reed, star of *Bubbling Brown Sugar*, is regarded as the reincarnation of Josephine Baker.

My novel *Sally Hemings* (translated under the title *La Virginianne*), about the liaison between Thomas Jefferson and his slave wife, was a best-seller in France, with over a million copies sold. Books about the life of black expatriates, *Harlem, Left Bank*, by the French writer Michel Fabre, and *Paris Noir* by Tyler Stovall, are similarly successful. The opera divas Barbara Hendricks and Jessye Norman are regulars on the Parisian social scene. Predominantly black jazz festivals are held year-round all over the country, but especially during the summer months on the Riviera; they have been a French tradition since the early fifties. Here, the all-American voice of Whitney Houston is heard almost as often on the airwaves in Paris (where she is number one) as it is in the Big Apple.

And the reciprocal love affair between the French and those they see not only as Americans but also as victims of a racist American society goes on.

Stephanie Ann Rush Wilson-Davenport

Finding the Right Stuff: Lessons in Bargaining

RED, BROWN, AND BLACK LEATHER PURSES SWAYED OVERHEAD, GENTLY PUSHED BY tropical breezes. Stacked on tables tightly arranged side by side were piles of handmade leather sandals, handcrafted musical instruments, and dark brown–skinned dolls with blue eyes. Behind these rows stretched an impromptu art gallery, dazzling those who strolled by with painted canvases of scantily clad, honey-colored women lounging on white beaches. Beyond that were fierce-looking wooden masks spread out on brightly colored mats on the ground. On each street corner, women dressed in white skirts and ruffled blouses made and sold spicy snacks: *acarajes,* or black-eyed-pea fritters filled with *caruru,* or stewed okra with dried shrimp. It was Sunday at the Hippie Faire in Rio de Janeiro, Brazil. Once again I had heeded the call of adventure and I was exhilarated to be shopping on foreign soil!

I could say that my love of travel was spurred by lofty inspirations; I could weave a tale of how I sat enthralled listening to my fourth-grade teacher lecturing about the cultures and traditions of faraway lands. But closer to the truth is the fact that I was fascinated by all the dolls, musical instruments, and artifacts that she kept inside a big black bag. To my ten-year-old self who rode the magic carpet around the world by reading books, seeing the stuff the teacher had collected made it all real. And this fascination with objects from foreign countries has never left me.

I inherited from my mother the ability to haggle, and I've refined it to a fine art. On a visit to a marketplace in Dakar, my heart leaped when I saw the beautifully crafted leather purses trimmed in snake skin. But my haggling instincts kicked in immediately, and I gave no outward indication of the slightest bit of interest in the purses. It was my first trip and I was on a mission to find a present to bring back to my younger sister. I exchanged polite greetings in French with the vendor and asked him for the price of the purse. When he told me, I shook my head in disbelief and started to walk away. It was then that he called to me to come back and tell him my "final price." I had no idea what it could be, but I knew that I wasn't going to pay his first price. When I started to walk away a second time, he called me back again. Finally, we settled on a price. I had the exact money in my blouse pocket.

Afterward, I showed our Senegalese guide my purchase and asked him to tell me how much he thought I had paid for them. He told me that there were three levels of prices. One was for the nonblack tourist and another for blacks. The third price was reserved for Senegalese. When I told him what I had paid, he marveled at the fact that I had paid the Senegalese price. I had just bought a stunning leather, snakeskin-trimmed purse for ten dollars! I was hooked on haggling.

Over the years, I have learned many lessons about haggling. One is that you must learn what the market will bear. Recently, my graduate school class traveled with our Chinese professor on a tour of universities in China. While in Shouzou, a few of us who were accustomed to shopping in the flea markets of Chicago decided to visit a *quon jin* (brightly lit markets that are set up at night). I was enchanted! Everything could be found there, from four-foot fans to wooden tea kettles shaped like turtles to food of every variety. Woks and grills were conveniently interspersed among the rows of merchandise so that shoppers could eat, browse, and stroll.

The secret to being taken seriously, we discovered, was to pull out your calculator. Then your image changed from that of a mildly interested tourist to that of a respected customer. And as soon as the calculator appeared, language barriers broke down. Black and Chinese fingers flew across the number keys punching in the latest offer of a "final price." One of our Chinese hosts had told us that the rule of thumb for negotiating was to arrive at one-third of the original asking price. If the vendor balked at that price, then he either had no more merchandise of that kind or the merchandise was difficult to obtain. I followed this advice and purchased a unique carved-bamboo tube that serves as an incense burner for a price well above the third, but I was satisfied that I couldn't find it elsewhere.

Not all haggling sessions have to be a contest of wills. Located near the edge of a huge canvas tent that served as a wholesale jade market in Hong Kong, I noticed a Chinese woman quietly stringing beads of jade on a cord. Amid scores of booths, several hundred vendors noisily mingled and hawked brightly colored kelly green jade necklaces or purple or pink jade earrings and beads. It was the woman's calm demeanor that intrigued me enough to stop and ask about her jade display. She spoke little English but gestured for me to sit on the stool next to her. When I sat down, I realized that I could examine her jade pieces much more carefully. Some of them were the color of green mint candy wafers. Finally, we agreed on a price that included creating a necklace using a piece I selected. While she sat making my necklace, I sat next to her, sipping tea she had poured for me. Today my antique piece of jade swings seductively on an extra long brown cord with an introductory yellow amber bead, and whenever I wear it I think about that calm woman in that bustling market.

When I went to work for the Wadsworth Atheneum I became the first full-time curator of African American Art at a mainstream museum in the U.S, so not surprisingly, I'm particularly interested in art when I travel and I always look for images of blacks. In Florence, Italy, I once saw a ceramic black madonna in the window of a shop. I went inside and there were four other black madonnas in the shop: one Gothic, one Hellenistic, one neoclassical and one Romanesque. Each cost in excess of three million lira. The Black Madonna is considered one of the most sacred symbols in all of Europe. Perhaps someday I will build a collection of black madonnas.

—Barbara A. Hudson,
"Travel Diary of a Research Trip"

I've learned not to regret that I cannot purchase everything I want. While shopping in a farmer's market in Salvador with my adopted sister from Bahia, I saw hidden among the sacks of grain and piles of collard greens, mangoes, and onions, sets of wooden bowls and pestles. How many times had I sat in the kitchen of my adopted family and watched as Eliene and her sisters crushed diced garlic and chiles as they prepared a fabulous Afro-Brazilian dish. I wanted to buy a set, but Eliene hurried me past the booth. Later, Eliene presented me with my very own wooden bowl set to carry back to my kitchen in Chicago.

Now I crush diced cloves of garlic, green chiles, diced onions, and freshly squeezed lime juice against the sides of the wooden bowl with a wooden pestle. Then I coat pieces of red snapper with the mixture before I put them into a hot oiled skillet. I sauté the fish along with more garlic and onions, then I add chopped tomatoes, green pepper, coconut milk, and palm oil. After simmering for about twenty minutes, I serve the *peixe de Baiana* over rice and decorate it with chopped cilantro. *Obrigada, minha irma,* Eliene. Thank you, my sister, Eliene. Your gift continues to be priceless. And as for all those other things I wanted and didn't buy, they're only *things,* and there are always more to see on the next trip! For me, it's not so much about owning things as about enjoying them, appreciating them. I find that I can do that without buying them.

Another lesson I've learned is that you can sometimes benefit from someone else's haggling skills. Once when I was visiting Dakar, Senegal, I made friends with two African American men. One of them was much older than I. On a visit to the jewelry market in Dakar, where world-renowned Arab artisans design and manufacture exquisite silver jewelry, he helped me out.

I viewed each booth while my older gentleman friend asked questions and commented in French to the artisans. Finally, at the last booth, my friend turned to me and whispered in English for me to select what I wanted to purchase and he would negotiate for me. I selected a few pieces, which included a silver bracelet with the Wolof motif of round balls placed at the open ends. After a brief haggling between the merchant and my friend, the merchant handed me a silver ring that matched the design carved in the bracelet. When I hesitated, my friend whispered that the merchant thought that my friend was negotiating to buy presents for his daughter, and the ring was to help sweeten the deal. Dutiful daughter that I was, I accepted the gift and thanked both the merchant and my papa, in French, of course.

> *D*ress modestly and simply. When traveling in non European countries, wear/buy clothes that the locals wear. Try not to look too much like a tourist to avoid being hassled and overcharged.
>
> —Torrie Nunnally,
> "Staying Well on the Road"

Getting to know people is as important as getting the best deal. In Salvador, Bahia, there is a restored area called the Pelourinho or Pillory, so named because it was the place where African slaves were brought and whipped as punishment. Today, Afro-Brazilians and their African American friends gather in outdoor cafés lining cobblestone streets (especially on Tuesday nights) to listen to Brazilian drums and cool out. When I visited there, an African American girlfriend who was staying in an apartment nearby introduced me to her Afro-Brazilian friends, Rosana and Luciene. Earlier that week, I had seen some very uniquely designed Afro-centric T-shirts; these were the designers of those T-shirts, explained my friend. Rosana wanted me to come and see their showroom.

It was late, but I overcame my reluctance to travel further into the Liberdade at night. Rosana and Luciene commandeered a friend and his Volkswagen to drive us. When we arrived, I realized that it was also their living quarters and on-site factory. It was my willingness to share in their enthusiasm in starting a new business that turned the usual haggling session into a gabfest with friends. When I returned the next morning to pick up my merchandise, I watched Rosana silkscreen my designs. Then I spent the next hour enjoying their hospitality, eating sliced melon and apples, drinking homemade tropical fruit juice, and listening to records sung by Dijivan, a popular Afro-Brazilian singer. I've returned to purchase T-shirts, but now it's done at a storefront in the Pelourinho. The special "opening-a-new-business" price consideration is still in effect, as is our friendship.

After years of shopping in markets all over the world, my son believes that we live in a museum that exhibits artifacts from African peoples in diaspora. I love the Senufu statues, Kuba headdresses, old wooden Chinese teakettles, Native American saddle blankets, and Senegalese sand paintings—they cheer me and inspire me. And I also treasure the tales, languages, recipes, and books I've collected and lifelong friends I've made while shopping around the world.

Earthlyn Marselean Manuel

Red Dirt on My Feet

I DECIDED TO GO TO INDIA. I BELIEVED THAT THERE, AMID THE RED DIRT, LUSH-green vegetation, humid heat, and thatched roofs of Auroville, in the state of Tamil Nadu, I could learn something important, something that would help me create the life I want.

Established in 1968 by followers of the Indian mystic Sri Aurobindo, Auroville is an experiment in human unity. Its early settlers, most of them French and German, joined with local Tamils to carve a spiritual oasis near the Bay of Bengal in southeast India. Many of these white settlers remained in Auroville, living among the Tamils and pursuing the dream of a place where people from around the world might transcend racial, social, and religious differences and devote themselves to "the practice of divine consciousness." It was this philosophy that drew me to Auroville. But my heart was also filled with anxiety about being a black woman in country that might not accept me.

My fears proved unnecessary. Three months later, landing in Madras, the capital of Tamil Nadu, I was surrounded by faces many shades darker than my own. Some had such black skin against the night that it seemed there was no skin at all. The faces were framed by gorgeous thick black satin wavy hair. When I engaged their stares, I felt that I was looking deep into midnight, and this darkness in the air made me part of a landscape of dark people in a way that was comforting.

I was delirious from twenty hours of travel as we packed into a small bus with our luggage tied insufficiently on top for the four-hour ride down a bumpy road at high speed, dodging trucks, amid ceaselessly blaring horns. The first thing I saw out of the window was a group of men wrapped in dingy white cloth, one small candle lighting their faces as they drank from cups. For a split second I expected to see a trash fire in a garbage can in the center of the circle; but no, these were not homeless black men in West Oakland hanging out on the corner at night. I'm in India, it's dawn on a December morning, already ninety degrees without a breeze. I later learned that in these small villages morning is a special time for the men to gather, drink tea, bathe near temple waters, and pray. The women and children draw artistic *kolams* (flower designs) in front of the home to protect the family, gather water in large urns, prepare breakfast, and then bathe and go to the temple mid-morning.

During these first hours in India, feasting my eyes on the women in their brilliant purple, green, yellow, and orange saris, I became conscious that my African self, unlike my American self, has no indigenous language, name, or way of being. Yet I felt in my bones the spirit of my African ancestry, and I was grateful that Taj and Colette, my dreadlocked sister-friends, were making this journey with me.

Seated on a thatched-roof patio in Auroville the next morning, I savored sweet black tea as I took in the intense greenness of my surroundings. I had dozed on my hard bed with two thick white candles softly bouncing flickers of light on the walls, my body exhausted but my mind racing with excitement, then fallen asleep to the rhythm of chirping frogs. I had awakened to amplified Tamil music from a nearby village, the Muslim call to prayer, and strange loud bird calls. (I learned that some of the music was from a wedding and the rest of it was from a

/ was on my way to India, and across from my seat I could feel a Korean man and his wife staring through my skull. I refrained from saying anything and allowed them the pleasure. I thought maybe my dreadlocks were a curiosity to them. It took me a few minutes to realize he had something to share with me. He struggled with his English as he expressed his love for Korea. It struck me then that love for country is love for oneself, for one's identity. Did I have this love for America? In some ways, yes, but I was saddened that my love was not as deep as his. He invited me to visit them and see his beloved land.

I had been sitting in my seat, worrying: What would the Tamil people think of this black woman with dreadlocks from America? Would I be loved or would I have to fight to be visible as I do in my own country? But the gesture of this man touched me and I caught myself. Never mind what the Indians think of me. How strong will I be in loving myself, protecting myself, and holding my spirit in a healing light? Do I love my own black-woman self?

—Earthlyn Marselean Manuel

Tiruvannamalai, a nearby village, which was preparing for a full moon ceremony.) Now I watched the Tamil men and women move effortlessly and work tirelessly in the humid vapors around the township. Washing, cooking, digging, sweeping—doing things for the local whites in much the same way as dark people in America do. But I refused to believe that the plight of dark people around the world is one of inevitable servitude. I was determined to learn new lessons about race in India, not just the same old ones.

*E*verywhere I go I hear American music. In the hill towns of Italy, the villages of Turkey, the cities of Africa—and now in India's holiest city, Varanasi. Guess who we hear the most? Tracy Chapman and Whitney Houston. What does it tell us when the whole world grooves to the music of black American women?

—Sylvia Harris Woodard,
"Postcards from the Global Village"

One afternoon, as onions were being sautéed for lunch, I lounged in the silent shadows of the thatched-roof patio. A breeze smoothed over my cheeks and nudged the top of my white muslin shirt open. A young Tamil woman floated by and peered into my face. I remembered her from the day before and the day before that. Her long, thick tail of hair swayed with her as she passed by me. I nodded hello. She smiled while carrying away the laundry, staring back at me, deliberately asking for my attention. Although we never said a word to each other (we had no language in common), I had a strong sense of being connected to her and that she felt the same.

After two days of intense heat, Taj and Colette and I bathed in the warm rushing waters of the Bay of Bengal. I invited the water to thrash up between my thighs and swirl down my leg muscles and trickle between my toes. The Indian men and boys watched us American women play—three dark women showing our bodies, our sensuality, delighting in the water's caress. I knew that most Indian women do not experience this pleasure; most cannot undress and feel the waves break against their naked thighs. This is an expression of what is rooted in India, where Hindus believe that individual souls manifest their own life conditions. If your soul incarnates as a woman and that life is oppressive, that is your fate. The only way out is to die and to be born again. I wondered if this is one reason for the high suicide rate among Indian women. The question crept into my knees and weakened them, forcing me to reach down to the wet sand and sit at the shore.

Several days later I spent an evening in a room full of Tamil women from many villages, some of whom had traveled fifteen to twenty miles to attend this meeting promoting the liberation of women. It took courage to attend. (Most of these women had to ask permission from their husbands, yet even the act of asking permission is an act of courage here.) I couldn't keep my eyes off the faces of these women; they were lit up by a determination to live a life beyond just surviving.

One of the most valuable things I learned in India was about the relative nature of wealth. One day our group went shopping. We loaded up into several dilapidated cabs and off we went listening to loud Tamil music, dodging cows, goats, people on bikes, people on bare feet, people everywhere. I exchanged three hundred American dollars, which translated into fourteen thousand rupees. The Indians stared at me as I tried to stuff this three-inch wad of money into my supposedly secret money belt. I walked around with a huge bulge on the side of my stomach; I'm certain that everyone knew exactly what was hanging there. It felt ridiculous and obscene to have so much money. Fourteen thousand rupees could feed and house a family of three in Tamil Nadu for more than a year. Our guide, Venkadesh, was stunned by the amount of money we spent on Indian clothes, sculptures, and costume jewelry. I had never felt wealthy before. Now I was a rich American in a poor village. It was jarring, but enlightening.

> On the day I left India, I watched a slow, red, hot Indian sun set just behind a cool lake between heavy green palm leaves. An ancient temple was behind me. I stood with my chest absorbing the heat and sweated out what felt like the tension of a lifetime. I gazed at the sun as if it was bowing to me and acknowledging my visit on this land. I closed my eyes in gratitude for its daily caresses which always reminded me that I am welcome and loved—all of my black woman self.
>
> —Earthlyn Marselean Manuel

On my flight home, as I reflected on my time in Tamil Nadu, an image stood out; Venkadesh had taken us to meet some friends. Their village home was muddy and dark, with flies, smells of cow dung, and stained white walls. Venkadesh's pride pushed through his chest as he announced us to his friends. We drank tea with them and ate a few *pooris,* trying not to show how tentative we felt. Then, while taking a bite, I saw my feet inches away from Venkadesh's feet. Two pairs of feet the exact same shade of black dusted in red dirt—our struggles as dark people so different and so similar. This image has remained with me as a reminder of how important it is to know one another across boundaries of race and geography; by opening ourselves to strangers, we can learn what we need to know about ourselves, and find, in the end, what binds us together.

Joy V. Harris

Whose Vacation Is this Anyway?

JUNE OF '95 MARKED A PROUD MOMENT IN THE LIFE OF MY NIECE, RONYA. SHE HAD accomplished one of the most revered achievements in African American life: graduation from high school and acceptance into college. What better gift to share with an African American princess than a guided tour of my most beloved city, Paris. For expanding her view of the world, Paris seemed to be the perfect place to start.

Paris in June. The very phrase brought up an image of cozy cafés and street musicians, quaint shops on narrow streets, centuries-old cathedrals, museums, and gardens in full bloom. And I haven't mentioned fashion and food. The last category alone would be worth the journey.

I had extended the invitation for this ten-day excursion the previous Thanksgiving, giving me more than six months to plan the details. Her mother agreed that this was an opportunity of a lifetime and would pay the airfare as a graduation present. I would cover other transportation, hotel costs, entrance fees, and dinner every night. When my other niece, twenty-one-year-old Helesha, got wind of the plans, she refused to be left out. The three of us would take Paris by storm.

I wasted no time, spending hours at local bookstores reading travel books. I spoke to everyone I knew who had been to Paris in recent years and even learned how to get on the Internet to find the best sights and locations. We would stay in an area I knew on the Left Bank in the sixth *arrondisement*, not far from the Sorbonne and the Luxembourg Gardens. We would have easy access to everything via Boulevards St. Michel and St. Germain, with the Louvre and Notre Dame a mile away.

After a flawless red-eye flight from Boston, we arrived in Paris shortly after noon; by 3:30, the girls were asleep in our Art Deco hotel. I napped for about half an hour, but even in my sleep my skin tingled, knowing that Paris was just outside the window, waiting beyond the balcony. I let the girls continue to snooze as I slipped into the street, literally dancing the four blocks to Rue de Seine. I bought a scrumptious chocolate fudge and bit into it. The Paris of my dreams came back to me; it felt just as I remembered it from my last visit. After pressing my nose against some antiques shop windows, I ducked into a *brasserie* and bought some bread and cheese for the girls' late lunch.

They were still asleep. Jet lag, I supposed. I sat on the balcony and ate, gazing at geraniums filling the apartment windows across the way. At ten o'clock, when the sun was beginning to fade away, Ronya turned over and smiled and asked about something to eat. By eleven, the three of us were cruising the streets of Paris on foot looking for a McDonalds. I let the choice of dinner pass this time, especially when I realized that the golden arches were just three blocks from Notre Dame. So, at midnight on our first day, we were walking along the Seine watching couples in the glow of the lights shining on the cathedral's buttresses. Paris had them hooked, or so I thought.

The next morning I woke up late and bathed quietly so as not to wake the sleeping beauties. The Luxembourg Gardens were just two blocks away; I decided to have a croissant and hot chocolate by the fountain and people-watch from a warm, comfortable vantage point. How could I be so selfish, I thought, sitting there so close to heaven and let my nieces miss this lovely scene. I forced myself back to the hotel a little past noon.

"So, what should we do today, Eiffel Tower or the Louvre?" I asked, spreading maps on the bedcovers while my nieces stirred beneath them.

"I'm a little hungry," Helesha answered, "but this is vacation. We really don't have to do anything."

"What's at the Louvre?" Ronya yawned. The stunned look on my face must have signaled that she'd better follow that up with something more. "I've seen it in a book somewhere, but I don't know what it is, or what's in it."

I started to explain to the two high school graduates that some of the world's finest art could be found there and that the building itself was once a palace. The only thing that got a hint of interest was the Mona Lisa. Winged Victory was pretty easy, right up the main stairway. Then, along with hundreds of other tourists, we crowded around Venus de Milo. The girls were smiling now, the Louvre had them hooked, or so I thought, until I found out they were laughing at the gum they had left at the base of another statue. I gave them that girl-I'll-kill-you look that has been passed down in my family for generations, and they retrieved it. After a few more notable paintings and sculptures got only a cool response, I decided to get the Mona Lisa over with.

"It's so much smaller than I thought. Why is this so famous?" Ronya asked, perplexed.

We had a brief art history discussion over bottled water and a croissant. They shrugged off my comments about the confident gaze, the use of color, and the approach to portraiture. It was still early, so I suggested a stroll up the Champs Elysées, or at least to the Tuileries gardens, which were right next door.

"If we have to walk, never mind. We walked here, we've walked around the Louvre, and we have to walk back. Let's just go back to the hotel."

> *I* carried with me my underdog self through the great halls of Europe so rather than being awed and thoroughly impressed by all I saw I was appalled by the vulgar display of conquest, the unashamed exhibit of bounty. There was more wealth of Africa in the four sub-basement floors of the British museum than presently in the continent. While all around me, people were snapping away at every window and dome, marveling and drooling over every monument, I was cringing, gritting my teeth, trying to erase the dead bodies, the wasted towns and villages, the misery. My head swam, my skin tightened and bristled.
>
> —Opal Palmer Adisa, "Spreading My Wings and Embracing the World"

For dinner that evening the only thing we could agree upon was pizza. We found a pizza café on St. Germain where the food was decent and cheap and a Heineken cost the same as a Coke. This place would become our second home.

"What do we do tomorrow?"

"We could go to Versailles Palace or Monet's garden at Giverny, maybe get out of the city," I offered.

"Shopping. It's time to shop," they said in unison.

By Thursday I had devised a strategy to satisfy my Paris sight-seeing addiction. I would rise in silence and sneak into the bathroom to write in my journal, then take off for breakfast in the Luxemburg Gardens and some close-by sites. I'd then double back to the hotel at around one, wake up the girls and wait for them get dressed until three, then we would head out. Today it would be shopping near Boulevard Raspail.

The lesson on prices turned into more than just calculating exchange rates. I had to agree with the girls that this stuff was expensive, even in the less chic shops. Shoes were seventy to ninety dollars and a simple T-shirt was close to forty.

"Where is the mall?" Ronya asked.

"Gallery Lafayette is not too far, and there is a bargain department store along the way."

We arrived at the department store, Tatee, just about the time office workers get out of work. Bedlam. People were packed in the narrow isles, speaking very brisk French or Algerian or Chinese with a French accent and with a more aggressive approach to shopping than I had experienced even in New York. We were badly battered as we considered purchases. At one point I looked over my shoulder and caught pitifully bewildered looks on my nieces' faces and suggested they go outside while I paid for our purchases. I went to rescue them with a couple of extra gifts, cheap umbrellas. It had begun to rain. We gave up on shopping and returned to the hotel in silence.

After a late dinner that consisted of nine-dollar sundaes at the Haagen Daz café, they finally let me have it full force.

"We came here for a vacation," Ronya started. "When I go on vacation, we sleep late, then go to the beach. And everybody speaks English and everything is real cheap. It's not like that here."

I began to explain that we were not in a resort or back home. We were

I arrived in Nimes, feeling very secure about traveling around southern France. I used travelers checks. I wore a hand-sized burglar alarm around my waist designed for joggers and had with me a garment purse to hide my money inside my clothes. My first stop was to the bank to exchange my dollars for francs. Then I set out to find the big attraction—the remains of the Coliseum built by the Romans. Standing just outside the gates were three women, two teenagers and an older woman, each holding one newspaper. I assumed they were news vendors but thought it odd that they only had one paper each.

As I left, I passed by the curious trio again. A block away, I heard rapid footsteps behind me and pitiful cries. The faster I walked, the more relentless were their cries. "Please, Miss. Give us, give us. Please, please!" Soon, one of them was on each side of me and one walking backwards in front of me, waving their newspapers around like fans. The more I resisted, the fiercer were their pleas.

When they began to stroke my arms to soften me up, I thought I would be sick. I reached into my fanny purse and pulled out a twenty franc coin, feeling proud of my generosity. But instead of leaving me alone, they stuck to me like leeches. To escape them I ran into the first open door I could find.

With the beggars out of sight, I continued enjoying my sightseeing. But in the evening when I returned to the train station to retrieve my luggage from the locker, I discovered that the locker key was missing from my fanny purse. Panic swept over me as I fingered the zipper to the second pouch. Just as I feared: every franc was gone. The thieves had used the newspapers to shield their hands from my eyes as they picked my pocket.

The police wrote up my case and told me that my tale of woe was typical. I could have kicked myself for failing to put the money in my undergarment money purse. My traveling partner was baffled as to why I had not used the burglar alarm buckled around my waist, especially after we had practiced using it many times. The only answer I could give was that the young women appeared to be harmless and I had felt pity for them. My advice: Trust your intuition (funny that they each only have one newspaper...) and use the security aids you buy for your trip!

—Pattie L. Harris, "Nimes"

in Paris. This a place where you see historical things you've read about and learn a little about another culture by watching, listening, and being curious. Then it was Helesha's turn.

"These are just old buildings to us. The people here are mean and try to run you over in those little cars. We came here to shop and we can't do that without more money; we don't know where to go and we can't ask anyone because we don't know what they're talking about."

And then the final blow.

"We were thinking we should leave, maybe go to London or just go home." Ronya nodded in agreement as Helesha spoke.

Go home? Leave Paris? After three thousand dollars and three thousand miles? I closed my eyes and began breathing deeply to push away the vision of tossing two young black bodies over the balcony. I checked my tone of voice and began what I thought was a reasonable defense.

"How could you leave Paris after only three days? You haven't even seen half of it. We are staying right where James Baldwin and Langston Hughes met friends in cafés. Josephine Baker sang not far from here. Friends of mine who are artists had studios and jazz clubs in the next block. You haven't even given it a chance."

"Those people are all dead. We have given it a chance," Ronya pouted. "We'd rather just chill." End of discussion.

I awoke on Friday depressed. In Paris! Unthinkable. After going through my normal routine, including some scorched expletives about these two young sisters in my journal, I returned from my garden breakfast and walk to find them still sleeping. I threw some francs on the table and wrote a note that I'd be back at three.

The closest travel agents were in the area near the Opera House and I walked toward them with a vengeance, talking out loud to myself. How could anyone not love Paris? Couldn't they see that there was life outside of Roxbury? You can take the child out of the ghetto, but....

The third agent spoke better English than the others and I began to explain my problem. As I asked about making reservations to return to the States early or taking a ferry to London the next day, tears began to roll down my cheeks. She looked at me sympathetically or maybe she thought that I was as crazy as I was beginning to feel. We came up with two plans of escape, but I would have to make a decision and confirm arrangements by the end of the day. I had an hour. I jogged passed the Louvre, across the Pont Carrosel, up Rue des Sts. Peres to Rue de Seine. I walked the rest of the way to the hotel and arrived breathless to find the room empty. I sat on the balcony and just as I began to feel a twinge of panic the two of them burst into the room, laughing, with arms full of shopping bags. For the first time in days, I was thrilled to see them.

"We found some good places to shop, up around the University," Ronya gushed, showing me the outfits and gifts she had bought.

"Yeah," Helesha said, unpacking her wares. "We walked in the store and they started talking in French. We stared at them and they laughed and started trying to talk in English. I can understand almost anybody if I'm trying to shop." They pulled out skirts, jackets, scarves, and barrettes purchased at some of the very places I had passed on my solo adventures.

Relieved that they were alive, and jealous that they were having a better time without me, I explained where I had been and the choices we had. We decided to compromise with a trip to London but to give me two more days in Paris.

"We think we can stand it two more days," Helesha smiled, "and anyway, I've got to bring back a picture of the Eiffel Tower."

For the next two days my routine changed. I got up and out early and went to see Giverny one day and the Rodin Museum and the flea market at St. Sulpice the next. I'm not sure what the girls did, but we met for a decent dinner each evening and finally found something that impressed them: the Eiffel Tower at night. I even got Ronya to try something other than hamburgers and pizza. I figured a ham and cheese crepe was at least a step in the right culinary direction.

London turned out to be delightful. Some brothers hit on the girls in English our first night, and we found blocks upon blocks of shopping on Praed Avenue. Somehow we squeezed in Buckingham Palace, Westminister Abbey, and the House of Parliament to appease me. Ronya and Helesha liked the city so much that they began planning to return the next summer.

On the flight home I pondered it all. True, they had acted a bit spoiled. On the other hand, maybe I had been heavy-handed in wanting to expose them to the things that touched my soul. But how would I have viewed Paris if I had taken Spanish and African American studies instead of French and World History? How would I have done if my first visit had been with a guide who had her own view of what was important instead of letting me discover Paris for myself?

I ended up seeing that it hadn't been such a bad vacation after all, just two different ones—theirs and mine.

Tonya Bolden

In the Land up Over

WHEN I TOLD THEM I WAS BOUND FOR ICELAND, A FEW FRIENDS AND FAMILY MEM-
bers misheard and thought I was off to scout out shamrocks and lepre-
chaun hideaways of gold. Others shivered for me, imagining Iceland
akin to Siberia. Which is pretty much what I thought.

So why was I going?

It was a free trip, a "fam" trip to be exact; and I was quick to adopt this
bit of travel industry lingo, what with "familiarization" being just too
much a mouthful. My benefactor was a magazine that I wrote for occasionally, and I was all flattered, until I realized it was only at the elev-
enth hour, when there'd been no takers among the magazine's staff and
star contributors, that someone thought of me and my unfettered curiosity. How else to explain that I had only three days to prepare for the
journey?

But I couldn't not go. How bad could it be? I'd be away for just a few
days, and in the company of about a dozen Americans, most of whom,
including two other African American women, turned out to be from
New York City like me. And since we'd be guests of Iceland's government, we would receive the red-carpet treatment. Still, I was disoriented
and something like scared. It wasn't a fear of physical danger, but something more basic: *Un*familiarization. I knew zip about the place. This was
in April of 1986, six months before the Reagan-Gorbachev summit in
Reykjavik and more than a decade after Bobby Fischer outchessed the
Soviets' Boris Spassky there. (I was thirteen at the time, and far more
interested in what was going on in my neighborhood handball court

than in some silent mind game between two odd men in a strange place.)

"What language do they speak?" was one of my first questions. As a by-product of high school French and Latin and my having majored in Russian in college and graduate school, I felt that having a fix on the language (or at least its language family tree) would help me get my bearings. When I found out that in Iceland they speak Icelandic, well, that didn't help much. Nor did a former college roommate's reminder of that stuck-up store in Princeton specializing in "world-famous" Icelandic wool in severe, soulless sweaters, hats, scarves, and such, the very sight of which gave me the itchies.

Would that I could have had some plum thoughts about this journey out of my world. The only abroadening I'd known was a trip to Jamaica, which hardly felt foreign either before or after my two-week stay there; and now, of all the places in the world, my first real trip would be to the land up over in the North Atlantic, an island right under the Arctic Circle.

Going in a hurry meant digesting the press kit on the fly. What a relief to find out that weatherwise the place was more benevolent than its name and location suggest. Neighbor Greenland, I learned, is the frigid, grueling place, with "moderately temperate" being Iceland's boast. Though I did not understand the geographics (something to do with the Gulf Stream), I did comprehend that I wouldn't be seeing Dancer and Blitzen look-alikes scrappling to prance in haunch-high snow. More to the point, I wouldn't be freezing my butt off.

Knowing that owing to Norwegian Vikings, Icelanders were, for the most part, of Nordic stock, I imagined meeting up with lots of tall, strong, blond people with names like Thor Thorsson and Brunhilda. Ninety-eight percent Lutheran and ninety-nine percent literate. What did I make of these stats? Icelanders would be an ordered people, I supposed, and at least not stupid.

Slightly twilight-zoned, that's how I felt when I stepped off the plane. Back home it was around midnight; up there, it was a bit beyond daybreak featuring a hollow wind and a firmament the color of dread.

The minibus transporting us to our hotel in Reykjavik hadn't been rolling long when a guide proffered Iceland's national tonic, so to speak. It was a schnapps, brand-named Brennivin, and nicknamed Black Death after the bubonic-pneumonic plague that ravaged so much of Europe, Asia, and North Africa five hundred years ago. To this day I've not even tried to fathom what naming a drink after a horror says of a people. But I do recall that a shot of Black Death seemed just the bracing thing for what looked to be a long ride through a silent, treeless landscape stalked by hills of black lava capped with green moss. How comforting was the sight of the U.S. military base and, here and there, a sign in English like "Hospital." Any port in a storm. Any taste of home.

Our first stop was not the hotel, but the Blue Lagoon, whose waters, we were told, could marvelize the skin. In this bizarre dawn none of us cared, but we did dutifully disembark for a look at this much vaunted wonder. Heeding the instructions to follow the well-worn path lest we plunge into a spring with water close to boiling, we walked carefully through reddish mud, through fog, and the stink of sulfur. And, to our surprise, the lagoon was truly blue and looked deliciously warm.

When traveling in foreign countries use the same airlines the locals use. The fares are generally cheaper.

—Brenda Joyce Patterson

I was soon to discover that crisp air and crystalline streams came with the territory, too. And stories about midnight sun, which I never saw, but how nice to know it was sometimes there, as it was to hear about terrain where reindeer really traipsed. But it was Nature, not in mere majesty but in might, that fascinated me the most. In this place born of volcanic eruption and tormented by many more over time, I knew awe as I never had before. From the bus window, and with my booted feet upon the hard ground, I snapped frame after frame of stern, soaring mountains (most peaked by active volcanoes I was told), fierce rapids, rugged gorges, thunderous, wondrous waterfalls, mammoth glaciers and geysers spewing hot-hot water high up into a slate gray sky. Real humbling sights for a born and bred city kid like me.

If it had been up to me, I would have done nature walks every day. But I was a captive guest and the city sights of Reykjavik were preordained.

I have few photographs or vivid memory-pictures of Reykjavik proper. I have a loose recollection of seeing sculpture at almost every turn, and around every corner, an art gallery, museum, or theater, and lots of restaurants. Spotting a Bennetton during a guided walking tour reminded me that it's a small world after all. Spotting a swastika writ large on a forlorn building while on a free-time stroll reminded me that it's an ugly world too.

I remember thinking after the fifth or sixth meal that it was a good thing I had a high tolerance for food from the sea: caviar, shrimp, salmon, etc., were on tap and herring was par for the course, many varieties of which I sampled during a luncheon fashion show of daywear, nightwear, everywhere, of the "world-famous" Icelandic wool, which was starting to look not so bad by day three, which is around when it dawned on me that I'd seen no hordes of full-bearded, ham-bone men, nor an inordinate amount of blonds. Nothing epic, awesome, or tangentially Vikingesque in that Hollywood way. Cold fish. That was my first impression of the natives.

Not until I went to Broadway, reputed to be the largest disco in Europe at that time, did I peep another side. I wasn't much into discos at home and saw no reason to get in the groove way up there. But I went, and oh, buddy, didn't I find the scene repellent, what with the punk aesthetic in coif, couture, and posture: hair on end, outfits in metallics, neon hues, and leather, accessorized by pushing and shoving.

In the U.S. I had spied in white eyes everything from fear to loathing at the sight of me; but there, at Broadway, I first knew something else— I felt strange, surreal even. For what might have been subtle daytime double takes became stares at the disco. En route from my table to the bathroom, I found myself in the middle of a crooked circle of Icelandic men with a coarse curiosity in their eyes. From a few mouths came rough bits of English intended, I gathered, to get me to stay and dance or stay and chat or stay and let this one guy continue to touch my arm. As I tried to move on, a short, youngish fellow with a scrawny beard, dashed a kiss on my cheek.

I had no impulse to smack him, because my gut told me that he wasn't getting fresh. For he hadn't really kissed me, just my color.

One of our guides, a strapping, big-boned, young woman, rescued me from Thor-the-Scrawny and company by yelling at them in German. I had not a clue as to what she said, and, as I later found out, she hadn't assumed they understood German but she did know that, to many ears, even the most innocuous German phrase can sound like a fist in your face.

What a great reconfiguring of the psyche this meant, adjusting to white people who merely found me a strange being, rather than an absolutely wrong kind of creature. The two other African American women in our group had similar encounters. I knew better than to assume that we three were the first black people these Icelanders had ever seen, because, for one, we were in the twentieth century, and for two, I had been told there were African Americans among the U.S. troops stationed in Iceland. So, okay, maybe there wasn't much heavy socializing between the troops and the natives, and, okay, maybe there were no sister soldiers at the base, and so, maybe we were indeed rare sights.

The morning after our encounter with Icelandic nightlife we were on a small plane on our way to Iceland's number-one fishing port, where colorful murals and brightly painted houses with bubbly-lovely curtains in the windows and knickknacked sills bore witness to the people's zest. Cézannesque." That's how one of my travel mates summed up Heimaey. Yet, amid the charm were reminders that it could be a perilous place. The crater fields and the house knee-deep in volcanic ash were mementos of a fury from below that had rocked the little island of roughly five thousand people something bad in 1973.

Heimaey had made a tremendous comeback. And, my Lord, what a Sunday morning I had, surrendering to Heimaey's vibrant beauty. In the afternoon it was just as good when we were at sea in a light rain, moving smoothly and with a little speed on tender waves, or drifting through sweet air toward a mountain flocked with gulls, or pulling into a grotto.

"This is the most beautiful cathedral I've ever seen," someone sighed as our captain treated us to his trumpet. "Amazing Grace" is what he played. My happy tears were on the rise as he brought this so sweet, so familiar hymn to a close and moved into a seaman's prayer.

I did not want to leave Heimaey and fancied that God had smiled on my wish, when a blanket of fog swept in, stranding us. Our predicament was easy to savor since our guides were obliged to make sure we knew only high hospitality. While they made the arrangements (including procuring toothbrushes), all we Americans had to do was be merry at a quaint and cozy inn. Most settled down to conversations, a few sang, and, true to stereotype, one or two found something to complain about.

I had a brandy-warm chat with our senior guide, Engilbert. He was a sober-faced, middle-aged man with an insatiable appetite for books, who spoke with great passion of his reading adventures. I was in shock when he said that even ordinary Icelanders consume upwards of sixty books a year and have a reverence for poets. Now that stat about Iceland's literacy rate had some flesh, and I was beginning to understand why many Europeans regard Americans as philistines. It didn't strike me as patronizing at all when Engilbert told me how much he'd learned from the mini-series "Roots," and that he'd read the book, too. I was so looking forward to waking up to a tomorrow on cheery Heimaey, but I was not to be spoiled. In the late evening, the fog lifted and with it the ban on air travel.

It was quick-quick back to Reykjavik. And there, on the day of departure, I succumbed to a temptation I had never known. I was in my hotel room, pretty much packed, and doing a tour of every drawer (whether or not I'd used it) when in the nightstand I found a Bible. A Gideon? You bet. And I had no qualms about stealing it.

Up until then my Icelandic was limited to the requisites: hello, please, thank you, the name of my hotel, and the main moola word, *krona*. Now I knew a sixth word: *biblóan. Guð* made seven. I browsed the book of books looking at a mass of Icelandic for the first time and feeling a quiet joy and comfort because, even though I couldn't read word one, I knew what it said. Like when I stared at "*Fyrsta Bók Móse: upphafi skapaði Guð himin og jörð. En jörðin var þá auð og tóm....*" I knew it was announcing: "In the beginning God created the heaven and the earth and the earth was without form, and void...." This *biblóan* became my most cherished souvenir, more so than my hunk of post-volcanic rock, a little ice blue cookbook with scores of herring recipes, the four shot glasses that came with the deluxe edition of Black Death, and the off-white supersized wool scarf, long ago given away, because the minute I unpacked it I got the itchies.

When I returned to my world, I didn't waste time writing up my experience. I was byline hungry and naive enough to believe that if a magazine handed you a trip, you were obliged to deliver a travel piece. Not so with this magazine; not so for this trip. The travel editor turned down my article. With pity in his voice he blurted, "Black people don't go to Iceland."

Gloria Wade-Gayles

How Not to Be a Gringo: Experiences with Color and Race in Mexico

THIS IS WHAT BEING A FOREIGNER MEANS, I THOUGHT TO MYSELF. YOU KNOW NOTHing and nobody and, therefore, you are in danger of making costly errors. Solution? Follow the white people. "Isn't that something?" I thought to myself. I came to Mexico to interact with people of color, bond with them, especially the women, and what must I do as soon as I arrive? Follow the lead of white people. They were everywhere in the airport, and many were seasoned tourists as evidenced by stickers their bags wore pretentiously: Paris, Stockholm, Milan, Berlin, Tokyo, Costa Rica, Rio de Janeiro, Portugal, and other places I hoped my children would one day visit.

I chose a white man with a kindly face and eyes that said, "Lady, you need help," to which I wanted to say, "Just give me a month and I'll do what my people always do. I'll close the gap. I'll fend for myself." Needing him desperately, I followed him like a duck, imprinting.

"Burth certifi-ket," the voice said when I reached the counter. It belonged to a man dressed in a brown uniform that resembled a police outfit. He was short, a bit on the stout side, dark, and with a bushy mustache. Was that really how he looked or how media massaging told me he should look?

"Burth certifi-ket" I heard again, only this time a tone of annoyance pronounced the words.

"*No tengo* burth certifi-ket," I said, regretting that I could not tell him *en español* that I was told back in the States, my passport would be sufficient.

"No burth certifi-ket. No enter. Next." He motioned for a man behind me to come to the counter.

"But. . . ."

"No burth certifi-ket. Next."

The man was not the kindly face I had followed, but he was kindly. Without my asking, he interceded on my behalf, speaking Spanish slowly but, apparently, well enough to advocate for my clearance. The Mexican official listened, interrupted only once with a question, shrugged his shoulders, looked at my "pass-a-port," and then gave it a loud stamp of approval.

"*Gracias,*" I said, to my white benefactor. "*Gracias.*" Trying not to show how wounded I was and how utterly lost, I followed other passengers who had been cleared, hoping they were going to the baggage area where, according to directions from the language institute, I would see the Mexican man who would drive me to Cuernavaca holding a large card that read my name. I saw him immediately and with a sigh of relief (and sufficient Spanish), I identified myself: "*Me llamo* Gloria Gayles."

A sudden turn, a Eureka sound from the driver, and we were pulling into a narrow driveway that deadended at a conclave of four lovely homes. He jumped from the Bug with jubilation, speaking excitedly to me in Spanish, and motioning me to follow him. He rang the bell, and a heavy-set woman in her mid-fifties appeared. "*Aquí,*" he said. "*Su casa.*"

The woman received me warmly and, with the translating assistance of a younger woman, apologized for having eaten before I arrived. They had tried to wait, but the hour was late, and they feared an error had been made and I had been sent to a different family.

"*No problema,*" I said, which was much too casual or lacking in respect for the occasion, but that was all I could remember to say. "*Yo hablo español un poco,*" I said, to make amends, which wasn't necessary since I was with them precisely because I spoke so little Spanish. Her name was María, and in complexion and facial features, she could have been a cousin on my mother's side of the family and, in the sweep of her hair from her face, my mother herself. She introduced me to the other women in my Mexican family: her mother, a thin and rather frail woman who fit the stereotype of Mexican matriarchs dignified by gray hair and a Spanish shawl; her older sister, Tía, whose effervescence made me think of a Mexican party; and her daughter, Lucía, newly turned twenty.

Only after the women had introduced themselves did she appear, and when I saw her, I gasped. Literally, I gasped. I had come all this way to be among people of color only to find myself forced to share my Mexican family with a white American. Her name was Linda, and she lived, of all places, in Atlanta. But, being white, she lived far from me, on the other side of the city, in Roswell, to be exact, a white community known to be politically conservative and created by white flight. Like a selfish child who, needing attention or wanting it, rejects the new "thing" brought home from the hospital, I rejected Linda. So much in my own racial conditioning made me believe she would bring into *mi casa* negative energy from the States.

The solution to the problem—and problem it was, for me—was simply to be polite to Linda without letting her assume importance in my experience. I was there to live and bond with Mexican women and that is what I intended to do. Alas, Linda spoke good and rapid Spanish, a fact that made me regret even more her presence in my house. Having been reared to be in all situations "a credit to the race," I didn't like being in language kindergarten in the presence of a white woman—and a Southerner at that!—who was in language college, if not graduate school. Since language permits you to belong, and empowers you, she would have a voice and I would not.

My accommodations were modest, but most comfortable. The house consisted of four bedrooms, a large dining room, a kitchen, two baths, and a patio, in the middle of which was a small swimming pool surrounded by flowers that grew in splendid profusion. What the home said about the status of the people depended on where you lived in Cuernavaca. If you were in communities where palatial homes were hidden behind large wooden gates that, when opened, showed large swimming pools, palazzos, uniformed men and women serving meals, and Jaguars and Mercedes polished to a shine, *mi casa* said the owners did not belong to Cuernavaca's elite. But if you were near *el centro,* where dwelling places were cardboard boxes, literally, and bathrooms were places hidden from view (and sometimes not), *mi casa* said the owners were privileged, just not wealthy.

My room was located directly in front of a bathroom Linda and I shared and to the left of a sewing/TV room where María and Tía gathered every Friday evening to hand-sew dresses that would go for a pretty penny in the States. While they sewed, they watched soap operas, the only difference between them and *Days of Our Lives* being language. My room was furnished with two twin-size beds, a nightstand, adequate closets, and a window that opened to a small garden at the back of the house.

On that first night I unpacked, took a long shower, and fell asleep as

*F*ind out the status of a country's water by contacting your local public health agency. If the water isn't safe to drink, it is best not to use it to brush your teeth or as ice. Instead, either boil water for twenty minutes or drink only bottled water. Remember, too, that alcohol doesn't purify water. Often hotels and restaurants have purification systems or will provide bottled water.

—Donna Mungen, "Eating Healthy Abroad"

soon as I began conjugating the most important verb of all: study. *Estudio, estudias....*

At seven the next morning, I was awakened by a light tap on my bedroom door. "Gloria," a voice said musically. "Gloria." I liked the sound the Spanish gave my name. I dressed and went down the hall to the kitchen, where everyone was gathered for the first meal of the day. I struggled to converse, but simple expressions like *"Buenos días"* and *"Buen dia"* were all I could remember. Foreigner? Foreigner is when you are sitting in a room with five women, hearing them talk and understanding nothing.

Before we finished breakfast, the door opened and the youngest of the matriarch's seven children appeared, a tall, slim, and black-haired young man in his late twenties. His name was Raul, which, in my media-contaminated mind, conjured up images of a matador, a Flamenco dancer, a mad revolutionary, or a combination of all three. He kissed the older women affectionately and teased the younger one, his niece. When María introduced him to me, she identified him as *mi hermano* and me as *la estudiante nueva*. Raul was cold enough to be hostile. He was there to drive me to the Institute, not to converse with me or even to be perfunctorily polite to me. That was clear in his eyes that refused to meet mine. His commitment was to his family; theirs was to me, a paying boarder.

The trip to the Institute took us up and down steep hills, through quiet neighborhoods of homes of splendor, and past congested corners where vendors, all of them dark in complexion, hawked their wares, to a complex of four or five buildings that faced a tree so magnificent in size and beautiful in the configuration of its leaves that it competed with the mountains for my awe. Raul never spoke during the trip, and neither did I. I didn't have enough facility to; he had no desire to. When he stopped in front of the building, he nodded the order, "Get out." I had trouble opening the sliding door of the van. He offered no assistance. Without saying, *"Adios,"* or *"Hasta la vista,"* he sped away.

Finally, I was where my dream had taken me: the Institute. As I had expected, few of the students were African Americans—perhaps four out of three-hundred-plus students—but as I had not expected, all of the administrators and teachers were fair-skinned. Mexicans of color were visible at the Institute only during the noon hour when, as vendors, they came inside the walls of the Institute to sell their crafts.

I performed well enough on the entrance exam to be placed in intermediate Spanish. My pride needed that victory. "You see, Gloria," I said to myself, "you knew more than you realized." The fact of the matter was that I could write the language and read it fairly well (as long as I had a *Cassell's Spanish Dictionary* with me), but the speed with which it is spoken made me appear comatose during the conversation portion of the exam. That is why I had chosen to spend a month at the Institute—to learn to converse in the language.

Much to my disappointment, however, the emphasis on conversation promoted in the brochures was sorely lacking in the actual program. The approach to teaching the language was decidedly traditional; we had a textbook, we filled in blanks, we conjugated verbs, and we completed homework. When we broke for lunch, I was anxious to find someone who, like me, wanted to struggle to converse.

> When traveling, allow yourself to give up control and be open, like a child, to learn about new things and new people. You will learn so much about yourself, that's the most wonderful part.
>
> —Mae Jemison

I was disappointed again. A majority of the students in my section of the campus were white businessmen enrolled in the classes at company expense, the better to corner a growing market, I supposed. I was passionate; they were disinterested. I held the language and the culture in reverence. They made jokes about sounds they could not pronounce. They were real *gringos,* who would willingly change the dividing line of the "border" when doing so increased sales, but always maintaining justification for the "border."

I approached a trio of Germans, all men. "Girl, Gloria," I said to myself, "you're some kind of brave. Bold." I literally showed off—an African American woman in Mexico speaking German to Germans, controlling the conversation, of course, so that it would not go beyond my ability and when it seemed to be headed in that direction, I quickly said, *"Ich habe mein Deutch vergessen. Das ist schade. Yah?"* No, it wasn't sad, because I had absolutely no interest in remembering German. I was in love with Spanish.

What was sad, however, was my inability to connect with the few African Americans at the Institute. They averted their eyes from me. I understood. The presence of other African Americans in a sea of whiteness sometimes causes some of us discomfort. I left them alone.

At the end of the day, as I was going to the bookstore to purchase a required text, I saw an African American woman in locks whom I thought I knew or whom my desperation told me I knew. I approached her and then screamed out her name with joy. "Bernice! Bernice Reagon!" If I were my aunt, I would have said, "Oh, but the Lord is good!" Imagine that! Bernice Reagon of Sweet Honey in the Rock standing before my eyes, sweeter than she had ever been because I needed her so. We embraced and within seconds another African American whom I had not seen joined us.

"What are you doing here?" I asked. What a foolish question! *"Que tal?"*

Bernice Reagon, right there at the Institute! I would be okay! I would be more than okay! She told me about a dinner/party planned that evening for students who were ending their stay at the Institute. She was among them. So, the Lord teases us. That left Linda as the only woman from the States with whom I would spend time and with whom I could converse in English when I became frustrated over not being able to do so in Spanish.

After dinner, Linda took me to *el centro*, where Mexicans far deeper in color than the Institute people stood in the hot sun selling their crafts. Such bright colors I had never seen. Blues and greens and yellows painted with broad strokes and fine strokes on stone, cloth, bark, straw, ceramic, leather, wool, and silver. There were baskets and hats and statues and medallions and jewelry and ponchos.

The marketplace itself, which stood in the middle of *el centro*, was a massive concrete construction of several tiers and passageways that led up steep steps to other passageways that led to avenues lined with meats and vegetables and produce. It was crowded with people, mostly women, wearing straw hats and holding the hands of children or carrying on their backs brown infants who slept soundly through the sounds of people conversing, guitars playing, vendors hawking, and cars revving their motors on the streets outside. Linda walked me through it with the expertise of a trained guide who loves everything in sight. There was nothing mean-spirited, arrogant, vain, or obtrusive about Linda. Clearly, she appreciated this culture of color.

After making our way from the top tier back to the street below, we sat in an outdoor café drinking coffee and bonding. Eventually, we came around to the subject of race in the States, our comments litmus tests we were administering to each other, relieved when we both passed. But mainly we talked about class in Cuernavaca, which was drawn rigidly along lines of color. Most of the vendors were dark, and all of the people I saw emerging from cardboard homes we passed en route to *el centro* were dark. The poor were dark; the not-poor were fair.

Fair was the dominant color among patrons in a store Linda and I walked to when we left the massive structure in *el centro*. The store was essentially off limits to the poor because everything inside cost a lot. It was a jewelry store where people purchased jewelry not much different from vendors' wares but far more expensive; a drugstore where white women from the States and elsewhere bought Retina-A to vanish away wrinkles; a bookstore where the latest in Mexican art and Mexican hardbound books was available, Frida Kahlo's work celebrated; and, in the back, a restaurant with premier service. Even the waiters and waitresses, dressed in white jackets, were fair.

Over dinner, Linda told me about the hard times *nuestra familia* had fallen upon after the death of María's husband, and why taking in student boarders was their livelihood, a job that denied them privacy and space. They were "on duty" seven mornings a week and seven evenings a week, free of us only when we were at the Institute on weekdays from eight to three-thirty. They prepared three meals for us—*el desayuno* (breakfast), *la comida* (the main meal served in the middle of the day), and a light snack at the time we would have eaten a full dinner in the States—and, at each meal, they were on duty to converse with us as their contract with the Institute must have stipulated.

Our efforts to wash dishes, sweep the floor, or feed their two cats—or to do anything other than study, sleep, and partake of their services—were rejected with politeness. For a family of four women without skills or beyond working age, in a city suffering from crippling unemployment, a steady stream of student boarders was an absolute necessity. It was the pain of this necessity that explained Raul's hostility and his infrequent visits to the family home. We were *gringos* whom women he loved served royally and daily. The brochures that publicized the delight of living with a native family failed to place the arrangement in the context of the country's economics.

My Spanish improved tremendously during the days I spent with Linda. She was good, really good, with the language. Linda was a retired high school Spanish teacher and, as the wife of a Delta pilot who could fly her anywhere, a frequent traveler to different parts of Mexico and Spain. She was patient with me, leading me into the language with creative skills the fair-skinned Mexicans at the Institute could do well to learn. We talked as mothers, as teachers, as wives, as women concerned about justice, as students loving Spanish with a passion. I regretted that my own experiences, and probably hers, had made us dance around each other before we were comfortable dancing with each other.

When she left for Atlanta, four days after my arrival, I was sad and found myself feeling like a foreigner again. Foreigner? That is when you are far from home, bereft of a friend you were recently blessed to find.

I missed Linda. I missed her when I could no longer endure my teacher's obvious disdain for me, her failure to recognize my hand when it was raised, her impatience with me, and her stroking, made-me-want-to-vomit indulgence of white students. For them, she had smiles. For me, she had a face with averted eyes. For them, there was understanding when the answer was not correct. For me, there was reprimand. That was it! No more! I went all the way to the top and was prepared to provide witnesses should I need them. I was transferred to another class to a teacher who gave to all students the benefit of her teaching. But I missed Linda.

I missed her when I walked the path she had shown me from the house to *el centro*, misjudging the distance of the trip when I walked it alone, hailing taxis that refused to stop for me, and more than once hearing "*Puta*," Spanish for prostitute.

I missed her when, en route home, I hailed a taxi at the busiest corner of *el centro*, giving him clear directions, *en español*, to *mi casa*. He took wrong turns. I knew that. I repeated the directions again. He was talking in rapid Spanish and when I heard him say "*mi casa*" rather than "*su casa*," I feared that he actually thought I was a *puta*.

The problem with VW bugs is that they only have two doors; you simply can't jump from them unless someone up front opens the door. My chant: "You can beat him. You are African. Your ancestors were Zulus in the mother country and revolutionaries in this one. You can beat him." He was stroking his crotch and repeating words I did not understand. "You can beat him. You can beat him."

Suddenly, with his left hand holding the steering wheel, he reached back with his right to pull up my skirt. My piercing scream and the fury of my English must have frightened him. He drove me home fast and as soon as I was out of the car, he sped away, not waiting to be paid, fearful that I would tell. And I would have, but there was no one to tell, no one to explain the pain of traveling from my native home, where the image of black women as whores, as available women, darker and therefore sweeter, penetrates the national psyche to find that image alive and well in a foreign land. Perhaps Linda could have understood some of this because I could have said it in English.

I missed her most when the new student finally arrived, two days later than her due date. The family, understandably, was concerned, for that was two days without pay. Had a mistake been made at the Institute? Had the student been assigned to another family? Did she change her mind and, if she did, was it possible to get another in her place as soon as possible?

The new student was no Linda! She was insufferably vain and arrogant. The first thing she wanted to do after meeting the family and putting her bags in her room—Linda's room in my eyes—was tan. She donned a swimsuit and sat for hours with her face tilted to the sun's rays. She wanted to know this and to know that, to impress in this way and in that way—to be the center of attention, the cherished guest, the prima donna whose dance everyone applauded. At meals, she attempted to dominate the conversation. The Spanish word for her was *gringo*. The African American word was "Miss Ann." "Some of my best friends are black" is the kind of expression you expect from a pretending-to-be-enlightened "Miss Ann," and, sure enough, this one told me about some of her best black friends.

As the veteran boarder, I did the right thing, following Linda's example, I offered to take Miss Ann to *el centro*. Wearing a short skirt and a sleeveless blouse scooped low, she caught the taxis I had had difficulty hailing after Linda's departure. She found the children selling straw baskets, bargaining with desperation and competing among themselves, cute.

María and her family knew immediately who this woman was as they had learned in my week with them who I was. I had won the respect of *mi familia* because I gave them mine. They liked me; that was obvious. They trusted me; that, too, was obvious. And though not as much as I would have liked, they identified me as a woman of color, which linked me to them in a way we understood though never articulated. Before the new student arrived, they had asked me about the civil rights movement, really about Dr. Martin Luther King, and the dogs, and the water hoses. Had I seen that? Yes. I had experienced that. I rose in their esteem. I knew I had when *la madre,* who rarely talked, listened with intense interest to María's Spanish translation of my responses to their questions. A religious woman who prayed throughout the day with her rosary beads, she nodded to me sympathetically and said, as Lucía interpreted, that white people would have to answer to God.

We talked about color problems in Mexico and, while they did not share my compassion for Mexicans living in abject poverty (somehow it was their fault), they seemed appreciative that I was saddened by the sight of young children selling wares in *el centro.* María considered that a sin before God, and she was convinced the children didn't have to do it.

Each night after dinner, I would sit with my notebook and my Spanish workbook in the large family room that opened to the pool at a table large enough to seat ten people and grand enough, with its authentically hand-carved oak, to be a museum attraction. The house was quiet and cool. Except for one of the family's two cats, who had decided to be my very own purring *el gato,* I studied alone. On Friday evening, however, I closed the books and spent time with María, Tía, and a friend who comprised the sewing circle that met in the back room to stitch and watch soap operas. They helped me with my Spanish; I helped them with their English. We laughed often at our mutual weaknesses, which often prevented us from understanding what was being said or asked. The spirit, however, we understood. We were all women, all of color, together in this "women's" room.

María was never without the serious look that said she alone carried the responsibility for caring for the family. Tía, the liveliest of the group, had never married, but I sensed that only recently had she given over her Fridays to needle and thread. I could picture her swirling on a dance floor, her hands in castanets and her painted lips singing a seductive song. María never wore makeup. Tía usually did. The three women made perfect stitches while watching soaps that were inane serials about blonde Mexican women embroiled in love conflicts with Mexican men who, if not always blonde, were never dark like the vendors in *el centro*.

Near the end of my visit, when my Spanish had improved and my fingers knew the needed pages in my dictionary, I chanced talking with the women about women's issues. For them, that meant caring for children, husbands, mothers, sisters, and brothers.

Mexico was poor, and the country was in political shambles, they admitted, and perhaps from the perspective of outsiders, Mexicans were lazy, but they were *muy felíz*. Very happy with and in their culture. I remember them joking one night about the hard-working Japanese. Mexicans would never work that hard, they admitted, because, unlike Japanese, who don't know how to live, Mexicans enjoy life. From the outside, we see Mexicans taking *siestas* in the middle of the day and stamp on them the image "lazy," not realizing that they began work early, left work to go home for the ritual of *la comida,* slept after the meal, and, awaking several hours later, they returned to work. Because of the intense midday heat, *siestas* are logical and healthful.

And finally, in the coolness of a Mexican night, I came to accept the woman who had taken up residence in Linda's room. She joined me at the oak table, interrupting my study with a desire to talk, a need to share her pain, apparently because something in my energy told her that my bosom was large and available. It was. I learned that she was in a love-hate relationship with her mother, a woman who was submissive as wife but domineering as mother. She had sought refuge in a marriage that ended in a bitter divorce. She was recovering from that bitterness and trying to heal from years of battering. Outside she was a flirtatious woman seemingly puffed up with vanity; inside she was a frightened and scarred child. "Never judge," my mother always taught me. "Never judge." One day I'll learn.

Four weeks after arriving in Cuernavaca, it was time to return home. Raul arrived delivering his usual kisses to his family and his expected silence to the *gringos*. He put my bags into the van and waited more patiently than I had ever seen him while I embraced María, Tía, Lucía, and the mother with genuine affection and gratitude. *En español!* My American compatriot rode with me in order to save Raul a trip back to *la casa*.

Not surprisingly, the people who crowded the bus terminal were dark in complexion, not fair. Police were waving their hands and blowing whistles, denying cars more than a second in front of the depot. Raul pulled from the traffic and quickly rushed over to open the door for me. Speaking in Spanish, my-soon-to-be-no-longer housemate advised Raul that he should help me with my luggage. *"No necesito la ayuda,"* I told Raul, hoping my Spanish was correct. She did not move to assist me. He scowled at her. I struggled with the luggage. I carried one bag to the front of the entrance, returned to the curb to get the second and began dragging it toward the terminal when I heard Raul calling my name. I turned around and saw him walking toward me, his stride balanced by a bag in each hand.

"You needn't do this, Raul," I said. "You'll get a ticket."

In silence, he walked me into the depot, put me in the line for the bus and, in full view of hundreds of Mexicans, he hugged me.

"*Gracias, Gloria,*" he said. "*Gracias.*"

He walked away quickly, turned around, and shouted loudly enough for everyone in the depot to hear. *"Gloria, buen vida. Buen vida."*

---

*T*he travel business and traveling have been a central part of my life. To me, travel is the best form of education. As an African American, travel has also helped me gain a sense of who I am.

Because the awareness of our racial differences is so deeply rooted in the U.S., we cannot help but judge our experiences as travelers by this reality. For example, I escorted a small group of African Americans to Brazil in 1979. We spent Carnival in Salvador da Bahia, a city rich in African tradition. Although we had an incredible time visiting this city—Brazil's historic capital and formerly a notorious center for the African slave trade—and although the tourist board representatives would have you believe that there is no racism, it was evident to our black selves that the class lines were clearly drawn along color lines.

We went on to Rio, one of the most exciting and beautiful cities in the world. We saw the mosaic sidewalks and the world-famous attractions of Corcavado, Christ the Redeemer Statue, and Sugarloaf Mountain, and the beaches of Copacabana and Ipanema. But an incident in Rio greatly disturbed me. I heard an African American woman announce in a very haughty manner, "These people can't even speak English." Someone reminded her that she was visiting a Portuguese-speaking country and one should not expect the people there to speak English any more than we should be expected to speak Portuguese when they visit the United States. I believe that one of the best lessons we learn as Americans when we travel is that we are not the center of the universe and, just maybe, our way is not always the best way.

—Stephanie Spears, "A Career in Travel"

Colleen J. McElroy

Journey to Ulcinj

NO MATTER HOW YOU CUT IT, YOU CAN'T GET TO ULCINJ FROM HERE OR ANYWHERE. On the map of Yugoslavia, all the roads are full of conflicting directions, all referring to some prehistory that only the Slavs understand. Ulcinj, I'd read, had been one of the harbors used by Turkish slave traders, and in the last days of the Ottoman Empire, the slave trading enterprise had simply been halted, "abandoning several hundred persons of African descent in Turkish ports all along the African and European coasts." One of those ports had been Ulcinj, located on what is now the southernmost tip of Yugoslavia, and according to travelers in that area, including my Serbo-Croatian language tutor, still containing descendants of Africans abandoned on those shores. I looked at a map. That explained the location, but nothing explained how all sense of roads had been abandoned. "Everyone has their reasons," my lover had once told me. And since he was a writer, living off his imagination, he said all I had to do was create reasons where none existed. Therein lies madness, I'd thought at the time. But that was before I needed a road to journey to Ulcinj. So I told myself: McElroy, use your imagination. Simple enough, except when I had to consider that you can't always get there from here, especially when here is Yugoslavia.

In the case of Ulcinj, all the maps were full of fuzzy lines. At first, I made formal inquiries—the polite American way—but I was in Eastern Europe, not America, and travel, by some inverse logic, seemed to become more difficult the closer my destination was to Belgrade. I spent weeks trying to cultivate the idea of time and motion with people who used time as a measure of determining what was due to them.

"Ulcinj?" they said in Belgrade. "That is in Yugoslavia?"

"On the southern tip. Near Albania," I said.

"Ah," they said. "Albania," they said. "But there is nothing there."

"Not in Albania," I began. "Near Albania. Montenegro. An old seaport for slave trade. When the Turks...."

I stopped. Their eyes had clouded over. I had crossed invisible borders—not once but twice. At the mere mention of the Turks, Slavs automatically replayed the five-hundred-year-old Ottoman invasion. Everyone was willing to talk about the invasion, but no one wanted to talk about the Turks. And as for Albania, no one talked about that—period. Somewhere in the middle of all that silence was Ulcinj.

Some people mistakenly believe that youth hostels are only for the young, but most are open to travelers of all ages. Many are in historic buildings, in beautiful locales. Contact American Youth Hostels in Washington, D.C., (202/ 783-6161 phone, 202/783-6171 fax) to get a directory and detailed information about hosteling. AYH also organizes inexpensive outdoors tours for teens, adults, and senior travelers, with an emphasis on education and cultural awareness.

—Elaine Lee

"The problem," Nada Obradovic said, "is simply this town that you wish to visit is in Montenegro."

"Yes," I said. "Montenegro. Crna Gora, the black mountain. Go tell it to the mountain. That be the place," I said in my best ghetto English.

Nada smiled brightly. "James Baldwin," she said. "Richard Wright, Langston Hughes, Gwendolyn Brooks."

This time, I returned her smile. Nada Obradovic was my translator, self-appointed before my arrival in Yugoslavia. I was flattered but disturbed that she'd bypassed all the copyright laws and provisions for intellectual property rights (a problem in many instances when a writer's work is translated without permission of the author). What it meant, simply, was that my work was being read in Eastern Europe, in towns where long names held two vowels and history was tied to men called Ivan the Terrible and Vlad the Impaler. And Nada, all apricot and peach and round as a plum, with a shock of red lipstick and bleached hair and nails like jeweled talons. At our first meeting, she had swooped me away from the male enclave of the Writer's Club on Avenue Vuk to her apartment several blocks away. That apartment more than equaled any dowager's flat on Park Avenue. French antiques, neoclassic Italian baubles, Victorian lamps, Austrian silver, Russian carpets, and an abundance of modern and expressionist art walled between an overflow of books, floor to ceiling on some walls. One room alone held the works of African and Caribbean writers.

And all this in a country where nobody seemed to know how to get to Ulcinj.

"I will take you to visit primitive painters in Korvacja. I have some of their works here," Nada said, waving a plump arm toward a nest of paintings on the wall behind her. "These artists are very famous in Yugoslavia. But Ulcinj is of no importance. And Montenegro, never. We have heard nothing of the literary life of Montenegro which holds any importance." She leaned forward to pour the coffee, her eyes filling with anticipation of a literary discussion. "Montenegro is no place for you," she said. "You should be here or in Zagreb, where many people will read your work. I know here a publisher who is anxious to speak with you. Yes, Belgrade is full of those who would translate your work." She offered a plate of chocolates. I declined. "Ulcinj. Interesting place," Nada continued. "But no one goes there." "Obviously someone has," I said. Nada sniffed.

I decided to try my own route. After all, I had been in the country for several months. I would simply book passage on JAT. My American friends in Belgrade had dubbed the airline Not Yet, and over the months, I had slowly learned why they harbored complaints about Jugoslav Air Transport. I placed a certain faith in any airline, believing it would generally go where they said it would, believing its comings and goings were regular, almost ordinary occurrences. Based on that, I ignored my previous JAT experiences, bought a ticket to Titograd, and triumphantly waved it in front of my doubting friends. Ulcinj, I told them, was now within my grasp.

"A ticket is easy," my friends said. "But the problem is finding the plane to go with it."

JAT lived up to its nickname. I lost count of how many times the departure was announced, how many times we were escorted to the gate only to find no plane, and how often I could walk from the newsstand to the lavatory and back without losing my seat in the waiting room. Six hours after the scheduled departure, we were finally in the air.

We landed at dusk when the sky was still cast in a pearlescent blue light. I was sitting in a window seat just forward of the wing, not a particularly safe seat, but given anyone's chances of surviving modern jet travel, as safe as any. From that vantage point, I could see a bus pulling away from the airport parking lot just as the plane descended. The bus wended its way down the spiraling road from the terminal and turned onto an access road. We bumped ground. The parking lot looked empty. I checked my watch and twisted in my seat. Surely those faint red taillights could not belong to the last bus to town. Forget that we were six hours late—even Balkan logic could allow some variation on schedules. I cursed JAT's inefficiency and for good measure glared at my seat partner, who had unbuckled his belt while we were still in the approach pattern, 10,000 feet off the ground. "Damn Slavic fatalism," I muttered. The plane swung toward a loading ramp, and I saw a set of stairs standing stark, like some dinosaur's spine, against the backdrop of the low slung terminal building. As we pulled closer, lights flickered off inside the terminal. One by one, the windows dimmed until there was only the yellow light over the entryway. For a second, the scene was too poetic: the taillights of a bus disappearing into the approaching darkness, stairs leading to nowhere, and now, the darkened terminal. Dreams of Ulcinj flickered with the lights.

"Your departure will be orderly," the cabin attendant said. Except that everything was already out of order with the terminal closing before the plane had landed and passengers plummeting into the aisle, frantically calling to each other and grabbing bags from the overhead bins as if we'd been ordered to life rafts right before some impending disaster. I rose from my seat with the sinking feeling the disaster might be mine. I reached for my bag. It was soaked with bad country wine leaking out of someone's poorly wrapped parcel. The canvas L.A. Gear pack would forever smell foul. I sighed. Yugoslavs looked at me with sympathetic eyes.

"We have three possible routes that might carry you to Ulcinj," the travel agent said. "The first route takes you from Titograd to Cetinje. And from Cetinje you proceed directly to Budva. From there, you might find a local bus to the town of Ulcinj or possibly a taxi. The second route takes you from Titograd directly to Petrovac. From there, of course, you might possibly hire a car. The third route takes you to Herceg-Novi, and you may catch the express bus to Petrovac, provided the bus to Herceg-Novi isn't full with passengers returning from Medjugorje. In which case, you may come back to Cetinje and proceed from there. But of course, you have arrived too late for this today."

She seemed really pleased with all of her "mights" and "possibles." I watched her trace the routes on a map, her red line jiggling through mountainous passes on the other side of Titograd. My heart jiggled along with it. I had already been on highways where the carcasses of cars were piled in cul-de-sacs like toys left to rust in the corner of some kid's room.

"We only put them there after the accident," a taxi driver had told me. "Then only to clear the road. Someone will take them away later." He'd shrugged when I'd asked him when, exactly, was later. But this was the same taxi driver who "saved on fuel" one night by turning off his headlights and coasting down the narrow road into the valley after discovering his gas gauge registered nearly empty.

"Tomorrow?" I asked the travel agent. "Can I go tomorrow?" She looked confused. "Do the buses run daily?" I asked.

Now her look was that of a kitten startled in the act of unwinding a ball of yarn. She gathered up all of the loose timetables scattered on the counter. "The buses south leave in the morning. The buses north leave in the evening. Unless you are leaving Titograd, then you may go north in the morning, provided you are going by express to Dubrovnik...."

"Can I purchase my bus tickets here?" I interrupted.

"I can only provide you with time schedules which reflect the arrivals and departures posted in each terminal."

I love everything about traveling—packing and figuring out what I'm going to wear, buying the tickets and negotiating the prices, deciding what hotel to stay at, sitting in the airport waiting for my flight to be called, or waiting in the train station to find out what track the train is going to come in on. I'm never happiest than when I'm on my way to somewhere.

—Tonya Pendleton, "Wanderlust"

Somewhere near Cetinje, I fell asleep, which was remarkable, considering how the motion of most Yugoslav buses seemed fixed on a sprung rhythm of bumpity-bump-hiccough. At least when I was asleep, I missed several dozen hairpin curves and villages the size of cowsheds. But I also missed my connection to Budva. I was awakened by a nudge from my seatmate and opened my bleary eyes wide enough to discover half the bus passengers had been staring at me while I slept—open mouthed, I was sure. What startled me all the more was that my seat partner was Japanese, and for one wild second, I thought I'd traveled back in time and was once again in Japan, lost and with no language referents. I forced myself from the twilight of a strange dream, one in which I'd been dancing to the music of a crazed string quartet under a canopy of palm leaves and rotting coconuts. Several people were eating goat's cheese, which explained the rotting coconuts, and the squeaky bus cushions explained the strange music, but I no longer knew what country I was in, much less where I was. I scrambled to find words. What came out was retarded German mixed with some sort of otherworld-Serbian: "Uh, Da li je ist moj?" I sputtered.

My seat partner smiled. Then slowly, with perfect diction, he said, "I am American. Do you speak English?" I nodded vigorously to show I really did, when I could speak at all. "I hope I didn't startle you," he continued, "but you've been asleep for a long time, and I wanted to know if you'd be going with us to the shrine of the Virgin?"

"Un-uh. I'm going to Ulcinj," I said. He frowned. "Ulcinj," I repeated. "On the other side of Budva."

A woman in front repeated "Budva," and the word spread throughout the bus. "Budva, ne," the woman said. People nodded. Even Ken Matsu, my American seat partner, nodded. "Budva je put sudje," the woman said. The mole on her upper lip danced into a smile line.

What did she know, I thought. So I asked again. "Koji je put Budva?"

Everyone, as if by command of some invisible captain of the guard, pointed south toward the back window of the bus. Meanwhile, we were climbing north, away from Budva, away from the mountains of Crna Gora.

"We are going to Medjugorje to the shrine of the Holy Virgin Mary," Ken said. "Have you seen the Virgin?"

I shook my head. "I haven't even seen Ulcinj," I muttered.

As one village dragged into another, I began to realize it would take twice as long to double back to Cetinje as it would to continue north to Mostar. In Mostar, I might catch the express to Dubrovnik rather than be stuck in Budva or Petrovac overnight. Besides, if I stayed on the bus, I'd have a chance to see what was being called the Miracle of Medjugorje, and that beat an overnight in a one-horse town any day of the week. I was beginning to think like a Slavic tour agent. And worse, my decision had a slight drawback: I was stuck in Medjugorje. The Christians, especially those who'd been on missionary assignments in Africa, took turns trying to save me, and even as we pulled into Medjugorje—a dusty little village where four teenagers claimed to have seen the Virgin Mary—my fellow travelers seemed undaunted by my stubborn refusal to embrace their beliefs

"I am as fascinated by biblical stories as you are," I said, "but these are teenagers, kids. Look, they keep saying Mary told them not to dance and watch television. You mean to tell me the Virgin Mary came all the way here to warn them away from the evils of television? Doesn't she have something better to do?"

"It was a sign for all of us," Ken Matsu said. "There are people here from all over the world. It is truly a holy place."

"Dusty, too," I said, and contemplated the sandy uphill trail to the site of the visitation. A hawker passed us selling maps, postcards, posters, souvenir statues, and bus tickets. I took a shuttle to the top of the hill.

The land rolled out like a worn carpet, patterns that had been worked and reworked by feudal rules, invasions, makeshift governments, and centuries of desperate peasants. It was a thought I frequently had in Europe, a feeling that the land was sagging under centuries of wars and constant change from ruler to ruler, language to language, and all the endless fighting that attempted to hold it still and in one piece. Europe was full of history, yes, but the burden was taking its toll. I only needed to look at the grim, unsmiling faces of people in Belgrade, or the forced joviality of Germans, or the carefully constructed mannerisms of the French and Italians. Like the pilgrims at Medjugorje, they all wanted that divine tie with the gods, a reason to keep it all going. Perhaps that was the difference between the Old World and the new one: In the States, there was a clear-cut definition of the conquerors and the vanquished, the country's history so new, those lines were still connected by the blood of Indian tribes and African slaves. The ties to the land were simpler: possession, bare knuckled, and may the best man win, provided we approve of who that man may be.

But looking out from that Medjugorje hillside, I could see that the ancient grudges were still there, rooted like those Inca markings I had seen on the Plains of Nazca in South America, fantastic animals of gigantic proportions, rising up the sheer walls of the cliff and carved ten feet deep into the bedrock of the plains—a strange code that had become a part of the soil, clearly visible from a distance but reduced to erosion cracks for anyone at ground level. Maybe I was too close to the ground at Medjugorje to see the big picture. Maybe I was simply distracted by my own journey to understand why so many had come so far on the strength of a rumor to see hillsides that were brown and webbed as sepia photographs.

If I looked really hard, I could almost imagine the purple mountains of Montenegro in the distance, and somewhere well beyond them, but still elusive, Ulcinj. All I really saw was a checkerboard of small wheat fields and dairy farms, a few scattered farmhouses, and the town itself, with its lone church and cobblestoned streets, lines of pilgrims trudging away from it like worker ants. The grainy soil was shallow, a fitting complement to the downcast eyes and lackluster sales pitch of some of the more enterprising townsfolk. There may have been only a handful of them, but they were vigorous, and at the top of the hill, they pressed their advantage by offering both audio- and videotapes of three thin children kneeling on the grassy slope, their faces turned in beatitude toward the sky. Those tapes were our only chance of seeing the children that day.

"Isn't it wonderful," a woman said as we boarded the evening bus to Dubrovnik. "I feel so privileged to get a chance to visit the place where the children saw our Blessed Lady."

"What children?" I asked. "I only saw souvenir vendors."

"Well, two of them are married and don't have visitations any longer," the woman whispered. Her tone was as confidential as an *Enquirer* columnist's. "The others are visited only on the weekends now."

"Weekends? How does the Virgin know it's OK on the weekends?" Silence. "There's a book on visions. I think it's called *Salem Revisited?*" I continued. "Those girls in Salem had visions too, you know. Different kind, but according to this book I read, it all has something to do with the way the wheat was stored. You know, a hallucinogen off the wheat germ. Mother Nature's LSD. That and puberty. All those hormones. Maybe that explains why the married ones don't get visions any more."

"I'm sure I don't know," the woman said, then pulled her lunch of bread and cheese from her rucksack of souvenirs and left me to my thoughts. I told myself: McElroy, ease up. Each of us is chasing some spirit. Yours is just in Ulcinj.

It would be equally true to say I arrived in Ulcinj by way of Medjugorje as it would be to say I finally made it on the magic of a Turkish carpet. Indeed, the Turkish carpet came as a result of my visit to Dubrovnik, but the only magic was how one quick look at Medjugorje could send me scurrying off to Dubrovnik to recover from the pilgrimage. Dubrovnik was a wonder city, an Adriatic Disneyland of castles, seashore, and tourists, where the sound of laughter, so foreign to Belgrade, was often heard. After months of wandering through the gray smog of Serbia, where dimly lit restaurants promised no more than boiled meat, clumps of radishes, and conspiratorial conversations, Dubrovnik offered succulent scampi turned pink with spices, black risotto steamed in inky squid, roast lamb, rich red wine, Turkish coffee, and some of the best desserts south of Austria. All of it served under bright umbrellas in outdoor cafés pocketed, table against table, along narrow streets and cobblestoned stairwells in the old walled city, the Starigrad of Dubrovnik. There, even the waiters smiled, and the competition for customers was carried on in loud, friendly echoes throughout the little nooks of the castle walls. But the life of the city was not exclusively in the castle, shops, and public square of the Starigrad. Dubrovnik was blessed by sun, sea, mountain air, and an overflow of foreign visitors. Under its mantle of sunlight and medieval glitter, the city carried its past as some modern members of royalty assume their crowns—to be admired without all the bother of wearing them every day. Its cachet of urbanity welcomed me as no other town in Yugoslavia had.

Dubrovnik was no Medjugorje full of suffering children who lived through visions, nor did it mirror Belgrade's impolite ruffians who had stared and taunted me. I discovered that difference earlier in the spring when I'd gone to Dubrovnik to attend a meeting of the International Congress on Women. Almost every country in the world had been represented at the conference, including America, and luckily for me, several of the writers were black women, two of whom I knew. The day I saw Geneva Smitherman and Angelita Reyes walking up the stairs of the University Admissions building, old home week had come to Dubrovnik. We greeted each other as if we'd been lost in the desert and found an oasis. Geneva and Angelita, along with four other black American women, were presenting papers at the conference. That first day, we had lunch together. The word spread: Black women have come to Dubrovnik. Had there ever been so many, and American, in town at the same time? Tongues wagged, as the gossip columnists would have said. Eyes followed our progress down the street. Not that we made any effort to be inconspicuous. Rosalind Griffin, a psychologist from Chicago, had me help her interview several young men who sold their bodies to tourists from Western Europe. "Ask them if they have a union," she insisted. "And what about health insurance?" The young men tried to answer, but it was easy to see that they were more fascinated with having a conversation with black women than they were with the questions Rosalind proposed. That was the contrast of Yugoslavia: the religious visions of Medjugorje, the political shortsightedness of Belgrade, and the ease of Dubrovnik, a city that had attracted every tyrant since Attila the Hun because of its access to the sea. All those invasions had made Dubrovnik cosmopolitan, more open to the world outside of Yugoslavia. The best shopkeepers in Dubrovnik were Albanians. Geneva and I visited a rug merchant in the Starigrad who held us in conversation so long, we almost missed a dinner appointment with the other women.

We met at one of the outdoor cafés in the old city. There were five of us, and as we waited—too long it seemed, for waiters to notice us, I began to think that some of Belgrade's coldness had reached the coast. Ten minutes passed. Twenty. This would have been slow even in Belgrade. Finally, a waiter came over. In a Slavic dialect heavily accented in Serbian, he began asking about a purple book. The women looked at me. "What the hell is he talking about?" Geneva said. I had understood *knjiga*, the word for book, but little else. "I don't know what he's talking about," I said. The waiter grinned. "I speaking English," he said. "Who is writing the purple book?"

"Purple book?" Angelita repeated.

Then I understood. "He wants to know which one of us is Alice Walker," I said.

The women laughed. "Get out," Anita said. "We don't look like Alice."

"Well, think about it," I said. "There's the conference, and here are five black women in one place at the same time."

"That doesn't mean one of us is Alice," Geneva said.

The waiter held out a battered book. The title was *Ljubicasta Boja*. "Well, until he holds out a menu instead of that book, one of us had better be Alice," I said.

"No problem," Rosalind laughed. "You're the writer."

I signed the book: LJUBAV, ALICE, in scrawling letters. And let me tell you, that dinner was the best one I had in Dubrovnik.

◦ ◦ ◦

Later, when I returned to Dubrovnik after my failed attempts to reach Ulcinj, I headed straight for Rafi, the rug merchant I'd met when I'd been with Geneva. The visit was old-fashioned, neither of us getting to the point until we'd had a bit of conversation. "Sit. Have a cup of tea. We will talk," Rafi said.

We talked about his collection of James Brown, and rock 'n' roll. "We have heard much of your music," he said.

I said, "Yeah. On my first day in Belgrade, I heard Terrance Trent D'Arby blaring out of a shop on Revolutionary Square. But I still had to go through six people before I could buy one grapefruit."

Rafi laughed. "But it is that way for everyone. Here in the state store, you have someone to select for you, someone to weigh for you, someone to price, someone to bag, and so on. Then everyone has work."

I looked around the shop. "You're the only one working here," I said.

"Yes, but you see, I have the work permit for selling to foreigners. Turkish rugs, Albanian rugs. I sell them all. It comes down through my family through the generations. That is what we have been doing for hundreds of years." He paused. "Where is your friend?" he asked, referring to Geneva.

"Gone home to the States," I told him.

"Pity," he said. "She never buys from me a rug." He shook his head.

I bought a rug. Then we talked about my perceptions of Yugoslavia. I bought a tapestry. Finally, the conversation moved to history. I bought several pieces of embroidery, and Rafi talked about Ulcinj. "I can get you there," he said. "I know many people in that town. A cousin of mine lives there."

I said nothing. I had once traveled with two Haitians who claimed every telegraph office in South America was manned by one of their cousins. And I once left a traveling companion on a lonely road in the middle of a country about to erupt into a civil war. He too was going to visit a cousin, although all I saw from the rear window of the bus was him standing in a swirl of dust and no houses for miles in any direction.

"How far from Ulcinj does your cousin live?" I asked.

"Oh, he lives no more than two kilometers from the center of the town," the rug merchant said. "It is easy to find his house."

"Good. So, how do I to get to Ulcinj?"

"That is not so easy," he sighed. "You must decide if you will travel by the bus or the boat. By the boat, you arrive six, seven o'clock, and next morning, you take the return boat. Or you may go by the plane or the train. Then you must take the bus. But I prefer the boat. Then you only need to take the taxi to my cousin's house." Boat, bus, plane, train? There were too many memories of the bus to Medjugorje still fresh in my head, but in the end, I had no choice but to trust Raji's route and his cousin.

◦ ◦ ◦

The beach at Ulcinj was anything but inviting. We entered at high tide under the shadow of the old medieval fortress. From a distance, all I saw was sharp rocks rising abruptly from the water into clumps of bushes that trembled under the force of the wind. Down the beach, there were thin patches of white sand among the rocks, but the day was overcast and blue sky was a distant dream from Dubrovnik. The air was sharp with the smell of salt and diesel fumes from passing fishing boats. Aside from myself, those few passengers who had come this far south from Rijeka, Split, or Dubrovnik were Germans and Swedes who seemed to relish the brisk air and swift current. Those on shore under the shadow of the fortress ruins, greeted us with the sour looks of people who had battled the weather all too often. Even in cloudy weather, the shadow of the fortress fell on everything, the skeletal shapes of Venetian, Turkish, and Slavic architecture looming like something left over from Mary Shelley's novel. At the end of the boat dock, I took a careful step, but land was elusive and the planks slippery with years of accumulated algae. My foot slipped, and the motion began to carry me back toward the sea when someone grabbed my hand. I looked up into the face of Rafi's cousin, and behind him, an older man whose features were so familiar, he could have been my own cousin, or uncle, or neighbor from any one of a dozen places in the States. And I knew I had finally reached Ulcinj.

What I remember most about Ulcinj was once there, time settled into place the way it does when I return home. Slobodan Tresic welcomed me into his house the way my mother's friends would welcome me home. His wife, shyer, never left the kitchen except to greet another neighbor come to see the "mala crna amerikanischa." Only the language was different, although after a while, no one really needed Rafi's cousin to translate for us. Neighbors dropped in to see the homesick wanderer, and like my relatives in the States, everyone brought food for the visitor. We ate. I ate far too much of everything. Some brought small gifts. Almost all brought children. Babies sat in my lap and looked big eyed and confused. Some fell asleep, their pale brown faces nestled in the crook of my neck. Others cried, burped all over my dress, and caused general distress for their mothers. Young children played with my finger rings, measuring their smaller hands against my long thin ones, all the while haltingly counting the number—jedan, dva, tri... each time surprised that my fingers and their vocabulary ended on the same digit. Women showed me their family heirlooms and needlepoint. I showed them pictures of my children, my books, my home in America. I listened to old men tell stories that I only half understood, but their laughter told me enough to understand that only half was true, anyway. And when the stories turned to war and hunger, I heard about young people who had been killed and others who had moved away to better jobs or schools. And how the Germans had taken scores of men during the war. How the others had hidden in the hills. Who trusted the Yugoslavs or Albanians or Turks. And who counted back far enough to find home in Africa, where faces like mine, Rafi's cousin said, were locked in some family albums. And toward midnight, when all the children were curled inside sleep, the singing began. An old man played a violin. I remember a particularly sad song about the sea, and how it always tries to return to land, only to be pulled away again. I remember the voice of the old woman who sang it, her weathered face brown like the sturdy trees near the cliffside. Several days later at Ohrid, Yugoslavia, I had my morning coffee under a striped umbrella by the lake, facing the distant shores of Albania. And I swear that woman's voice was singing still.

Elaine Lee

Creating and Sustaining a Trip around the World

FOR YEARS, I THOUGHT IT WOULD BE GREAT TO TAKE OFF SIX MONTHS TO A YEAR TO sample, savor, and celebrate the culture, food, and natural wonders of life on this earth. One day, I pulled my dream down from the ethereal plane and made it happen. With a thirty-pound backpack, a hope, and a dare, I began a remarkable solo adventure through eight countries in Central and Southern Europe, Africa, and Southeast Asia. I returned home seven months later, my spirit rejuvenated and the borders of my inner and outer world greatly expanded.

I began the journey in 1991, a full year before my departure, when I announced my vision to friends and neighbors at my annual New Year's party. During a ritual, each of us shared an important goal. We pretended that we had already accomplished or received the thing we wanted. We discussed how it felt, acted it out, made it come alive, as a way of making our goals more real. A few days later, I pinned a big map of the world to the wall next to my desk. I even bought earrings, fashioned like globes of the earth, and wore them to keep me thinking and talking about my trip. I immersed myself in travel literature, went to travel workshops, slide shows, and took a class on how to pack for long-term international travel.

What follows is a detailed explanation of exactly how I did it. So many black women tell me they could never do it (because it would cost too much, be too complicated to figure out, too scary to do). It's not any of those things. I hope this demystifies the process.

Travel Clubs

I joined a local travel club. The members were hard-core international travelers who met bimonthly in members' homes. A potluck and a slide show of one of the member's recent trips would be followed by a general discussion of the region. Then we would go around the room for a "check in period," in which each of us had a chance to talk about our travel plans and ask questions; most often other club members were able to respond or provide a referral. The meetings were always inspiring and informative. Talking with so many women who had traveled solo around the world helped to curb my fears about my upcoming trip. They eagerly shared fascinating and helpful travel tips and leads. I loved tasting all the exotic dishes folks had learned to prepare during their travels and to see the colorful ethnic garb they had purchased or bartered for. It was also edifying to see that they were just regular folks, not necessarily rich or brilliant, but ordinary people who had chosen to make travel a priority in their lives.

I joined the Youth Hostel organization, but no one ever asked to see my membership card at any of the hostels I stayed in. I also joined an international home and hospitality exchange club, which is an organization of people who love to travel but do not like to pay high hotel bills or just like living like the locals do. It cost between sixty and one hundred dollars to join and membership affords you the opportunity to list your home for exchange or list your need for a hospitality exchange. Members stay in other members' homes and in turn extend that same courtesy to travelers coming to their city. You receive a book annually that lists all the members, information about their homes, availability, preferences, etc. If time had permitted I would have applied for membership in Servas, which has an international network of member homes where people can stay free of charge, if the traveler is sincerely interested in cultural exchange.

Planning My Route and Buying Tickets

Five months before I left, I decided which countries I wanted to visit. My original plan was to travel westward from California to New Zealand, Australia, Fiji, Bali, Singapore, Thailand, China, Egypt, Madagascar, Greece, France, the British Virgin Islands, Jamaica, and several U.S. cities. I then had to locate an airline or brokerage company to arrange the most affordable travel to those countries. I solicited the names of travel agents/services from other travelers and combed the travel sections of the *San Francisco Chronicle,* the *Los Angeles Times* and the *New York Times* for bargains. I also called each of the major airlines for price quotes.

After extensive comparison shopping, I could not find a price below four thousand dollars, which was more than I wanted to spend. I was forced to streamline my trip, finally settling on visiting several US cities, France, traveling by train to and through Switzerland and Italy, by boat to Greece and several Greek Islands, and flying to Egypt, Thailand, Singapore, Bali, and Lombok, Indonesia.

I ultimately utilized the services of a ticket brokerage firm that specialized in round the world (RTW) packages. My airline tickets cost twenty-one hundred dollars, the train and boat fares approximately three hundred dollars. Had I been more flexible with my departure date and itinerary, I could have gotten airline tickets for only thirteen hundred dollars. Comparable packages purchased from the airlines would have cost approximately three thousand dollars.

Many of the RTW packages let you choose from about forty to sixty cities but rarely include the South Pacific, the Caribbean, or the hearts of Africa and South America without extra charges (approximately two hundred dollars each). The theory is that they can only offer affordable deals on their most traveled international routes. Additionally, RTW tickets require travel in one continuous direction, which must be completed within six months to a year.

Finding Friendly Faces or Simply a Place to Stay

As soon as I settled on a route, I set about renewing and establishing contacts in many of the countries I planned to visit. I wrote to friends, and friends of friends, as well as members of my home and hospitality exchange club, and asked if I could stay in their homes during my visit or if they could recommend a place for me to stay. I found homestays in Paris, Rome, Aswan (Egypt), and several cities in Thailand.

In places where I didn't have homestays or personal recommendations, I relied on my trusty guidebooks for suggestions. I always had a hotel in mind when I arrived in a new country. After I cleared customs and converted some money, I would call the hotel to make sure they had a room. (I did not make hotel reservations in advance because I didn't want to be tied down to specific dates and I also wanted to see the places before I agreed to stay there.) Sometimes I

> Be selective about using local tourist bureaus to arrange accommodations, particularly those in airports and train stations. In my experience, they sometimes appear to be government tourist service centers but are really fronts for private companies, who dress up their agents in official-looking outfits with badges, etc., to win your confidence and ultimately your business. The lodging through these pseudo–tourist operations is often much more expensive than the lodging you can locate on your own. On the other hand, some are legitimate and very helpful.
> —Elaine Lee

asked a cab driver to take me to several of the hotels that were listed in my guidebook, before I decided on one. The few times I was dissatisfied with my choice, I simply moved to new accommodations the next day.

The first day in a new country was usually the hardest, but within twenty-four hours I had settled into a room, found places to eat, met new friends, and a new adventure had begun.

Guidebooks

About four months before departure I began to seriously study travel guidebooks. My favorite budget travel guide was the *Let's Go* series, published by Harvard Student Agencies. My second favorite was the *Lonely Planet* series. It really helped to read two books for each major destination but since they are cumbersome to carry I consolidated by writing notes from one into the other or I tore out the parts I wanted. Some books are stronger on some things than others, so blending them can result in more comprehensive information. For example, *Let's Go* is weak on history but very good at helping to locate affordable lodging and restaurants. I wish Thalia Zepatos's *A Journey of One's Own: Uncommon Advice for the Independent Woman Traveler* had been available back then. It's a storehouse of essential information. I also recommend *Intrepid Traveler* by Adam Rogers and *22 Days Around the World*, by Roger Rappoport and Burl Willes.

I wanted to be able to reread material en route to each new destination, but my backpack would have been too heavy to carry with the books for eight countries. So I mailed them to myself via an American Express office or a reliable friend in the preceding country. Purchasing books written in English outside of America is prohibitively expensive, even in the least expensive countries, and they can be extremely hard to find, although some travel destinations have used-book shops and sometimes you can trade with travelers going in the opposite direction.

If you are planning extensive travel with open travel dates, you may want to wait to get your visas in the country preceding the one where you need the visa, otherwise they may expire before you use them.
—Elaine Lee

Documents

Three months before my departure, I made sure all of my travel documents were in order. I renewed my passport, having learned the hard way on a previous trip that several countries do not permit entry with a "soon to expire" (within six months) passport.

I made copies of my credit cards, passport, birth certificate, and airline tickets to carry with me and got several extra passport pictures. (I also took the negative.) I wrote the U.S. State Department and got its current listing of visa requirements for other countries (this is also available at a local library or on the Internet). I didn't use a private visa preparation service. I got an International Driver's License for ten dollars from a local AAA office. I never used it but was glad I had it.

Health

Two months prior to departure, I contacted my local health department's immunization division for information about required medications or precautions for each of the countries I planned to visit. I took malaria pills with me but followed Bill Dalton's advice in *Indonesia Handbook* and never took them as a preventive measure for fear of getting sick and/or weakening my immune system. Many travel clinics recommend carrying a single dose to be taken if symptoms occur.

To help prepare my body for the rigors of international travel, I increased my exercise program to include aerobics and weight training, and increased my swimming to a mile three times a week. I got physical and dental exams, had my teeth cleaned and put together a first aid kit that included Flagyl for parasites, whole psyllium husks for diarrhea or constipation (works like magic!), condoms, water purifiers, insect repellent, antibiotics, pain killers, two pairs of contact lenses and their preparation (this was fairly easy to find along the way), sterile syringes, two pairs of eyeglasses, and copies of prescriptions for medicines and eyeglasses.

I wrote to the International Association for Medical Assistance for Travellers (736 Center Street, Lewiston, NY 14092) to obtain their directory of English-speaking doctors.

Managing Money

For my solo, low-budget, no-frills trip around the world I spent six thousand dollars including transportation costs. My out-of-pocket expenses varied from five hundred to a thousand dollars per month (which would probably be seven hundred to fifteen hundred in 1998).

∫ix thousand dollars (with inflation it would probably be eight thousand by now) is a lot of money to come up with. I brainstormed all my options such as: buying fewer clothes or jewelry, holding off on major purchases, raiding my savings account, refinancing my home, cashing in on an investment, getting a second job, getting a loan, etc. I decided to refinance my home.

I also used the team approach. A friend and I agreed to help each other take off work for two years. When one of us "retired," the other would continue to work and be willing to help the "retired" one financially if she got in a rut. Luckily neither of us had to "cop a lean" but it was great for each of us to know that the other one was there and that we had "each other's back."

—Elaine Lee

Some countries were more expensive (most European), some less (most non-European). Many people have told me that traveling with a partner would have cost less (because you can split the costs of lodging), but of course traveling with a partner can also cost more because you are less likely to be invited to stay in someone's home.

I converted twenty-five hundred dollars into Travelers Checks, took five hundred dollars worth of French francs (since that was my first foreign stop), an American Express card, a debit card, and a MasterCard. I wish I had taken a supply of U.S. dollars in ones and fives because many non-European people like to do business in dollars and give much better prices when they see U.S. cash. I found out midway through my trip that it was cheaper and easier to use my debit card to get cash instead of hassling with traveler's checks (you get the best exchange rate and are charged a low transaction fee). I found MasterCard was the most widely accepted credit card.

I relied heavily on a currency converter calculator, which allowed me to convert the cost of items from U.S. dollars to foreign value and from foreign value to U.S. dollars at the touch of a finger. It also converted weights, temperatures, and measurements. A waterproof money/passport pouch gave me complete freedom from worry, particularly while I went swimming or to the shower, since I often had no one to watch things for me.

Travel Insurance

I read a *Consumer Reports* article on the best companies to use and settled on Travel Guard. I purchased their deluxe plan, which cost me $243 and included insurance for trip cancellation, $5,000 for medical insurance, $500 for lost baggage, and $50,000 for life insurance. (Travel Guard International, Inc., 1145 Clark St., Stevens Point, WI 54481 715/ 345-0505. Another good choice would be Travelers' Emergency Network (TEN).

Setting up a Home Secretary

Some people have their mail forwarded to them at American Express offices around the world and handle their own affairs from abroad, but I didn't trust the mail and I didn't want to be bothered with business affairs during my travels. I asked a trusted friend to handle my affairs (it's also possible to use a bonded bookkeeper or financial manager), and I prepared detailed instructions for her. I had a rubber stamp made so she could endorse and deposit my incoming checks.

I set up an automatic payment system to cover the minimum payment due on my MasterCard each month. I also put overdraft protection on my checking account so possible overdrafts could be picked up on my MasterCard. I paid off all my other bills with the exception of my mortgage, for which I wrote out checks to have mailed monthly by the person handling my finances. I took several personal checks, which allowed me to write checks for unexpected expenses that arose at home.

I called my friend weekly for the first few weeks to discuss problems and slowly reduced the frequency of calls as it became clear that everything was under control. I gave her an itinerary and names of people to call in each country, who could reach me within a reasonable period of time. (I checked in with those people after entering each country.) I also registered with the American Embassy in many of the countries I visited for more than a week, so there could be some trail established if something unforeseen (gawdforbid) was to happen to me. I set up an account with a phone messaging service so that the friend handling my affairs could leave me messages. My plan was to check my messages weekly; however, I soon discovered that in many countries the phone system did not have the capability to allow me to access my message center.

Bella, bella, the handsome young man said looking at me with a wide smile. I beamed in return. It didn't matter that I was on a street in Paris and his greeting was in Italian. The sound was music to my ears as I walked past him in my red dress and full brim black hat. And I couldn't resist looking back just to check. Yes, he had stopped in his tracks to watch me. I turned and strutted on down the street. (You all know that strut. It's the one some of us black women who've reached the age of forty and realized that we have survived and things are pretty damn good, take on. It's the one Maya Angelou likes to talk about.)

—Eleanor Jacobs,
"Paris, Wonderful Paris!"

Departure Strategies

I decided to rent out my home, and since I couldn't find a friend to rent it to, I placed a listing with the local university's faculty housing office and located an instructor who needed a place to live for the length of time I was going to be gone. (I reduced the rent to offset pet-care duties.) I set up an apartment-sharing agreement instead of a strict sublease, to protect myself in case I needed to return home in an emergency. I prepared detailed house and pet-care instructions, which included a chart of daily, weekly, and monthly activities, and displayed it on the refrigerator door. I also left him a list of repair people to call in case they were needed, as well as a list of all the things in a state of disrepair.

I prepaid my water bill to create a substantial credit on my account so no payments would need to be made during my absence. I transferred the phone, gas, and electric service into his name. Since that meant I no longer had a phone line, I had no access to my long-distance privileges, so I acquired a nonsubscriber long-distance calling card.

I moved all of my personal belongings to a secure off-site location and hired a housekeeper and a lawn maintenance person on a biweekly basis to increase the likelihood that the house and yard would be properly cared for.

I groomed my dog and put in an ample supply of food, medicine, and flea combatants. I registered my credit card number with my veterinarian so that the caretaker could take him for help without worrying about bills.

> *T*ake earplugs if you're sensitive to noise (yes, the roosters really do crow every morning at 5:00 a.m. in Bali, and it's also the time the local mosques in Egypt begin their daily chant, *"Allah a Akbar"* over high-powered outdoor loudspeaker systems).
>
> —Elaine Lee

I loaned my car to a friend in exchange for her paying the cost of my insurance and maintaining the car on an established schedule. Our written agreement also included information regarding what to do in case of vandalism, accident, or necessary repair.

Luggage

I was very satisfied with my three foot by four foot back pack/suitcase convertible luggage. I used it both ways, depending on the circumstances. I cheerfully utilized a luggage cart when walking long distances with my luggage. (Now there are versions made with built-in wheels.) I also carried a compartmentalized knapsack for my daily excursions.

I took a class at Easy Going Traveler's Store, in Berkeley, California, on how to pack lightly (thirty pounds) and comprehensively for international travel and found that effective packing is a strategic science. We learned how to bundle our belongings into groups to reduce the need for ironing, to maximize accessibility, and to best utilize space.

What I Took with Me

Our instructor urged us to restrict our color scheme to two colors for easy interchange. I chose khaki/beige and black and found those to be quite versatile but boring. I used accessories to brighten up my wardrobe a bit, but since I was a woman traveling alone, I wanted to dress conservatively to avoid unwanted attention.

I took one pair of pants, one pair of knee-length hiking shorts, a pair of leggings, one skirt, one dress, a heavy and a light shirt, a long T-shirt that doubled as a nightshirt, three pairs of shoes (pumps, walking/hiking shoes, and sandals). I also packed four pairs of panties, two bras, one small purse, two pairs of socks, a rain poncho and a jacket, one hat, a light cotton robe, swimsuit, and a kanga (long cotton body wrap that can also be used as a sheet and/or ground cover). I bought clothes along the way and mailed extra clothes home or gave them away when my pack got too heavy.

I took small containers of the bare essentials of personal grooming articles and was particularly glad to have brought lots of packaged moist towelettes, small packages of Kleenex (many bathrooms outside of the U.S. do not have toilet paper), and several toilet seat covers.

I developed a greater appreciation for this country's attempt to create a "melting pot," after seeing for myself that we come from such amazingly distinct and diverse heritages, with such varied priorities and rhythms!
—Elaine Lee

A few things that proved invaluable were a hardy supply of first-rate earplugs, small gifts to give away, cassette recorder and tapes, a small computer game, travel scrabble game, several novels, a small needlepoint/crewel project (you're often stuck for hours waiting for first one thing and then another, and it helps to have something to do when you don't feel like writing or socializing). I found my braided rubber clothes line to be indispensable; it was great because it did not require clothespins, the clothes are attached in the braid. I loved my watch with the capability for military time and regular time, since timekeeping varies from country to country. Its alarm and timer proved very helpful. I utilized my flashlight quite a bit (it doubled as a reading light often when I was in hostels and the lights were turned out), sewing kit/scissors, several large resealable plastic bags for opened bottles or wet clothes. (I also used my rain parka once when I had to leave somewhere in a hurry and my recently washed clothes were still wet. Yikes!)

I found it useful to gather several different traveler's checklist/trip planners from bookstores, hostels, and travel clubs to help avoid oversights. I worried before I left that I might find myself without something I needed, that I might lose things, or have things stolen, but my best friend said, "Elaine, as long as you have your passport and your credit card you'll be fine," and I carried that reassurance with me and, fortunately, I was never reduced to those bare essentials.

Traveling Alone

I considered finding a travel partner but felt that it would be hard to find someone with the time, money, and interests similar to mine. So I ventured out into my odyssey alone, but I was never alone for long. I met local people and fellow travelers, hooked up with friends, contacted friends of friends, and checked in with the members of my international hospitality exchange club.

I was never bored or lonely. If I found myself stuck in a train station or airport, there were almost always interesting locals to converse with or other English-speaking travelers with whom I could swap travel tales. I always kept a book, a journal, my needlepoint kit, cassette tape player, and a small travel game to entertain myself with if company was unavailable or undesired.

It is important to remember that there are few places on the planet as dangerous as the United States, so I had little fear for my safety when traveling solo abroad. I always dressed modestly and used my intuition and my street smarts to guide me. I never encountered a dangerous or life-threatening situation on my round-the-world or any other trip. And I'm sure I learned the languages, terrain, currencies, and customs faster than I would have if I had had someone else to depend on.

Traveling alone led to some very intense personal encounters. Many people feel safe sharing their innermost secrets with strangers they figure they may never meet again. I was continually amazed with the deep connections and openness I experienced with other travelers and locals during my seven-month sojourn.

If I Can Do It...

Yes, *you* can do it, too. You can dive for lobster off the coast of the British Virgin Islands, "people watch" from an outdoor café in Paris, attend the Montreux Jazz Festival in Switzerland, sunbathe on a Greek Island, climb inside a pyramid in Egypt, visit the hill tribes of Northern Thailand, watch a fire-walking trance dance in Bali. Don't shortchange yourself and settle for being an armchair traveler when affordable travel is a real possibility. We as black women have been reluctant travelers for far too long. The world is waiting for you.

RESOURCES

SOME TRAVEL BOOKS BY AFRICAN AMERICAN TRAVEL WRITERS

Caribbean Bound: Culture, Roots, Places, and People by Linda Cousins (The Universal AfriCAN Writer Press, 1995), 226 pages, $14.95. Geared toward the Afro-centric and culturally aware traveler. Features historic sites, galleries, museums, regattas, festivals, markets, etc.

Historic Black Landmarks: A Traveler's Guide by George Cantor (Visible Ink Press, a division of Gale Research, Inc., 1991), 400 pages, $17.95. Lists over 300 sites in the U.S. and Canada, has a brief history of black Americans. Maps and photos.

African American Historic Places, edited by Beth Savage for the National Park Service (Preservation Press, National Trust for Historic Preservation, 1994), 693 pages, $25.95. Lists over 800 places in the U. S. and places the sites in a historical and cultural context.

Hippocrene Guide to the Underground Railroad by Charles Blockson (Hippocrene Books, 1994), 370 pages, $22.95. Traces the many roads that lead from the Mid-Atlantic states to Canada and the stops and safe havens along the way.

Hippocrene U.S.A. Guide to Black America by Marcella Thum (Hippocrene Books, 1991), 384 pages, $11.95 Lists sites in alphabetical order by states.

In Their Footsteps: The American Visions Guide to African American Heritage Sites by Henry Chase (Henry Holt Publishers, 1994), 584 pages, $35. Organized by region with brief, powerful essays by well-known writers from those regions. Covers U.S. and Canada.

Open Road Publishing's Hawaii Guide by Rachel Christmas Derrick (Open Road Publishing, 1997), 540 pages, $17.95.

SOME AFRICAN AMERICAN TRAVEL MAGAZINES

Black Meetings and Tourism, published monthly for travel agents and convention coordinators/bureaus, 20840 Chase Street, Winnetka, CA 91306 (818/709- 0646).

So You Goin' to Carnival, a comprehensive carnival guide published annually by Ah Wee Tours, Ltd., 411 Utica Avenue, Brooklyn, NY 11213 (800/MON-JUMP).

African Americans on Wheels, a quarterly magazine for black auto enthusiasts, 2034 National Press Building, Washington, D.C. 20045 (202/588-9459; email: AAOW@aol.com).

Cultural Traveler Online Newsletter, published monthly by Linda Cousins of Cultural Travel Publications, POB 5, Radio City Station, NYC, NY 10101 (email: Akan@aol.com).

Black Traveler, published monthly by A&E Publishing, 116 Victory Blvd., Suite 201, North Hollywood, CA 91606 (818/753-9198).

Pathfinders Travel Magazine, published quarterly "for people of color who love to travel," 6424 N. 13th Street, Philadelphia, PA 19126 (215/927-9950).

SOME AFRICAN-AMERICAN-ORIENTED TOUR AND TRAVEL COMPANIES

Association for the Study of Classical African Civilization has an annual international conference and study tour (213/730 -1155) or contact Consolidated Tours (800/554-4556).

Kemet Nu Educational Tours: Ashra and Merira Kwesi organize tours to Egypt and Ghana, POB 41005, Dallas, TX 75241 (214/371-0206; email: kemetnu@aol.com).

Kultural Arts Network produces an annual Gullah excursion and conference in the South Carolina Sea Islands. It includes traditional Gullah storytelling, sing-offs, tributes to the ancestors, craft demonstrations, lectures on Gullah linguistics, and African connections. They also offer other Afro-centric tours such as the annual Underground Railroad Journey; POB 40-0199, Brooklyn, NY 11240 (212/439-1026; email: QueenMut@aol.com).

GIGI Travel Agency handles over 100 tours annually, including tours to Europe, Africa, South Pacific, Caribbean, festivals, and cruises; 799 Nostrand Avenue, Brooklyn, NY 11225 (718/778-8500).

The Sphynx Connection provides fourteen-day Egyptian odyssey/study tours, 345 Haddon Road, #5, Oakland, CA 94606 (510/839-7804).

Alken Tours handles a wide range of retail and wholesale travel services, 25 W. 43rd St., New York, NY 10036 (212/764-0244).

Sebayit Tours coordinates numerous study and conference tours to Africa and Gullah Islands, 11 E. Chase Street, #7A, Baltimore, MD 21202 (800/639-3556).

SOME AFRICAN AMERICAN OWNED OR OPERATED HEALTH RETREATS

Ann Wigmore Institute, Leola Brooks, Director. Their mission is to promote the science of self-healing through detoxification of the body and the exclusive consumption of living foods. Their one- and two-week programs provide a focused and results-oriented curriculum teaches the basics of nutrition, indoor gardening/sprouting, yoga, lymphatic exercises and colon care; POB 429, Rincon, Puerto Rico, 00677 (809/868 6307).

Women of Color as Warriors of Light. This four-day retreat is held annually on an Oregon Indian Reservation. It provides a transformational environment conducive to renewal, self-discovery, celebration, and healing. Activities include yoga, massage, storytelling, meditation, workshops, and hiking; 2942 Chesapeake Avenue, Los Angeles, CA 90016 (303/443-3656).

Jackie's on the Reef, Negril, Jamaica. This retreat/hotel offers yoga classes, massages, herbal scrubs, tai chi sessions, and a vegetarian menu; c/o 364 Washington Avenue, Brooklyn, NY 11238 (718/783-6763 or 809/957-4997).

Royal Court Hotel and Natural Health Retreat, Montego Bay, Jamaica. This holistic resort offers massages, colon cleansing, yoga, a gym, Jacuzzi, steam room, and vegetarian meals (876/952- 4531).

Cottonwood Hot Springs Spa and Motel, POB 277, Cottonwood, AL 36320 (800/526-7727).

Inner Visions Retreats/Spiritual Life Maintenance, facilitated by Iyanla Vanzant. Three-day retreats help participants clear blocks, transcend their pasts, and create a viable future through the use of universal spiritual laws and African spiritual practices. Locations vary (888/POWER27).

Family Reunion Institute holds annual spring conferences. Workshops include: how to start a reunion, how to revive/strengthen reunions, trying out new themes/activities. Dr. Vargus, School of Social Administration, Temple University, Ritter Hall Annex, Philadelphia, PA 19122 (215/204 6244).

African American Women's Advance: Sharing, Healing, and Renewal is an annual retreat held in Shelton, Washington; c/o Masterminds, 22810 30th Ave. South, #C101,

Seattle, WA 98198 (206/878-8163).

Omega Institute is a holistic learning center that has a number of its retreats/work-shops run by African Americans; 260 Lake Drive, Rhinebeck, NY 12572 (914/266-4444; Web site: http://omega-inst.org).

Creative Escapes offers spring and fall health retreats; POB 1257, Piscataway, NJ 08855 (908/463-3794).

Afrikan Center of Well Being, POB 1596, Stafford, TX 77497 (713/639-3571).

SOME BLACK OWNED OR OPERATED ACCOMMODATIONS AND RESORTS

Cane Garden Bay Beach Hotel, POB 570, Cane Garden Bay, Tortola, British Virgin Islands (809/495-4639).

Sandals Resorts, with locations in St. Lucia, Jamaica, Antigua, Turk, and Caicos Islands (800/SANDALS).

Great House Beach Resort, POB 157, The Valley, Anguilla (800/583-9427; email: flemingw@zemu.candw.com.ai).

Negril Tree House Resort, POB 29, Norman Manley Blvd., Negril, Jamaica (800/NEGRIL1).

Bedside Manor, Bed and Breakfast Inn, Oakland, CA (510/452-4550).

Martha's Vineyard Resorts and Racquet Club, POB 255, Boston, MA 02130 (800/874-4403; email: Jackerobin@aol.com).

Shangri-La Historic Inn, Resort and Spa, Bonita Springs, FL (800/279-3811).

Villas and Apartments Abroad (800/433-3020).

SOME AFRICAN AMERICAN CRUISES

Festival at Sea: Cruising with an African American Twist. Seven-day voyages in the Eastern Caribbean that include celebrity performances, sports/bid whist/domino/dance/black trivia competitions, step show, and gospel hour. Blue World Travel, 50 First Street, #411, San Francisco, CA 94105 (415/882-9444).

National Professional's Network hosts an annual cruise on the Royal Caribbean Line that includes professional development seminars and cultural celebrations; 1150 Connecticut Ave., NW, Washington, D.C. 20036 (800/340-1965 or 301/565-0070).

National African American Travel and Entertainment Network hosts a variety of music-oriented cruises (gospel, blues, jazz) and festivals (NY, NJ, CT 914/654-0500, other states 800/955-4646).

SOME BLACK PROFESSIONAL ORGANIZATIONS RELATED TO TRAVEL

InterAmerican Travel Agents Society is the largest and oldest association of black owned and operated travel agencies; 248 S. Alden, Philadelphia, PA 19139 (215/471-5321).

Organization of Black Airline Pilots, POB 50666, Phoenix, AZ 85076 (800/jet-OBAP).

Black Flight Attendants of America, 1060 Crenshaw Blvd., Suite 202, Los Angeles, CA 90019 (213/299-3406).

National Coalition of Black Meeting Planners, 8630 Fenton Street, Ste. 328, Silver Spring, MD 20910 (202/628 3952).

National Association of Black Hospitality Professionals, POB 8132 Columbia, GA 31908 (email: NABHP@aol.com).

African American Convention and Tourism (contact Roy Jay, 800/909-2882).

Blacks in International Affairs provides mentorships, conferences, scholarships, and a newsletter. POB 11675, Washington, D.C. 20028 (301/953-0815).

SOME AFRICAN AMERICAN SPORTS AND TRAVEL CLUBS

National Bowling Association, 377 Park Avenue South, NYC, NY 10016 (212/689-8308).

American Tennis Association, 16th and Kennedy Streets NW, Washington, D.C. (202/291-9893).

National Black Scuba Divers (over 30 chapters is the U.S.), 1605 Crittendon Street N.E., Washington, D.C. 20017 (800/521-NABS).

National "Brotherhood" of Black Skiers (over 80 chapters in the U.S.), 1525 E. 53rd Street, Ste. 402, Chicago, IL 60615 (312/955-4100; Web site: http://www.nbs.org).

Ebony Queens Motorcycle Club, POB 311021, Flint, MI 48504 (517/355-4500 ext. 113; Web site: http://mlss15.cl.msu.edu/~bambam/eqmc/eqmc.html).

Minority Golf Association, POB 1081, Westhampton Beach, NY 11978 (202/829-0596).

SOME LEADS ON EDUCATIONAL TRAVEL

Operation Crossroads Africa offers summer work/travel/study programs to address development needs in Africa and the diaspora. 475 Riverside Drive, Suite 831, NYC, NY 10115 (212/870-2106; email: ocainc@aol.com).

Opportunities in Africa is a guide produced by the African American Institute that provides resources for students and professionals interested in teaching, studying, or visiting in Africa. Interbook, 130 Cedar Street, New York, NY 10006 (212/566-1944), $3 per copy.

Council on International Education Exchange provides two travel scholarships for minorities: The Bailey Minority Scholarship for Education Abroad and the Bowman Award, 205 E. 42nd Street, New York, NY 10017 (212/822-26000; Web site: http://www.ciee.org).

Foreign Affairs Fellowship/Student Intern Program: U.S. Department of State. These programs are intended to encourage outstanding students to consider a diplomatic career. Recruitment Division, POB 9317, Arlington, VA 22219 (703/812-2261 or 7242; Web site: http:/www.state.gov).

Peace Corps places 3,000 volunteers annually in 90 developing countries. This two-year program requires a bachelor's degree. POB 948, Washington, D.C. 20526 (800/424-8580).

Rotary International offers scholarships for undergraduate and graduate study abroad. Rotary Foundation, 1 Rotary Ctr., 1560 Sherman Ave., Evanston, IL 60201 (847/866-3000).

Fulbright Scholarships for graduating seniors and graduate students, USIA Fulbright, 809 United Nations Plaza, New York, NY 10017 (212/984-5330; Web site: http://www.cies.org).

Online Directory for Study Abroad is created and maintained by the University of Minnesota Study and Travel Center (Web site: http://www.isp.acad.umn.edu/istc/Default.html).

SOME HOME AND HOSPITALITY EXCHANGE GROUPS AND INFORMATION

Women Welcome Women fosters international friendship by enabling women of different countries to visit one another. 88 Easton Street, High Wycombe, Bucks HP11 1LT, United Kingdom (phone and fax: 01494-465441).

Intervac, POB 59054, San Francisco, CA 94159 (800/756-HOME).

Servas is a cultural exchange program that opens homes and hearts to travelers in over 100 countries. 11 John St., Rm. 706, New York, NY 10038 (212/267-0252).

Vacation Exchange Club (800/638-3841).

Trading Places: Wonderful World of Vacation Home Exchanging by Bill and Mary Barbour (Rutledge Hill Press, 1991), 192 pages, $9.95.

A SAMPLING OF FESTIVALS OF INTEREST TO THE AFRICAN AMERICAN TRAVELER

Spring: Louisiana Blues and Jazz Festival (New Orleans); Saint Lucia Jazz Festival; Barbados Gospelfest; Yoruba Ancestor Festival (Sheldon, SC); Gullah Festival (South Carolina Islands); National Black Arts Festival (Atlanta, GA) even years only; Carifesta (Montreal, Canada); Goombay Summer Festival (Nassau, Bahamas); African Street Festival (Brooklyn, NY).

Summer: Essence Music Festival (New Orleans); Crop Over Festival (Barbados); Caribana (Toronto, Canada); Reggae Sunsplash (Jamaica); Fete des Cuisinieres (Guadeloupe); North Sea Jazz Festival (Amsterdam); Boa Morte Festival (Cachoeira, Brazil); Tobago Heritage Festival; Sinbad's Summer Jam (variety of locations).

Fall: Mississippi Delta Blues Festival (Greenville, MS); Annual West Indian Day/Labor Day (Brooklyn, NY); Belize International Music Festival; Pirate Week (Cayman's Islands); Mojo Art Festival (Charleston, SC).

Winter: Zora Neal Hurston Festival of the Arts (Eatonville, GA); Crucian Christmas Fiesta (St. Croix, U.S.V.I.); Hatillo Mask Festival (Puerto Rico); Day of the Virgin Festival (El Carmen, Peru); Jazz Festival (Barbados).

Pre-Lenten Carnivals take place in: New Orleans, LA; Port of Prince, Trinidad; Rio de Janeiro, Brazil; Venice, Italy; and Nice, France.

FESTIVAL LOCATORS

So You Goin' to Carnival, a comprehensive carnival guide published annually by Ah Wee Tours Ltd., 411 Utica Avenue, Brooklyn, NY 11213 (800/MON-JUMP).

Caio Travel Services focuses on European and Caribbean Jazz Cruises and Tours, and publishes a bimonthly newsletter; 2707 Congress Street, Suite 1F, San Diego, CA 92110 (619/297-8112; email: bsnider@caiotravel.com).

Guide to World Fairs and Festivals (Greenwood Press, 1985), 309 pages, $39.95.

Music Festivals: From Bach to Blues by Tom Clynes (Visible Ink Press 1996), 582 pages, $18.95.

Food Festivals by Barbara Carlson (Visible Ink Press, 1997), 428 pages, $14.95.

Festival Web sites: http://www. Festival.com; http://www.Festivalfinder.com; http://www. jazzcentralstation.com/jcs/station/index.html

MISCELLANEOUS

A Journey of One's Own: Uncommon Advice for the Independent Woman Traveler, 2nd ed. by Thalia Zepatos (Eighth Mountain Press, 1996), 360 pages, $16.95. This is the best single resource for detailed information on every aspect of traveling: choosing guidebooks and luggage, avoiding theft, staying healthy, dealing with sexual harassment, etc.

Adventures in Good Company: The Complete Guide to Women's Tours and Outdoor Trips by Thalia Zepatos (Eighth Mountain Press, 1995), 420 pages, $16.95. The definitive resource for all kinds of organized trips and tours, including spiritual journeys and leadership-development programs. Includes a directory of 100 companies worldwide.

Go Ware produces colorful maps of major U.S. cities that feature sites of African American clubs, restaurants, churches, historic landmarks, galleries, and hotels. POB 55126, Hayward, CA 94545 (510/247-9793)

Fodor's Net Travel: Your Map to Travel on the Internet and Online Services by Mary Goodwin, Kristin Miller, and Shaun Witten (Michael Wolff and Co. Publishing, 1996), 386 pages, $22.00.

Transitions Abroad: The Guide to Learning, Living and Working Overseas is a bimonthly guide to practical information needed for cultural-immersion travel as well as alternatives to mass tourism for travelers of all ages and interests. They also publish a variety of planning guides. Dept. TRA, POB 3000, Denville, NJ 07834, $19.95.

Maiden Voyages: The Indispensable Guide to Women's Travel is a quarterly magazine, 109 Minna Street, Suite 240, San Francisco, CA 94105 (414/526-8405; email: info@maidenvoyages.com).

Almanac of International Jobs and Careers by Ronald L. and Caryl R. Krannich (Krannich Impact Publications, 1994), 350 pages, $19.95.

Jobs for People Who Love to Travel by Ronald L. and Caryl R. Krannich (Krannich Impact Publications, 1995), 247 pages, $15.95.

Overseas Placement Services for Educators, University of Northern Iowa, SSC#19, Cedar Falls, IA 50614 (319/273-2083).

Spa-Finders is a resource center that can help you find a spa to meet your needs (800/255-7727).

Mapquest sells maps to over 78 countries and 34 U.S. cities; driving instructions between 150,000 points in the U.S. (Web site: http://www..mapquest.com).

Escapes Unlimited is a tour company that specializes in trips for single parents and their children; 626 E. Chapman Ave., Orange, CA 92666 (800/243-7227).

The Unofficial Guide to Ethnic Cuisine and Dining in America by Zibort, Stevens, and Vermont (A Bob Schlinger Publication, Macmillan Travel, 1995), 421 pages, $13.

Sarah Tours offers the Moroccan Imilchil Annual Betrothal Festival and Tour (800/267-0036).

The Black Woman's Guide to Financial Independence by Cheryl D. Broussard (Penguin, 1996), 191 pages, $15.95.

ABOUT THE EDITOR

ELAINE LEE is an attorney in San Francisco with a private law practice in family law, probate, estate planning, and personal injury. She is also a program director for the San Francisco Foundation, a community fund that disburses forty million dollars annually to a wide array of nonprofit organizations in the Bay Area.

From 1981 to 1991, she was the executive director of the Family Law Center in Berkeley, a legal assistance and support center, where she worked extensively with battered women. Prior to that she was adjunct professor of law at the New College of California School of Law, a hearing examiner for the San Francisco Residential Rent Stabilization and Arbitration Board, and a staff member of the San Francisco Neighborhood Legal Assistance Foundation.

She received her J.D. at the University of Denver School of Law and also studied at Howard University School of Law. She studied at the Columbia University/Union Theological Seminary, majoring in political theology. She received her B.A. at Western Michigan University.

She has received awards from the Women Lawyers of Alameda County for outstanding contributions to the community, and from the City of Berkeley Commission on the Status of Women.

She is an avid swimmer, reader, dancer, skier, stargazer, whitewater-rafter, sailor, cyclist, and bibliophile. She traveled solo around the world over a two-year period several years ago and continues to travel regularly. She has visited forty-three countries.

CONTRIBUTORS' NOTES

Faith Adiele grew up on a farm in Washington State and began traveling overseas at the age of fifteen. Her essays have appeared in *Life Notes: Personal Writing by Contemporary Black Women, Tanzania on Tuesday: American Women Abroad, Testimony: African Americans on Self-Discovery and Black Identity, Names We Call Home: Autobiography of Racial Identity,* and *Miscegenation Blues: Voices of Mixed Race Women.* She is currently the Christa McAuliffe visiting professor in English at Framingham State College in Massachusetts. She is working on a memoir about traveling to West Africa as an adult and meeting her father and siblings for the first time.

Opal Palmer Adisa, Jamaican born, is a literary critic, writer and storyteller. Her published works are: *It Begins with Tears, Tamarind and Mango Women, traveling women, Bake-Face and other Guava Stories,* and *Piña, the Many-Eyed Fruit.* Her poetry, prose, and essays have appeared in numerous anthologies and journals. She is associate professor and chair of the Ethnic Studies Program at the California College of Arts and Crafts.

Maya Angelou is an author, poet, director, playwright, performer, singer, and stage/screen producer. Her many books include *I Know Why the Caged Bird Sings, Just Give Me a Cool Drink of Water 'fore I Die, Gather Together in My Name, Oh Pray My Wings Are Gonna Fit Me Well, And Still I Rise,* and *Wouldn't Take Nothing for My Journey Now.*

Daphne E. Barbee-Wooten is an attorney, video producer, and freelance writer who lives in Honolulu, Hawaii. She has contributed articles to numerous publications, including *Essence, Afro-Hawaii News, Mahogany,* and *Rastamon Times.* She coproduced two videos with her husband, attorney André Wooten: *Reclaiming Our African Heritage* and *Ode to Pharaoh Hatshepsut/Temple of Philae for Isis.*

Rosemary Blake is the owner of Uzima Services in New York City, a company that works with businesses, groups, and organizations on goal setting and implementation, investment strategy, financial management, program design, and communication. She is the founding member and president of Women's Economic Circle. She is a partner of BlakeMapp Productions, a video production company currently working on a documentary, *Sister Soldier.*

Tonya Bolden is the author of *The Book of African-American Women: Crusaders, Creators, Uplifters, Just Family,* and *Through Loona's Door.* She is the editor of *Rites of Passage: Stories About Growing Up by Black Writers from Around the World.*

Gwendolyn Brooks was the first African American to win the Pulitzer Prize. She has also received the National Medal of Arts and the National Endowment for the Arts Lifetime Achievement Award and served as a consultant in poetry to the Library of Congress. Since 1968 she has been the Poet Laureate of Illinois. She has published many books, including poetry for adults and children, a novel, writing manuals, and an autobiography.

Barbara Chase-Riboud is the author of *Sally Hemings, The President's Daughter, Echo of Lions,* and *Liberty.* Her sculptures are in major collections in Europe and the United States. She recently received the commission to create the African Burial Ground Memorial Sculpture for the Federal Building in New York City.

Dawn Comer is an actress and writer/producer who lives in Los Angeles. She has written and produced radio dramas and feature films, and has numerous stage and television credits. She has also worked extensively as a commercial voice-over actor.

Linda Cousins is an internationally published poet, playwright, and historical researcher. She is the author of *Caribbean Bound! Culture, Roots, Places, and People,* and the founding publisher/editor of the Universal AfriCAN Writer Press. She produces *The Cultural Traveler,* a monthly online newsletter. She is a Brooklyn high school teacher.

Rosalind Cummings-Yeates is a freelance writer. She has contributed articles to numerous publications, including the *Chicago Tribune, Bride, Yoga Journal, Chicago Sun-Times,* and *Mojo.* She is currently completing a collection of short stories, *Dancing Like a North-Sider.* She resides in Chicago.

Aya de León is a contributor to the anthology *Spooks, Spies, and Private Eyes: Black Mystery, Crime and Suspense Fiction of the 20th Century* and has contributed articles to *Essence.* She recently completed a collection of nonfiction prose entitled *Sneaking Back in the House: A Long Lost Latina Daughter of the Caribbean Returns.* She is the founder of Mothertongue Institute for Creative Development, where she conducts writing and creativity workshops.

Rachel Christmas Derrick is a freelance writer. Her travel writings have been published in numerous publications, including the *New York Times ,Washington Post, Boston Globe, Los Angeles Times, Travel & Leisure, Newsweek, Essence, Heart & Soul, Emerge,* and *Ms.* She is the author of Open Road Publishing's *Hawaii Guide.*

Tahra Edwards is working on her Ph.D. in anthropology. As part of her studies, she recently served as an intern with the Center for African Research and Transformation in Durban, South Africa. She is currently working on a compilation of poems and essays written about her travels in subsaharan Africa. She is a playwright and former staff writer for her college newspaper, the *Spelman Spotlight.*

Barbara Ellis-Van de Water is a public affairs officer for the Federal Emergency Management Agency. She has worked as a writer, producer, and editor of television and film. She has engaged in extensive international travel throughout her life and currently resides in St. John, U.S. Virgin Islands.

Toni Eubanks is author of *Journey Home,* the first in a series of books focusing on the coming-of-age experiences of African American girls. She is an educational resource coordinator for a national youth serving organization and an adjunct instructor of English at the College of New Rochelle.

Constance García-Barrio resides in Philadelphia and teaches at West Chester University. She has contributed articles to numerous publications, including the *Philadelphia Inquirer, Essence,* and *Maiden Voyages.* Her fiction has appeared in *The Antietam Review, The MacGuffin, Talk That Talk: Anthology of African American Storytelling,* and *Black Erotica.* She recently completed a novel entitled *Jerusalem Stone.*

Sharony Andrews Green is the assistant national editor for the *Detroit Free Press.* She is currently writing a biography and documentary film about her husband's father, the late jazz guitarist, Grant Green, as well as a story-art book entitled *Cuttin' the Rug Under a Moonlit Sky.*

Dale Grenier is an environmentalist who enjoys hiking, birding, and camping. She has her Ph.D. in Environmental Planning from the University of Washington.

Joy V. Harris is a Boston native and former teacher of African American literature. After a successful business career, which included owning her own shipping franchise, she is now seriously pursuing a writing career. She resides in Berkeley, California.

Loretta Henry resides in East Flatbush, Brooklyn, New York, and is currently working toward a career in the media.

Marianne Ilaw is a corporate communications specialist and freelance writer. She has contributed articles to numerous publications, including *Today's Black Woman, Chocolate Singles, Black Enterprise, Young Sisters and Brothers, Quarterly Black Review of Books,* and the *New York Voice.* She resides in Queens, New York.

Kristin M. Jefferson is an international art dealer, digital artist, writer, and documentary videomaker.

Adrienne Johnson is a freelance writer and copyeditor for the *Los Angeles Times.* Her travel dreams include visiting Cuba, the Seychelles, a ride on the Orient Express, and a lazy week eating crabs at a Sea Islands bed and breakfast located off the coast of South Carolina.

Charisse Jones is a national reporter for *U.S.A. Today.* She is a former staff reporter for the *New York Times* and *Los Angeles Times.* She shared a Pulitzer prize for coverage of the L.A. riots. She has contributed articles to numerous publications, including *Essence, Vibe,* and *Glamour.*

Renée Kemp is a TV news reporter in San Francisco. She is an award-winning journalist who has contributed articles to numerous magazines and newspapers, including *Essence, San Jose Mercury News,* and the *Oakland Tribune.* Her work is included in *Spirits of the Passage.*

Dorothy Lazard is an Oakland, California–based fiction writer and essayist. She has contributed articles to numerous magazines, including *Essence, Deluge,* and *Spectacle: A Literary Journal.* She is a contributor to *Storming Heaven's Gate: Women Writing About Spirituality* and is currently working on her first novel. She is an information resources coordinator at the University of California, Berkeley, Women's Center.

Audre Lorde (1934–1992) was a prolific writer, essayist, poet, and international activist. Among her many books are *From a Land Where Other People Live, Coal, The Black Unicorn,*

Our Dead Behind Us, The Cancer Journals, Zami: A New Spelling of My Name, and *Sister Outsider.*

Emma T. Lucas is an associate professor of social work and political science at Carlow College in Pittsburgh, Pennsylvania, and the author of *The Recognition of Elder Abuse Among Health Services Professionals.*

Earthlyn Marselean Manuel is the author of *The Black Angel: A Healing Tool for African-American Women.* She is president and cocreator of Shoké Foundation, which provides workshops, products, and processes for healing in the black community. She has contributed articles to *Essence* and *Deluge.*

Colleen J. McElroy is a professor and poet with a yen for travel that goes back to her youth as an army brat. Among her many books are *A Long Way Home, What Madness Brought Me Here: New and Selected Poems 1968–1988, Lie and Say You Love Me, Bone Flames, Queen of Ebony Isles,* and *The Mule's Done Long Since Gone.*

Lydia A. Nayo is a writer who lives in Oakland, California. Her commentaries on life and culture have appeared in the *Los Angeles Times* and have been aired on National Public Radio's "All Things Considered." She is currently working on her first novel.

Jill Nelson is a journalist and the author of *Volunteer Slavery: My Authentic Negro Experience.*

Brenda Joyce Patterson is a poet, bookworm, and wanna-be world traveler. She works at the Lakeland, Florida public library and coedits the literary magazine *Onionhead.*

Viki Radden resides in Marin County, California.

Lucinda Roy is the Gloria D. Smith Professor of English at Virginia Technical College in Blacksburg Virginia. She is the author of two books of poetry, *Wailing the Dead to Sleep* and *The Humming Birds,* and a novel, *Lady Moses.* She is currently at work on her second novel and a series of oil paintings depicting the Middle Passage.

Andrea Benton Rushing is professor of Black Studies and English at Amherst College. She is the coeditor of *Women in Africa and the African Diaspora.* She has contributed articles to numerous magazines and journals on the subjects of African and African American literature.

Jennifer Sanders is the director of Project Maes da Historia (Mothers of History), whose objective is to record the life stories, folklore, knowledge of natural medicine, African remembrances, and spiritual beliefs of Afro-Brazilian women. She currently lives in Salvador, Brazil.

Gwen Shervington resides in Oakland, California. She grew up in the South Bronx, New York.

Linda Villarosa is executive editor of *Essence.* She is the editor of *Body and Soul: The Black Women's Guide to Physical Health and Emotional Well-Being.*

Gloria Wade-Gayles is a poet, novelist, literary critic, and professor of English and Women's Studies at Spelman College, in Atlanta, Georgia. She is the author of *No Crystal Stair: Visions of Race and Sex in Black Women's Fiction* and *Pushed Back to Strength.* She is editor of *My Soul Is a Witness: African-American Women's Spirituality.*

Alice Walker is an author, poet, and activist. Her many books include *Anything You Love Can Be Saved, The Same River Twice, The Color Purple, In Search of Our Mother's Gardens, The Third Life of Grange Copeland,* and *You Can't Keep a Woman Down.*

Sheila S. Walker is the director of the Center for African and African American Studies and the Annabel Irion Worsham Centennial Professor at the University of Texas at Austin. She is the author of *Ceremonial Spirit Possession in Africa and Afro-America* and *The Religious Revolution in the Ivory Coast: The Prophet Harris and the Harrist*

Church. She has contributed articles to numerous anthologies and scholarly journals as well as magazines, including *Black Scholar, Ebony, Essence,* and *The Black Collegian.* She is an anthropologist, filmmaker, development consultant, and field researcher.

Wuanda M. T. Walls, an eighth-generation Pennsylvanian, has traveled extensively throughout the world. She has contributed articles to numerous publications, including *Essence, Boston Globe, Denver Post, Bon Appetit, Black Enterprise,* and *Emerge.* She is a contributor to the anthology *Season of Adventure.*

Evelyn C. White is a visiting scholar in Women's Studies at Mills College in Oakland, California. She is the editor of *The Black Women's Health Book* and author of *Chain Chain Change: For Black Women in Abusive Relationships.* She is currently writing the official biography of Alice Walker.

Stephanie Ann Rush Wilson-Davenport is a high school teacher. She loves to travel, read, cook, and design clothes. She resides in Chicago, Illinois.

ACKNOWLEDGMENTS

I CHERISH AND THANK MY CIRCLE OF PARENTS—CHRISTOPHER LEE, MARY LOU LEE, Juana Long, and J.D. Shook—for teaching me how to create and achieve goals by using the magic formula of love, creativity, discipline and perseverance. I offer thanksgiving to my dear sista' friends Evelyn C. White and Karen James for inspiring me, encouraging me, challenging me, and supporting me prior to, during, and after my sojourn around the planet and through this book. Their unwavering belief in me and my dreams sustain me.

I send my blessings and gratitude to my wondrous circle of friends and family. Without their generous, loving, consistent, and expansive support, this book could not have come into being. Richard Allen, Ida Baker, Scott Banks, Linda Brunson, Mildred Carlysle, Insoah Chionesu, Paul Cooper, Chic Dabby, Aliona Gibson, Joy Harris, Stanley Hébert III, Paulette Houston, Eva Jefferson-Patterson, T.C. Jefferson, Haki Madhubuti, Kaari Martin, Pam Moore, Shirley Nakao, Naeem Masjied, Prestine Nash, Harini Oken, Kit Pappenheimer, Jewell Parker, Shelly Parker, The Rainbow Collective, Retha Robinson, Jeff Sanders, Kweli Tutashinda, Dick Walker, Eileen Williams, Sonya Williams, Theo Williams, James Winbush, Donald Yates. Because of you, I am.

My thanks to Cheryl Williams, through whose dissertation I learned more abut early black women travelers.

I give thanks and praise to my business associates for their talent and tenacity—Carol Canter, Virginia King, Ron Madson, Jerry Mays, Stella McHenry, Mishla Schwartz, Pearl Stewart, Ellovoy Thomas, and Sylvia

Turner—and especially to Ruth Gundle and the staff at the Eighth Mountain Press for pruning and publishing *Go Girl,* the world's first travel book by and for African American women. I admire their courage to venture into this uncharted territory.

The Fearless Flyer
How to Fly in Comfort and without Trepidation

CHERRY HARTMAN and
JULIE SHELDON HUFFAKER

$10.95
192 pages
trade paperback
ISBN 0-933377-33-9

Overcome Your Fear of Flying

It's not difficult to do. **Cherry Hartman,** a Licensed Clinical Social Worker who has specialized in treating anxiety—including aerophobia—for twenty-five years, shares the methods that have worked for her clients.

- Understand why you are afraid to fly.
- Acquire easy-to-learn techniques to dispel preflight jitters and make your flying time easy and restful.
- Discover how even a rudimentary knowledge of aerodynamics and air travel regulation can be powerfully reassuring.

Be Comfortable on Your Next Flight

The air aboard a plane is drier than the Sahara Desert. Your hair goes limp. Your feet swell. You are stuck in a space substantially smaller than a phone booth. For hours. To top it off, the company is not of your choosing. *This is not home.* What can you do about it? Much more than you might think. **Julie Sheldon Huffaker** offers the benefits of her extensive research and air travel along with tips and tricks from the experts to transform your next flight into an efficient business session or a rejuvenating window of personal time.

- Tired of feeling weary and irritable when you deplane? Does your back ache? Do you come down with a cold or flu within days of flying? Learn how to feel good and stay healthy.
- Make informed choices about where to sit, what to eat, how to manage luggage, and when to schedule your flight.
- Learn about your rights as an air traveler and everything else you need to know to become a truly fearless flyer.

FOR ORDERING INFORMATION PLEASE TURN TO THE LAST PAGE

Adventures in Good Company
The Complete Guide to Women's Tours and Outdoor Trips

Adventures in Good Company

The Complete Guide to Women's
Tours and Outdoor Trips

THALIA ZEPATOS

THALIA ZEPATOS

$16.95
432 pages
trade paperback
ISBN 0-933377-27-4

With her familiar warmth, humor, and expertise, Thalia Zepatos demystifies the burgeoning world of organized travel options for women. Chapters on bicycling, canoeing, horseback riding, sailing, rock climbing, dog sledding, trekking, etc.—as well as leadership development programs, cultural exchange opportunities, and spiritual journeys—encourage the reader to be adventurous and help her to choose a trip wisely. Issues that are particular to group travel (insurance, safety, medical concerns, unrealistic expectations, etc.) are fully explored.

More than a hundred companies worldwide that offer trips for women are profiled. Full information on their philosophy, number of years in business, qualifications of group leaders, types of trips offered, and typical cost is provided in an easy-to-use format. Programs tailored to women and children, physically challenged women, lesbians, and older women are highlighted.

No book by Thalia Zepatos would be complete without her trademark travel stories—both her own, and those from a wide array of women adventurers. Wise, funny, instructive, and inspiring, they convey the unique challenges and joys of traveling in the company of women.

FOR ORDERING INFORMATION PLEASE TURN TO THE LAST PAGE

A Journey of One's Own, 2nd Edition

Uncommon Advice for the Independent Woman Traveler

THALIA ZEPATOS

$16.95
360 pages
trade paperback
ISBN 0-933377-36-3

Tales of cross-cultural encounters and self-discovery from a wide array of women travelers add spice to expert and detailed advice on practical matters such as dealing with sexual harassment, staying healthy, traveling safely, avoiding theft, finding the cheapest airline tickets, managing a long trip, and much, much more.

"Superlatives generally make us suspicious, but we must say: This is THE best women's travel resource we've seen, ever.... It's authoritative; it's supportive; it's amusing; it really does have it all." — *New York Daily News*

"Realistic and constructive." —*Travel Holiday*

"Sensitive, intelligent and inspirational." —*San Francisco Chronicle*

"Thalia Zepatos is teacher, spokeswoman and heroine of sorts to a generation of travelers, both women and men, who understand travel as more than the periodic recreational migration that our commercial culture promotes." —*Seattle Times*

"This book is not just for women, and it's not just for those who travel alone. It is for those who want to truly experience cultures other than their own. Packed with the odd bits of wisdom that one collects on the road, it prepares the unseasoned adventurer for the myriad dilemmas of the less-traveled road.... Travelers will find this book invaluable." —*Whole Earth Catalog*

FOR ORDERING INFORMATION PLEASE TURN TO THE LAST PAGE

ORDERING INFORMATION

EIGHTH MOUNTAIN books can be found in independent and chain bookstores across the U.S., Canada, Great Britain, and Australia. If your favorite bookstore is out of the title you want, ask them to order it for you. You can also order books directly from Eighth Mountain if you are anywhere in North America. Please add $2.50 for the first book ($3.50 in Canada) and 50¢ each additional book for postage and handling. Send a check payable to The Eighth Mountain Press. Books will be mailed book rate. If you need speedier delivery, call us to discuss other options.

Eighth Mountain titles are distributed to the trade by Consortium Book Sales and Distribution, 1045 Westgate Drive, Saint Paul, MN 55114-1065 (800/283-3572 or 612/221-9035) and are carried by all major book wholesalers and library jobbers.

For specialty, bulk, and catalog sales contact the Eighth Mountain Press directly.

The Eighth Mountain Press
624 SE 29th Avenue
Portland, OR 97214
phone: 503/233-3936
fax: 503/233-0774

DEAR READER, I would love to hear from you! Send your comments, questions, travel tips, and story ideas to:

Elaine Lee, PO Box 2603, Berkeley, CA 94702
Email: laneybug@aol.com
Web site: http://www.geocities.com/yosemite/rapids/1271